They Coulda Been Contenders

TWELVE ACTORS WHO SHOULD HAVE BECOME CINEMATIC SUPERSTARS

by Dan Van Neste

FOREWORD BY BOB KING

THEY COULDA BEEN CONTENDERS
TWELVE ACTORS WHO SHOULD HAVE BECOME CINEMATIC SUPERSTARS
©2019 Dan Van Neste

All rights reserved.

No part of this book may be reproduced in any form or by any means, electronic, mechanical, digital, photocopying, or recording, except for in the inclusion of a review, without permission in writing from the publisher.

Published in the USA by:

BearManor Media
1317 Edgewater Dr #110
Orlando FL 32804
www.BearManorMedia.com

ISBN: 978-1-62933-461-5 (alk. paper)

Book design and layout by Valerie Thompson

"You was my brother, Charley. You shoulda looked out for me a little bit. You shoulda taken care of me, just a little bit, so I wouldn't have to take them dives for the short-end money . . . I coulda had class. **I coulda been a contender.** *I coulda been somebody . . ."*

— Terry Malloy as portrayed by Marlon Brando in On The Waterfront (1954) directed by Elia Kazan, script by Budd Schulberg.

Table of Contents

FOREWORD BY BOB KING . . . 1

INTRODUCTION . . . 3

ACKNOWLEDGMENTS . . . 7

PART I — THE PROFILES

CHAPTER ONE — "NANCY CARROLL: ONE OF THE FIGHTING IRISH" . . . **13**

CHAPTER TWO — "GLORIA DICKSON: WE WON'T FORGET" . . . **55**

CHAPTER THREE — "CLAIRE DODD: DIMPLED AND DANGEROUS" . . . **77**

CHAPTER FOUR — "RICHARD GREENE: SWASHBUCKLER WITH A DOUBLE-EDGED SWORD" . . . **103**

CHAPTER FIVE — "JOHN HODIAK: THE HERO FROM HAMTRAMCK" . . . **123**

CHAPTER SIX — "MARIAN MARSH: LITTLE MAID MARIAN" (Two-Part Profile) . . . **151**

CHAPTER SEVEN — "KAREN MORLEY: MAVERICK IN WHITE SATIN" . . . **201**

CHAPTER EIGHT — "EDWARD NORRIS: BABY FACE GANGSTER" (Two-Part Profile) . . . **241**

CHAPTER NINE — "JEAN PARKER: THE CINDERELLA GIRL" (Two-Part Profile) . . . **289**

CHAPTER TEN — "PAULA RAYMOND:
A WORKING ACTRESS" (Two-Part Profile) . . . **323**

CHAPTER ELEVEN — "ZACHARY SCOTT:
A SCOUNDREL WITH STYLE" . . . **353**

CHAPTER TWELVE — "GLORIA STUART:
CHASING RAINBOWS IN DREAMLAND" . . . **375**

PART II — THE FILMS

FILMOGRAPHIES . . . **413**

SELECTED BIBLIOGRAPHY . . . **513**

END NOTES . . . **525**

PHOTO CREDITS . . . **559**

ABOUT THE AUTHOR . . . **561**

INDEX . . . **563**

Foreword
by Bob King

Surprisingly, the dawn of the classic film fanzine appeared over the small town of Indiana, Pennsylvania. It was there that one Samuel K. Rubin, a local furniture store owner, published #1 of his brainchild, "8mm Collector," back in June of 1962. Things have never been the same since. "But why," younger readers may wonder, "that strange name?" And, "What does '8 mm' possibly refer to?"

Well, yes, it was a different world then. In 1962, the home video revolution was coming, but few people knew about it. If you did show movies in your home it was mostly on a sheet or a white wall and you used a projector that accommodated narrow gauge motion picture film, 8 millimeters in width. And more likely than not you showed old movies originally made before the technological revolution of the "talkies" drove "silent" movies from the nation's theaters.

Not surprisingly, Sam's publication at first focused on films featuring the likes of Mary Pickford, Wallace Reid, Barbara La Marr, and Lon Chaney Sr. As time passed and film buffs began to watch their movies on VCRs, Sam gradually increased his coverage of films made after the 1920's, and he changed the name of his publication to *Classic Images*, the name it still bears to this day.

Film fan magazines existed long before Sam Rubin came along, but let's not make the mistake of confusing *Classic Images* with the movie gossip mags sold by the millions in drug stores throughout most of the 20th century. Much of what appeared in the old film fan mags consisted of fictional accounts of movie stars, crafted with the help of studio publicists, all with the intent of increasing sales of tickets at the nation's theaters.

Classic Images on the other hand, had a more serious approach. *CI* was focused more on film history with the intent of increasing our understanding of the motion picture medium and the people who created and developed it. This is not to say that *CI* ever aspired to be a stuffy academic journal. No, at *CI* we always aimed to serve people of all walks of life who were drawn together by one thing: an intense and passionate interest in the movies. Our goal was and is to serve these highly intelligent and discerning readers with meaningful and well written articles that not only enlighten but also provide the simple pleasure of a good read.

Thus when a new writer named Dan Van Neste began offering articles for publication in *CI* it was obvious from the start that he was just the sort of person we needed. Readers embraced his intelligent and well-researched articles. They particularly noted Dan's ability to shed new light on subjects they thought they already understood. This is because his writing had a freshness that many found remarkable, especially if they had been reading Hollywood history for decades. Even more remarkable is the fact that after all these years, Dan's writing retains its freshness. Even when he writes about a subject you don't think you'll care about, don't be surprised to find that your time and attention to each and every story will be amply rewarded.

Finally, we extend our thanks and gratitude to Dan for all the work he has done over the years. Without writers like Dan Van Neste, our understanding and appreciation of our film heritage would be sadly diminished.

BOB KING, EDITOR & GENERAL MANAGER
CLASSIC IMAGES & FILMS OF THE GOLDEN AGE

Introduction

"Westward Ho!" "Go West, Young Man!" In 19th century America, those familiar clarion calls inspired countless men and women to pull up stakes, and head west of the Mississippi River to a land of opportunity to seek their fortunes and fulfill their dreams. One of the most popular destinations was America's West Coast, more specifically California, which became part of the U.S. as a result of the Mexican War (1846-48), and a state in 1850. It's coastal location, mild Mediterranean climate (well-suited to agriculture and fruit production), and the discovery of gold in 1848, were among the many factors which attracted the masses to California. The completion of the first Transcontinental Railroad, mass innovations in transportation modes, and the development of the road and highway system accelerated the migration in the latter portion of the 19th and early 20th centuries.

Various new industries sprang up in coastal areas of California. Among them was motion picture production. Previously headquartered in New Jersey and New York, American film producers and movie studios began relocating to the Southern California coast in the early years of the 20th Century. Their new base of operations was a neighborhood in central Los Angeles named Hollywood. Relocating in or near Hollywood presented several advantages to film executives and creative personnel. The mild, sunny weather and southern California's topographical variety (which included mountains, green fields, orchards, deserts, and ocean), allowed producers to film almost every day of the year, and tell a variety of stories with a broad range of settings. Additionally, the new West Coast location allowed film companies to escape the heavy hand of Thomas Edison's Motion

Picture Patents Company known as, "The Trust." Headquartered in New Jersey, "The Trust" held patents on movie processing and projection equipment and charged licensing fees. Yet another advantage was the cost of labor. In the early 1900's, the Los Angeles area was known as a center of non-union labor where movie companies were able to employ skilled craftsmen for much less money. All these assets inspired enormous growth in the motion picture business in California. By 1925, American film production had become the seventh largest industry in the United States, and Hollywood its hub.

The massive growth of the West Coast motion picture industry inspired yet another wave of immigration. Beginning in the 1920's, and continuing throughout the period in film history recognized by classic movie enthusiasts and historians as the "golden age of the cinema," (roughly extending from the mid 1930's through the 1950's), a new flood of immigrants (mostly young adults), decided to take up residence in Hollywood. They came from every corner of the earth, from all races, ethnic backgrounds, languages, and religions. Some came to escape lives of poverty and despair, some to distinguish themselves in families of wealth and influence, while others to satisfy a variety of financial, and psychological needs. In spite of their disparate backgrounds and stories, these new immigrants shared one overarching goal: to become employed in the ever expanding motion picture industry. Many sought to become motion picture stars. A relatively new phenomena, movie stars consisted of a small elite group of film actors who, over time, had become popular with film audiences and developed a large following of adoring fans.

Sadly, for the vast majority of the new dreamy-eyed immigrants, their naïve quest to find fame and fortune in the movies would soon end in disillusionment. Discouraged, and financially challenged, most abandoned the "city of dreams," and returned home to their families and their previous lives.

Of the small group of determined individuals who stayed, few could legitimately claim any significant success. Some ended up in chorus lines, bit roles, or on the periphery of the industry as support staff, technical assistants, secretaries, etc. Only the tiniest minority achieved their initial dreams of becoming actors and filmmakers who made a living in their chosen professions.

The twelve unique life stories you're about to read are culled from the microscopic group of aspiring actors who beat the immense odds — the "crème de la crème" if you will. Like the large group from which they emerged, these twelve individuals represented a wide diversity of backgrounds and personalities — from a fiery Irish beauty from the Bowery, to an artistically inclined "blueblood" from Texas, from a sweet stage actress from Idaho, to the defiant daughter of a wealthy West Coast realtor, from a handsome British stage actor, to a blonde bombshell from the Midwest. Add a demure chocolatier's daughter from Boston, a humble immigrant's son from Michigan, a teenaged artist from Montana, a gynecologist's son from Philadelphia, an ambitious model from San Francisco, and a beautiful dreamer from southern California, and you have the subjects of this volume. Utilizing talent, determination, and industry, all twelve of the subjects showcased in this book overcame enormous barriers and realized their initial goal of becoming film actors. All achieved fame and were recognized for their significant abilities and contributions, **yet** despite their successes, none of them was able to reach the pinnacle of their profession — defined as superstardom a.k.a. silver screen immortality. Today, sadly, some of their names are unfamiliar to the masses, even to some classic film enthusiasts. Given their significant assets, and impressive resumes, how could this be? What were the reasons? With the invaluable assistance of various library and archival records, recollections from some of the subjects themselves and those who knew and/or worked with them, each of the detailed profiles in this book is an examination of the lives and careers of the twelve with the primary goal of answering those key questions. The essays herein are also an opportunity to offer a long overdue "tip of the hat" to a dozen gifted, creative and hardworking individuals who coulda been contenders!

Acknowledgments

Hello again. Dan Van Neste here. I'm an author, biographer whose main focus is on vintage filmmakers and entertainment history. *They Coulda Been Contenders* is my third book, and a very personal one. While working on it, I celebrated an important anniversary: 30 years of writing about the movies. Perhaps this may not seem like much of an accomplishment in comparison to some, (after all, many writers have been working in excess of 50 years!), but to me, it was an achievement. Back in April 1988, when I began work on my first movie-related article, I couldn't possibly have imagined three decades later, I'd still be at it, and writing books to boot. Over 50 major articles, and two books later, here we are. Let me just say, it's been quite a ride!

Doing this volume was akin to a formal commemoration of that anniversary. You see, the twelve essays in this book are lightly edited versions of twelve articles I penned over the last three decades — twelve of my most popular pieces, all published in two acclaimed magazines: *Classic Images* and its sister quarterly, *Films of the Golden Age*. The oldest dates back to 1995, and the most recent, to 2012. Assembling this collection turned out to be an extraordinarily nostalgic experience for me, inspiring a flood of personal memories and emotions — smiles, frowns, laughter, and not a few tears. I remembered the vital help I received on each, the satisfaction I felt seeing them in print, the lasting friendships I made along the way including treasured ones with some of the people I was writing about and interviewing. On the minus side, I vividly recalled the difficulties I faced doing the research, the distractions I felt at the time in my personal life, the anxieties I experienced doing some of my first interviews. The tears came as I relived hearing the news of the deaths of most of those I interviewed including six of the individuals profiled here. I mourned their passing both as a fan and as a friend.

As mentioned above, the production of each of these mini-biographies was not done without key help from multiple sources. Among the libraries and archives consulted on one or more were: The Academy of Motion Picture Arts and Sciences — Margaret Herrick Library in Los Angeles, The Wisconsin Center for Film and Theatre Research in Madison, New York Public Library, The Museum of Modern Art, Warner Brothers Archives, University of Southern California, RKO Archives, Charles E. Young Library, University of California, Los Angeles, Library of Congress, University of Wyoming Library, Laramie, University of Georgia Library in Atlanta, and the Michigan State University Library in East Lansing. My thanks to all the librarians and archivists for their kindness, time and attention.

The list of individuals who assisted on one or more of these pieces is very long and sadly, includes many who are no longer living. Let me say here and now, I sincerely appreciate their assistance! I have endeavored to list as many as possible, but if any names were omitted, it was strictly inadvertent, and I sincerely apologize. My deepest thanks to: Janet Lorenz, Lois Peyton, Richard Braff, Peter Hawke, Tony Greco, John Drennon, Laura Wagner, Charles Stumpf, Hal Snelling, Steve Tompkins, William Studer, Jerry Ohlinger, Claire Brandt of Eddie Brandt's Saturday Matinee, Tom Stuto, David Heck, Al Raker, Betty Heater, Joan Seaton, John Cavallo, Gunhard Oravas, Gene Massimo, Marvin Paige, David Marowitz, Laura Shetenhelm, Nancy Norris, Gary Travis, Blackie Seymour, Mike Hawks at Larry Edmunds Bookstore, Tom Weaver, Robert Hanks, Doug McClelland, Jerry Anker, Gary Hamann, Joanne Greene-Fields, Dan Pierson, Scott Ratner, the staff of *Classic Images* and *Films of the Golden Age* magazines, and my family for their support.

Special thank yous are in order to Richard Finegan for the wonderful Gloria Stuart photos, and to the terrfic people at BearManor Media including Ben Ohmart, Sandy Grabman, and ace designer Valerie Thompson for their patience, kindness, and for being a genuine pleasure to work with!! My sincere gratitude also goes out to Bob King, the longtime editor of *Classic Images* and *Films of the Golden*

Age for working so hard for so many years to produce two very fine magazines commemorating the golden age of the cinema and vintage filmmakers. Bravo!! On a personal note, I also want to thank Bob, for taking a chance on this lowly writer in 1994, continuing to support me all these years, AND for graciously agreeing to write the foreword for this book! In appreciation for their many contributions, this volume is dedicated to the extraordinarily talented, innovative, hard working, and underappreciated actors and filmmakers who made B movies in the 1930's and 1940's.

For their great benevolence and thoughtfulness, I would also like to express my special thanks to the following individuals who agreed to do interviews for one or more of these pieces. They include Patricia Kirkland Bevan, Don Bevan, John Springer, Will Hutchins, Suzanne Benedetto, David Chierichetti, Vincent Sherman, Sybil Jason, John Cooper, Brand Cooper, Josephine Hutchinson, Virginia O'Brien, John Wiegman, Ann Rutherford, Marian Shilling, and Richard Gordon. And lastly, and most importantly, I want to express my profound appreciation from the bottom of my heart to six of my subjects who so graciously agreed to lengthy interviews with me about their lives and careers including Marian Marsh, Karen Morley, Edward Norris, Jean Parker, Paula Raymond, and Gloria Stuart. I will never forget their kindnesses, encouragement, and friendship! My most sincere hope is this volume will inspire a renewed interest in these talented, underrated actors and their film legacies.

Before letting you go to hopefully, become engrossed in the individual stories in the book, I want to take a few moments to briefly discuss its contents. It is divided into two main parts. Part I consists of twelve chapters corresponding to the twelve individuals profiled. Each essay is an account of the lives and careers of the twelve with an emphasis on their careers. Each has been lightly edited from the original. Some of the twelve include separate interview sections, while others integrate interview material within the article itself. Please note, the twelve essays featured here are not meant as substitutes for full-fledged, in-depth book biographies of these individuals (which will hopefully, someday be written and cover *every* aspect of their lives and careers), but as discussions of their ability and potential, and summaries of their contributions. Having said that, I do believe these mini-biographies and interviews (both with the subjects and others who knew them), are very revealing and valuable on a number of levels.

At the end of each chapter is an "Update" section which consists of additional, mostly new information which has come to light since the publication of the original articles. This new information includes a wide assortment of material having to do with the particular person, including their later years, notable events surrounding them including their death dates, and information about their families, friends, acquaintances, etc. In addition to the "Updates," some of the twelve essays also have "Extras" a.k.a. addendums which include additional articles and/or interviews done on the particular person, some of which have never been published. Part II of the book is devoted to filmographies of the twelve. Each entry includes title, date, studio, director, and main cast members.

Finally, let me say a few words about the title of this book. As most classic film enthusiasts know, the title refers to a famous line of dialogue penned by scenarist Budd Schulberg for the 1954 classic crime drama, *On the Waterfront*. In the movie, the protagonist, dock worker, Terry Malloy (Marlon Brando) battles the mob and his guilty conscience. He utters the famous quote, "I coulda been a contender," lamenting the fact, that despite his ability and promise as a boxer, he was never able to attain fame, at least partially due to the intervention and interference of others. Although the overall lives and experiences of the twelve subjects in this book are all *very different* from that of Malloy, the quote does seem to wring true for them as well. Like Malloy, they had the ability and drive to achieve their potentials (a.k.a. superstardom), under the right circumstances with the right kind of guidance and assistance.

Part 1
The Profiles

CHAPTER ONE
"NANCY CARROLL: ONE OF THE FIGHTING IRISH"

(Originally published in *Films of the Golden Age*, Fall, 2000)

A persuasive case can be made that titian-haired, baby-faced Nancy Carroll was the first important new star created by talking pictures. Between 1929-31, she quickly climbed to the pinnacle of Hollywood, topping popularity polls and generating big box office receipts, not to mention tons of fan mail. For depression-era audiences smarting from stock market crashes and long unemployment lines, the pretty, perky Irish colleen was just the antidote. She literally sang, danced, and charmed their blues away in some of the period's most popular comedies and musicals. Occasionally, she abandoned escapist fare to demonstrate a surprising ability as a tragedienne.

Around Paramount studio they called her, "Irish." Some said her quick ascension to stardom was a stroke of Irish luck, but those who knew the hardworking, fiercely determined young lady, knew her rise to fame was no mere happenstance. Her Irish roots and upbringing (as one of twelve children of immigrants), was a source of much of the confidence, fortitude, and toughness which propelled her to stardom, but sadly, Miss Carroll's heritage would also contribute to her downfall. By the end of the 1930's decade, Nancy's filmic heyday was but a fading memory. For Nancy Carroll had a disposition to match her fiery red hair, and even her significant talent was not sufficient to overcome a reputation for being temperamental and uncooperative.

The future star debuted as Ann Veronica Lahiff (Lahiff with a small h), on November 19, 1903, in Manhattan. Miss Carroll claimed her birthdate was 1908, and most reference books list it as 1905 or 1906, but Nancy's daughter Patricia Kirkland Bevan corrected the record in an interview with the author. "My mother lied about her age. She went to the church where she was baptized and charmed one of the priests into making the 3 into an 8!"¹ Nancy gave a fascinating account of her early years in a 1929 article.

"I was the seventh child of a seventh child. My mother from County Roscommon, Ireland was a seventh child. She married Thomas Lahiff from County Clare. I was their seventh gift to their adopted nation. There would be twelve altogether. . . We were all born in New York City. We lived in an apartment at Tenth Avenue and Sixty Eighth Street. My father worked in a garage, later he owned two taxis. I can remember when he made twenty five dollars a week and kept us all in porridge and shoes. . . Father played the concertina. We danced; we jigged; we had great, bubbling with enthusiasm parties. We slept cross-wise on the bed. All the girls together. It was hard on the older ones. Their legs hung over the edge and from under the covers. We were all in school together. One Lahiff for each grade. . . People ask me if we used to fight, and I always answer, 'We are Irish.' But I was the fightingest fighter of the family. My tongue or my fists were always ready. I was brought up on my own and had to fight for what I wanted. It wasn't a bad training for the motion picture business!"²

Although Nancy's Uncle Billy would become a successful businessman (as owner of the famed, "Tavern," a favorite celebrity restaurant/watering hole on New York's 48th Street), life was hard for brother Tom's brood in turn of the century New York. After attending a local Catholic grade school, each member of the family was expected to find work.

"When a child in our family reached fourteen, he or she began to work for a living. You had to be fourteen in New York State to get a working permit. . . I was only thirteen at my eighth grade graduation. . . In spite of my Irish free-for-all disposition, I was wild about studies. But in our family it just didn't seem sporting to go to school when all the rest had started working. . ."³

Thus the intelligent 13-year-old Ann gave up her first important dream (of a high school education), and went to stenographic school. Just prior to her first job interview, the nervous youngster ended up in Loew's Theatre hoping to let the movies, as she put it, "help whistle back my courage." She remembered, hanging over the railing of the tops of the gallery to watch Norma Talmadge play *Poppy* with Eugene O'Brien. "To me it was the most beautiful sight I'd ever seen!"[4]

Eventually she and sister Teresa landed detestable positions as typists in a mail order house. Later, Ann became a secretary on Wall Street. In their spare time, the two girls made up dancing and singing routines which were tried out at the local Knights of Columbus hall. In the spring of 1923, the duo's popularity attracted the attention of the Shuberts who auditioned them for their vaudeville revue, *The Passing Show of 1923*.

"Terry and I were pretty well frightened. . . And right in the middle of our song and dance, I felt my slipper string untying. We were to end with a cartwheel. I didn't want to trip and be hurt so I went right on singing and Terry went right on dancing and singing, while I bent and tied up the little meanie. Mr. Shubert laughed. 'Anyone who has poise enough to stop and tie a shoe is good!' he told me. On the day of our dress rehearsal we gave up our jobs"[5]

The show opened to mixed reviews and lasted only three months, but the little Irish upstart's show business dream survived the disappointment. Shubert liked both girls, especially the angelic-looking Ann nicknamed, "The Cherub." He hired the duo later for his *Topics of 1923*. By this time, both girls had discarded their family name in favor of Carroll (the last name of a show business friend). "The Cherub" decided to change her name entirely. An attractive rotogravure photograph of Ann (now Nancy Carroll), eventually found its way to *New York Daily News* reporter and budding playwright, Jack Kirkland who became determined to meet this stunning young girl. When his goal was accomplished a few weeks later at a dance, he was smitten instantly. "Jack wanted me to marry him almost since I first met him." Nancy later confided. "But I was crazy with ambition. I'd had a taste of the stage; the taste was good. I wanted a full meal . . ."[6]

In June, 1924, Jack's persistence paid off. The couple were married in a small simple ceremony in New York. After honeymooning with friends in Akron, Ohio, Nancy resumed her show business career,

This 1920's photo of vibrant, vivacious young Miss Carroll clearly illustrates why she was nicknamed, "The Cherub."

joining the Shuberts,' *Passing Show of 1924*, appearing (sans sister Terry), with another ambitious youngster, Lucille Le Sueur, (Joan Crawford). Nancy told an interviewer,

"Jack and I were each making sixty a week. We didn't have any time to spend money. All of a sudden we found we had a thousand dollars. Then I realized I was going to have a baby . . . Jack said, 'You need

one last fling dear. Let's just take that thousand and scoot to Paris. We'll live in a garret and I'll write the great American novel and you'll have the great American baby . . ."[7]

Thus the happy couple ended up in France for the next few months where Jack served as press agent to Tom Mix who was touring with his horse, Tony, while Nancy wrote a "chit-chat" column.

Just prior to giving birth, Nancy became homesick. "All of a sudden I decided I wanted my baby to be born on New York soil where the twelve little Lahiffs had first seen the light of day. So we crossed the ocean just in time to give the little colleen her Irish American birthright."[8] Patricia Kirkland was born in the Bronx in July, 1925. "I was born in a Jewish hospital called Mount Morris Park, which my mother quickly renamed Mount St. Morris Park!" said a laughing Patricia.[9] By spring, 1926, Jack, Nancy, and bundle had found their way to Hollywood where Jack, encouraged by Mix, hoped to secure work as a scenarist. With the baby in the care of a nurse, the ambitious Kirklands set out on a quest to conquer the filmmaking world.

The film capitol's initial enthusiasm for the young couple was at best tepid. In fact, their first few weeks in California were rugged. When Jack's job leads didn't pan out immediately, tenacious Nancy felt an added pressure to succeed in her own employment search. Countless rejections, and a few pairs of worn out shoes later, she secured stage work and an MGM screen test. Metros' verdict was negative. "In 1926, they had the idea that faces must be lean and classical in appearance. Mine was frankly roly-poly Irish."[10] After two Lupino Lane stage comedies and an unsuccessful play, (ironically entitled, *Nancy*), Miss Carroll finally scored her first major theatrical break, as tough girl Roxie Hart in the melodramatic, *Chicago*, presented by the Macloons in Los Angeles. Her good reviews landed her a second lead and a blonde wig in her first film, *Ladies Must Dress* (Fox-1926). Multiple screen tests followed, one of which found its way to Paramount.

There are conflicting stories regarding Miss Carroll's first big break in the movies. Even Nancy gave contradictory accounts to the Hollywood press. One story had her submitting a screen test to Paramount in the midst of casting the lead in their adaptation of the Broadway smash, *Abie's Irish Rose*. When author, Anne Nichols saw it, she was said to have exclaimed, "That's my girl!" A more colorful version, (most likely a publicist's invention), had Nancy in the midst of a violent argument with the gatekeeper at Paramount when she was refused admittance to a luncheon appointment. Legend has it she was making such a ruckus, kicking and screaming, she attracted the attention of Miss Nichols who found her Irish Rose. Whatever the truth, the result was indisputable: newcomer Nancy Carroll landed the title role in a grade-A motion picture, one which would secure her a place in film history and pave her pathway to stardom.[11]

The familiar story of culturally incompatible lovers, the comedy drama, *Abie's Irish Rose* (Paramount,1928), was directed by Victor Fleming and enacted by a fine cast including veteran Jean Hersholt, and young Charles "Buddy" Rogers. Originally a silent, a sound sequence was added after it premiered in New York. Nancy's rendition of the song, "Rosemary" (written by Anne Nichols and J. S. Zamecnik), was said to have been one of the first ever performed into a movie microphone; and her tap dance number, the first ever on a motion picture sound stage. Although the film was greeted by mixed reviews, Nancy's notices were excellent. The result was a long term Paramount contract.[12]

No time was wasted putting the exhuberant, 5 foot four inch, 118 pound, blue-eyed "Cherub" to work. Paramount loaned her to Fox to play a carefree chorine in the silent comedy, *Chicken A-La King* (1928). At her home studio, the fiesty ingenue was a businessman's daughter in love with a naive radio announcer (Richard Dix) in *Easy Come, Easy Go* (1928), and a spoiled rich kid who finds love and maturity out west in *The Water Hole* with Jack Holt. After *Abie's Irish Rose*, Nancy's best opportunity to attract attention came in Paramount's melodramatic, *Manhattan Cocktail* (1928), which boasted a good cast, and director, Dorothy Arzner. As a Broadway wannabe who becomes disillusioned with life in the big city, Nancy was called upon to dance, sing two Victor Shertzinger songs, "Another Kiss," and "Gotta Be Good," and look spectacular. Her success inspired audiences and critics to stand up and take note of the of the actress with the pretty heart-shaped face, the cupid's bow mouth, and the unusual singing voice who was able to be sexy yet demure. Even

1920's photo of Miss Carroll.

with the crude recording devices utilized in early sound film sequences, Miss Carroll's "funny, cooing" vocals delighted moviegoers. Little did they know that behind that charming facade lurked a formidable dramatic talent.

On the strength of her work in *Manhattan Cocktail*, Paramount opted to give Nancy a dramatic vehicle. Their choice: *The Shopworn Angel* (1928), a tear-stained tale of a tough chorus girl's (Carroll) life-changing love for a naive, frightened soldier (Gary Cooper) headed off to World War I. Assisted by director Richard Wallace, Nancy's skillful, multi-layered portrayal of hard-as-nails Daisy Heath surprised even her most ardent admirers. Especially memorable were her final scenes in which Daisy envisions her lover's tragic fate as she tearfully performs the Lou Davis and M. Fred Coots' composition, "A Precious Little Thing Called Love," (part of a sound sequence added to the film). Critics were properly impressed. *The New York Sun* opined, "Richard Wallace has turned out a thoroughly fresh and fascinating film. . . Nancy Carroll and Gary Cooper give expert and charming performances." *The New York Daily Mirror* went further, calling Nancy's work, "magnificent."

The critical acclaim and box office success of *The Shopworn Angel* quickly propelled little Miss Carroll to the forefront of film newcomers. As Paramount counted their tidy profits, they set their star-making machine in motion, parceling out more prominent roles to the talented young starlet. All in all, she would have seven films releases in 1929 alone, including the first in a series of musicals which would make her a significant star, and mark the beginning of the all-too-brief peak period of her career.

With the emergence of sound, and the immense box office receipts of MGM's *The Broadway Melody*, all the major studios were eager to produce their own musical extravaganzas. The increasingly popular Nancy's singing and dancing abilities made her a natural to star in Paramount's spectacles. Although the plotlines were flimsy, the characters underdeveloped, depression era audiences enthusiastically embraced the new talkie musicals in no small part due to the talents of some of the best songwriters around, and the sheer charm and charisma of performers like Nancy Carroll whose infectious smile, and sincerity transcended the films' clichés, and incongruities.

Paramount's *Close Harmony* was a case in point. The first of three musicals Carroll would make in 1929, it reteamed her with Buddy Rogers (in their first all-talking motion picture), in a cliché ridden tale of a bandleader befriended by a successful singer/dancer. Of course, they fall in love with predictable complications. Directed by John Cromwell and Edward Sutherland, based on a story by Elsie Janis, a summation of the picture could be found in the film editor's name: "Tay Malarkey," but audiences were enthusiastic. Both Carroll

Nancy's performance as the worldly chorine in *The Shopworn Angel* (Paramount, 1928), touched the hearts of filmgoers and won critical accolades. Critic Walter Kerr called it, "a model of movie acting."

and Rogers gave totally committed performances, ably aided by memorable Leo Robin and Richard Whiting songs like, "I Want to Go Places and Do Things."[13]

Cromwell and Sutherland also directed *Dance of Life* (Paramount, 1929), a substantive movie based on the successful stage play, *Burlesque*. This time, Carroll was costarred with musical-comedy star Hal Skelly who recreated his acclaimed Broadway role as a troubled comedian saved from self destruction by the love of his dancer/wife (Carroll). A critical and box office smash, the movie's success was attributed to the fine Benjamin Glazer screenplay, the music supplied by Mssrs. Robin, Whiting, and Sam Coslow, and the team of Skelly and Carroll who made you care. As the psychologically abused wife (a challenging role played on stage by young Barbara Stanwyck), Nancy received the best reviews of her career thus far. She followed *Dance* with an even greater success, one which would cement her stardom: the collegiate musical, *Sweetie* (Paramount, 1929). If the tale of a football star's (Stanley Smith) love for a chorine (Carroll) who inherits the college for which he plays, was pure nonsense, no one seemed to notice. Chock full of song and merriment, it was just the prescription in late fall, 1929, at the time of the stock market crash. Pert and pretty Nancy Carroll was on hand to help moviegoers escape their woes for one hour and 35 minutes, and they loved her for it.[14]

Just when Carroll's career was headed to the summit of Mt. Hollywood, her private life would fall on jagged rocks. Talented husband, Jack toiled several months as a scenario writer at Paramount, but failed to make an impression. When offered the opportunity to produce one of his plays, *Frankie and Johnny* in New York, he jumped at the chance. His move to the East Coast in 1929, separated the couple for the first time. At the outset, Nancy kept up the appearance of marital bliss.

"We learned early in our marriage that it is a give and take proposition, He must live his own life; I must live mine . . . I want him to stay in New York until he accomplishes his purpose, just as I must stay in Hollywood to accomplish mine. . ."[15]

The separation would take a heavy toll, however.

Carroll had little time to dwell on her personal problems. After an outrageously melodramatic role as a musician menaced by lechers in *Dangerous Paradise* (Paramount, 1930), she resumed her musical exploits. In the trivial, yet spectacularly popular musical/comedy, *Honey* (Paramount, 1930), she was an aristocrat posing as a maid (a singing maid, mind you). Hardly a great classic movie by any measure, depression audiences were wild about the film, flooding Paramount with tons of fan mail. The studio responded by placing Carroll in their all-star revue, *Paramount on Parade* (1930), dancing and singing

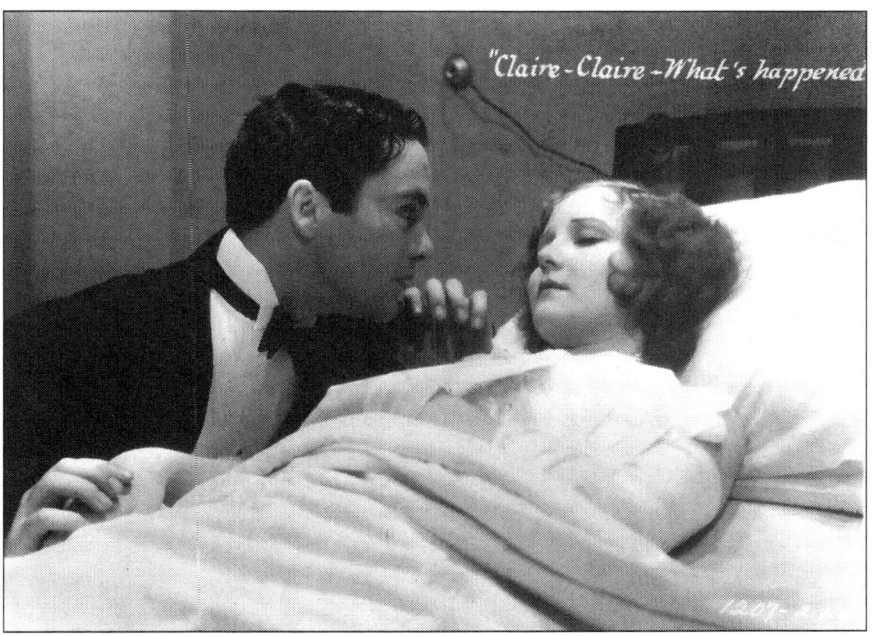

The team of Charles "Buddy" Rogers and Nancy Carroll was a popular one with early sound film audiences. Here they enact a melodramatic scene from *Illusion* (Paramount, 1929), the third of their four film pairings.

the Wolfe Gilbert and Abel Baer composition, "Dancin to Save Your Sole," after emerging from behind a giant shoe. The technicolor musical, *Follow Thru* (Paramount, 1930), reteamed Nancy with pal Buddy Rogers (for the fourth and final time), as a champion golfer in love with her instructor. Important critics scoffed at the film, but moviegoers jammed theaters. If the plot wasn't much, the music was. Lew Brown, B. G. DeSylvia and Roy Henderson's song, "Button Up Your Overcoat" became a major hit, and an all-time standard. Other standout songs included, "I'm Hard to Please" (written by Richard Rogers and Lorenz Hart), and "A Peach of a Pair" (penned by Richard Whiting and George Marion Jr.). In reference to Carroll's career, *Follow Thru* was notable as the first film to present the fiery red hair, beautiful complexion, and dazzling blue eyes of Nancy in living color.

Amidst popular trivialities like *Honey* and *Close Harmony*, Nancy would contribute what most consider the two best performances of her career. In *The Devil's Holiday* (Paramount, 1930), America's "sweetie" was transformed into a hard-hearted golddigger whose best laid

Nancy is beaming in this publicity photo for Paramount's *Dangerous Paradise*, (Paramount, 1930), but rumor had it she wasn't smiling on the set. Her feud with costar, Richard Arlen would become legendary.

plans run afoul when she falls for the object of her diggs, a millionaire's son (Phillips Holmes). As the mercenary manicurist, Hallie Hobart, Miss Carroll proved to all doubters she was a dramatic actress to be reckoned with. Under the skillful direction of Edmund Goulding, her understated performance earned her a Best Actress Oscar nomination and the unqualified approval of the critics. *Variety* called Carroll's work, "no less than a revelation. Hers is no pretty-faced ingénue, but a genuine trooper with imagination and power." Unfortunately, the Academy Award did not follow. She would lose narrowly to Norma Shearer in *The Divorcee*. (Vote totals were reported in 1931.)[16]

In late autumn, 1930, Carroll was reunited with husband Jack in New York where she filmed, *Laughter* (1930), at Paramount's Astoria Studios. A precursor of the witty, sophisticated comedies which found enormous popularity in the latter 1930's, the film weaved a bittersweet tale of a millionaire's wife (Carroll), a former "Follies' beauty," who forsakes material possessions to run away with a composer (Fredric March) who enriches her life with love and the gift of "laughter." A favorite of audiences and critics, a conventional adult drama with some clever comic scenes was transformed into a

For her sterling performance as the mercenary manicurist in *The Devil's Holiday* (Paramount, 1930), Nancy won her first and only Academy Award nomination. On the left is Phillips Holmes.

work of art by skillful Harry D'Abbadie D'Arrast's direction, David Ogden Stewart's scintillating dialogue, and the utter excellence of its leads. March, in one of his favorite roles, was magnetic as the impertinent, carefree composer, as was Carroll whose intelligent performance effectively communicated the maturation of the protagonist who realizes wealth is not her ticket to happiness.

With the premiere of the acclaimed, *Laughter*, Nancy's career reached its zenith as she topped several polls as Hollywood's most popular actress — perhaps the first star of significance to be generated by talking pictures. Her stunning ascension to stardom had come in just three years. On the gentle breezes of popularity, acclaim, and enormous success, the young elfin star should have been able to sail smoothly, but it was not to be. For beneath a surface of calm, tempests were brewing whose gale force winds would soon blow the lid off little Miss Carroll's career. Essentially a kind, generous, exceedingly loyal, if slightly eccentric person, Irish Nancy could be cunning, obstinent, and downright contrary when frustrated or provoked. Hurricane Nan a.k.a. the legendary Carroll temper was said to have

One of the many charming scenes Nancy shared with costar, Fredric March in the witty, critically acclaimed comedy-drama, *Laughter* **(Paramount, 1930), Miss Carroll's personal favorite of her thirty nine films.**

first surfaced while making, *Sweetie*. Stories of her blowups, demands, and disputes with other actors, producers, directors, and technicians were to become numerous and very colorful. Early on, Carroll became resentful of the roles given her, the way she was treated by Paramount, and by the invasion of her privacy. Her frustration sometimes boiled over into angry outbursts — sudden sharp discharges, like flashes of lightning for which she was usually sorry. She said the main reason was professional.

"I don't know what it stood for, but I was cast in everything. Out of one film into another — comedies, dramas, musicals. . . I had no choice of stories or roles. I couldn't offer a word as to how I'd like to do a scene. Everything was too fast and furious." [17]

If Carroll's rise to the stardom had been meteoric, her fall from grace would be even quicker. By decade's end, the luminous star that was Nancy Carroll was but a fading memory. Nancy's tantrums, public complaints, and refusal to do certain photo sessions, and interviews alienated many Hollywood influentials: from studio heads to technicians and important writers and columnists. Famed portrait photographer John Engsted, who worked in Paramount's publicity department during Carroll's heyday, was one of many who were distinctly unimpressed with the volatile Miss Carroll's demeanor. According to noted film historian, David Chierichetti, who knew Engsted, "John often talked about how difficult Nancy Carroll always was, how hard it was just to get her to sit down and pose for pictures, schedule an interview, or anything the publicity department wanted from her. . ."[18] In movie magazine articles Carroll was publicly chastised for being, "disagreeable." In one entitled, "An Open Letter to Nancy Carroll" (1931), influential writer Adele Whitely Fletcher called Carroll on the carpet for, "being difficult and temperatmental . . ." "It's your own fault, Nancy," she opined. "You ruin all the grand things you do by the way do them . . ."[19]

Carroll's professional difficulties were compounded by personal problems. By the end of 1930, the Kirkland marriage was over. As happy as they had once been, they had grown apart and could not sustain their long distance union. In the spring of 1931, they separated. By June, their seven-year marriage came to an official and amicable end, a victim of separate careers, and interests.[20] Nancy's daughter, Patricia told the author they remained on good terms.

"They were just great with each other. I never heard them argue. She never said a nasty word about Pop, and he never said a nasty word about her. Daddy went into deep mourning when she died. He didn't talk for about three days! When I see what happens with friends of mine, (i.e. breakups), I really respect the way they acted, for my benefit I'm sure."[21]

A few days after her divorce, Miss Carroll married husband #2, Bolton Mallory, editor of the humor weekly, *Life*. The resulting negative press disillusioned many of her fans. The notoriety combined with her temper, and a disappointing film titled, *The Night Angel* to make a lethal mixture.

Although Nancy acquitted herself well in the melodramatic *Stolen Heaven* (Paramount, 1931), costarring Phillips Holmes and Louis Calhern, the movie was not a worthy follow-up to *Laughter*. Burdened by uninspired direction and a mediocre script, Nancy's touching performance as a down on her luck street walker was lost in a sea of weak dialogue and inconsequential scenes. The mildly diverting comedy, *Personal Maid* (Paramount, 1930), which featured sister Terry in a small role, also did nothing to enhance her standing. With her reputation muddied, Nancy pinned her hopes of sustaining her momentum on a reunion with Fredric March and director Edmund Goulding. Unfortunately, the film was a bonafide disaster from which Carroll's career would never recover.

Originally slated for Marlene Dietrich, *The Night Angel* (Paramount, 1931), cast Irish Nancy as the daughter of a notorious Czech cabaret operator (Alison Skipworth) who becomes enamored of the prosecutor (March) who sends her mother to prison. Inanely plotted with ludicrous dialogue, the rather dull melodramatic hodge-podge damaged all the involved talents. For once, audiences and reviewers spoke in unison. Moviegoers stayed away in droves. March and Goulding (who also wrote the script), were each taken down a peg. Both would soon recover, but not Nancy. Miscast as a gamine from Prague, the film damaged her professionally at a time when she needed a successful picture to counter the negative press and personal turmoil which engulfed her. In his review of the film, a *Photoplay* critic summed up Carroll's predicament in one line. "If this sort of thing keeps up, Nancy Carroll's name at the box office won't be worth an apple . . ."[22]

A wounded Carroll made five motion pictures in 1932, but failed to reinvigorate her movie career. She was wasted: as a chorine who suffers when she marries into wealth in *Wayward* (Paramount), as a girl setting out to avenge the mob murder of her brother in the modestly budgeted, *Under-Cover Man* (Paramount), and as a meek serving maid in love with her aristocratic boss (Doug Fairbanks Jr.) in *The Scarlet Dawn* (on loan to Warner Bros.). Despite a showy lead role and a first rate supporting cast (including Cary Grant and Randolph Scott), the drama, *Hot Saturday* (Paramount), was also a non-starter. Nancy was captivating as a small town girl whose love for a playboy (Grant) makes her the target of gossips, but Paramount gave the movie little promotion, and her performance went largely unnoticed.

Carroll's best opportunity for a comeback in 1932, came as the sweetheart of a German soldier killed in World War I who falls for

Irish Nancy Carroll was miscast as a gamine from Prague in director Edmund Goulding's drama, *The Night Angel* (Paramount, 1931), costarring Fredric March. The film was such a disastrous flop, her career never fully recovered.

the Frenchman (Phillips Holmes) responsible in *Broken Lullaby* a.k.a. *The Man I Killed* (Paramount). With guidance from master director, Ernst Lubitsch, a fine cast delivered exceptional performances which powerfully presented the film's pacifist theme. One affecting scene had Nancy reading the last letter she received from her fiance to the man who killed him. *New York Times* critic, Mordaunt Hall spoke for the majority when he called the film, "further evidence of Ernst

Two attractive and talented actors: Miss Carroll and Douglas Fairbanks Jr. appeared in the minor melodrama, *The Scarlet Dawn* (Warner Bros, 1932).

Lubitsch's genius. . . its story is unfurled in poetic fashion with an unexcelled performance by Lionel Barrymore, and fine acting from Phillips Holmes and Nancy Carroll." Unfortunately for Nancy, the film failed at the box office precisely for the reason it succeeded with critics. Its realistic portrayal of war's grim realities was a downer, and depression-era audiences were in no mood to feel sad when they went to the movies.[23]

The tumult surrounding the cantankerous colleen continued unabated. Her reputation for being "difficult" proliferated with reports of her clashes with Lubitsch over billing and the size of her role in *Broken Lullaby*. Stories also circulated chronicling Carroll's feud with her *Wayward* costar Richard Arlen, whom she thoroughly disliked and would not speak to off the set. Still another colorful tale related by author David Chierichetti (as told to him by John Engsted), had Carroll turning around and slapping a seamstress in Paramount's costume department when the girl accidentally pricked her with a pin during a fitting.[24] When asked to comment, Nancy branded many of the negative stories as fiction, and defiantly challenged magazine writers to "prove" she was difficult, but all the fuss was continuing to take a toll on her professional standing. Burdened with a temperamental star in the midst of a career downturn, Paramount began having second thoughts about picking up Carroll's option in 1933. In a stinging rebuke entitled, "What's Going to Happen to Nancy," Carroll critic Adele Whitely Fletcher summed up Nancy's status at her home studio,

"Everyone from the stage hands to the executives themselves seem pretty well fed up after years of Nancy's antics. From what I have seen they've ceased caring what happens to her; they'll be glad 'to see her heels' as the old Irish expression goes. . ." [25]

Paramount's financial losses, (a staggering 15.8 million dollars in 1932), also factored into their decision to have a "long talk" with the gutsy redhead who agreed to be more cooperative. It was too late. By years end, the petite firebrand would be packing her bags.

Under the guidance of director Ernst Lubitsch, Nancy gave one of her finest film performances opposite Phillips Holmes in *Broken Lullaby* a.k.a. *The Man I Killed* (Paramount, 1932), but sadly, the film's downbeat theme doomed box office receipts.

Before her departure from Paramount, Nancy had two good roles both on loan to other studios. In the modest, *Child of Manhattan* (Columbia, 1933), she was vibrant as a dance hall hostess who becomes mistress, then wife to a wealthy landowner. She was also excellent as the unfaithful wife of an attorney ironically defending a man for killing his straying spouse in the psychological drama, *A Kiss Before the Mirror* (Universal, 1933), stylishly directed by James Whale. Her final Paramount films were weak entries. The melodrama, *Woman Accused* (1933), was both odd and perplexing. Even Carroll's committed performance as a beautiful murderess who evades punishment through the bravura efforts of her attorney beau (Cary Grant), couldn't bring sanity to the incredible proceedings. The melodramatic plotline of *I Love That Man* (1933), was even worse. With main characters named Brains, Driller, Mousey, and Labels, at least it was good for unintentional laughs. As the innocent girlfriend of confidence man (Edmund Lowe), you could almost see Carroll gritting her teeth. It was time to seek greener pastures.

As Nancy left her home studio amid press reports branding her a temperamental troublemaker, she still hoped to re-ascend popularity polls and reshape her tarnished image. Some soul searching was in order. Most assuredly her Irish temper had been the main source of her image problems. What had been her greatest strength: her fighting spirit, had turned into a significant impediment once she'd achieved her show business dream. In Nancy's defense, if she had occasionally lost her cool, she'd had plenty of provocation. While Paramount had made her a star, they hadn't always nurtured her apparent talent, squandering her momentum on such nonentities as *Personal Maid*, and *Wayward*, while reneging on promises to loan her to Sam Goldwyn to star in *Street Scene*, or giving her the lead in *A Farewell to Arms*, a property originally purchased for Carroll and Fredric March. With no regard for her feelings, the studio ordered her to do interviews and photo sessions while her marriage was crumbling, and pressured her to keep the existence of her daughter hidden from the public. Patricia Bevan recalled the circumstances this way.

"From the beginning, Paramount insisted that I be kept a secret. That's when mother and Marlene Dietrich got together. Dietrich had the same problem with Maria. They both asked the studio, 'What is going on?!';

Based on a ten chapter novel written by ten different novelists, the melodrama, *Woman Accused* (Paramount, 1933), cast Nancy as a woman on trial for murder.

and each in their separate and very loud ways made a big thing out of it." [26]

For their part, the Hollywood press was frequently unfair and unduly critical, forever blaming Nancy and floating rumors about her family and personal life. Miss Carroll eventually realized she was in a no-win situation. "If I walk into a restaurant and sit by myself, they say, 'Nancy Carroll — trying to be ritzy.' If you're late and you don't stop to say good morning to the gateman — that's being snooty."[27] Daughter Patricia related a particularly cruel press incident in a recent interview with the author.

"I remember we were living in Beverly Hills and I used to go down to

Rodeo school riding my bike like any normal kid. A girl and I were playing jacks out on the front sidewalk one day when a guy came over to us. The next day there was a newspaper story, 'Nancy Carroll's Daughter Threatened With Kidnapping.' When I got home from school, my mother had put a newspaper with the headline right there at the front door. She had put a chair under the door handle, and Grandpa's shalele across. And she said, 'Just let'em try!!!' Just so I wouldn't be scared." [28]

After a failed attempt at Broadway success in the dramatic, *Undesirable Lady* (The play closed after only 24 performances.), the Irish firecracker returned to Hollywood to begin freelancing. In 1934, she appeared in the film adaptation of Ben Levy's successful stage comedy, *Springtime For Henry* (Fox, 1934), contributing yet another charming performance as a philandering wife whose husband surrenders her (to wealthy lover, Otto Kruger), as part of a lucrative business deal. Despite Carroll's best efforts, the film was unsuccessful. What had been a sparkling, and sophisticated comedic romp on stage, was turned into a sexy slapstick farce by director Frank Tuttle which offended the Legion of Decency whose "condemned" rating doomed its distribution. Nancy fared better in *Transatlantic Merry-Go-Round* (United Artists, 1934), an all-star Busby Berkeley-esque musical comedy extravaganza with a mystery plotline thrown in for good measure. A "Grand Hotel" at sea, the film was a literal smorgasbord of entertainment delights including lavish production numbers, ace jokesters Jack Benny, Sid Silvers, and Mitzi Green, not to mention Richard Whiting and Sidney Clare songs. Ravishing Carroll's engaging performance (as the show's star), was yet another highlight which caught the attention of director Frank Capra who promptly signed her to a four picture contract with Columbia in hopes of orchestrating her comeback. Capra planned to feature her in his upcoming film, *Broadway Bill*, but problems forced a postponement of production. By the time it commenced, Columbia had placed Nancy in a ludicrous melodrama, *Jealousy*, and she was unavailable. The plum role eventually went to Myrna Loy.

Nancy is said to have hated the four pictures she made for Columbia between 1934-35. Each was decidedly grade B with few distinguishing qualities excepting Carroll's poise, and professionalism.

Nancy gave a scintillating performance opposite Otto Kruger in the sexy slapstick farce, *Springtime For Henry* (Fox, 1934).

The musical melodrama, *After the Dance* (1935), was perhaps the best of the bunch. An attempt to recreate the magic of Astaire and Rogers, Columbia paired Carroll with George Murphy (whom Nancy disliked), both modestly talented dancers. Although the result was fairly pleasing, the lack of studio investment doomed the venture. After three other Columbia mediocrities: *Jealousy* (1934), *I'll Love You Always* (1935), and *Atlantic Adventure* (1935), Nancy became disillusioned. According to Paul Nemcek's informative book, *Films of Nancy Carroll*, she became anxious to complete her studio contract when she realized, "the B pictures were doing little for her career and actually lowering her stature."[29] In the fall of 1935, Miss Carroll fled the film capital.

By 1934, it was clear Nancy's second marriage was a mistake. The basic incompatibility between Carroll and former Princeton professor, Bolton Mallory was compounded by long separations and rumors of infidelity. In July 1935, Carroll began divorce proceedings only to find that Mallory had already been granted a Mexican divorce and had married 13-year-old Carlotta Labato. Still suffering from scandal fatigue, the independent-minded, strong-willed Miss Carroll obtained her own Nevada divorce and would remain single for the next 18 years. Patricia Bevan remembers accompanying her mother while she untied the marriage knot to Mallory. With the thrill-seeking Nancy Carroll, things were never boring.

"Mother was physically without fear! She loved doing hazardous things. When we were in Nevada for the famous six weeks when she was divorcing Bolton, we went to the Hoover Dam. The guys ask her if she would like to go up on the wooden platform (with ropes on it) that goes way up to the top of the dam way out in the open. 'Oh yes!!' she said . . . She laughed, smiled, and waved at me while being hauled all over the Hoover Dam! I'll never forget it!" [30]

In 1936, Carroll opted to take a long needed vacation to catch up on her rest, to plan her future, and to be with 11-year-old Patricia. They sailed to Europe for an extended stay visiting London, Paris, Venice, and Budapest. During the trip, Nancy received numerous film offers: mostly leads in low budget productions, which she flatly refused. Finally, in 1938, she was persuaded to accept a showy featured film role in a comedy starring old friend Fredric March, and Virginia Bruce. The bright and breezy, *There Goes My Heart* (United Artists, 1938), should have propelled Carroll back into the limelight, but her fifth-billed part was severely cut prior to release, stripping it of most of its substance. One month later, Carroll accepted another disappointing assignment as the fiancé of Melvyn Douglas in the Deanna Durbin vehicle, *That Certain Age* (Universal, 1938). Unfortunately, (and somewhat surprisingly), the movie would be Carroll's last. There would be frequents rumors (published and unpublished), of a comeback film, but none materialized. It now seemed as if Nancy's legendary Irish luck had turned bad.

Filmdom's loss was the theater's gain. Nancy had always preferred the excitement of an audience and the electricity of live theater. Although Hollywood would tempt her from time to time, she would devote the remaining 26 years of her life to entertaining and inspiring theater audiences, and living life to the max, finding the personal satisfaction, fulfillment, and joy Hollywood had never afforded her. By 1939, she was back on the "Great White Way" replacing Martha Sleeper in the risque comedy, *I Must Love Someone*

At age 35, Nancy contributed what would be her final film performance as Melvyn Douglas' fiance in the Deanna Durbin vehicle, *That Certain Age* (Universal, 1938). From left to right: Miss Durbin, Mr. Douglas and Nancy.

penned by ex-husband, Jack Kirkland (now an acclaimed playwright whose *Tobacco Road* had one of Broadway's longest runs). Her excellent reviews encouraged Carroll to travel back to the West Coast to test for the role of Henry Hull's wife in producer Edward Small's film, *My Son, My Son*, but the part eventually went to Sophie Stewart.

The 1940's brought particular joy to Carroll's life. Even though she participated in one of the decade's biggest Broadway flops, *For Heaven's Sake, Mother* (1948), opposite Molly Picon, Nancy, (now a New York resident), found success in summer stock appearances in such diverse plays as *Mr. and Mrs. North* (1941-43), *Stage Door* (1942), *Too Many Husbands* (1944-47), and *The Two Mrs. Carrolls* (1945, 1949). She also took great satisfaction in her daughter's burgeoning interest in acting. In 1942, a very proud Nancy witnessed the theatrical debut of her 17-year-old daughter in *Susan and God* at the Bucks County Playhouse (in Pennsylvania). Later, she applauded Patricia's much-lauded performance as Corliss Archer in the touring company of *Kiss and Tell* (1943), and her acclaimed Broadway opening in *Years Ago* (1946), costarring Fredric March, and Florence Eldredge.

In the latter 1940's, Nancy witnessed the marriage of talented Patricia to gifted playwright and caricaturist, Donald Bevan (*Stalag 17*), and the birth of her first grandchild (a grandson) in 1949, the same year Carroll visited the beloved land of her forefathers, Ireland.[31]

During World War II, the patriotic Miss Carroll worked tirelessly entertaining American troops, taking the comedy, *Mr. and Mrs. North* to U.S.O. camps using soldiers as actors. At one of her many wartime appearances, she was approached by a young college graduate now working as a fledgling newspaper and radio reporter. His name was John Springer, and he would eventually become one of the entertainment world's most successful publicists and most celebrated film history writers whose works include *All Talking, All Singing, All Dancing*, and the much beloved *They Had Faces Then*. Years later, in an interview with the author, Springer remembered Carroll's kindness and charisma that day.

"She was every bit as pretty as I had expected, warm and friendly too, unlike some stars who would brush off a newspaperman of no particular distinction. I'd see her again over the next couple of years when now in uniform, I did public relations for the Air Force show, 'ATC Contract Caravan'." [32]

Eventually Springer and Carroll would become devoted friends.

In 1950, Nancy was tempted back to the screen, (the small screen), replacing Jean Muir as Mrs. Aldrich in the popular NBC comedy series, *The Aldrich Family*. Even though Carroll enjoyed the experience, she opted out of the show in 1951, in time to do several guest shots as the mother on her daughter's new sitcom, *The Egg and I* costarring John Craven. During the next two decades, Nancy would be an occasional guest on such popular TV series as *The Further Adventures of Ellery Queen* (1959), *U. S. Steel Hour* (3 episodes 1961-62), *Naked City* (1961), and *Going My Way* (1963).[33]

Since her divorce in 1935, Nancy had kept her personal relationships fairly discreet. During her Hollywood heyday, she had been burned by negative reports of her private life, and had learned a valuable lesson. Of course, that didn't stop gossip columnists from linking her with several distinguished men over the years including writer

Nancy and her actress daughter Patricia Kirkland rehearse a scene for Miss Kirkland's TV situation comedy, *The Egg and I*. Nancy did several guest shots on the series playing Miss Kirkland's mother.

Quentin Reynolds, high-powered attorney William Van Rensselaer Smith, Senator Jacob Javits, and young John Springer. Regarding Mr. Springer, one columnist even suggested they had tied the knot. Though they never married, Springer and Carroll would remain close pals, and loyal Nancy Carroll was a good friend in a pinch. In 1927, she had been a character witness for her friend, Paul Kelly during his infamous manslaughter trial. In the 1950's, Nancy came to the aid of John Springer who had a distinctly different kind of problem.

"She was a terribly generous person. When my wife June and I were

going to get married, we ran into Nancy at a party. She adored June on sight. I told her we were going to be married by a justice of the peace. Nancy said, 'What about the Catholic church?' I said I wanted to set it up, but the priest said June would have to go through six months of instruction. . . When she heard this, Nancy went to Cardinal Spellman and said, 'You've turned a good Catholic boy away from the church.' And he said, 'Don't be silly, they can be married here in St. Patrick's Cathedral.' And we were. And it was the wedding of all weddings! Janet Leigh and Tony Curtis were our best man and maid of honor. Everyone was there from John Steinbeck to Marlene Dietrich, Hank Fonda, and many others. Nancy did all that!!" [34]

In 1953, Nancy surprised everyone by marrying wealthy Dutch sports car manufacturer, C. H. J. "Jappe" Gruen (not Groen as is listed in reference books), and moving to Indonesia, the location of his fiber glass plant. In 1956, they were back in New York where Mr. Gruen received treatment for tuberculosis. Afterwards, they moved to Mexico City where he recuperated. During these years, Nancy finally had the opportunity and the financial means to explore her many interests like traveling, gourmet cooking, oil painting, and deep sea fishing. Apparently she had a real aptitude for the latter two hobbies. The first exhibition of her art was in New York's Salpeter Gallery in 1952.[35] Son-in-law Don Bevan, told the author Nancy's fishing exploits made her a legend in the Florida Keys.

"When she died we got a letter from Barbara Bel Geddes who said, 'Maybe you don't know this about your mother, but we were at Sloppy Joes on Key West where Hemingway's prize fish was mounted over the bar, and of course, he got credit for it. But the bartender told us that he didn't really catch the fish. A little actress by the name of Nancy Carroll caught it. She couldn't pull it in. She fought the fish for hours and hours. And Hemingway takes the credit!'" [36]

In 1957, the 54-year-old Mrs. Gruen began attending Mexico City College studying art in hopes of obtaining a degree. Nancy had always regretted her lack of a formal education, and attending college was thrilling. While a student, she took part in various English speaking dramatic productions, and was chosen to direct.

Eventually, she accepted an offer to teach an acting course, but by 1960, the hyperactive Carroll was restless. Bored with the tranquility of Mexico, she longed for the hustle and bustle of New York. Her trips to visit her family (The Bevan brood now included four grandchildren.), became more frequent as her homesickness became acute. Nancy was above all else, a genuine American trooper. She had literally grown up on the American stage, and she wanted to go home.[37]

In the early 1960's, the indomitable redhead became involved in numerous stage, television, and radio projects. She did several candid interviews in which she acknowledged responsibility for problems in her film career and expressed regrets for any hurt feelings she had caused. She even buried old enmities. In 1961, Miss Carroll turned up as a surprise guest on an episode of TV's *This Is Your Life* saluting Richard Arlen. Older columnists who remembered the famous Carroll/Arlen feud, had a field day. In July, 1963, Nancy heard from another voice from the past when *Stolen Heaven* director George Abbott asked her to read for the lead in the national tour of the smash Broadway hit, *Never Too Late*, costarring William Bendix. Her tour-de-force audition won her the part (originated on Broadway by Maureen O'Sullivan), of a middle-aged wife and mother who discovers she is pregnant. Nancy was ecstatic, telling the press,

"I dearly love our company, and oh, I'm so glad to be back in show business. Bill Bendix and I had signed five-year contracts to do a television series together, but we got out of them. We had a final run through here the other evening and everybody was so wonderful to me — Maureen and Paul Ford, and our director, George Abbott. We used to call George a carpenter, but now I'm convinced he's a genius."[38]

In August 1963, the ever beautiful Miss Carroll embarked on a difficult eight-month cross-country tour of *Never Too Late*, delighting audiences, and dazzling critics. It soon became apparent that the youthful redhead had lost none of the ability, charm, and charisma which had so captivated the multitudes 30+ years before. One of the lucky few who had the pleasure of Nancy's company during those days was a member of the supporting cast, a talented actor who had become a big television star on the hit western series, *Sugarfoot*, Will Hutchins. In an interview with the author, Mr.

Hutchins shared fond memories of the production, and his magnetic costar.

"Nancy was such a beautiful lady. I loved her to death! I had heard reports about her, but I have nothing but great things to say. 100%, no ifs, ands, or buts! She was one of the top actresses I ever worked with who had one of the loveliest voices I ever heard. . . I met her in New York where we rehearsed. I knew she was a big movie star, singing, dancing, and acting. When we did our first read through, I thought she was a bit stuffy. She had the last line in the play. There's an old superstition that you don't read the last line of a play during rehearsal, and she made a big thing about it. I thought she was kind of hoity-toity then. But boy, was I wrong. . . When we hit certain towns, we would all do things together. I remember, she took us to movies, a concert with the Chicago Symphony, and art museums like the National Gallery in Washington. . . I came to realize over the long haul, Nancy was the best thing in the show. It felt great on stage with her. She really came across to the audience. She had great stage presence — magic! . . . I think it hurt William Bendix's feelings when she got the best reviews. He was a great talent himself, but he had throat cancer and was so blasted sick! The run should have been much longer, but he just didn't have the energy. . ." [39]

By September 1964, the "child of Manhattan" was back in New York appearing as a Jewish stepmother in an off Broadway production of *Cindy*, a modernized version of *Cinderella*. After wintering in Mexico, she returned to the "Big Apple" in the spring of 1965, this time for good. Apparently, her frequent trips to the states had created difficulties in her twelve-year marriage. Rumors of the Gruens' separation were confirmed when Carroll took up residence in New York. In late June 1965, Nancy began a short engagement of *Never Too Late* at Long Island's Mineola Theatre costarring Tom Ewell. On August 2, the 61-year-old actress took the comedy to the Tappan Zee Playhouse in Nyack, this time with Bert Lahr. On Friday, August 6, 1965, her failure to appear for a performance prompted telephone calls to her apartment. When there was no answer, daughter Patricia was summoned, and she and Don rushed to Nancy's Upper East Side residence and found her dead, clad in a

Nancy's last acting triumph came in 1963 when she portrayed a middle-aged woman who unexpectedly, becomes pregnant in the road company version of the hit Broadway comedy, *Never Too Late* (1963), costarring William Bendix.]

nightgown and slippers, kneeling near a flickering television set. An autopsy listed her death from "natural causes."[40] Apparently, Nancy had died shortly after returning home from the Thursday night performance. According to Patricia,

"It was an aneurism. She did the show and went out afterward with someone she had went to high school with who turned up lo these many years; and when she came home, that was it. She did know something was wrong because she'd had bad headaches during the last week, and went to someone in the Army Medical Corps who did an ultra-sound which took the pain away instantly. She thought it was a miracle. Unfortunately, it just covered up what was going on." [41]

Tributes poured in from around the world. Although Nancy had ceased making films almost three decades earlier, the stars of the silver screen had not forgotten her. Through the years, several of her costars like Cary Grant, Gary Cooper, and Gene Raymond had weighed in, crediting Carroll with immeasurably aiding their careers, and teaching them valuable lessons in filmmaking. Of the many published obituaries and tributes at the time of her death, none was more heartfelt and poignant than John Springer's in *Films in Review*. In an obituary piece, he recalled taking Nancy to the screening of *Honey* at the Theodore Huff Memorial Film Society in the 1950's.

"I hadn't told her where we were going, and when she entered, there was a standing ovation. William K. Everson's program notes for the night referred to her as, 'the most neglected fine actress, because of the unavailability of her films,' and reading this brought quick, happy tears to Nancy's eyes. Later, Everson and Dan Talbot arranged a showing of one of her favorite films, Laughter for her grandchildren who had never seen her on the screen before." [42]

A small private memorial service was held for family only. Interment was alongside her parents in Long Island. Scores of her famous friends visited the funeral home prior to the services including such luminaries as ex-hubby Jack Kirkland, Henry Fonda, Gene Raymond, Myrna Loy, Robert Preston, Helen Hayes, Mary Pickford and Buddy Rogers. Mr. Springer remembered one of the most illustrious visitors.

"I recall when Nancy died, the funeral home was right around the corner from where we lived. I remember Ginger Rogers coming. She said, 'Nancy was just one of the greatest actresses. She was someone who could do it all!' And you know what? She did!" [43]

Nancy's son-in-law, Don Bevan summed up Carroll this way.

"With very sweet Nancy Carroll there was always high drama. As Pat has said about her mother, when she walked into a room, the lights turned on. If a window was closed, she opened it. If it was open, she'd close it." [44]

Today, too few recall the sparkling charm and incredible sincerity of the actress known as Nancy Carroll. She, with the pretty heart-shaped face, the fiery red hair, dazzling blue eyes, the funny little vocals, dancing to escape her heartbreak, the tough little chorine discovering a conscience and the pain of regret, all indelible images of one of the talkies' first stars, now unfortunately, one of the movies' forgotten ladies.

At first glance, the beguiling Miss Carroll's obscurity seems perplexing. After all, she was one of the early sound era's most popular and successful actresses, but there's a simple obvious explanation. If Nancy's temper impeded her career, neglect has sabotaged her memory. With the notable exception of John Springer, film historians have largely failed to recognize the historical significance of Carroll's career, and her importance as a symbol of her era. The lack of availability of her films, and their scarcity on classic film channels are also factors. Hope springs eternal, however. With the information age and the internet, new forms of communication are springing up. Classic film buffs, and movie fans across the country are designing websites to honor their neglected film favorites. On January 30, 1999, an extraordinary one was launched to commemorate the life and career of Nancy Carroll. It's called, "Baby Face" and includes a biography, filmography, photographs, classic Carroll quotations, and various other interesting facts. Its designer, Suzanne Benedetto describes her creation this way.

"Having always been interested in vintage Hollywood, I wanted to create a beautiful and fun website in honor of an actress from the early years, one which would not only pay respect to her talent, but preserve her memory as well as educate current and future generations about her. I wanted to do this for someone who had been forgotten, but didn't deserve to be. The very first name that came to mind was Nancy Carroll. To me, she embodied all things wonderful: talent, beauty, independence, feminism, commitment to motherhood, perseverance, living her life her way. Who could be more deserving than the original musical sweetheart! . . ." [45]

Yes indeed, Suzanne. "Baby Face" stands as an impressive if long overdue memorial to the little colleen who captured America's heart during the depression. The fighting Irish actress from Manhattan would be proud!

UPDATE

Nancy's daughter, noted TV and stage actress, and casting director Patricia Kirkland Bevan died of a cancer-related illness two months after doing interviews with the author on August 14, 2000. Publicist/author, John Springer passed away on October 30, 2001. The cause was listed as congestive heart failure. Pat's author/artist husband, Donald Bevan died on May 29, 2013. Of Nancy's four grandchildren, two: Mark and Nan (named after Nancy), eight grandchildren and three great grandchildren survived Mr. Bevan. Author and costume designer David Chierichetti died unexpectedly on November 28, 2016. Actor Will Hutchins lives in Long Island, New York. Suzanne Benedetto's wonderful tribute website, "Baby Face" renamed, "Child of Manhattan" is still online, reminding classic film devotees of the beauty and unique charm of Nancy, and inspiring new fans of this unjustly forgotten actress.

Check it out: **http://childofmanhattan.com/**

EXTRA

Legendary publicist and acclaimed author, the late John Springer was often referred to as the "Guardian of the Stars." An unassuming, quiet individual, his success was based on trust. His clients trusted him to guard their secrets, and he considered their trust a sacred bond. No wonder he represented the biggest names in show business, from the Burtons (Richard and Elizabeth Taylor), and Marilyn Monroe, to Judy Garland, Henry Fonda, Robert Mitchum, Gary Cooper, and Joan Crawford to name only a few. Classic film enthusiasts also remember Mr. Springer as an acclaimed author. Among his written works were such volumes as *All Talking! All Singing! All Dancing!* his homage to the Hollywood musical, and the much beloved *They Had Faces Then*, his tribute to the feminine actors of the 1930's, both the stars and supporting players.

In May 2000, the author had the privilege of interviewing Mr. Springer about Nancy Carroll. The following is the complete, never-before published interview. As you will see, despite the fact Nancy had been gone for over thirty years when this interview was conducted, time had not diminished Mr. Springer's love and devotion for his friend and favorite actress.

"LOVING NANCY: AN INTERVIEW WITH JOHN SPRINGER"

DAN: It's always great to speak to you again. This time, I know the topic is one that's close to your heart: Nancy Carroll!

JOHN SPRINGER: I adored her!

DAN: You have said you met her during World War II.

JOHN SPRINGER: Yes. I was with Josh Logan's flying soldiers show. Nancy did a guest spot with us entertaining the soldiers, and I got to know her then. I was already in love with her before I met her. I dated Nancy in the late 1940's, early 1950's. I also knew her former husbands Jack Kirkland and Bolton Mallory very well.

DAN: Jack and Nancy remained good friends after their divorce, didn't they?

JOHN SPRINGER: Indeed they did. The first time I ever met Jack, he came over to me at Sardies, after my book had come out. (my first book) And he said, "Hey my name is Jack Kirkland. I want you to know I appreciate so much what you wrote about Nancy Carroll. I loved her. Everybody that knew her loved her. And you captured it." I was glad to know he felt that way.

DAN: You really fell for her, didn't you?

JOHN SPRINGER: At one point I had such a crush on her! I remember going into the office one Monday. The secretary said, "Call your mother." They had been calling. Jimmie Fidler had announced over the radio that Nancy and I were secretly married. I called my mother and father who were beside themselves; my mother because I was a good

Catholic boy and she was a divorced woman, and my father because she was x number of years older than I. I said, "Come on, I haven't even seen her for months." We had a big break up at least four or five months ago."

DAN: Did Nancy ever talk about her films when you knew her?

JOHN SPRINGER: Sometimes.

DAN: Was she nostalgic about the old times? How did she feel about her film work?

JOHN SPRINGER: She thought it was good. And it **was** good! She didn't like the last ones. She had done some pictures for Columbia that she didn't like at all. And she didn't like them particularly because Frank Capra had already given Jean Arthur a real turn around and made her a bigger star than she had ever been. Capra signed Nancy for Columbia and planned to use her in Broadway Bill. In the meantime, Columbia had put her in Jealousy and I'll Love You Always, and by the time Broadway Bill commenced, Myrna got it, and she was marvelous.

DAN: Did she ever mention what her favorite films were?

JOHN SPRINGER: I know she loved both Devil's Holiday and Laughter. Laughter, I believe, was her favorite. She loved Freddie March. And didn't we all! She had fun doing things like Sweetie and Honey, Follow Thru, and Close Harmony. She loved The Shopworn Angel. It was great, way beyond the Margaret Sullavan version.

DAN: In The Devil's Holiday, she acts the whole cast off the screen.

JOHN SPRINGER: She sure does! Incidentally, I was with Doug Fairbanks Jr. recently. He is a nice guy. I said to him, "One time I was so jealous of you because you were playing opposite my favorite actress in a very uncharacteristic role, Scarlet Dawn." And he said, "Oh yes, Nancy Carroll, she was a sweet little thing!" And I thought,

"Boy, that wasn't the way I would have described Nancy, even when she was playing Sweetie and Honey!!" (laughter)

DAN: *She was an original! She seemed to transcend her material. Many of her films were not particularly great, but she made you care about the characters she played.*

JOHN SPRINGER. *Exactly! The only film of hers I couldn't get into was The Night Angel. I just felt she was miscast. Laughter is my favorite as well, but I also liked some of the films she made after her heyday like Child of Manhattan, and I'll Love You Always. Springtime for Henry is fun.*

DAN: *What about Broken Lullaby? It was said she quarreled with the great director Ernst Lubitsch when they were making it?*

JOHN SPRINGER: *I liked Broken Lullaby, but it just seemed that it was not right for Nancy.*

DAN: *Since you were a friend of hers for decades, and knew her well, what was your assessment of her as a person?*

JOHN SPRINGER: *She was very warm and loving, but she could be nasty as hell to someone whom she didn't like. With me, she was warm and sweet.*

DAN: *She had quite a reputation for being temperamental. What was your impression?*

JOHN SPRINGER: *She could be temperamental. She could get very angry. I saw her blow her stack a couple of times, but mostly she was warm and charming.*

DAN: *According to the press, her outbursts of temper were short but intense.*

JOHN SPRINGER: *Oh, yes! She was warm and charming to everyone, unless she was in a bad mood. I never knew him, but I know she* hated Richard Arlen. They had a terrible feud. That's not unusual because my other dream girl, Sylvia Sidney hated him too!

DAN: *The film historian David Cheriechetti knew legendary costume designer John Engsted, and said Engsted told him Nancy had slapped him after he accidentally pricked her with a pin.*

JOHN SPRINGER: She was very capable of that (much laughter), but I'm sure she was so full of regret for doing that. I'm sure she went back and apologized all over the place. She would come back.

DAN: *Since you dated her, there's a chance she got mad at you. Did she?*

JOHN SPRINGER: I remember one time I took her to the Stork Club, and my younger brother was still in uniform. He had just come back from Japan. We had some kind of quarrel, and she stamped out of the club. I chased her. I left my brother alone at the table. I don't remember any of the details! (laughter).

DAN: *You said in one of your writings that she acknowledged making a lot of mistakes in her career, and admitted she had lost her temper too many times. Did she really feel that way?*

JOHN SPRINGER: Oh yes. She realized that.

DAN: *During her heyday, many gossip columnists and writers were negative about her because she was not cooperating with them, doing interviews etc.*

JOHN SPRINGER: She was not, but the only person I know about that she was quarreling with regularly was Richard Arlen. She couldn't stand him. He was nasty to Louise Brooks who was also one of my buddies . . . She didn't like him either.

DAN: *Did she ever talk about the press to you?*

JOHN SPRINGER: I can remember one day, I took the editor of

Photoplay, Adele Whitely Fletcher, a very imposing woman, to lunch with Nancy, and they couldn't have been warmer to each other. Adele called me afterwards and was so grateful, and said Nancy was such a marvelous person.

DAN: You told me she liked to play jokes and joke around.

JOHN SPRINGER: Oh sure. I remember, for instance, one day when she was doing shows for our Army Air Force group. We also had Danny Kaye. Well, Danny Kaye went on stage and talked and talked and talked!! He was funny for a while, then he became boring. Nancy, who was backstage, took my arm band and put it on her arm. She then came out with a little club and arrested him, and took him off stage. Everybody loved it except Danny who didn't like it at all. It was better than the hook!! (laughter)

DAN: Did she have any close pals in the Hollywood?

JOHN SPRINGER: I know Arline Judge was a pal. They were real buddies. In between Arline's many marriages, Nancy used to hang out with Arline at at a bar called Glennons. That's when I first knew her.

DAN: After she helped you with your wedding to your wife, June, you continued to stay in touch, didn't you?

JOHN SPRINGER: Oh yes. I remember running into Nancy. She was doing a play in Nyack New York. I was on the Coast sharing an office with Mike Nichols who was about to do Who's Afraid of Virginia Woolf. Nancy called, and said, "Oh god, I'd love to play that woman in Virginia Woolf." I said, "Well, I'm afraid Elizabeth has beaten you to it. She's doing it." She said, "Oh, I know, but I'd still love to do it sometime, and I will." Then, I said, "You know, it's been so long since we've gotten together. When are you coming back?" She said, "Well, I'll be doing this play, why don't you come see me? It's just a few miles from New York City." And, I agreed to meet her and get together after the play. Then my closest friend, Hank Fonda called me and he said, "Hey Johnny, I'm coming in. I'll only be here for a couple of days. Let's go out!" And I said, "Oh jeez, I promised Nancy Carroll that I'd go and see her show." He said, "Oh, you can see that another time." So I called Nancy and said I can't come. Something has happened. She said, "Well, come Saturday, it's our closing night, and we're going to have a party." This was Tuesday or Wednesday. So, I went out and had a few belts with Fonda. And the next morning, Nancy was dead. I always felt so guilty! Apparently, they dropped her off after the performance. They found her kneeling by the television set. They couldn't reach her. People had tried to call her. They finally called Pat, and she and Don went over there and found her.

DAN: I assume she didn't suffer.

JOHN SPRINGER: I'm quite sure she didn't.

DAN: It must have been a shock.

JOHN SPRINGER: It sure was! She was a terribly generous person!

DAN: Will Hutchins told me she kept the Never Too Late tour going. Bendix was very ill with throat cancer, and he was often down, not feeling well, not up for the performances. He said she would watch over him and help him through the performance.

JOHN SPRINGER: She did it with other people.

DAN: What is your fondest memory of her? You've probably already told me.

JOHN SPRINGER: Well, all the fondest memories that I'm going to tell you! (much laughter) Seriously, my fondest memory was how she went to Cardinal Spellman.

DAN: I want to thank you for all your time.

JOHN SPRINGER: It's awfully nice to talk to you. Obviously, I'm an admirer of your work already. I think its time that someone who cares did a piece about Nancy. She's almost a forgotten woman.

John Springer receiving Marquette University's College of Journalism's By-Line Award in February, 1971.

DAN: Well, I will do my best not to let you down.

JOHN SPRINGER: I'm sure you will not. Just talking to you makes me realize you can do it. Sometime, I'll give you the whole story about Louise Brooks! [47]

CHAPTER TWO
"GLORIA DICKSON: WE WON'T FORGET"

(Originally published in *Classic Images*, January, 2000)

Although she was proclaimed one of Hollywood's premier young actresses in 1937, today only the most devout classic film enthusiasts recognize the name Gloria Dickson. Even film historians have largely overlooked her work. Like many talented actors of her era, her star flickered briefly, promisingly, then dimmed, a victim of inferior vehicles, poor choices, and a tempestuous private life. In 1945, when tragedy claimed her at the tender age of 28, few remembered the promise Gloria had demonstrated eight years earlier when she made her film debut in Warner Bros.' grade A emotional drama, *They Won't Forget*. Her intense, riveting performance in that motion picture had led to predictions of superstardom for the talented 19 year-old blonde, but it was not to be. At the time of her death, her career was on a downward spiral, and she was wasting away in minor roles. To those who enjoy B-movies, and good acting however, she's a standout — a prime example of the failure of the studio system to fulfill the potential of an actress of considerable natural ability. Film historians may have forgotten Gloria Dickson, but those who are familiar with her work will never forget her!

"She's just a little girl from potato country," was the description Jack Warner gave Hollywood columnists regarding his new contract player when Gloria made her film debut in 1937. Born Thais Alalia Dickerson on August 13, 1917, in Pocatello, Idaho, the future Gloria Dickson was the youngest daughter of banker, Fred Dickerson and his wife Emma. In early childhood, Thais became firmly attached to her devoted father who communicated his love for the great outdoors to his baby girl. In his free time, he took her on holidays in the mountains where they went horseback riding, and trout fishing.

At night, he would spend long hours reading biographies, classic literature and plays to the young girl. Both Mr. and Mrs. Dickerson were interested in literary and artistic endeavors and encouraged their daughter's early aspirations to become an actress. In grade school, she was given diction and poise lessons as well as a spot in their basement where she organized neighborhood theatricals. Her father told her over and over, "If you retain your ideals of good theater, and keep your feet on the ground, you will go far."

Those words echoed in the young girl's mind when her idyllic childhood came to an abrupt end in 1929, with her father's sudden death. It was a traumatic time for the entire family (including elder sister, Doris), but for 12-year-old Thais, it was heartbreaking. In 1930, Mrs. Dickerson moved the children to Long Beach, California (30 miles from Hollywood), where her youngest graduated from junior high, and enrolled at Polytechnic High School majoring in dramatics. [48]

During her high school years, the increasingly attractive young lady appeared in amateur theater productions. Encouraged by her acting coaches, she moonlighted doing dramatic readings (to organ accompaniment), at social clubs, and on KFOX radio station in Long Beach. "In California, I began reading poems on the air. I don't quite remember how it began, but my success with that made me want to work harder than ever in dramatic class." she said years later. [49]

Indeed, her hard work landed her a job with a tent show troupe shortly after her high school graduation in 1935. While a member of the Hart Players, she appeared in every kind of play from Shakespeare to modern. Every night, the troupe would divvy up their modest take among all the players. Young Miss Dickerson's nightly share was, to say the least, modest. She recalled those tough years in a 1937 interview.

"It was my first professional engagement, with a salary that ranged from seventy-five cents a week when business was poor, to three dollars a week when business was good. More often than not, business was poor, and I had to get along on six-bits. I've heard of rubber dollars and how far they'll go, but it's really surprising how far you can stretch a ten cent piece!" [50]

Things began looking up in April 1936, when she applied to join the Federal Theater Project, a government sponsored program designed to promote young talent. Her audition at L.A.'s Mason Opera House ended with a move (with her mother), to Los Angeles. The innate naturalness and subtlety of her acting landed her the lead, Diane in *Seventh Heaven*. She followed with leads in *Smilin Through* and *The Devil Passes*. The latter attracted the attention of Warner Bros' talent scout, Irving Kumin who went backstage and left his card on her dressing table during a performance. Legend has it that she tossed it in the wastebasket, but her work had so impressed Kumin, he looked her up again. Soon a screen test was arranged. Two days later, Thais Alalia Dickerson landed a three year Warner Brothers contract at $200 a week, and a new name, Gloria Dickson. The young actress was thrilled!

"Mother and I could hardly believe that I was suddenly really an actress. It had been my only ambition ever since I could remember. It seemed that all my dreams had come true when we moved to Los Angeles, and I went to work studying parts — rehearsing one role during the day and playing another at night. I didn't give a thought ever to playing in pictures. I didn't have time!" [51]

As the studio began grooming their new contract player, director Mervyn LeRoy (*Little Caesar, I Am a Fugitive From a Chain Gang*), was busy planning his next project, a film adaption of reporter Ward Greene's novel, *A Death in the Deep South*. Filmed previously in 1915, it was the true story of the lynching of a northern Jewish man in Atlanta. On the heels of the success of Fritz Lang's socially significant drama, *Fury* (MGM, 1936), LeRoy and Warner Bros. decided to make their own mob violence film, and Greene's novel seemed the perfect vehicle. With the exception of Claude Rains, LeRoy opted to cast a largely unknown group of actors to heighten the film's impact. When he saw Gloria's impressive screen test, he immediately began thinking of her for the pivotal role of the accused's wife. After he met the intelligent, down-to-earth young lady, he was quickly convinced unknown Gloria Dickson would have the lead feminine role in her first motion picture — an important grade-A production which had the potential to launch her star into the heavens.

Based on Atlanta's infamous Leo Frank case, *They Won't Forget* (Warner Bros., 1937), was the tale of an amoral, ambitious Southern district attorney's (Claude Rains) successful attempt to gain political prominence by charging a northern schoolteacher (Edward Norris) with the brutal murder of one of his teenage pupils (Lana Turner, in her first important film role), despite less than convincing evidence. Assisted by a cynical reporter (Allyn Joslyn), Rains prosecutes his case, stirring up a frenzy of rage in the surrounding community. Sensational media coverage across America inspires a New York newspaper to hire an attorney and detective to help defend the hapless Yankee schoolteacher which, in turn, infuriates the Southerners and poisons the atmosphere. Despite the weakness in Rain's case, and obvious witness tampering, the jury convicts the unfortunate man and sentences him to death. Aghast at the unfairness of the entire trial, the state's governor commits the teacher's sentence to life in prison, but during Norris' journey by rail to the penitentiary, a mob storms the railroad car, and forcibly removes the terrified handcuffed man who is subsequently lynched. In the film's final scene, the young man's widow (Gloria Dickson) denounces both Rains and Joslyn for their responsibility for the murder of her beloved husband. As she leaves, Joslyn turns to Rains, "I wonder if Hale really did it?" To which Rains replies, "I wonder?"

Straightforward, uncompromising, *They Won't Forget* packed a powerful punch with 1937 audiences and critics. Its indictment of mob violence, unscrupulous politicians, and the amoral, circulation-hungry press are timeless themes — ones that still reverberate as powerfully today as they did decades before. Intelligently written, photographed and enacted, the film made several "ten best" lists including the prestigious *New York Times*. *Times* critic Frank Nugent called it, "perfection . . . a brilliant sociological drama and a trenchant film editorial against intolerance and hatred." Kudos were spread to all involved. Inexplicably, the film is undervalued today. If it is mentioned at all, it is usually in the context of sweater-clad Lana Turner's famous scene walking down the city streets, her bosom bouncing to the beat of a local orchestra performing at a Confederate day parade (LeRoy's inventive way of suggesting the sexual nature of the crime while avoiding the censor's scissors).

Gloria scored a triumph in her film debut. As the tragic Sybil Hale, whose life is ruined by her husband's trial and murder, she demonstrated a rare assurity for so young a performer. Especially powerful were her final scenes. After the prejudiced jury has convicted her husband, she stands, turns and faces the voracious crowd who are cheering the decision, "Well, you've got your conviction. What more do you want? What more do you want?!" Gloria's last scene is even more memorable and constitutes the finest moments of her career, as she confronts Rains and Joslyn.

"You're the ones who killed him. You're the ones who stirred up all the hatred and prejudice down here . . . But it isn't over with, his death. The kind of thing you've done is never over. It will stay with you as long as you live, no matter how hard you try to shut it out of your mind, no matter how high and how far you go. And all the money in the world won't be able to rid you of it. Because deep down in your hearts and souls, you know its the truth!"

In a recent interview with the author, one of the film's stars, the handsome and gifted actor Edward Norris (*Show Them No Mercy, Boys Town*), fondly recalled his former costar and her contribution to the film.

"She was absolutely delightful, a very hard worker, knew everything there was to know and really didn't need direction. Her last scene was so beautifully delivered — from the heart . . . I liked her enormously. There was a warmth and friendliness about her, like someone I had known all my life. . . There was a rare intimacy between the two of us that worked so beautifully in our scenes. I wish we could have made more films together. If we'd gotten a good script, we would have been off to the races. But no, it didn't happen for either of us . . ." [52]

The film was an important milestone for Gloria in several respects. Her auspicious film debut landed her on the top of Hollywood's short list of important up and comers, a distinction which allotted her enormous publicity. In the fall of 1937, her face adorned multiple magazine covers. She was the subject of several major movie magazine articles with titles like, "The Luckiest Girl in the World," "New

Gloria Dickson and her screen husband Edward Norris enact a emotional scene in director Mervyn LeRoy's critically acclaimed drama *They Won't Forget* (Warner Bros., 1937).

Director Mervyn LeRoy sets up a shot of Gloria during the filming of *They Won't Forget* (Warner Bros., 1937).

Star of the Year." One magazine proclaimed her, "One of the greatest American actresses yet discovered." Even Jack Warner was singing her praises. At the premiere of *They Won't Forget*, he called her an "important new discovery . . . In presenting her in this role we express a confidence we have never before accorded an unacclaimed player."[53] During the making of the film, Gloria's likeness became the first natural colored photograph to be transmitted by *International News Pictures* from Hollywood to the East Coast, a process which involved four-color separate negatives. *They Won't Forget* turned out to be significant on a personal as well as professional level. On her first day on the Warner's lot, Gloria met make-up artist Perc Westmore. The romantic sparks between them soon blossomed into a serious relationship. His influence over Gloria and her career (for better and for worse), would be very strong for the next three years.

On the strength of her work in the acclaimed *They Won't Forget*, Gloria was offered several film projects from various studios. Even Broadway producers were interested. Jack Warner quickly nixed all the film offers, but consented to her appearance as a vain young actress in the New York stage drama, *Wise Tomorrow* (October, 1937).[54] The positive reception she received from audiences and critics thrilled the talented newcomer, and would be one of the highlights of her life.

When Miss Dickson returned to Hollywood in the winter of 1938, she harbored high hopes for her career. After two critical successes, she sensed she was on the fast track to becoming a actress/star of the first rank, but was wise enough to realize it wouldn't be easy.

"I'm deeply grateful for all the nice things said about me, but I'm smart enough to know that one picture doesn't make a permanent success. I'm not a good screen actress yet, and there's a lot to learn before I am."[54]

Gloria had to have been disappointed however, with the follow-up roles she received from the studio which professed such admiration for her. If Jack Warner was as enthusiastic about Dickson as he proclaimed, and cared to develop her obvious potential, it is hard to fathom why he assigned her the four films she made in 1938. Each was decidedly low budget, and gave her few opportunities to show her versatility and continue her climb to stardom. Despite a charming cast made up of other Warner Bros. contract players, the comedy/musical *Golddiggers in Paris*, had few distinguishing features. Gloria's second banana role as the estranged wife of Rudy Vallee, gave her little to do. The same can be said for her supporting role in *Secrets of an Actress*, starring elegant Kay Francis. Rumor had it Miss Francis had been giving Warner Brothers lots of static (since losing the lead of *Tovarich* to Claudette Colbert), so the studio responded by assigning her this tired tale of a glamourous star in love with an architect (George Brent) whose wife (Dickson) will not give him a divorce. Even the time-tested talents of a distinguished cast and the efforts of director William Keighley couldn't salvage the mediocre script.

Gloria had the feminine lead in Warner Bros. organized crime melodrama, *Racket Busters*, costarring George Brent and Humphrey Bogart, but had little screen time as the pregnant wife of an honest trucker (Brent) fighting gangland attempts to control the American produce business. The Canadian Mountie adventure *Heart of the North* (Warner Bros., 1938), gave Gloria a more substantive role as the daughter of a trapper falsely accused of murder and theft, but all the performances were dwarfed by the sensational on location technicolor photography.

One of the screenwriters (in collaboration with Lee Katz and Robert Rossen), of *Heart of the North* was a talented ex-actor who would become one of Warner Bros. most respected and successful directors, Vincent Sherman. When recently contacted by the author, Mr. Sherman spoke amusingly of the production and his contributions to it.

"Oh god! I got it when I first started at Warner Brothers because I had worked (as a scriptwriter) on the successful Crime School with the Dead End Kids and Bogie. Heart of the North was being made in the middle of the woods with Lewis Seiler directing. Briney (Brian) Foy said to me, 'Why don't you go to work on this and see what you can do with it.' I said, 'Gee, Briney. It's not my cup of tea.' And he said, 'Do what you can.' So I did, but don't know to this day if I had six lines in the goddam thing! I don't think I ever saw it! . . . It was funny. It's the same thing that goes on today. If your name is on a hit picture, regardless of whether you like it or not, or whether you really contributed or not.

They say get him on this one! . . ." [56]

If Miss Dickson's professional fortunes appeared to have hit a bump in the road, she could take solace in the apparent happiness of her private life. She married Perc Westmore in June 1938. At first, their union seemed ideal as they appeared to have many common hobbies and interests. During their first year of marriage, Perc took Gloria on several mini-vacations, camping and deep sea fishing during which they shared their mutual love for the great outdoors. When a writer asked her to access the impact of her marriage on her career, Gloria was upbeat.

"Marriage isn't going to interfere with my career any more than it is with Perc's. Why in the world should it? I know he is going to be as proud of my progress as I am going to be of his. We're both in the movies, but we're in different fields, so far as eventually being bored talking shop is concerned, we really ought to and will learn a lot from each other." [57]

Unfortunately, not all Miss Dickson learned from her new husband was of a positive nature. A notorious lothario and an avid partier, Westmore was also very controlling and exceedingly jealous. During the next two years, he and Jack Warner would do much to damage Gloria's chances of ever becoming a first ranked star actress. Vincent Sherman told the author.

"I knew her, but knew very little about her. The only thing I knew was that in her first picture, she was a very good actress, very interesting. Then she married Perc Westmore, and he insisted that she have a nose job, and it changed the whole quality of her face. Instead of merely improving her looks, it changed her whole appearance entirely." [58]

In 1939, Miss Dickson appeared in six motion pictures for Warner Bros., only one of which was worthy. Her best chance came in *They Made Me a Criminal*, the story of a corrupt, newly-crowned middleweight champ (John Garfield) who sobers up from his victory celebration to learn he is accused of murder and thought to be dead (supposedly killed in an auto crash). A dogged detective's pursuit of

The Dead End Kids, John Garfield and Gloria Dickson enact a scene from *They Made Me a Criminal* (Warner Bros., 1939).

Gloria played the manager of a fruit ranch/rehabilitation center who falls in love with a troubled boxer (John Garfield) in *They Made Me a Criminal* (Warner Bros., 1939). Here she is seen with Claude Rains and Mr. Garfield.

the truth, and fighter's eventual rehabilitation form the crux of the dramatic content. Although young Garfield's dynamic lead performance tended to dominate the proceedings, Gloria had some very fine moments as the warm-hearted manager of a fruit ranch (which also serves as a rehabilitation center), whose love inspires the troubled champ to mend his ways.

Gloria's five other assignments were sadly typical of her post *They Won't Forget* work in which she had supporting roles (usually as the other woman), in better films, and leads in second features. Warner Bros. grade A adaptation of the successful stage musical, *On Your Toes*, was a case in point. It had a capable cast headed by Vera Zorina, and commendable production values (including a ballet sequence choreographed by none other than George Balanchine), but Gloria's 7th-billed part as a ballet patroness was at best incidental. Although she had more important roles in two 1939 Warner Bros. program pictures, *No Place to Go*, and *Waterfront*, (both of which cast her as the devoted wife of Dennis Morgan), her performances were largely lost in the movies' cheap sets and inferior scripts. (*Waterfront* had the distinction of being the first and only film in which she received top billing.) Gloria fared no better in her two other Warner Bro's outings: as a murder suspect in the Torchy Blane-ish mystery/comedy, *Private Detective* (1939), starring Jane Wyman, and as a feminine menace in the inept football comedy, *The Cowboy Quarterback* (1939). In a 1939 review, one critic summed up Gloria's situation perfectly, thanking her for facing her assignments, "bravely," and for "majoring in minor roles."

1940 would prove a turning point year in the life of Miss Dickson. By this time, it was becoming painfully clear that her career was in a rut, and Warner Bros. appeared oblivious to her unhappiness. Not only was she dissatisfied with the size and scope of her roles, but the quality of the scripts. Gloria viewed herself as a lead actress of the Bette Davis ilk. She desired meaty, challenging parts, and realized she would have to leave her home studio to have a chance to play them. In 1940, she quietly completed her three-year contract with the studio which had given her career such a promising start. Her last two Warner Bros. films: *Tear Gas Squad* and *King of the Lumberjacks* (made in 1940), were second features which were not without merit, but like the vast majority of Gloria's Warner Bros assignments, were ultimately defeated by lack of studio investment.

Gloria began her freelance career promisingly; celebrating her contractual freedom with a emotional, eye-catching supporting performance as a socialite whose disintegrating marriage casues her such anguish she commits suicide in *I Want a Divorce* (Paramount, 1940), a drama chronicling the joys and problems of matrimony. Frequently preachy, but engrossing, the film starring Dick Powell (in his first non-singing role), and his real life spouse, Joan Blondell was a favorite of audiences and critics. Its excellent notices gave Gloria's flagging spirits a well needed boost, and a renewed hope she could ressurect her career by freelancing. *I Want a Divorce* also held a strange irony in Miss Dickson's personal life. By the time the production commenced in April 1940, her marriage to Perc Westmore was in shambles. By the picture's completion in August, she would be divorced and romantically involved with its director, Ralph Murphy.

It took only a few months for the shine to wear off of the Westmore marriage. After a promising start, the previously married Perc resumed his extramarital affairs which had been his pattern. The couple's problems were further compounded by his intense jealousy and controlling nature. From the outset, he insisted innocently attractive, but not technically beautiful Gloria re-invent her image. He pressured her to undergo facial plastic surgery then presented her in several pictorial layouts in numerous magazines as a glamourous, sexy siren. At first, Gloria was entirely obedient, deferring to his wishes in every way, but as time progressed and her career faltered, she began to question the wisdom of his decisions, his interference in her career, and resent his indiscretions. Also of significance, was Westmore's drinking. In the beginning, the conservative girl from Pocatello attempted in vain to moderate her husband's bad habits, but eventually she too fell victim to his wild and wooley lifestyle. By the end of 1939, things had gotten particularly rocky with both Mr. and Mrs. Westmore drinking heavily and quarreling incessantly. One of their more notorious rows was documented by Perc's brother Frank Westmore and Muriel Davidson in the book, *The Westmores of Hollywood*. According to Westmore and Davidson,

"Every year at Christmas, for example, the House of Westmore gave a

lavish catered party — costing thousands — for the employees and their families. It was always a raucous, no holds barred affair. One such party stands out in my mind. Perc was in love with Ola (Ola Hall who would become his fourth wife), and she with him, though neither acknowledged it for sometime thereafter... Perc was dancing with Ola when Gloria suddenly smashed her highball glass and rammed the sharp edges into Perc's face. As I watched the blood pour down Perc's cheeks, I recalled hearing about a similar incident between George (Perc's father) and my mother, Ada..." [59]

Gloria's first husband, legendary make-up artist, Perc Westmore pressured her to undergoe plastic surgery which changed her appearance and screen persona from the "girl next door," to a sexy siren.

Gloria in 1940.

Another notorious incident involving the couple occured while Gloria was traveling cross country in February 1940. When she stopped off in Utah to see her old friend, actor singer, Cliff Edwards, Perc reported her as a missing person. For several days, her "mysterious disappearance" made headlines in newspapers across the United States. When she turned up a week later, she stated her husband had known her whereabouts all along. Hollywood insiders chalked up the whole affair as "a cheap publicity stunt." In June 1940, the Westmore marriage came to an official end, but the two years of "wedded bliss" between Gloria and Perc had taken a toll on Mrs. Westmore both professionally and personally. [60]

Sadly, Miss Dickson would never be able to reestablish herself as a star actress of top grade productions, but in 1941, (her first full year as a freelance actress), she did manage to secure some interesting roles in multiple low budget films which she handled admirably. In *The Big Boss* (Columbia, 1941), she was a newspaperwoman who chronicles the struggle between a crusading reform governor (John Litel) and his brother a crooked political boss (Otto Kruger). Well paced and credible, this melodramatic second feature owed much of its popularity to its performances. *Variety* called Dickson's, "skillful, sincere, and . . . moving." Gloria was also excellent as the wife of fisherman Ray Middleton who loses his sanity and his life in the action-packed thriller, *Mercy Island* (Republic, 1941), and as the argumentative wife of an attorney in *This Thing Called Love* (Columbia, 1941), a delightfully naughty sex comedy about newlyweds (Melvyn Douglas and Rosalind Russell) who encounter problems when new bride, Miss Russell, insists on a three month celibacy period. Penned by George Seaton, Ken Englund, and P.J. Wolfson, this witty literate movie impressed audiences and critics who called it, "Fun with a capital F." It seemed everyone was charmed except the legion of decency which condemned the film for militating, "against the Christian concept of marriage." Censors banned it in several countries including Ireland and Australia.

In 1940, Gloria embarked on another unfortunate marrriage — this time to *I Want a Divorce* director Ralph Murphy, a 46-year-old man (22 years her senior), who shared Perc Westmore's roving eye and penchant for partying. Problems surfaced after a few months, when it was revealed she had married Murphy before her divorce was final. On October 10, 1941, Gloria was forced to remarry Murphy, further perpetrating the negative publicity which now appeared like a dark cloud over her life and career.[61] Hollywood's moral "puritans" took note. Regrettably, this was not the last negative news. In the next few years, Gloria colorful private life would become more interesting than her work. She would make five films in the period between 1942 -1945, none of which restored luster to her tarnished career.

One of the good ones was the low budget comic melodrama, *Affairs of Jimmy Valentine* a.k.a. *The Unforgotten Crime* (Republic,1942), which debuted in 1942. Miss Dickson had a 3rd-billed supporting

Gloria and her screen husband, Allyn Joslyn in a scene from the critically acclaimed sex comedy, *This Thing Called Love* **(Columbia, 1941).**

role (as a radio station employee caught up in a publicity stunt), but had some impressive scenes. Today, film historians fondly recall the film as one of Republic's best. In his groundbreaking volume, *B Movies*, film historian Don Miller called it, "the apogee of Republic's B picture output . . . whatever inspiration was injected into the cast and crew, they performed as if they were involved in the movie of the year."[62] Gloria followed with another good performance as the faithful secretary to honest editor Lee Tracy who exposes his corrupt boss in *Power of the Press* (Columbia, 1943).

During her last years in Hollywood, the demand for Miss Dickson's services declined dramatically. There were multiple reasons. All the negative press, rumors of her heavy drinking, and the alterations in her personal appearance caused producers to have second thoughts about casting her. The refreshing innocence which had so impressed Hollywood in the early years of her career, had by this time, been replaced by a worldly toughness. Photographs taken in the early 1940's, reveal the toll her failed marriages and controversial private life had taken. Only in her mid twenties, Gloria, now overweight, looked at least a decade older.

Miss Dickson played murder suspects in two of her last three films: *The Crime Doctor's Strangest Case* (Columbia, 1943), and *Lady of Burlesque* (United Artists, 1943). The former was the second installment of the entertaining B mystery series starring Warner Baxter as a psychiatrist who moonlights as an amateur sleuth. The latter was a medium budget whodunit elevated by the expertise of newly independent producer, Hunt Stromberg, formally employed (for 17 years) by MGM. Based on Gypsy Rose Lee's novel, *The G-String Murders, Lady of Burlesque* was the story of a series of killings at a New York City strip show, and the search for the murderer among many who had the opportunity and the motive. What might have been merely another in an endless series of melodramatic program pictures became top notch entertainment in the experienced hands of director William Wellman, photographer Robert DeGrass, and Oscar-nominated composer Arthur Laye. Especially memorable was Laye's risque composition, "Take It Off the E String, Play It on the G-String" delivered in bravura style by the film's unlikely star, the legendary Barbara Stanwyck. Sharing acting honors were such reliable featured players as Gloria, Iris Adrian, J. Edward Bromberg, and two talented newcomers: Stephanie Bachelor and Michael O'Shea (fresh from his successful stage performance in *Eve of St. Mark*.)

Although 6th-billed, Miss Dickson was poignant as a veteran stripper who has a wayward husband and a hot temper. Despite the brevity of her time onscreen, she still managed a standout performance, proving that the ravages of her hard life had not diminished her ability. As Dolly Baxter, the tough, yet sensitive exotic dancer, she proved to all doubters she was still an actress to be reckoned with, one who enriched her work with great sensitivity and emotional vulnerability. To this particular role, Gloria brought a unique understanding. Like her character, she had suffered more than a few hard knocks including the humiliation of a straying husband. Her final scene was exceptionally affecting. After the police have arrested her two-timing screen husband, concerned friend, Stanwyck asks Dickson, "Where are you goin, honey?" Gloria replies quietly, "Who me? Well, I'm going down to the Peerless Bar and Grill with the rest of you

Gloria was a murder suspect in *The Crime Doctor's Strangest Case* (Columbia, 1943), the second installment in the entertaining B mystery series starring Warner Baxter.

guys for a midnight snack, (her voice then cracks), and a whale of a time."

By 1942, Gloria realized her second marriage was doomed. She had made a valiant effort to make a go of it with Murphy, but to no avail. Like Westmore, his bohemian lifestyle was well established, and wishful thinking could not alter it. Whispers linked his name to several women most notably would-be actress, Ann Corio whom he was directing in a San Francisco stage production. Miss Dickson became legally separated from Murphy in February 1943, and divorced him in April 1944, on grounds of mental cruelty. "He wouldn't come home for four or five days at a time," she testified at the divorce hearing. "It made it difficult to establish a home at all. He told me he didn't love me and wasn't happy . . ."[63] Once again, Gloria was free, but not for long. A month later, in 1944, she would marry yet again to ex-middleweight boxer, former bodyguard (to Jean Harlow), William Fitzgerald. Unlike her previous unions, this marriage would not conclude in a courtroom. It would end on a sunny spring afternoon in 1945, when Gloria Dickson would make headlines for the last time.

CHAPTER TWO: GLORIA DICKSON

Miss Dickson had a small 8th-billed role as a lady barber in the comedy, *Rationing* (MGM, 1944) starring Wallace Beery. Sadly, it would be her last film.

If Gloria harbored any illusions her acclaimed supporting performance in *Lady of Burlesque* would resurrect her career, she was mistaken. Although she continued to appear on radio, the only film work she landed in 1944, was a small (8th-billed) role as a lady barber in MGM's *Rationing* starring Wallace Beery. This minor league comedy would be her last film. During its production, she met Fitzgerald whom she quickly married. By all accounts, her last marriage was a happy one. Recently discharged from the Marines after being wounded in the South Pacific, Fitzgerald resumed working for MGM where he had been employed prior to the war. In the summer of 1944, the couple leased a large West Hollywood hillside home overlooking the Sunset Strip owned by Mr. and Mrs. Sidney Toler. It was an unusual house with many large windows on the main floor and very small ones upstairs which were 20 feet above the ground.[64]

On Tuesday, April 10, 1945, Gloria was to meet her agent Leon Lance to discuss some promising new film projects. For a year, she had been keeping a relatively low profile in hopes of acquiring film work. Her attempt to clean up her image was apparently beginning to pay off. When she failed to keep the appointment, Lance chalked it up to her usual tardiness and her habit of taking afternoon naps. Shortly after 2 p.m. one of Gloria's neighbors smelled what seemed like burning leaves, but thought nothing of it. Two hours later, he reported seeing, "a burst of flame, coming from the front of the Fitzgerald house . . ." When he ran to the house, several people were already there. Flames were shooting from the roof of the building.

Five fire departments were summoned from Hollywood and Beverly Hills. Gloria's husband, William was notified and rushed to the scene. By the time he arrived, the house was an inferno. Even though he had been told no one was at home, Fitzgerald immediately sensed Gloria was in there, and frantically attempted to enter, screaming, "My baby's in there — I've got to get to my baby!" He was denied entrance. The fire crews did an exemplary job extinguishing the fire, but they had arrived too late. Gloria's body was found face down by a bathroom window. An autopsy revealed she had died of asphyxiation from inhalation of flames which seared her lungs. She suffered first and second degree burns over her entire body. The lifeless body of her pet boxer was found a few feet away.[65]

Police and fire inspectors theorized the fire began while Dickson was napping upstairs. Apparently an unextinguished cigarette had ignited an overstuffed chair on the main floor spreading throughout the downstairs area. It was believed Gloria's dog probably woke her after the main floor was engulfed in flames. With the upstairs windows too high to reach, Gloria apparently tried to escape through the small bathroom window, but was eventually overcome by smoke. Police believed she may have spent at least an hour in the bathroom waiting to be rescued.[66]

Once again, Gloria Dickson made headlines. Her face adorned the front of newspapers across the country. Most of the articles recounted the details of the fire in grizzly specificity, aided by macabre photos. Most of the published stories devoted a few paragraphs to Dickson's three marriages and two messy divorces, but shamefully little space was allotted to her acting ability and her films which were her true legacy. A day after the fire, another incredibly sad event transpired when Mrs. Emma Dickerson, Gloria's grieving mother, visited the scene of her daughter's death. While police and fire investigators probed the debris, Mrs. Dickerson, near hysteria, combed the charred ruins for any personal keepsakes of her youngest daughter.[67] Services were held on April 17, 1945, with interment in Hollywood Forever Cemetery in West Hollywood, Los Angeles County. Gloria's tombstone reads, "Thais A Dickerson, My Baby," and is located under a large tree.[68] Gloria's widower, William Fitzgerald would also have a short life. Records indicate he died on May 5, 1958, in the Nebraska State Penitentiary at age 47.[69]

Recounting her troubled private life and sad demise, it is tempting to view Gloria Dickson only in tragic terms. While it cannot be denied she led a difficult life and died way too soon, it is also important to remember she had accomplished much during her 28 years. In 1937, when she first arrived in Hollywood, Gloria summed up her life's goal in an interview. "My ambition is just to be the very best kind of actress. I don't mean a star particularly. I mean just a really fine actress."[70] Although she never became a mega star, a careful review of her filmography is verification she accomplished what she set out to do. Through talent and hard work the "little girl from potato country" had become an exceptionally fine actress whose naturalness and emotional intensity added considerable depth to each and every one of her 21 films. If the scripts and production values were sometimes beneath her, she still managed to shine, playing sympathetic heroines as well as tough girls with equal aplomb. Her characterization of Sybil Hale in Mervyn LeRoy's masterpiece, *They Won't Forget* lingers in our memories as powerful testimony to her unique gifts. Like the film, Gloria Dickson's performance was simply unforgettable!

UPDATE

Since the publication of the above article in 2000, a few more facts have come to light regarding Miss Dickson's life and family. Gloria's mother, Emma Starrett Dickerson died in 1975, and is buried in Forest Lawn Memorial Park in Orange County, California.[71] Gloria's third husband, William Fitzgerald was still in the military five years after Gloria's death in 1950, when he was arrested for desertion in time of war while driving a long-haul truck in New Hampshire. He was dishonorably discharged in 1951. Four years later, in 1955, Fitzgerald married again, this time to a woman from Nebraska. The marriage ended one month after it began, when she discovered he had been writing bad checks charged to her bank account. He was arrested, and convicted a few months later. He was sentenced to a five-year prison term in the Nebraska State Penitentiary where he died in 1958, from venereal disease. He was buried in the prison cemetery.[72] Little is known about Gloria's older sister Doris, who apparently married a man named Martinson and moved to Texas. Legendary director Vincent Sherman died on June 18, 2006, at the Motion Picture & Television Fund Hospital in Woodland Hills less than one month shy of celebrating his centennial birthday. The cause of death was listed as "natural causes." For information on Gloria's costar, Edward Norris, consult his biography which is also featured later in this volume.[73]

CHAPTER THREE
"CLAIRE DODD: DIMPLED AND DANGEROUS"

(Originally published in *Films of the Golden Age*, Winter, 2012)

"Who's the dame with the platinum chassis?" inquires Blondie Johnson (Joan Blondell) as her boyfriend Danny (Chester Morris) makes goo-goo eyes at a sexy blonde (Claire Dodd) who just entered the room on the arm of his mobster boss. "Why that's Gladys LaMann the musical comedy actress, Max's sweetie," says the mesmerized Danny. Blondie is suspicious of the dimpled dish with the dazzling smile, and she has every right to be. Before she knows it, the smitten Danny is engaged to the man-eating coquette, and she's playing him for a sucker. Danny eventually regains his senses, but by then, his money is gone and his life is in tatters. Lucky for him, ever faithful Blondie is around to help pick up the pieces.

Like Warner Bros. comic melodrama, *Blondie Johnson* (Warner Bros., 1933), many an early sound era movie script revolved around challenges faced in a budding romance between a brash, naïve, corruptible young man and his cuddly, ever loyal best girl. One of the romantic obstacles depicted in the aforementioned screenplays, involved competition from another woman, who like the destructive Gladys, arrives on the scene to turn the hero's head and complicate the relationship. Beautiful, smart, and always bad to the bone, these lovely looking troublemakers bewitch the young man who succumbs to temptation and abandons his faculties. The fact that she is a deceitful, conniving, two-timing she-devil never once occurs to the poor sap until it's almost too late.

There were several talented actresses who specialized in "other woman" roles during the 1930's. One of the best was Claire Dodd. A tall, stunningly attractive blue-green-eyed blonde, Dodd was a gifted thespian who could effectively essay a wide range of characters, but was particularly effective in villainous roles. Her delicate features, sly dimpled smile, sophisticated demeanor, and uniquely effective way of delivering an acid barb made her a formidable screen vixen — as pretty as a picture and as toxic as Three Mile Island! Memorably cast as bored society snobs, scheming career women, golddiggers, and assorted molls, minxes, and chiselers, her deliciously nasty characterizations lifted many films and won accolades, but superstardom eluded her. The reasons were multiple, but Claire's off-screen personality seemed to impede her progress. After a dozen years (1930-42) trying to ascend the ladder of cinematic success, Claire finally gave up. Mired in low budget movies and supporting roles, in 1942, she walked away from the bright lights and scrutiny of the film business into a richer, more personally satisfying career as a wife and mother.

The "dame with the platinum chassis" began life's journey in America's heartland. Born Dorothy Ann Dodd on December 29, 1908, she was the only child of veterinarian Walter W. Dodd and the former Ethel Cool, daughter of a postmaster. Authoritative sources reported her birthplace as Des Moines, Iowa, but Dodd often told reporters she was born in Little Rock, Arkansas. Accounts of her early life were likewise confusing and contradictory. One source stated she grew up in Iowa. Another said she spent her formative years in Little Rock and subsequently resided in Kansas City, Denver, and Phoenix. A 1931 Paramount studio biography, said she was born in New England, then lived in Europe. In a 2011 interview with the author, Miss Dodd's son, John Cooper sought to set the record straight.

"My mother was born in Des Moines, Iowa while her mother was on a trip. She was embarrassed about that. She had nothing against the Midwest, but she was a Southerner. She had Southern pride, unwarranted or not. Her family was from Little Rock where she grew up." [74]

When Dorothy was ten years old, her father abandoned the family. Ethel Dodd subsequently contracted tuberculosis and found it difficult to make ends meet. While in her teens, Dorothy quit school, and began working to help support herself and her mother. Mr. Cooper believes the events of his mother's formative years had a profound affect on her.

"She would not talk about anything she didn't want to talk about. During my lifetime until she died, I never met a relative of hers . . . I suspect her early life was very traumatic, especially when her father left . . . She had trust issues with everybody. It's clear, the things that happen to you early in life are the bottom layer of who you are. It was part of the reason she turned into who she was . . ." [75]

By the late 1920's, the five-foot-six-inch tall, 120 pound blonde Dorothy had blossomed into a curvaceous beauty who turned heads.

Beautiful young Claire in *Whoopie* (United Artists, 1930). All Claire Dodd photos courtesy of the Cooper family.

She was working as a model in Burlingame, California in 1929, when she was spotted by a talent scout and brought to Hollywood for a screen test. Producers Sam Goldwyn and Florenz Ziegfeld liked what they saw, and cast her as a "Goldwyn Girl" in the lavish Eddie Cantor comic musical, *Whoopee* (United Artists, 1930). Later that year, Dorothy, who took the name Claire Dodd, was seen as a mannequin in MGM's Joan Crawford musical, *Our Blushing Brides* (MGM, 1930).

Claire was back in Burlingame in 1930, when Ziegfeld summoned her to New York to make her Broadway debut in the Marilyn Miller musical, *Smiles* (1930-31). When the production closed after 63 performances, the budding actress was signed by Paramount Pictures who put her to work in tiny, mostly uncredited roles in such film nonentities as the weepie, *Working Girls* (1931), the Clive Brook/Buddy Rogers drama, *The Lawyer's Secret* (1931), and the screwball comedy, *Girls About Town* (1931). The latter is notable as Miss Dodd's first of three screen appearances in support of glamorous Kay Francis. On May 12, 1931, twenty-two-year-old Claire married New York real estate developer John Milton Strauss in Tijuana, Mexico.[76]

If the ambitious Miss Dodd harbored any grand illusions about film acting and Hollywood, they were quickly dashed soon after she arrived in the film capital. In a 1934 interview, she recalled her initial months in Hollywood.

"I did almost nothing much for a year. Publicity photographs, greeting exhibitor's parties, dancing group scenes, odds and ends . . . Any extra could have done what I was assigned, and yet I was receiving a very decent salary check regularly."[77]

Things finally began looking up in the winter of 1931, when one of her assignments was to play opposite a well-known New York stage actor in a screen test. Warner Bros. head of production, Darryl Zanuck happened to see the test and was impressed, not with the actor, but with the photogenic young woman who played the scene with him. Striking a deal with Paramount to borrow her services, Zanuck cast the aspiring film actress in tiny roles in two dramas: *Under Eighteen* (Warner Bros., 1931), and *Alias the Doctor* (First National, 1932). Claire's camera friendly good looks and charisma stood out, inspiring Zanuck to request a contract sharing agreement with Paramount. According to Claire's son John, he (Zanuck) became Claire's mentor at this time.

"She had great admiration for him (Zanuck) and he thought there was something special about her he could use . . . He shepherded her through her career . . . This caused some of the problems my mother had. She was the only starlet at the studios to have her own dressing room, whereas

The stunning Miss Dodd at the outset of her career. All Claire Dodd photos courtesy of the Cooper family.

the others had to share. It was a source of great envy and irritation to them, but my mother refused to chum with people. She didn't want to be with them listening to gossip, and she didn't sleep around. Zanuck respected her, and that's one of the reasons he helped her. . ." [78]

Dodd would make 10 films in 1932, and in the process, establish her screen persona. Her Paramount appearances were mostly tiny

Claire played a blackmailing showgirl in the entertaining crime drama, *Lawyer Man* (Warner Bros., 1932). Seen here with Kenneth Thompson. All Claire Dodd photos courtesy of the Cooper family

uncredited roles which gave her little screen time. The one good part she received before departing the studio in 1933, was as a married woman who poses as a young aviator's wife in order to save his life in the Lupe Velez vehicle, *The Broken Wing*. Claire fared better at Warner Bros. who cast her in showy, significant supporting parts as elegant "other women" in three dramas. In *Man Wanted*, she played a high society party girl who successfully snags a magazine editor's (Kay Francis) husband, and in *Crooner*, a sexy matron on a quest to lure a singer (David Manners) from the arms of his best girl (Ann Dvorak). Dodd's best early opportunity came in *Lawyer Man*, as Virginia St. Johns, a double-dealing temptress out to fleece brilliant attorney, Anton Adam (played by William Powell). The initial verbal exchanges between Virginia and Anton are classic Dodd.

Virginia: "I've heard about you in all the papers and I made up my mind I just had to meet you . . ."

Anton: "   What's an experienced guy like me supposed to do when a beautiful woman tells him he's fascinating?

Virginia: "Usually he tries to live up to her expectations."

Claire's scintillating performance as the charmingly malignant Virginia netted her excellent reviews and more film offers. By the end of 1933, she was working exclusively for Warner Bros., joining a dynamic roster of contract players which included James Cagney, Bette Davis, Kay Francis, Joan Blondell, Pat O'Brien, Allen Jenkins, Frank McHugh, Glenda Farrell, and Ruth Donnelly. Although she could persuasively play saintly heroines, Dodd's delicate beauty, sophisticated manner, devilish sparkle in her eyes, and singular way of delivering a sarcastic quip made her a natural for villainous roles as high society women and scheming golddiggers who use their beauty and refinement for destructive purposes. She would make more than 20 films (almost all low budgeters), for Warner Bros. during her peak period (1933-1936), gaining fame and valuable experience while filling a niche in the studio's repertory company. Lamentably, it all came at a price. Because she was so believable as sophisticated troublemakers, she soon became typed, and once an actor began appearing regularly in low budget movies, it was exceedingly hard to win a promotion.

1933 was a particularly memorable year in the career of young Miss Dodd who held her own in support of some of Hollywood's finest actors. Her vehicles were mostly unremarkable 60-70 minute program pictures, but Claire gave 100%, and left us some of the bitchiest, most delightful performances of 1930's cinema. A case in point is the action drama, *Parachute Jumper* (Warner Bros.), in which Dodd portrayed the mistress of a racketeer who employs a handsome former transport pilot, Bill (Douglas Fairbanks Jr.) as her chauffer and "handy man." Basically a dull, thinly-plotted affair which wasted an expert cast (headed by Fairbanks, and young Bette Davis), the film is nevertheless worth a look for one scene which has the seductive Mrs. Newberry (Dodd) describing Bill's job duties.

"It'll require a lot of handling. I suppose you're used to heavy work . . . In the past my chauffeurs have been rather handy around the house. I

Douglas Fairbanks Jr. played an ex-Marine who becomes the chauffer of a mobster's mistress (Claire Dodd) in the melodramatic, *Parachute Jumper* (Warner Bros., 1933). All Claire Dodd photos courtesy of the Cooper family.

mean fixing little gadgets, taking care of things. Have you had any experience of that sort? You seem to be a very well built young man."

Hurricane Claire wreaked more havoc in 1933, as a radio field scout in the Joe E. Brown comedy, *Elmer the Great* (Warner Bros.), a snobbish high flyer who steals Helen Twelvetrees' husband in the dramatic *My Woman* (Columbia), a gangster moll who turns the head of tough-guy Chester Morris in the comic melodrama, *Blondie Johnson* (Warner Bros.), the daughter of a shady land developer who takes hard-as-nails shyster James Cagney for a ride in *Hard to Handle* (Warner Bros.), and as an alcoholic night club singer whose accidental death is prosecuted as a murder in the affecting drama, *Ann Carver's Profession* (Columbia, 1933). Dodd's most indelible part also came in 1933, as golddigger, Vivian Rich who casts a spell over fast-talking musical producer, Chester Kent (James Cagney) in the lavish musical comedy *Footlight Parade* (Warner Bros.). Several reference books

Miss Dodd had a showy role as an alcoholic nightclub singer whose death is blamed on an ex-football star turned singer (Gene Raymond) in Columbia's *Ann Carver's Profession* (Columbia, 1933).

cite the latter as the highlight of Dodd's career, recounting a witty, well-crafted sequence in which Kent's sprightly secretary, Joan (played by the inimitable Joan Blondell), literally kicks black-hearted Vivian to the curb.

>Vivian: *"But where do I go?"*
>
>Joan: *"Outside Countess! As long as they have sidewalks, you have a job!"*

Despite her beauty, obvious ability, and charisma, Claire Dodd never progressed into lead roles in grade A pictures. Some of the reasons were beyond her control, but her negative attitude toward the Hollywood press and cinema elites did not help. Although she performed all obligatory duties and gave polished performances, the intensely private Claire resisted reporter's attempts to pry into her past and refused to massage massive egos and socialize with costars. Someone in the press dubbed her, "Ice Bucket" at this time, and the sobriquet stuck. By the mid 1930's, her standoffishness was already impacting her career. John Cooper says his mother enjoyed the creative process of making films, but was basically unwilling to make some of the "sacrifices" necessary to become a major star.

"She worked in films because she loved to act, and it made her money which she used to take care of herself and her mother, but she wouldn't play the game . . . One of the people Claire would not 'play the game' with was influential producer Howard Hughes. One day, my mother was in her dressing room when she got a phone call from Hughes' secretary saying he would like to meet her. She told the secretary, 'If Mr. Hughes wants to talk to me, tell him to call me himself,' and hung up. The next day she got a call from Warner Bros. 'Miss Dodd, if Howard Hughes calls up and asks you to meet his gardener, you go. Do you understand?' Well, she had to call back and make an appointment to meet him which made her furious. The secretary made her wait for a half hour. When she was finally allowed in, she shook his hand across the desk, and he asked her to sit down. She told me they then had a staring contest. After about 20 minutes, he said, 'That will be all, Miss Dodd.' They never really spoke! He wanted to find out what she was about, and possibly have sex with her, but he met his match in my mother!" [79]

Encountering Claire Dodd in a film was a little like seeing a beautiful wild bird singing a lovely song just outside your window. You are charmed by its delicate plummage, and want to let it in and have it near you. Eventually, you work up the courage to open your window; and much to your delight, it flies in, and perches daintily on your shoulder and coos. You are so charmed by its presence it becomes the center of your universe. You spend all your time and money on things you believe might keep it content. Just when you are convinced you have miraculously tamed this gorgeous creature, without warning, it starts squawking like a vulture, sinks its talons in your neck, and tries to peck your eyes out. When you finally manage to get the vicious bag of feathers out of your house, you realize your abode is in ruins and you're a mess.

Such was the fate of multiple lead male characters who succumbed to the song of dainty but dangerous Dodd in 14 films during the period 1934-35. Most of these pictures like Warner Bros.' *Massacre* (1934),

Claire waged war with spunky Joan Blondell in three films including the mega-musical, *Footlight Parade* (Warner Bros., 1933) costarring James Cagney.

Watch out, Jimmy, there's danger in those dimples! Dodd was at her best as the predatory Vivian Rich opposite James Cagney in *Footlight Parade* (Warner Bros., 1933), directed by Archie Mayo. All Claire Dodd photos courtesy of the Cooper family.

Journal For a Crime (1934), *The Personality Kid* (1934), *Babbitt* (1934), *I Sell Anything* (1934), and *Roberta* (RKO, 1935), presented Claire as spoiled, scheming debutantes, predatory socialites, or gold digging sexpots who delight in wrecking lives. One particularly inspired Dodd performance of the period was delivered in *Gambling Lady* (Warner Bros., 1934), a mediocre drama distinguished by the spirited acting of a top flight cast. Dodd portrayed Sheila, a haughty jet-setter intent on breaking up the marriage of her wealthy ex-boyfriend Garry (Joel McCrea) and his professional gambler wife, Lady Lee (Barbara Stanwyck). To achieve her unsavory objective, Sheila stages a posh New York party. Sparks fly at the event when the two feminine rivals (superbly played by Dodd and the legendary Miss Stanwyck), bare their claws.

Sheila: *"Lady, dahling, why don't you show the doctor some of your card tricks, the professional ones, you know the ones you used to win those fabulous sums."*

Lady: *"Sheila, dahling. I don't feel like doing any tricks unless you want to put up some money."*

Sheila: *"Naturally I couldn't play with you. I'm not in your class!"*

One of Claire's favorite costars was Fred Astaire with whom she appeared in the memorable musical romance, *Roberta* (RKO, 1935). All Claire Dodd photos courtesy of the Cooper family.

It wasn't easy to hold your own with Barbara Stanwyck, but Claire Dodd did as a haughty upper crust home wrecker in Warner Bros.' minor drama, *Gambling Lady* (1934), costarring Joel McCrea.

A successful commercial artist (Dodd) amuses herself with a brief fling with a married boxer (Pat O'Brien) in *The Personality Kid* (Warner Bros., 1934). All Claire Dodd photos courtesy of the Cooper family.

She was even more ferocious as the selfish, shrewish wife of a sports writer (James Dunn) who sacrifices her devoted husband in order to live the high life in the low budget drama, *The Payoff* (Warner Bros., 1935). Claire's mesmerizingly evil portrayal inspired virtually unanimous critical applause even from the unlikeliest quarters. The *New York Times* critic Andre Sennwald was particularly enthusiastic. "Miss Dodd has played vindictive women all during her screen career, but this one is her masterpiece . . ." he gushed.

Although Claire was undoubtedly pleased with the enthusiastic embrace of her work in *Gambling Lady* and *The Payoff*, by 1934, she was becoming bored playing vixens. She went public with her displeasure, and took a suspension when Warner Bros. demanded she play another "vamping hussy." Eventually the studio relented. In a rare interview, she explained.

"I more or less won my point. Of course, I don't care if they (the parts) are all good, so long as they vary them a bit. I refuse to go on getting caught in hotel rooms by indignant wives in every picture I make. Fun's fun, but there's a limit to that sort of thing. And I've just about reached it." [80]

The brothers Warner kept their word, and beginning in 1934, gave their number one vixen more varied assignments, albeit in B movies. On loan, Claire had her one and only starring role as an art thief who goes straight to catch a murderer in the ultra low budget mystery, *The Secret of the Chateau* (Universal, 1935). She was the cold vengeful sister of a murder victim in the George Raft melodrama *The Glass Key* (Paramount, 1935), and an ingénue in love with a naval officer and a young child in *Navy Born* (Republic, 1936). Back at her home studio, Dodd was a radio writer in *One Fatal Hour* a.k.a. *Two Against the World* (1936), the daughter of a Kentucky colonel in the amusing triviality, *Don't Bet on Blondes* (1935), and a glamorous jewel thief in the minor-league Kay Francis comedy, *The Goose and the Gander* (1935). Claire's best 'good girl" roles at Warner Bros. came in two Perry Mason mysteries: *The Case of the Curious Bride* (1935) and *The Case of the Velvet Claws* (1936) in which she portrayed Mason's indispensable secretary Della Street opposite debonair Warren William. Both entries were well-paced with attractive casts,

Although unimpressed by Hollywood elites, Claire had high praise for several of her costars including Humphrey Bogart with whom she made *One Fatal Hour* a.k.a. *Two Against the World* (Warner Bros., 1936). All Claire Dodd photos courtesy of the Cooper family.

plenty of action, and witty repartee between William and Dodd who worked well together. If there were questions regarding Dodd's ability to play sympathetic parts, the Mason entries dispelled all doubts. Dodd's Della was extremely persuasive: beautiful, spunky, and resourceful. So appealing was she, it made perfect sense when Warner Bros. opted to marry the confirmed bachelor to Della in *Velvet Claws*.

In 1936, Miss Dodd completed her Warner Bros.' contract with a 3rd-billed murder suspect role in the conventional grade B mystery, *Murder By an Aristocrat* (Warner Bros.). It is not known if the studio tried to renew, but Claire certainly would have declined the offer had it been made. Warner Bros. had made her a motion picture star, but ultimately failed to exploit her proven assets by assigning her material commensurate with her talent. One source reported Dodd was also under contract to RKO at the time she left Warner Bros. but this fact could not be confirmed. One thing is certain, however.

After departing Warner Bros., Claire Dodd's film career declined further. She made the rounds of several studios, admirably played a variety of supporting parts during the final five year, 13 film phase of her career (1937-42), but none of her latter projects did her the least bit of good.

After taking time off to give birth to son, Jon Michael Strauss in December 1936, Claire returned to moviemaking and to her patented Queen Bitch portrayals, "vamping and hussying" her way through seven motion pictures for assorted studios in a two year period (1938-39). For MGM, she made three movies. The best of them was the intriguing low budget whodunit, *Fast Company* (1938), about the search for the killer of a crooked book dealer (George Zucco). To no one's surprise, his lovely mistress (Dodd) is the culprit, a particularly dangerous one who almost succeeds in eliminating the detective (Melvyn Douglas) who solves the crime. Dodd was a uppity Countess out to snag a famous singer in the A-level musical comedy *Romance in the Dark* (Paramount, 1938), murder victims in *Charlie Chan in Honolulu* (20th CenturyFox, 1938), and Walter Wanger's melodramatic *Slightly Honorable* (United Artists, 1939), and a manipulator who attempts to steal the affections of a married man and his young daughter in the dramatic *Woman Doctor* (Republic, 1939). The latter, costarred Dodd with Frieda Inescourt, Henry Wilcoxen, and young Sybil Jason. In a 2011 interview with the author, Miss Jason, who also appeared with Dodd in *The Singing Kid* (Warner Bros., 1936), recalled *Woman Doctor* and her relationship with the actress known around Hollywood as "Ice Bucket." She described Claire Dodd as anything but icy.

"I am happy to say that I have GREAT memories of Claire. She was the exact opposite of the femme fatale characters she portrayed. I found her a warm and really quite funny lady . . . Incongruously, Frieda Inescourt portrayed my mother for the second time, but it was Claire who I was closer to during that time . . . As you know, the leading man was Henry Wilcoxen, and the three of us and my elder sister Anita, who was my guardian, ALWAYS had lunch together at a restaurant right near the studio . . . They had a joke about me because every time we ordered lunch, without fail, I would always order the fresh fruit salad!!!! Throughout the filming the two always referred to me as 'fruit

Crime does not pay! Gangster's mistress, Alma Behlmer (Dodd) learns this valuable lesson the hard way in the crime drama, *Slightly Honorable* (United Artists, 1940), with Pat O'Brien and Edward Arnold. All Claire Dodd photos courtesy of the Cooper family.

salad Jason.' Although in the story, Claire was nasty, it was Claire and Henry who had a fine friendship. No romance because Henry was very happily married to Joan Woodbury . . . Unfortunately, for a number of reasons, I did not see Claire again, much to my regret. I was signed to a contract with Fox and did The Little Princess and Bluebird with my friend, Shirley Temple, and I don't think Claire made many movies at Fox during the time I was there . . . Needless to say, I have the fondest regard for Claire, and I honestly feel that she did not get her due as an actress. She was VERY easy to relate to during our scenes together, and generous in the give and take from one character to the other which is essential for a good scene . . ." [81]

In March 1938, Claire filed for divorce from John Milton Strauss after almost seven years of marriage. At the hearing, she charged her husband with constantly criticizing her, "dress, speech, and management of their home" in front of friends and guests. She was granted custody of the couples' 16-month-old son and $200 a month child support. John Cooper said the primary reason Claire ended her first marriage was Strauss was, "a gambler who lost a bunch of her money."[82] She would remain single until 1940, when she met and married the love of her life, automobile distributor H. Brand Cooper.

In 1940, Miss Dodd accepted a 6th-billed role as the snobbish wife of social climber, Allyn Joslyn in Universal's Bing Crosby/Gloria Jean musical drama, *If I Had My Way*, then signed a pact with the studio. If she had any remaining hope Universal would be the studio to finally feature her in good pictures, she was again disappointed. Although she was given the feminine lead as a reporter opposite the popular comic duo, Abbott and Costello, Dick Powell, and the musical Andrews Sisters in the middling musical comedy, *In The Navy* (1941), all too soon, she was back grinding out Universal programmers like the inferior mystery comedy, *The Black Cat* (1941), the B-crime drama, *Mississippi Gambler* (1942), the serial adventure, *Don Winslow of the Navy* (1942), and the campy, grade-Z island thriller, *The Mad Doctor of Market Street* (1942). The latter presented elegant Claire as the potential victim of an evil mad scientist portrayed by scene-chewing Lionel Atwill. Peppered with enough ludicrous scenes and dreadful dialogue to make any bad movie lover's hall of fame, the film received scathing reviews. Claire left Universal after its release. She made one more film, the disappointing Joe E. Brown spy comedy, *The Daring Young Man*, (Columbia, 1942), then quit show business and rarely looked back. Says John:

"When we lived in Beverly Hills, people would invariably come up to her and ask for an autograph. She was flattered, and would give it to them, but she moved on . . . She discouraged me from entering the film business. She said it was filled with 'nasty,' vane people. She told me there was some amazing talent like Bogart, Cagney, and Fred Astaire, but not to become involved."[83]

Claire (second from left) did the conga with Bing Crosby in the entertaining musical, *If I Had My Way* (Universal, 1940).

In Universal's Abbott and Costello wartime comedy, *In the Navy* (1941), Claire played a reporter on the trail of a radio singer (Dick Powell) after his enlistment. All Claire Dodd photos courtesy of the Cooper family.

In 1942, Claire Dodd Strauss Cooper began the second phase of her life, one which seemed to suit her. After 60 + films and a dozen years in the limelight, publicly suffering the frustrations of a disappointing film career, the very private star seemed to take comfort in her new anonymity and in her new found freedom to pursue her myriad of interests and hobbies. A well-rounded individual who had always exhibited abilities outside acting, Claire was a licensed pilot, an excellent cook, an expert seamstress and jewelry maker, and an antique collector who bought and sold valuables. According to her son, John, despite a lack of formal education, Claire was also an extremely intelligent, articulate, and well-read person whose opinions were widely respected even by those who were not easily impressed. A case in point, was publisher William Randolph Hearst.

"My father told me that he and my mom used to frequent San Simeon, Hearst's castle on the California coast. One morning my dad got up late, and my mother was gone. After dressing, he went to inquire where she was. It turns out she had gotten up early and was traipsing about the grounds having a one-on-one discussion about geopolitics with Hearst who apparently delighted in her perspective." [84]

Claire also found contentment and great personal satisfaction in her home life. Her marriage to Brand Cooper would be a happy and enduring one, lasting 31 years and producing four children: a daughter, Austene, and three sons: twins Brand and John, and Peter. The Coopers eventually purchased Rock Candy Farm: 400 acres and a red New England style farm house outside Beverly Hills where they raised the children. John has fond memories of his childhood years.

"I'm a Beverly hillbilly. I grew up in the hills of Beverly. You remember The Andy Griffith Show where he whistles and throws a rock in the lake? That was filmed in the neighboring yard. It was beautiful. It belonged to the Department of Water and Power, and no one was allowed in there except us because our property bordered it, and my dad used to give a bottle of whiskey to the guy who took care of it. My mom initially did not want to live in 400 acres of wilderness with only three or four houses. It was wild! There were coyotes, deer, great horned owls and hawks. The road out of Beverly Hills was half dirt." [85]

Claire decided to end her acting career after marrying businessman, H. Brand Cooper in 1940.

Outside of their remarkable wilderness home, the Coopers basically lived like regular folks. Claire and Brand were not poor, but they weren't wealthy either. The kids wore Sears clothing, and did chores around the house. Claire supplemented the family income by making jewelry and buying and selling antiques.[86] She rarely spoke of the past except on rare occasions when one of her famed coworkers would telephone and/or stop by. John Cooper recalled one particularly memorable visitor to Rock Candy Farm: Claire's two time costar, Bette Davis.

A woman of many interests, Claire was an expert seamstress, jewelry maker, antique collector, and a licensed pilot. All Claire Dodd photos courtesy of the Cooper family.

"My mother hadn't seen Bette in years. Well, she (Bette) shows up, comes in and sits down on our L-shaped couch. In front of the couch was a Louis umpteenth style coffee table, my mother's prize. Bette put her feet on the table and her arms over the back of the couch and said, 'I like this place. It's lived in.' This made my mother furious. I can still see the

1930's portrait of Claire Dodd.

flash go through her eyes because that was insulting to her. I don't know if Bette meant it like that. I think probably she was trying to compliment my mother . . . Because of that, my brother and I spent the entire summer painting the house! (much laughter)" [87]

During the late 1960's, the Coopers decided to vacation in Holland. Claire's family was of Dutch heritage, and she'd always wanted to visit. She was going through menopause at the time and received a massive injection of estrogen just prior to the trip. Months after their return, she was diagnosed with cancer. She battled the disease for two long years before succumbing at home on November 23, 1973, age 64. Funeral services were held on November 27, at the Church of the Good Shepherd (Catholic) in Beverly Hills with interment in the Brand Family Cemetery in Glendale.[88] She was survived by her husband, daughter, four sons, and countless film fans then and now who admired her sparkling beauty, charisma, and exceptional talent, particularly her uncanny ability to make even the most ruthless, despicable characters interesting and entertaining, even likeable. Her son, John remembers Claire as "a wonderful mother, an amazing person." He believes she was proud of her career in films, but prouder still of her self-reliance.

"She was driven by a depression-era mind set. It drove her entire life. She didn't say it, but the proof is in the pudding. She was always planning for disaster. We had cupboards full of food stored up and stacked. When she died, there were 50 pairs of shoes in her closet. She could only wear Triple-A Italian shoes. She would buy them when they came on sale and stock them. She was always prepared." [89]

UPDATE

Claire's son, John Cooper has retired from his work as a construction professional and is currently recuperating from a recent illness. His twin brother Brand owns a law firm, and Claire's youngest son, Peter is the owner of a computer software company. They all live in the Pacific Northwest. According to the younger Coopers, their older siblings, Jon Michael Strauss, and sister Austene have been estranged from the family for many years, thus their whereabouts and status is unknown.[90]

CHAPTER FOUR
"RICHARD GREENE: SWASHBUCKLER WITH A DOUBLE-EDGED SWORD"

(Original Publication: *Classic Images*, October, 1997)

Before achieving his greatest fame as the titled hero in the hit television series, *The Adventures of Robin Hood* in 1955, handsome Richard Greene had a noteworthy film career. During his moviemaking years, he was frequently compared to Tyrone Power. Both were approximately the same age, had matinee idol looks, worked for the same studio, and played similar type roles. Like Power, Greene's handsome appearance turned out to be a double-edged sword, aiding his entry into films, but ultimately, proving detrimental to his acting ambitions. In a movie magazine interview in 1938, (his first year in the film capital), the naive Mr. Greene stated his acting goal to Hollywood and the public. He said, "I would like to get into character roles with some real meat to them."[91] Unfortunately, no one was listening, least of all his bosses at 20th Century Fox studio, and Greene's legion of female admirers who cared more about his trademark dimples than his acting abilities. Greene persevered however, managing to turn in several skillful leading man performances before becoming typed in routine costume adventures. His early film work continues to leave his admirers wondering what might have been.

The Richard Greene story began in the port city of Plymouth, Devonshire, England on August 25, 1914, with the birth of a son to Richard Greene and his wife, Kathleen Gerrard Greene, both prominent British stage character actors. Just two weeks later, Richard Marius Joseph Greene was placed in the care of a nanny so his mother could return to acting. It seemed destined that young Richard would become a film actor. He was the product of four generations of thespians, and his grandfather William Friese-Greene was one of the pioneers of motion picture making in Great Britain. Friese-Greene's famous 1885 exhibition, *Girl With the Moving Eyes* was commemorated in the 1951 film, *The Magic Box*.

Upon completion of his studies at Cardinal Vaughn School at Kensington, in 1933, nineteen-year-old Richard made his stage debut at the Old Vic as a spear carrier in Shakespeare's *Julius Caesar*. By then, he had grown into an extremely good looking, athletic young man — 6 foot 1 1/2 inches tall, 170 pounds with dark brown, wavy hair. He was so handsome, that between acting jobs, he obtained employment modeling shirts and hats for one pound a sitting. In 1934, he obtained a small role in a revival of *Journey's End*, and a bit part in a film, *Sing As You Go* (Ealing Studios), starring Gracie Fields. His entire role consisted of two words, "Not yet." Greene laughingly recalled the role years later.

"For me, it was the entire script! I rehearsed for two whole days. I said, 'Not yet' in every possible intonation and inflection. I murmured the words, and I shouted them until I grew hoarse in repeating them." [92]

This rather intense preparation was all for naught when the scene was deleted in the editing room.

In 1936, Greene joined the Brandon-Thomas Repertory Company, traveling to every corner of the British Isles in various productions. Later that year, he won the juvenile lead in the Terence Rattigan play, *French Without Tears*, a critically acclaimed hit on the London stage. The part was an important break for the young man that brought him to the attention of British producer Alexander Korda who tested him for films, but made no offers. In the fall of 1937, a 20th Century Fox talent scout saw the play, and quickly cabled Darryl Zanuck he had found, "an important new talent." The scout was impressed with the young man's performance, but more by his dashing good looks a-la Tyrone Power. On Christmas Eve, 1937, the whirlwind began when young Greene was approached by Fox representatives, and on January 17, 1938, signed to a seven-year contract at a considerable sum. One week after his autograph was affixed, Greene was at 20th Century Fox studios in Hollywood being groomed for stardom, posing for photographs, having his teeth capped, and being fitted for costumes. By February, he was on a soundstage working on his first motion picture.[93]

Greene's first film role under his new contract was as the youngest of four brothers who set out to clear their deceased father's name in acclaimed director John Ford's dramatic *Four Men and a Prayer* (20th Century Fox, 1938). The cast also included such significant stars as Loretta Young, and David Niven. "I was so bewildered!" (during the making of the film)," Greene recalled, "I still don't know how I ever got through the scenes. If Loretta hadn't kidded me out of my fright, I might never have made it."[94] The film debuted in New York on May 8, 1938, to enthusiastic reviews. *The New York Times* said,"Miss Young has found a handsome new leading man in Richard Greene." That observation was echoed by scores of "swooning" female fans who swarmed into movie houses and deluged the studio with adoring fan letters. Zanuck was ecstatic! All the quiet, rather shy Mr. Greene could feel was embarrassment.

Greene was given little time to enjoy his sudden fame. He was immediately cast in three more 20th Century Fox motion pictures. First, he romanced skating sensation, Sonia Henie in *My Lucky Star* (1938). then young T.C.F. contractee, Nancy Kelly in the grand action adventure, *Submarine Patrol* (1938). The latter film reunited him with the legendary John Ford who requested him for the lead. Ford liked this inexperienced young actor, referring to him as "Bouncer" because Greene never seemed able to sit still. Next came the popular sentimental drama, *Kentucky* (1938), with Loretta Young in which he played a banker's son turned horse trainer. If the plot appeared a bit farfetched, the film had many redeeming features including beautiful Technicolor photography, great on-screen chemistry between the two stars, and an Oscar-winning supporting performance by Walter Brennan. On his infrequent days off, the ever conscientious Greene often put on old clothes and spent time in downtown Los Angeles observing people. "I would wander around for many hours among those quite poor but always interesting humans. I learned a lot about America there." he said.[95]

1939 would be a peak year for Richard Greene on the silver screen in which he appeared in four major 20th Century Fox releases which solidified his popularity and increased his visibility. In *The Little Princess*, he romanced Anita Louise in Victorian England while helping poor little Shirley Temple (in her first Technicolor feature), find her missing father. In *The Hound of the Baskervilles* based on

After the release of Greene's first films, female fan letters flooded 20th Century Fox studios asking for an autographed photo. This is one Mr. Greene sent to young Elizabeth Van Guilder in 1939.

Arthur Conan Doyle's eeire mystery, Greene had the lead in a film now considered a classic. His performance as the nephew and heir of a murdered Devonshire baronet was widely hailed, but largely

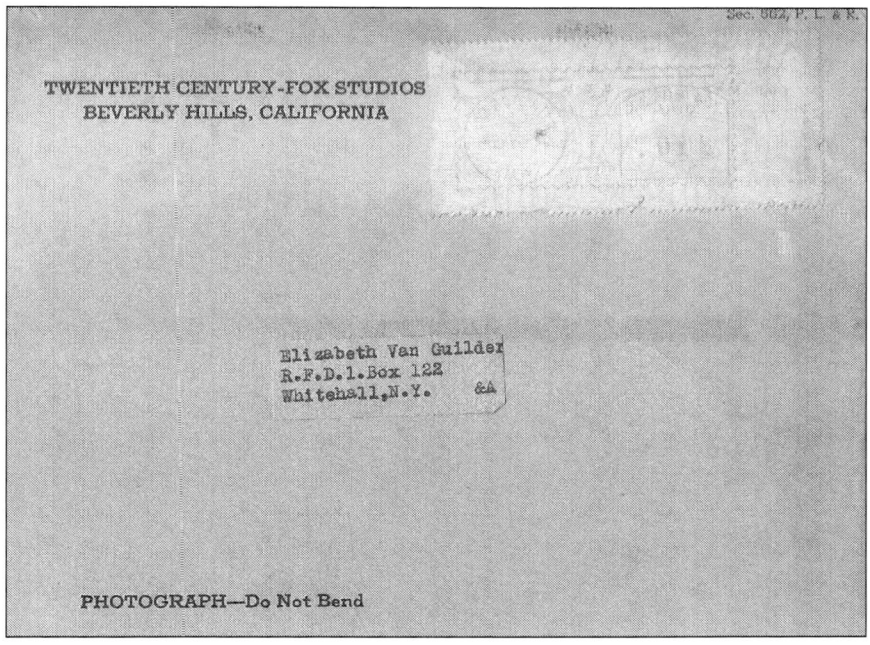

Envelope addressed to Ms. Van Guilder dated 1939.

overshadowed by the film's atmospheric quality, and the classic performances of Basil Rathbone and Nigel Bruce as Sherlock Holmes and Watson. A *Boston Globe* review did single young Greene out however, saying, "Richard Greene is the only really romantic leading man since Robert Taylor and Tyrone Power on the horizon."

While filming the prestigious biopic, *Stanley and Livingstone*, Greene carefully studied stars Spencer Tracy and Cedric Hardwicke, hoping to gain knowledge and techniques which might prove valuable to his aspirations of becoming a serious dramatic actor. As directed by Henry King, with the assistance of a large quantity of on location African footage, the familiar story was filmed with restraint and intelligence. Greene's role as the love interest of female lead, Nancy Kelly, was clearly a supporting one, but the film's excellent reception aided his career. In *Here I Am a Stranger*, Greene portrayed a young college student who becomes re-acquainted with his estranged, alcoholic father (well played by Richard Dix). Their relationship was the theme of this well-handled drama. Critics noted Greene's "strong portrayal," and cited his work in the picture as proof there was talent hidden behind the handsome facade.

A scene from *The Hound of the Baskervilles* (20th Century Fox, 1939). From left to right: Basil Rathbone, Greene, and Lionel Atwill.

Greene had another showy role as a young college student who comes to know his estranged father in the affecting drama, *Here I Am a Stranger*, (20th Century Fox, 1939).

Greene played steamboat inventor Robert Fulton in the fanciful film biography, *Little Old New York* (20th Century Fox, 1940) costarring Alice Faye.

In 1940, Greene landed another significant part, this time as steamboat inventor Robert Fulton in the entertaining, *Little Old New York* (20th Century Fox, 1940), opposite popular Alice Faye. Historians were horrified at the film's "Hollywoodized" screenplay, but Greene and Faye fans could not have cared less about the fanciful movie's historical inaccuracies, making it a major box office hit. In the comedy-drama, *I Was an Adventuress* (20th Century Fox, 1940), the young film star gave another sincere performance as a millionaire who singlehandedly reforms a beautiful jewel thief (Vera Zorina). Richard Greene was on a roll!

With his career clearly on the upswing, and fan mail rivaling Ty Power, in 1940, Greene asked 20th Century Fox to release him from his contract so he could return to his beloved Britain to aid in the war effort. When they grudgingly obliged, Greene enlisted in the Royal Armoured Corps of the Twenty-Seventh Lancers. This brave and patriotic move won admiration on both sides of the Atlantic, but did nothing but harm to Greene's movie career which would never quite recover its lost momentum. Beginning in the fall of 1940,

Greene served in France, the Netherlands, and Belgium, later becoming an officer cadet and a second lieutenant.[96]

While serving in the military, on Christmas Eve, 1941, Richard married beautiful 21-year-old British actress, Patricia Medina, after a whirlwind courtship. After a two day honeymoon, Greene returned to the army at Yorkshire for a year of training, eventually becoming a first lieutenant. One year later, he was relieved of duty on two occasions to appear in two British war propaganda films, *Unpublished Story* (Two Cities-British, 1942) and *Flying Fortress* (Warner Bros.-British, 1942), and the following year, was given yet another furlough to costar with Anna Neagle in *The Yellow Canary* (RKO, 1943), a mystery film about British spies. In May 1943, Greene sustained a leg injury which could have resulted in a discharge if he had not insisted on staying on. He was eventually given a staff liaison post and captain's rank until he was discharged in December 1944. When asked about his war experience, he stated,

"Many of them were horrible days, and others were unpleasant, and yet I wouldn't give up a single day . . . That experience has given me thought and a maturity I never would have had if I had remained in Hollywood."[97]

After the war, 31-year-old Richard and his young bride resided for a time in Britain where both appeared in British films and on the London stage. Greene made two British motion pictures at this time, the first of which was the delightful, *Don't Take It to Heart* (Two Cities-British, 1944), with wife, Patricia. Critics loved this charming romantic comedy, giving the Greene's rave reviews, but the film had only limited success in America. Richard followed by appearing as Irish theater impresario George Howard in the musical biopic, *Gaiety George* (a.k.a. *Showtime*) (Embassy Pictures-British, 1946). Greene hoped the movie would re-invigorate his film career, but it was unsuccessful. In between these pictures, he toured Europe, entertaining allied troops.

In 1946, the Greenes moved to U. S. West Coast after Miss Medina was offered a screen test by 20th Century Fox. Both had high hopes of becoming important Hollywood stars, but sadly, despite their abilities, neither would achieve their professional dreams. One of

In 1940, at the height of his popularity, patriotic Richard Greene returned to Great Britain and enlisted in the British Army to assist his beloved country fight for its survival, serving in the Royal Armoured Corps of the Twenty-Seventh Lancers. This press photo shows him stepping out of a light tank used by his unit.

Richard Greene and his lovely wife, Patricia Medina and their dogs "Kippy" and "Pfui" posed for this photo outside their country home in 1944.

Richard's first acts upon his return was rushing to the nearest hamburger stand. "Hamburgers," he said, "are one of America's greatest contributions to civilization!"⁹⁸ His next acts were to turn down several films offers. All were leading man type roles he felt were inconsequential. In what has to be the most unique interview ever given by a Hollywood star of either sex, Greene decried his still youthful good looks. "I don't want to become Lionel Barrymore, but I've been waiting to get a few wrinkles, or character lines, as actors say, in my face, but I haven't got any good ones yet," he said.⁹⁹

Richard's first post-war Hollywood film would be a famous one, and signal a new phase of his career. *Forever Amber* (20th Century Fox-1947), adapted from the popular sensual novel, was a sanitized version of the amorous adventures of Amber St. Clare, a 17th century harlot. Problems and delays plagued the film adaptation from the beginning. Production was halted after a few weeks, when it became painfully apparent to producer William Periberg and director, Otto Preminger that actress Peggy Cummins was miscast in the lead. Miss Cummins was eventually replaced by glamorous Linda Darnell. By the time filming resumed, Vincent Price (formerly cast as Lord Almsbury, the cynical friend of leading man, Cornel Wilde), had also departed. When Greene was offered Price's showy role, he eagerly accepted, rightly sensing it would be a way to reintroduce himself to American audiences. "In *Forever Amber*, I've gotten what I wanted, an older, more mature part. For the first time in my career, I won't win the girl," he announced happily.[100]

The richly produced movie was a triumph at the box office. Greene's performance was called, "a standout!" *Motion Picture* magazine said he gave the character, "humor and charm." It would seem logical that Richard's auspicious return to American films would have led to richer and more varied offers, but it was not to be. Instead, the success of *Forever Amber* paired with Greene's still-youthful good looks, to type him in costume adventures like his follow-ups: *The Fighting O'Flynn* (Universal, 1948), and *The Fan* (20th Century Fox, 1949), neither of which were as good as *Forever Amber* or further enhanced his reputation.

In August 1949, the freelancing Mr. Greene crossed the Atlantic once again to appear in the minor British men's prison film, *Now Barabbas Was a Robber* (Warner Bros.-British, 1949), filmed in Italy, then returned to England to support Myrna Loy and Roger Livesey in the unsuccessful drama, *If This Be Sin* (London Films-British, 1949). It was at this time that rumors began regularly surfacing regarding friction between Mr and Mrs. Greene, which Medina confirmed when she announced the couple's separation in April 1950. "We're quarreling all the time," she said. "He doesn't like the way I keep house, and I find fault with him, but we both care more about each other than anyone else."[101] It was not enough however. A divorce decree was granted on June 25, 1951. Once again, a marriage between actors had been broken by the pressures of competing careers. The irony of this particular breakup was that both Mr. and Mrs. Greene had the same career problems. Both were too good looking and became typed in costume pictures which stifled their development as top ranked star/actors. Shortly after the divorce, Miss Medina was asked about her ex-husband. She said,

"I will always be his friend, maybe his best friend, but not his wife. It didn't work, and heaven knows we both gave it a fair chance. Marriage is not for me, and I'm sure I won't get married again." [102]

She did get married again however, and to another handsome and gifted actor, the distinguished Joseph Cotten in 1960. Her second marriage would be a happy one, lasting until Mr. Cotten's death in 1994. She remained friends with Richard Greene until his death.

1950 was another turning point year in the life and career of Richard Greene who bought a new home in Hollywood, and acquired a 12 foot dinghy, he named, *Arachnid*. He also initiated a romantic relationship with heiress, Nancy Oakes (1925-2005), the daughter of legendary entrepenuer, investor, and philanthropist, Sir Harry Oakes. Richard and Nancy's relationship produced a daughter, Patricia Luisa Oakes in 1951.

1950 was also the year Greene solidified his new screen image and the new phase of his film career, inheriting (along with Stewart Granger, Cornel Wilde and Louis Hayward), the swashbuckling mantle of the aging Errol Flynn. He would appear in ten more costume adventure films during the period between 1950 to 1961. Each had him as a bigger-than-life hero, defending the lowly and oppressed, and winning the hand of a fair maiden in the bargain. None were particularly distinguished, but each had Greene looking dashing and believable, (amazingly youthful for a man in his forties), colorful characters, beautiful women, and a few thrills particularly for the junior set. During the making of the swashbuckler, *Shadow of the Eagle* (Valiant-1950), Greene admitted he had given up all hope of becoming a great dramatic actor, and instead, settled comfortably into the costume adventure genre. "This swashbuckler stuff is a bit rough on the anatomy," he stated, "But I find it more exhilarating than whispering mish-mash into some ingénue's pink little ear." [103]

Greene played John Ridd, a humble farmer who fights oppression and wins the hand of a beautiful landlord's daughter in Columbia's romantic adventure *Lorna Doone* (1951).

Among his notable films of this period were *The Desert Hawk* (Universal, 1950), *Lorna Doone* (Columbia, 1951), *Rogue's March* (MGM, 1953), *Captain Scarlett* (United Artists, 1953), and *Contraband Spain* (Associated British Producers, 1955).

Two films are most representative of his work during these years. The very popular, *The Black Castle* (Universal International, 1952), had the heroic Greene traveling to a menacing Bavarian castle owned by an evil, one-eyed count (Stephen McNally) in search of missing friends. There, he must endure black panthers, crocodile pits, and lethal drugs to defeat the dastardly count, and rescue the count's beautiful unhappy wife, (played by Paula Corday). He is aided by a wise, but ill-fated doctor portrayed by horror legend, Boris Karloff in a rare sympathetic role. *The Bandits of Corsica* (United Artists, 1954), a sequel to the entertaining 1942 swashbuckler, *The Corsican Brothers*, gave Greene the challenge of playing dual roles, and a chance to costar with beautiful Paula Raymond, who described the film as, "a very pleasant experience," and her former costar as, "A charming guy! Just as beautiful a person as he looked!"[104]

From left to right: John Hoyt, Greene, Stephen McNally, Paula Corday, and Michael Pate in a scene from Universal International's *The Black Castle* (1952).

From left to right: Lon Chaney Jr., Richard Greene, Stephen McNally and Paula (a.k.a. Rita) Corday in *The Black Castle* (Universal International, 1952).

As none of the swashbucklers were earning him any notable distinction, and with fewer film offers coming in, Greene turned his attention to the stage in the middle 1950's, producing and appearing in the British play, *The Secret Tent* (1954). When it failed to reach London's West End, it was a bitter pill. Richard was also disappointed when he bought the rights to Don Martin's comedy-western, *The Dude From Montana*, and no film producers expressed interest.

In 1955, at a professional low point, Greene's career was rescued by an unlikely source: television. Lured by sizeable monies and better than average scripts, Greene first began appearing on American television in 1951, guesting on several popular series including, *Studio One in Hollywood* (1951), *Lux Video Theater* (1951), *Somerset Maughm Theater* (1951), and *Robert Montgomery Presents* (1951-52). To his surprise, he found these the assignments both challenging and enjoyable, thus when Yeoman Films of Great Britain approached him with a chance to star in a modestly-produced television series in England for American audiences based on the Robin Hood legend, Greene readily accepted. The result was one of the most popular adventure series of the decade, one which would make Greene into a big television star, and enrich his emptying wallet.[105]

Produced at Nettlefield Studios in Great Britain, *The Adventures of Robin Hood* series based on the Robin Hood legend, was premiered on CBS television in September 1955. Embraced by the public, it was an enormous success, running four years, and 143 half-hour episodes. An interesting sidelight of its production, was the employment of several black-listed writers including Ring Lardner Jr. under assumed names. Also hired were talented young directors including Terence Fisher and Lindsay Anderson whose job was to guide Robin in his fight against Norman injustice. Richard described the series' success this way,

"Kids love pageantry and costume plays. But the most important thing is: Robin can be identified with any American hero. He's the British Hopalong!"[106]

Greene's lucrative flirtation with television (both British and American), would continue when *The Adventures of Robin Hood* was rerun in America in the 1960's. In the 1970's, he appeared on the

Richard Greene won his greatest fame and fortune playing the famed Robin of Locksley in the immensely popular TV version of *The Adventures of Robin Hood* filmed at Nettlefield Studios in Great Britain.

medical drama series, *The Doctors*, as well as many other TV projects on both sides of the Atlantic including Yorkshire television's production of the comic drama, *A Man for Loving* (1970) costarring Lorne Greene.

In addition to occasional acting jobs, Mr. Greene kept his final years busy by pursuing some of his many interests and hobbies. As a result of wealth acquired from TV, he bought a fifteen-ton sloop, and an Irish country estate where he farmed and became a top horse

Latter day portrait circa. 1968.

breeder. Occasionally he was lured away from hobbies, and TV projects to appear on the stage, and in a handful of minor, mostly British-made films including, *Beyond the Curtain* (Rank, 1960), *Sword of Sherwood Forest* (Columbia, 1961), a spinoff from his hit series which he co-produced, *Dangerous Island* (British, 1967), *Blood of Fu Manchu* (AA-British, 1968) and *Kiss and Kill* (Commonwealth United, 1969) His last movie, *Tales from the Crypt* (Amicus, 1972), was comprised of a quintet of ghoulishly entertaining tales of terror. Richard was among many top stars to appear in this British horror hit.

After the breakup of his relationship with Nancy Oakes, in 1960, Greene wed Brazilian heiress, Beatriz Summers who shared his passions for travel and horses. When they weren't at home in Ireland, they were jet-setting around the world with their wealthy friends. The couple eventually separated in 1980.[107] Two years later, Richard suffered serious injuries in a fall, followed by a diagnosis of a brain tumor. In the autumn of 1982, he underwent brain surgery from which he never fully recovered. Richard Greene died three years later on June 2, 1985, in Norfolk, England of cardiac arrest at the age of 70 years. He was cremated and his ashes were scattered at sea. He was survived by daughter Patricia, and a grandson.[108]

In retrospect, Greene's career in films was respectable, but unremarkable mainly because he was given too few opportunities to showcase his abilities and realize his potential. Unfortunately, his Hollywood experience was typical of many actors whose looks won them a ticket inside the studio gates, but proved a hindrance to the achievement of their ultimate acting goals. In the end, when we think of Richard Greene, we forget his acclaimed early film work. Instead, we remember him on his trusty steed, his sword or bow intact, fair maiden at his side. Let's face it, film and TV producers needed good looking heros, and Richard Greene cut a dashing figure in costume epics. Without all his Hollywood heroics, just think of all those lowly oppressed peasants who would have remained in bondage, all those filmic wars of independence lost, and the scores of pre-teens left unentertained. And, one can only speculate what might have become of poor, beautiful Paula Corday in that black castle? Would she have been the breakfast for a hungry crocodile, the victim of lethal drugs, or other untold abuses perpetrated by her one-eyed, teeth knashing husband? Lucky for her Richard Greene was there, and lucky for us!

UPDATE

Since the publication of the article in 1997, several interesting bits of information have come to light about Mr. Greene's family and his former lover, gold-mining heiress Nancy Oakes. After her relationship with Greene ended, Ms. Oakes married German Baron von Hoyningen- Huene in 1952. She divorced him in 1956, and later, married Patrick Tritton. She died January 21, 2005 at age 80. In 1977, Richard and Nancy's daughter, Patricia Luisa married Franklin D. Roosevelt Jr., the son of the 32nd U.S. president and his wife Eleanor. During the couples' four year marriage (1977-81), they produced a son, John Alexander Roosevelt born October 18, 1977. Patricia Oakes Roosevelt later married Robert Leigh-Wood, a prominent London stockbroker and gave birth to a daughter, Shirley Alice Leigh-Wood in 1985. Patricia currently lives in the Caribbean where she and her husband are restoring the Oakes family home as a hotel. Richard Greene's grandson, John Alexander "Jack" Roosevelt works in the financial industry. In 2010, he married Elizabeth Garcia, a prominent lawyer's daughter. The couple resides in the Northeastern United States. Greene's granddaughter, Shirley Alice Leigh-Wood is an actress and model. Richard's first wife, Patricia Medina died of respiratory failure on April 28, 2012, age 92.[109]

CHAPTER FIVE
"JOHN HODIAK: THE HERO FROM HAMTRAMCK"

(Originally published in *Classic Images*, August, 1998)

October 19, 1955 — Tarzana, California. "John Hodiak, motion picture, stage, and television actor died this morning at his home here while shaving before going to work at Twentieth Century Fox Studio. The 41-year-old leading man succumbed instantaneously to a coronary thrombosis."[110]

Such was the *New York Times* brief description of the untimely end to the life and career of one of Hollywood's golden boys. Like John Garfield three years earlier, death had claimed a prominent Hollywood actor in the prime of life. The obituary went on to list the career highlights of Hodiak, a humble young man from Michigan including his 1954 Broadway triumph in *The Caine Mutiny Court Martial*, and impressive film performances in such diverse productions as *Lifeboat, The Harvey Girls, A Bell For Adano,* and *Battleground*. During his Hollywood years, John Hodiak's primary goals had always been to demonstrate his versatility and range as an actor, and be a good person. Although he never became a movie superstar, a close examination of his life and acting career clearly shows how well he succeeded!

The son of immigrants, the future film star was born on April 16, 1914, in Pittsburgh. His Ukranian father, Walter had met the Polish Anna Pogorzelliec while harvesting wheat in Bohemia. After their marriage, the couple emigrated to the United States in 1912, and settled in Pennsylvania. The first born, John was followed by Walter Jr., and sister Ann. Later, the Hodiaks adopted John's first cousin, Mary. In 1922, the family moved to Hamtramck, Michigan, a city near Detroit known for its immigrant population, where Walter Sr. found work at an auto plant.

Life was hard for the young family during the 1920's, residing in a very small house on a narrow street in a poor part of town. Young John was often found loitering on the streets, fighting with other kids, and scrounging for scrap iron to earn some money for himself. "I was a dese, dem, and dose kid back then," he said. "Foreigners find it hard to pronounce the English "th" and most of the kids had foreign born parents like mine."[111] His troublemaking often landed him in hot water with his tough, but loving parents. What might have been a life of failure and crime was rescued however, by the Hodiak's devotion to their eldest boy, and by an unlikely source: John's utter infatuation with acting and the movies.

John first caught the "acting bug" while appearing in several plays staged regularly by the local Catholic church. He enjoyed his initial forays into the arts, but was insecure about his looks and accent. "I was an awfully homely kid," he recalled, "but even then, I wanted to be an actor. And I must have had plenty of ham in my system not to be discouraged by a mirror."[112] In fact, at age 11, he became determined to be a movie actor after seeing a Douglas Fairbanks film 20 times at the local theater. As much to escape the unpleasant realities of his disadvantaged life as to become a film star, he began skipping school to pursue his celluloid passion. The truancy officer eventually caught up with him and reported to his parents. After a persuasive meeting of boy and father in the woodshed, John temporarily gave up his silver screen devotion, and took up the clarinet. "It was then I realized that an actor had to suffer!" he laughingly remembered.[113] He also began to take school more seriously.

In 1927, he was selected by neighbors to make a campaign speech for Wilbur Bruckner, a candidate for Michigan governor. Upon winning the election, Bruckner arranged an audition with a Detroit radio station for his enthusiastic young supporter. John's poor diction doomed him, but the experience made him resolute in pursuit of an artistic career. "The fact is he (the program manager), was right at the time, but I didn't quit playing that emotional hunch," John recalled.[114] In high school, John briefly abandoned his acting obsession to play third base for Hamtramck High School. His strong throwing arm attracted a minor league baseball scout from the St. Louis Cardinals, but after consultation with his family, John abandoned "America's pasttime." While a high school senior, he received a dramatic scholarship to Northwestern University, but turned it down in an attempt to enter West Point, only to meet rejection due to educational deficiencies.

After graduating, Hodiak worked as a caddy, then as a stockroom clerk at the local Chevrolet plant. His duties included reading invoice figures back to coworkers which helped his enunciation. By the early 1930's, he had decided on radio as a way to pursue his acting goals. He even made recordings of his rich baritone which he took to the same WXYZ program manager who had turned him down earlier. This time, he met with success. "They took me on as a bit player with no salary. But that was all right. I had a daytime job . . ." said John. Eventually, he was promoted and salaried, allowing him to abandon his factory job. "I went into radio full time for considerably less money than I was getting at Chevrolet, but felt I was still following that hunch."[115] His parents were not particularly pleased with the career move, but recognized their son's single-minded quest as positive and uplifting.

In the latter 1930's, John traveled to Chicago to "test the waters," landing a short-lived job at a prominent radio station. He decided to remain in the "Windy City" despite being fired a few weeks later for nonconformance with the station's bureaucratic policies. After existing on "hamburgers and donuts" for weeks, he heard of an audition for the radio role of "Lil Abner." "I spent hours trying to create a voice — a sort of portrait of that naive, gangling hunk of hillbilly muscle," he said.[116] His winning creation was a combination of his father's Ukranian accent and a southern friend's "you-all" idiom. This led to appearances on several significant Chicago radio programs during the period 1939-42.

In 1942, MGM movie scout Marvin Schenck heard Hodiak and arranged to meet him. Now 28, John had matured from a skinny, homely kid into a 6 foot, husky, virile, square-jawed young man with strong arms and a winning toothy smile. Although not handsome in the formal sense, John emanated an air of reserve, intelligence, and integrity that were apparent in the way he spoke and carried himself. He had an "all American" wholesomeness which combined with an old world chivalry to endear him to both women and men. He was the kind of strong, disciplined-looking guy you would want on your side in times of trial. No wonder Schenck instantly recognized his potential as a screen hero, and arranged a New York screen test. Mayer and company were sufficiently impressed to offer him a long term contract. They didn't have to twist the young man's arm to sign on the dotted line. John had been preparing for this moment for years.[117]

Hodiak's first year in the film capital was one of adjustments. MGM, the most prestigious of studios, immediately set about "processing" their newest contract player, cutting hair, suggesting clothing, photographing him for publicity. Mayer even had new names picked out to go with John's new Hollywood life. Hodiak's response was swift and direct. He would submit to all other modifications, but altering his proud family name was out. "I look like a guy named John Hodiak," he argued, and I don't intend making any changes."[118] Mayer and company backed down. Another "culture shock" for the conservative young man was the sudden loss of his privacy. The shy John resented having to squire strange women (mostly starlets), around town and seeing his name (in print), linked with girls he barely knew. During 1943, his first full year as an MGM employee, the studio introduced him to filmgoers in four films. He was the silent crony of a corrupt small town political boss in the serio-comic *A Stranger in Town*, with Frank Morgan. In *Swing Shift Maisie*, with Ann Sothern, he had one line which consisted of, "All green card holders follow me." The zany *I Dood It*, starring Red Skelton, had him as a stage actor turned bomber, and in the strange and affecting drama, *Song of Russia*, he was a Russian peasant farmer whose son is killed by the Nazis.

1944, Hodiak's breakthrough year, started out routinely with a supporting role in *Maisie Goes to Reno* (MGM) and a second lead as a busy husband whose neglect of his wife causes her to turn to an old beau in the mediocre, *Marriage Is a Private Affair* (MGM). His costar in the latter was baby-faced, blonde sexpot, Lana Turner in the ascending stages of her explosive career. Although the familiar storyline had critics turning up their noses, box office receipts were respectable due to Miss Turner's popularity. The movie turned out to be significant to Hodiak as the first major film to present him as a military man. Early on, MGM recognized the young would-be star's sturdy solid appearance would make him an excellent choice to play soldiers.

The film was also memorable because lovely Lana lavished attention on the star-struck young man. "If there's a word for John Hodiak, it's intense . . . File his name under tall, tan, and terrific!" gushed the blonde beauty. According to Joe Morella and Edward Z. Eptstein in their biography, "Lana," Turner was:

"briefly involved with John Hodiak, her costar. Their first date was originally for publicity, but it soon went beyond that stage . . . Insiders at the studio remember however, that Hodiak was one of the few stars at MGM who wouldn't give in to Lana's charms, and this infuriated her." [119]

Whatever happened or didn't, the film raised Hodiak's visibility.

John's first great film role came as a result of a favor he generously granted another actor. Director Alfred Hitchcock, fresh from a series of acclaimed thrillers, had been contracted by 20th Century Fox for two projects. He had always wanted to shoot a film in a confined setting, and conceived the allegorical idea of a lifeboat, filled with characters representing participants in the ongoing military conflict exploding across Europe. Hitchcock took his ideas to novelist John Steinbeck who developed them, then to poet MacKinlay Kantor. Neither would agree to write the screen adaptation. The task eventually fell to old pro, Joseph Swerling (*The Westerner, Pride of the Yankees*) who scripted the tale of nine survivors of a torpedoed passenger ship afloat in a *Lifeboat* (20th Century Fox, 1944). Their relationships during their troubled journey to safety formed the crux of this unusual dramatic film. Eight of the characters, including a parasitic jewel bedecked socialite (Tallulah Bankhead), an opportunistic millionaire business man (Henry Hull), an injured sailor (William Bendix), and a black steward (Canada Lee) are powerful symbols of the free but flawed democratic culture. Their near fatal acquiescence to the rescued captain of a German U-boat (Walter Slezak), was Hitchcock's way of making a forceful point.

To maximize impact and realism, Hitchcock purposely set out to cast unfamiliar faces. Someone suggested the accomplished African American actor, Canada Lee for the steward role. John Hodiak had become friendly with Lee while in New York, and had voluntarily appeared in Lee's test as a favor. Viewing the result, Hitchcock hired

Lee, and urged 20th Century Fox to acquire Hodiak's services to play John Kovac, a left-wing crew member of the ship. A loan agreement was subsequently arranged.

The difficult filming was restricted to a boat secured in a large studio tank. To further replicate reality, the ever fanatical director insisted the craft never remain stationary, causing all nine cast members to become seasick. Several mishaps marred the proceedings, including the near drowning of actor Hume Cronyn who got caught under a large metal water activator used for making waves. The young and inexperienced Hodiak was intimidated and nervous about working with the quirky, difficult Hitchcock who had a well-deserved reputation for his unsympathetic treatment of actors. During his first day on the set, Hodiak's tenseness became apparent to the director who remarked, "What's there to worry about, John? Remember this is just another picture." Then Hitchcock paused dramatically before adding, "on which your whole future depends."[120]

Despite the difficulties, Hitchcock's controversial, technically brilliant motion picture was a great success on all levels, and is today considered a classic. John's performance as the tough, embittered Nazi-hating Kovac was widely admired, and as Hitchcock had predicted, it was the film that put the name Hodiak on the Hollywood map. *Lifeboat* also established John as a sex symbol. Women flocked to see the very masculine, shirtless John romancing costar, Miss Bankhead who he described as, "a real trouper." "It was my chance and I think I made the most of it," he said. When asked about his new status as a screen lover, John brushed it off, "I don't think I'm the type. I just want to be a credit to my profession — a good actor."[121]

20th Century Fox production head Darryl Zanuck was so impressed with the young actor he again borrowed Hodiak to play the title role in his production of *Sunday Dinner For a Soldier* (1944), the tender, funny story of a poor family living on a Florida houseboat who scrimp and save to invite a soldier over for a chicken dinner. Essentially a modest film, the sensitive performances of Hodiak and talented veterans Charles Winninger, and Anne Revere lifted the the material from mediocrity. Critics and audiences applauded, adding another feather to the Hodiak cap. To John, the movie's importance was magnified by the camaraderie he developed with its leading lady, versatile and charming 21-year-old Anne Baxter. According to

The relationships of nine survivors of a torpedoed passenger ship formed the plot of the riveting melodrama, *Lifeboat* (20th Century Fox, 1944), directed by Alfred Hitchcock. From left to right: Tallulah Bankhead, Hodiak, Hume Cronyn (in the background at the oars, Henry Hull and William Bendix.

Anne, their friendship, which would eventually blossomed into romance, then marriage, was definitely not love at first sight.

"Hume Cronyn had pointed him out to me in the studio cafe, and kidded, 'Now there's a nice eligible bachelor you ought to meet,' John had just made Lifeboat and he was interesting to plenty of unmarried young actresses around Hollywood. 'Don't be silly,' I answered. 'I'm not interested in eligible actors. Two careers —.'"[122]

Hodiak won a legion of new feminine fans with his onscreen romance of costar Tallulah Bankhead in *Lifeboat* **(20th Century Fox, 1944).**

In fact, during the initial days of production, both referred to each other as 'Miss Baxter' and 'Mr. Hodiak.' That changed when they became acquainted on an Easter egg hunt, and made plans for a night on the town. In the next two years, they would become inseparable, the darlings of the Hollywood gossip columnists.

Arguably, John's finest film performance came in 1945, again on loan to Darryl Zanuck, this time for the lead role in the poignant, *A Bell For Adano* (20th Century Fox). Based on John Hersey's Pulitzer Prize winning novel, the film was adapted for the screen by Lamarr Trotti and Norman Reilly Raine. A talented cast including Hodiak, Gene Tierney, and William Bendix, was assembled to enact the story of the humane administration of a small Sicilian town by an compassionate U.S. Army Major (Hodiak) at the end of World War II, and his valiant attempts to bring democracy to a community that barely knew the meaning of the word. Henry King's superb direction, and a literate script added pathos and excitement to the simple story presented in a series of colorful, and moving sequences. From the major's arrival in town to a suspicious Facist-weary reception, to the touching conclusion when the townspeople honor him after he restores their church bell, the movie was an almost perfect filmization of the popular book. As Major Joppollo, the stern yet sentimental administrator who is displaced after he ignores a superior's command (in order to assist the citizens of Adano), John turned in a sensitive, multi-faceted performance. The *New York Times* critic Bosley Crowther called the motion picture, "moving and thrilling . . . as fine a job as is physically conceivable on the commericial screen." Of its lead performance, Crowther said, "John Hodiak is excellent as Joppollo, firm and unquestionably sincere with just the right shades of emotion in his response to human problems." It would be John's favorite role, and audiences concurred. Of the movie, and his part, John said this.

"They (filmgoers) think it's wonderful because it's so real. That just about sums up my own reaction to the role of Major Joppollo. . . . I thought it was wonderful because it seemed so real to me. I was born of foreign parents, just as Joppollo was, and I had worked at unimportant jobs before getting the chance to do the thing I most wanted to. Like him too, I had inherited a deep sympathy for the unfortunate people left in the wake of the armies that marched across Europe . . . Fully as inspiring, was the emphasis put by this role on how much a man could accomplish, despite difficulties, if he just did his best. And the Major did his best!" [123]

Since arriving in Hollywood, John had lived frugally in a single-room apartment, doing his own cooking, setting aside monies to purchase a home for his parents. In 1945, he bought them a six- room house in the San Fernando Valley with a three-car garage, orchards of citrus, fig, and walnut trees, and plenty of room for vegetable and flower gardens. He promptly moved his entire family there including his parents, two sisters (and their families) and brother Walter. (back from Okinawa). Of his career, he said,

"I've been so absorbed and thinking of nothing else . . . Now it is time to think of my family. Happiness starts in the family and sort of ripples out of the community to the world at large. All the best fun is in

John's favorite film role was as Major Joppollo, the firm yet humane administrator of a small Sicilian town during World War II in 20th Century Fox's affecting drama, *A Bell For Adano* (1945) directed by Henry King.

sharing . . . I shall never have money. There are too many things that need to be done with it." [124]

True to his word, throughout the remainder of his life, John Hodiak continued to share the fruits of his success with his family, friends, and the community which had so loyally supported him. He donated generously to many charities in both Michigan and California, including setting up "kid's club centers" in Hamtramck, where youngsters could go for games and athletic activities. His own childhood troubles inspired him in this, and many other such endeavors. "A lot of people claim to have discovered me, and a lot of people have helped me," he said. "Frankly, everyone of them is right, and I'm one actor who is plenty grateful." [125]

In the fall of 1945, Hodiak appeared poised for superstardom. In the next year, he would make three more motion pictures, further demonstrating his versatility. Although a poor script and fumbling direction substantially weakened the comic melodrama, *Two Smart People* (MGM, 1946), which costarred him with Lucille Ball and Lloyd Nolan, John acquitted himself well as a confidence man headed for jail. He was also very good as a Marine amnesiac, who sets out on a danger-filled mission to discover his true identity in the thriller, *Somewhere in the Night* (Twentieth Century Fox, 1946). Directed and scripted by Joseph L. Mankiewicz, the film was jam-packed with gripping scenes and good performances. *Variety* called it, "a zingy melodrama, and Hodiak's performance, "strong . . . making every scene count and giving his character plenty of punch." According to Kenneth L. Geist's biography, *Pictures Will Talk, the Life and Films of Joseph L. Mankiewicz*, the film's only weakness was the lack of "Bogart and Bacall type chemistry" between the sullen, sensitive Hodiak and his leading lady, newcomer, Nancy Guild. Miss Guild explained the relationship to Mr. Geist.

"John was a very sweet man, but very cold. I remember when we were playing the scene in the derelict mission house, I made the cavalier statement, 'Gee everyone really looks very poor and like a bum.' Hodiak misinterpreted this as a cruel remark and snarled, 'That's what I come from!'" [126]

Another of his costars had fonder memories. When the veteran actress Josephine Hutchinson (*The Story of Louis Pasteur, Son of Frankenstein, Cass Timberlane*) was contacted by the author, she had this to say of the film and its star,

"I remember that once we went on location to Los Angeles, there was a steep hill where an accident of a runaway car was to be photographed. Suddenly, as the action was just about to start, there was a woman singing in a window in one of those old apartment houses. The first assistant and the production manager tried desperately to find her as she was holding up valuable time. Eventually, when she was discovered, she was doing it to force the studio to give her a film test. I was told that during all this pandemonium, Hodiak was holed up in his trailer reading Chekhov. I've always thought that gave one a marvelous picture of a dedicated actor." [127]

Undoubtedly, John's best film of 1946 was the lusty musical/western, *The Harvey Girls* (MGM), directed by George Sidney. The superior song writing talents of Johnny Mercer and Harry Warren, and the singing and acting abilities of Judy Garland were among the highlights of this riproaring, honky-tonking fun fest. Originally slated as a film comedy vehicle for Lana Turner, the story of Fred Harvey's waitresses' civilizing the Old West, was made into a musical after *Oklahoma* became a mega hit on the stage. The stellar supporting cast including such versatiles as Angela Lansbury, Ray Bolger, Virginia O'Brien, and Preston Foster, added further joy and ticket sales, making it one of the year's biggest hits. John's portrayal of Ned Trent, the tough manager of a dance hall, who is softened by a mail-order bride turned Harvey girl (Garland), was a change of pace, and first rate. Some insiders and critics said he was miscast, but audiences thought otherwise. When asked how he approached a role, John said he relied on instinct. "I never had a drama lesson . . . It's my belief that acting's essentially a quality within a person and not a mere bag of tricks and mannerisms to be exhibited externally."[128]

After a two-year courtship, John married Anne Baxter on July 7, 1946, at the Burlingame, California home of her parents. It was a simple garden wedding with a few invited guests. It appeared an odd match. The poor son of immigrants marrying the patrician daughter of a distillery executive, and granddaughter of the great architect, Frank Lloyd Wright. The quiet, kindly, contemplative, John tying the knot with the talkative, quick-tempered and impulsive Anne. Fortunately, both shared things in common as well, including their love of music, travel, and an all-consuming devotion to their

John had a change of pace role as the manager of a dance hall who falls for a mail order bride turned "Harvey House" waitress (Judy Garland) in the mega-hit musical, *The Harvey Girls* (MGM, 1946).

craft. After a brief honeymoon in Colorado Springs, the young marrieds took up residence in Anne's small Hollywood home on her suggestion. On their third anniversary in 1949, Anne publicly proclaimed her love and admiration for her husband this way.

"Once when I was young, foolish, and unmarried, I sounded off recklessly . . . that I'd never marry an actor . . . Now a correction is in order. . . by now, I know that two careers don't menace a marriage. They make it better!"[129]

Domestically content, with a string of acclaimed screen appearances on his resume, John Hodiak felt very positive about his life in the winter of 1946. Unfortunately, dark clouds hovered on the horizon. He couldn't possibly have known, but his film career was now at its summit, and a slow yet steady decline would follow, precipitated by a string of mediocre films and his demotion from a leading man to predominantly supporting roles. John's three 1947 releases precipitated his decline. Each had John in villainous roles with menacing results.

In the slow, predictable drama, *The Arnelo Affair* (MGM), directed by Arch Oboler, known as, "the wonder boy of radio," Hodiak portrayed a slick night club owner who weaves a murderous web around the neglected wife (Frances Gifford) of an attorney. The passion-packed *Desert Fury* (Paramount), presented him as a psychotic gambler who victimizes the sexy runaway daughter (Lizabeth Scott), of a gambling house proprietor (Mary Astor) with whom he was once involved. Reviews of the latter were as scorching as the hot desert sand. The *New York Times* called it, "a beaut of a technicolor mistake from beginning to end . . ." which also could be said of *Love From a Stranger* (Eagle Lion), which resurrected the old Bluebeard story. This disappointing remake had Hodiak as a sinister South American gentleman who sweeps an attractive London sweepstakes winner (Sylvia Sidney) off her feet into marriage. During its production, John accompanied his young spouse to the Academy Awards, loudly cheering her triumphant win as best supporting actress for her excellent work in *The Razor's Edge*. Even as early as 1947, it was becoming increasingly apparent to John, his wife's career was taking off just as his was becoming stalled in second gear. He proclaimed,

"So far as the actor is concerned, the attitude of producers seems to be this: 'You're getting parts and you're getting paid, so what are you beefing about?' . . . But there are such things as honesty and integrity to be preserved. If you keep betraying these qualities you'll eventually lose them. This I do not want . . . I'd like to play in simple stories that have warmth, humanity, and charm about them. For instance, I felt that Sunday Dinner For a Soldier put these qualities over . . . I got the film on loan-out. . . So it does seem that my own studio could do as well for me on the home lot." [130]

Paramount Pictures portrait of John during the production of *Desert Fury* (1947).

The MGM brass was not listening however, and appeared confused on how best to present their star.

As a result of the public drubbing he took from critics and filmgoers in 1947, combined with the return of many of the film industry's top male star/actors from active duty in World War II, John found quality leading man scripts to be a scarce commodity. He realized if he wanted to work in worthy productions, he would have to be content with roles of lesser importance. Thus Phase Two of his movie career

John Hodiak, who met his future wife, actress Anne Baxter while filming *Sunday Dinner For a Soldier* in 1944, was reteamed with her in 1948, in the World War II drama, *Homecoming* (MGM).

began in 1948, when John reteamed with his award winning wife, both in support of MGM's biggest stars, Clark Gable and Lana Turner. Hodiak's fourth-billed performance as the dedicated doctor/best friend of a self-centered physician (Gable) in the World War II drama, *Homecoming* (MGM, 1948), was excellent, but the role was relatively minor.

One year after the completion of *Homecoming*, Hodiak was again cast in support of Clark Gable in the war drama, *Command Decision* (MGM, 1949), about a brigadier general's (Gable's) controversial decision to conduct the costly, but crucial aerial bombardment of Germany, despite the objections of his superior officer, (Walter Pidgeon). A suspenseful and poignant screenplay, and superb performances highlighted this unusual and credible war film. Hodiak had the small key role of Colonel Edwin Martin, a noble flyer killed the day his wife gives birth to their first child. MGM's well-acted melodrama, *The Bribe* (1949), also gave John a good character part as a boozy ex-bomber pilot who sells his mechanical talent to crooks. This time, he supported Robert Taylor, as a secret service investigator, and Ava Gardner as his (Hodiak's) barroom singing wife.

Certainly one of the best films of Phase II of the Hodiak career was William Wellman's stark unadorned tribute to the average G.I., *Battleground* (MGM, 1949). Adapted from a Robert Pirosh story (based on his own war experiences), the movie chronicled the transformation of a detail of American troops from crisp glider soldiers into foot-slogging riflemen who suffer the fear, grief, and bewilderment of the Battle of the Bulge. Although ultimately a significant success, the film had an extremely difficult history. Dore Schary, the new #2 man at MGM, had brought the project with him from RKO where he had unsuccessfully battled Howard Hughes who resisted producing it. Upon his arrival at MGM, Schary was forced to wage another skirmish, this one with MGM head, Louis B. Mayer, who like Hughes, felt the movie would bomb at the box office. Luckily for everyone, Schary prevailed, and the result was one of the best war dramas of all time.

A uniformly fine ensemble cast brought "the battered bastards of Bastogne" to life including, George Murphy, Van Johnson, Hodiak, and James Whitmore, assisted by some of the original "Screaming Eagles" of the 101rst Airborne division, playing themselves. John's quiet, dignified supporting performance as Jarvess, a newspaper columnist who discovers the grim gallantry of war, was highly regarded. Nominated for six Academy Awards including Best Picture, the film won for Pirosh's screenplay and the photography of Paul Vogel. *Battleground's* phenomenal critical and box office success was a particular triumph for Schary, who would soon replace Mayer as head of MGM.

If his career as a lead actor now seemed off track, John could take solace in the apparent tranquility of his private life. His beloved family expressed happiness with their new life in sunny California, and his three-year marriage to Miss Baxter seemed on a solid footing. The thankful John expressed his gratitude to his creator, "I pray all the time; I count my blessings and thank God another day has passed with safety and comfort for my loved ones," he told the press.[131] During this period, Anne penned an article for *Modern Screen* magazine extolling the virtues of matrimony and expressing the contentment of her life with John.

"When I start a picture, I always get yellow roses on the set from John. And when he starts one, I send a little horseshoe of carnations. I don't

Hodiak's last great film role came in 1949, as a former newspaper columnist who becomes part of the heroic 101st Airbone Division resisting the Nazis at the Battle of the Bulge in the Oscar nominated war drama, *Battleground* (MGM). Seen here with actress, Denise Darcel.

know how John and I will spend our wedding anniversary this year . . . , but I can tell you one thing about it. We'll be looking over the past year and making plans for the next, checking up on our happiness and finding as usual, that it gets better every year . . ." [132]

In addition to his wife, John also found support from good friends in the film capital, people like the talented, innovative John Wiegman, one of the legends of radio, who was instrumental in founding the

KTLA radio and television station in Los Angeles. Mr. Wiegman had this to say about his friend when contacted by the author.

"There was a whole group of us in the business that hung out together: John Hodiak, Richard Long, Steve Brodie, Dennis O'Keefe . . . John would try to sneak away for an hour or two, looking for comradery, tell war stories, lies . . . (laughter) He was a good buddy to all of us, and an underrated actor. He didn't talk about acting, but the other fellows did, and they respected him as a pro. As a man, he was kind, gentle, soft-spoken, giving of himself and his wealth. He did a lot of great things without applause." [133]

During his busiest filmmaking period 1949-51, (eight motion pictures, all for MGM) John solidied his new status as a supporting player, only once taking on a leading role. He was a straight-laced army captain boldly battling the Apaches, while vying with Indian scout (Robert Taylor) for beauteous, Arlene Dahl in the western, *Ambush* (1949), an FBI agent in support of stars Spencer Tracy, and James Stewart in the World War II yarn, *Malaya* (1949), and an American colonel who falls for the titled heroine (Greer Garson) in the disappointing sequel to the Oscar winning *Mrs. Miniver*, titled *The Miniver Story* (1950).

John briefly re-ascended to star billing in the minor romantic melodrama, *A Lady Without Passport* (1950), about an immigration officer (Hodiak) who uses an alien (Hedy Lamarr) in an attempt to trap a smuggling ring, but even the first-rate Everglades chase conclusion which gave John the enviable task of saving gorgeous Miss Lamarr from the clutches of a smuggler (George Macready), couldn't save this flop which effectively dashed any hopes he still harbored of reinvorgorating his status as a lead actor at MGM.

By 1951, John had concluded his career as a Metro-Goldwyn-Mayer contract player was going nowhere, and accepted his last four character assignments in MGM productions with resignation. He was the colleague/friend of a college professor (Ray Milland) who suffers the anguishing loss of his entire family in a fire in *Night Into Morning*, a sympathetic district attorney up against a heavy drinking criminal lawyer (Spencer Tracy) in the interesting, but unsuccessful *People Against O'Hara*, and a white man who lives with the Indians in the colorful adventure, *Across the Wide Missouri*. The latter, beautifully photographed on location in Durango, Colorado, reunited John with old friends Clark Gable and director William Wellman in a well-intentioned tale of an Indian-fighting trapper won over by the native American culture. In spite of an interesting premise, good acting, and Wellman's expert hand, the film was not well received, however. According to Frank L. Thompson in his book, *William Wellman*, "Wild Bill" placed most of the blame on the editing process supervised by Dore Schary, which he said stripped the movie of subtlety and substituted narration. Schary also lopped off most of John's role as a Scotsman who lives with the Blackfoot tribe.[134]

Hodiak completed his seven year studio contract by filming a small role in MGM's *The Sellout*, (1951), a minor entry about small town corruption starring Walter Pidgeon. Also in the supporting cast was another Metro-Goldwyn-Mayer contract player completing her own studio pact, Paula Raymond. When the author asked Miss Raymond about Mr. Hodiak, she expressed great admiration for him as an actor and a man. "Charming! I liked him enormously. He was a total professional!"[135] During the filming, on July 7, 1951, John and Anne became the proud parents of Katrina Baxter Hodiak. The birth of his daughter, coupled with his departure from MGM, temporarily lifted John's spirits. Professionally, he looked forward to freelancing and accepting stage roles.

While an MGM contract player, John had been offered numerous stage opportunities which he had been forced to decline. In his first act as a freelance artist, he accepted the role of a masochistic sheriff of a *Peyton Place* type small town in, *The Chase*, which opened on Broadway in April, 1952. Although his performance was praised, winning the prestigious Donaldson Award, and the play won favorable notices, its short run was a disappointment. (Marlon Brando would play John's role in the 1966 film version.)

In the summer of 1952, Hodiak returned to Hollywood to film, *Battle Zone* (Allied Artists), a minor-league venture focusing on the exploits of two combat photographers in the Korean War. It was at this time whispers of trouble in the Hodiak/Baxter marriage became clearly audible. Both Anne and John initially denied problems, but rumors persisted. The truth was they were now having major disagreements exacerbated by two careers headed in separate directions. Although they tried to keep the union together for the sake of young Katrina, their attempts ultimately failed. A divorce decree was granted on January 27, 1953. According to the settlement, John agreed to pay financial support for both Anne and the child (who was placed in her mother's custody). With the stroke of a pen, one of Hollywood's "safest" marriages was relegated to the scrap heap, and Anne Baxter's 1949 proclamation, "Two careers don't menace a marriage," seemed wishful thinking.[136]

The breakup of the "perfect" marriage of Hodiak and Baxter inspired an unusual amount of speculation at the time. The "fault" depended on whose "camp" you spoke to, but in reality, there were no simple answers. Anne's booming career and recent decision to drastically alter her image were undoubtedly factors. After her Oscar-nominated triumph as the scheming title character in *All About Eve* (20th Century Fox, 1950), Anne made a very public attempt to change her screen persona from an all-American girl next door, to a sexy siren. She cut her hair, bleached it blonde, posed for suggestive photos, and made provocative statements to the press. During the filming of *The Blue Gardenia* (Warner Bros., 1953), interviews surfaced in which she described her old image as, "inhibited and dull." "I've been presented as terribly nice, a good actress, wife, and mother," she said. "This is wonderful, but it wasn't interesting. That's not what actresses are supposed to be."[137] On the set of *My Wife's Best Friend* (20th Century Fox, 1952), she wore strapless bras and midriff clothes, posed for pictures smoking cigars, and stated she would like to put as much fervor in her movie love scenes as possible. "If we could make love scenes as we feel them," she said. "we could drag a lot of people back into movie theaters."[138] Most who knew both Anne and John were confused by all of this. Others blamed the couple's difficulties on interference by Anne's mother, as well as the "chasm" between their backgrounds and temperaments. One thing is certain. John was not amused and impressed with Anne's "transformation," but as in most failed relationships, it was not one sided. John brought his own baggage to this union.

John's declining acting career aggravated the inferiority complex he had carried with him always. Since his childhood, when he was the homely, streetwise kid from the poor side of town, he had a negative self-image which he had worked very hard to overcome. But fears and self-doubts lingered, now centering on his acting abilities and stature as a star. Even after his acclaimed film successes, these inner demons occasionally reared their ugly heads in a sudden burst of temper, but most often, they lay simmering just below sea level, flooding him with worry and apprehension. In a 1947 interview, John revealed some of his insecurities.

"I suppose that my whole life has been bent toward acting. However, I still don't feel satisfied with myself. I still think I've missed. Just how I don't know. But I keep looking for something that I've never found."[139]

His wife's ascending career in contrast to his decline impacted John's troubles, and further deepened the problems between them.

The divorce left John heartsick. He took an apartment in Hollywood for a time, but eventually moved back with his parents. He played a great deal of golf (his passion), and increasingly sought out the company of his old pals. Gossip columnists noted his presence at several nightspots with a variety of beautiful and interesting women, but those who knew him well said he continued to carry a torch for his ex-wife. In 1953, John starred in three minor motion pictures for Columbia: *Mission to Korea*, a salute to American Air Force valor on the Korean peninsula, and two okay westerns: *Ambush at Tomahawk Gap*, about four ex-cons searching for buried loot, and *Conquest of Cochese*, (the title role), a dramatization of the plight of Native Americans in the Old West. He followed with the grade-Z war adventure, *Dragonfly Squadron* (Allied Artists, 1954) which was so low budget, critics didn't bother to review it. In between these movie nonentities, he made a few top notch television appearances including the, *Hollywood Playhouse* production of "Task Force Smith" (1952), and the *Ford Theater* drama, "They Also Serve" (1953) costarring Maureen O'Sullivan and Virginia Grey.

In the summer of 1953, John was finally offered a project which would allow him to flex his acting muscles again. Producer Paul Gregory and actor Charles Laughton had persuaded Pulitzer prize-winning novelist, Herman Wouk to adapt a portion of his novel, *The Caine Mutiny* into a play. The excellent result was submitted to Henry Fonda who eagerly accepted the lead role of Lieutenant Barney Greenwald who has the difficult task of defending an

Hodiak played the title role in *Conquest of Cochise* (Columbia, 1953).

executive officer being court-martialed for mutiny against the tyrannical captain of a destroyer. The trial serves as the focus of the shattering, *Caine Mutiny Court Martial*, as Greenwald gradually breaks through the cool, collected, surface demeanor of the deranged Captain Queeg (Lloyd Nolan) to expose his demented cowardice. Hodiak was selected by Laughton to play the defendant, Lt. Stephen Maryk based on his many distinguished soldier performances.

Rehearsals began in Los Angeles with Dick Powell directing. At the last minute, Powell was replaced by Laughton after Fonda and company complained. After its initial engagement to critical raves, the cast took the play on the road, fine tuning it for its Broadway opening in January 1954. New York reviews echoed previous notices, with the cast scoring solidly. Critic Brooks Atkinson said John's portrait of the accused, "had strength, charm, candor, and the stamp of a human being. Every stroke in it is genuine and pertinent." These well-deserved superlatives and the audiences' grateful cheers lifted John's sagging spirits. He continued with the play for most of the year, and began dreaming again of important stage and film projects, but tragically, the heavy hand of destiny would soon step in.

In 1955, Mr. Hodiak accepted the role of an ethical district attorney prosecuting a Mexican boy for murder in *Trial* (MGM). A tale of racial prejudice and corruption, the film packed a wallop thanks to a taut Don Mankiewicz screenplay, and a sterling cast headed by Glenn Ford, Dorothy McGuire, Arthur Kennedy, and Hodiak. John was pleased with his work in the movie, and eagerly awaited its October release. Upon its completion, he accepted another co-starring role in *On the Threshold of Space* (20th Century Fox, 1956), a tribute to Air force aviators and physicians who test supersonic aircraft. Directed by Robert Webb, most of the movie was made on location at Elgin and Holoman Air Force Bases in Florida and New Mexico. John's role as an Air Force surgeon who specializes in rocket sled experiments required a great deal of strenuous physical exertion, in and out of the jets.[139] After finishing his climatic scenes on location the first week in October, he headed home to California, just in time to read the laudatory New York reviews of *Trial*. On October 16, he appeared in an acclaimed episode of *The Loretta Young Show* (television series) entitled, "The Last Spring," about an army reservist (Hodiak) unhappily recalled to active duty.

Things were looking up for the 41-year-old John Hodiak when he arose at 5:50 a.m. on the morning of October 19, 1955, complaining of "gas pains" to his mother and sister. He was due back at 20th Century Fox studio later in the morning to put the final touches on *On the Threshold of Space*. At 6:50 a.m., he was shaving in the bathroom when his sister, Anne heard him fall to the floor. The fire department was summoned immediately, and the inhalator crew worked over him, but he had succumbed instantly to a massive heart attack.[141]

A stunned Hollywood greeted the tragic news with disbelief. A 20th Century Fox studio representative spoke of John's popularity on the set, "always kidding, always pleasant to everyone." His pal John Wiegman said he was dumbfounded. "I couldn't believe it! Why? He seemed so healthy! Nobody had any idea there was anything wrong with him. He had been keeping to himself. No one had seen him in a while."[142] Anne Baxter described his death, "as very very sad. He suffered from a lack of self-confidence and never realized how damned good an actor he really was." Most typical of his colleague's reaction was given to the author by Josephine Hutchinson when she said, "John was a fine actor, and at the time of his death, I really mourned his loss, not only for himself, but our profession."[143]

On October 21, a private funeral was held with a few invited guests. John was buried in the Calvary Cemetery in Los Angeles. One of the newspapers covering the event reprinted a statement he had made in a 1940's interview,

"When I die, I hope people will say this of me. 'He always did his best. He liked people and enjoyed life. He always tried to share his happiness. So the world was a little better place for his having lived."[144]

The throngs of weeping fans and admirers that lined the street outside the rosary services were a testament to the achievement of this, John's ultimate life goal.

Mr. Hodiak was survived by daughter, Katrina, his parents, brother Walter, and sister Anne Sliva. Shortly after his unexpected death, it was revealed he had left no will. Documents were filed with the Superior Court which listed his estate at approximately $25,000 including stocks, cash, and the home he had purchased for his family in Tarzana. On March 1, 1956, John's parents petitioned the court to transfer the title of the house that John had given them, but had neglected to place in their name. Under the law, his entire estate would have gone to his young daughter. It was reported in the *Hollywood Citizen News* on April 21, 1956, that Anne Baxter intended to lay claim to the estate (including the house) for Katrina,

It is believed the physical exertion of his role as an Air Force aviator testing supersonic aircraft in 20th Century Fox's *On the Threshold of Space* (1956) was one of the contributing factors to Hodiak's fatal heart attack which came as the film was being finished. Seen with Hodiak here are Dean Jagger and Guy Madison.

but apparently, she must have had second thoughts. On May 29, the title was transferred to Walter and Anne Hodiak with no opposition.

Although one cannot discount John Hodiak's substantial acting ability and acclaimed film performances, he was never able to ascend to the pantheon of screen stars. His versatility and range as an actor were obvious and proven, but he lacked that undefinable quality, many refer to as "it." In addition, MGM, (his home studio for much of his moviemaking years), appeared unsure of how to cast him to maximum effect, too often squandering his talent on supporting roles.

In retrospect, what touches us most about John Hodiak was not his masterful acting or his insecurities, but the story of his rise to fame. It is comforting to know that such a decent human being could achieve his dream in America. Like sports, the movie industry allowed many disadvantaged, yet talented youngsters a way to pull themselves up "by the bootstraps," from selling scrap iron on the poor

Alamagordo Daily News **(New Mexico) headline October 18, 1955.**

streets of Hamtramck, to dining at Romanoff's with the rich and famous. Through talent, hard work, and single-minded perseverance, John beat the odds and achieved the goal he had set at the tender age of 11. Like his idol, Douglas Fairbanks, he became a movie star, known and admired throughout the world, but unlike many of his counterparts, he never forgot from whence he came and all who had paved his way. When he died so suddenly, so tragically on October 19, 1955, he remained largely unaffected by the fame, fortune, glitz, and glamour of the city of dreams. "While it's exciting to have people screaming for autographs, I'd like to go along learning, and trying to be well thought of by my friends . . ." he said. With all that in mind, it seems entirely appropriate most of John Hodiak's best screen roles were heroic. It was type casting!

UPDATE

Anne Baxter died at the Lenox Hill Hospital in New York City on December 12, 1985, eight days after suffering a cerebral hemorrhage while hailing a cab on Madison Avenue. Josephine Hutchinson passed away on June 4, 1998, at the Florence Nightengale Nursing Home in Manhattan. She was 94 years old. Katrina Hodiak eventually became an actress who appeared with her mother in *Jane Austen in Manhattan* (1980), then in 1982, married Michael Von Ditter, the wealthy great grandson of novelist, Thomas Mann. They had a son, Tobin Von Ditter in 1984, before divorcing. Currently, Katrina, now 67 years old, lives in the northwest United States with and her second husband, logger, Jeff Lenore. They own five-acres in a remote area where they raise vegetables and keep a variety of animals. Katrina also designs custom jewelry and is renowned throughout the Pacific Northwest and beyond for her creations.[146]

CHAPTER SIX
"MARIAN MARSH: LITTLE MAID MARIAN"

(Two-part article originally published in *Films of the Golden Age*, Winter, 1998)

PART I

"Isn't she beautiful?" — an oft repeated expression on the lips and ink-stained dissertations of innumerable movie executives, critics, journalists, and millions of moviegoers when referencing doll-faced actress, Marian Marsh who burst on the Hollywood scene as the movies found their voices. Surprisingly, not a publicist's invention, the quotation originated with Miss Marsh's actress sister who tirelessly promoted her until she hit it big as John Barrymore's leading lady in the 1931 classic, *Svengali*.

After the release of *Svengali*, critics and journalists who applauded Marian's performance and dubbed her an "overnight sensation" wondered out loud if she had the ability, and character to sustain her position atop Hollywood. In the next four years, the gifted, intelligent, and wise young woman proved her excellent work was no fluke, turning in several distinguished performances opposite some of Hollywood's finest actors. Marian Marsh never became a film superstar, but her youthful wide-eyed innocence combined with her delicate beauty to make a storybook movie heroine, a perfect counterbalance to the evil licentious characters who menaced her in many of her memorable films. In the latter 1930's, as she matured, unfortunately, the quality of her scripts declined as did her interest and enthusiasm for filmmaking. In 1942, she abandoned the silver screen, setting out on a happier, more fulfilling existence as a wife, mother, and philanthropist. This is her story.

Born Violet Ethelred Krauth on October 17, 1913, on the island of Trinidad, British West Indies, the future leading lady was the granddaughter of an English engineer, and the daughter of a chocolate manufacturer. The youngest of four children of Leo and Harriette Krauth, Violet's family consisted of a sister Jean and brothers George, and Edward. When she was ten years old, the Krauth's moved to Massachusetts. Marian recalled her parents in multiple interviews.

"My father and mother had started a chocolate candy factory in Trinidad. They did all the work themselves at first. From nothing, they built up a good trade. When World War I knocked the bottom out of his market, my father moved us to Boston. There he became vice president of a very large chocolate manufacturing company." [147]

Although not an actor, Mr. Krauth was enamored of the theater and performing. He took his children to stage productions at every opportunity and spoke respectfully and affectionately of the arts. He instilled in each a sense of individuality, self-confidence, and self-reliance, and emphasized performing as an avenue of achievement.

During the mid 1920's, the Krauth's eldest daughter, Jean became a student at Paramount's Astoria Studio in New York City where she was taught the basics of acting, poise, dancing, etc. When the winter holidays approached in 1925, the homesick Jean sent for her sister, Violet, a buddingly beautiful 12-year-old with blonde curls, large blue/gray eyes, and a shy smile. "Isn't she beautiful?" Jean would say to all of her classmates, teachers and anyone who would listen.

When her school term ended, Jean received a six-month Paramount contract. Young Violet continued her visits, and was introduced to everyone from the doorman to Jessie L. Lasky. When her contract expired, Jean found work at F. B. O. Studios (which later became RKO), in Hollywood. Under the name Jean Morgan, later Jean Fenwick, she appeared in large and small roles in F.B.O.'s program pictures and for a variety of studios. The Krauths moved to the West Coast in 1926, to be closer to their eldest daughter. While Jean worked in pictures, Violet enrolled at Le Conte Junior High School, then transferred to the legendary Hollywood High in 1927, where she excelled in dramatics and basketball. An adept athlete and tomboy at heart, Violet seemed more interested in shooting free throws than motion pictures, but she was maturing quickly into a striking beauty, and becoming increasingly curious about her sister's profession.

Violet's "hoop dreams" ended suddenly in 1928, when Jean arranged a screen test for her at Pathe Studios who were in the process of building a stock company. Marian vividly recalled the test.

"She (Jean) was determined that I should crash the studio gates, and with that end in view, spent weeks haunting casting offices, telling them all about 'little sister,' even forgetting her own career. . . I finally did get a chance to make a test at Pathe . . . We waited for six hours before I received any attention. My make-up had to be done over and my hair dressed. When the big moment arrived, I was so tired, I really didn't care whether I stepped before the camera or not. The director, supervising

the test, told me to cry — it was exactly what I wanted to do. I cried all over the place and he thought it was great acting. I got the contract..." [148]

Lamentably, her promising start came to an abrupt conclusion when Pathe dropped her after only two months and one small film appearance in the short, *Fairways and Fouls* (1929). "Then Sam Goldwyn put me under contract. I was there five weeks and spoke two lines in *Whoopie* (Goldwyn, 1930), an early sound musical starring Eddie Cantor," she said. [149]

By 1930, the former Violet Krauth had changed her name to Marilyn Morgan, and made a momentous decision. "By this time, I was crazy to act!" she recalled. [150] Under the guidance of her sister, she contacted famous stage star, Nance O'Neil, and arranged voice and poise tutoring, hired master Ernest Belcher for dance lessons, and contracted a noted voice specialist to learn the art of singing. Four days after her release by Goldwyn, she was at Warner Bros. for a screen test. The impressive result ended with her autograph enthusiastically affixed to a long term contract. Her initial euphoria soon waned, however. Despite being featured in over 30 shorts starring James Gleason and his wife Lucille, and a small role in the 1930 classic, *Hell's Angels* (on loan to Howard Hughes/United Artists), she felt her career was stagnating. "For six months, I was forgotten," she complained. Fortunately, that was about to change. [151]

In 1930, the starlet met stage director Edgar McGregor while walking down a Hollywood street. Marian told interviewer, Don Leifert, it was a fateful meeting.

"He asked me what I was doing. I told him I was under contract to Warner Brothers, but I didn't think they knew I was there . . . He said he had this wonderful play called, Young Sinners and I was perfect for it . . . So, he called the studio and in no time at all — three or four days — I had the part . . ." [152]

Warner Bros. agreed to allow her to appear in the production with the stipulation she change her stage name so as not to be confused with another studio contract player, the highly touted dancer, Marilyn Miller. "We shortened Marilyn to Marian and my mother came up with Marsh because she remembered Mae Marsh from silent pictures," she told an interviewer.

Young Sinners starring silent star, Molly O'Day opened in Los Angeles, then San Francisco to packed houses. Marian's critical raves were the first indication there was talent behind the lovely blonde façade, but her triumph was tinged with sadness. While on a trip to Boston, Leo Krauth contracted pneumonia and died suddenly, leaving his devoted family in a state of grief stricken shock. Leo had been an inspirational figure to all his children, especially his youngest daughter. When asked in 1932, what she looked for in a man, Marian said, "When I meet someone and I think . . . why, you're not as cultured not as brilliant as my father. He was a remarkable man!"[153] Despite her sorrow, Marian pressed ahead, more determined than ever to attain stardom to honor her father's memory. With her next film, she would fulfill his most cherished wish, and conquer the city of dreams.

First published in 1894, George du Maurier's popular romantic novel, *Trilby* had become a successful British stage play in 1895. In 1915, it was filmed with Clara Kimball Young in the tragic title role of a young innocent milkmaid/model who becomes a great singing diva under the "hypnotic" tutelage of her malevolent music teacher, Svengali, played by Wilton Lackaye. In 1923, another feature was produced with Arthur Edmund Carewe in the villainous male lead. Seven years later, in 1930, Warners optioned the property (to be titled, *Svengali*,) as a vehicle for legendary actor, John Barrymore.

Several prominent actresses including beautiful Evelyn Laye actively sought the challenging role of Trilby. Marian recalled,

"I was doing a play called Young Sinners at the old Belasco Theatre. Jack Warner and his brothers came to see the play and inquired, 'Who is that girl?' I found myself in the embarrassing situation of having to inform the Warners that I was under contract to them!" [154]

Jack Warner recognized the 17-year-old dreamy-eyed beauty as a prime candidate for Trilby, but before ordering screen tests, wisely decided to take her to meet Barrymore. In an interview with writer, Gregory Mank for his 1985 *Films in Review* article, *Svengali*, Marian described her first meeting with the film legend.

"When I first met John Barrymore, he was sick in bed at his house up on Tower Road. He was in this great big enormous bed in this great big enormous room. I walked around for him, and he said, 'Umm, ummm, very good!' and I showed him my profile. He said, 'Profiles are very famous in the Barrymore family,' and agreed to test me," [155]

Marian was tested multiple times prior to her selection for the plum role. Legend has it Barrymore favored her because of her uncanny resemblance to his current wife, Dolores Costello.

Filming began on January 12, 1931, with Archie Mayo directing a stellar cast which also included Bramwell Fletcher, Luis Alberni, and Donald Crisp. The teenaged Marian was excited but nervous. She shrewdly understood Trilby would be a make or break role, and was apprehensive about working with Barrymore who had a disreputable reputation both in front of, and behind the cameras. The ever suspicious Jack Warner shared her concerns and kept a pedagogic vigil. Their fears proved groundless. In one of his "contented periods," Barrymore behaved beautifully, referring to the ingénue as his, "Little Maid Marian." Miss Marsh told Mr. Mank she retained positive memories of Barrymore and the filming.

"These were happy days for Jack Barrymore. He was on his best behavior, I might add; he was happily married to Dolores Costello; and he wasn't drinking . . . Mr. Barrymore (as I always called him), worried so about me, which was very pleasant. Whenever we rehearsed, he would say, 'Are you comfortable? Don't worry about anything — just be natural.' I remember he spoke to me about my diction; he said at times I spoke too clearly, and that I should 'jumble it up' sometimes to sound more natural. . . ." [156]

The chemistry between Barrymore and Marsh, blue ribbon supporting performances, exceptional cinematography and art direction helped make *Svengali* (Warner Bros., 1931), a critical and box office triumph! Among the highlights were multiple awe-inspiring sequences brilliantly photographed by Oscar-nominated Barney McGill. From the famous vignette near the beginning of the movie as the camera leaves the evil bleached eyes of Svengali, panning out over the city to the bedroom of the sleeping Trilby, to its unforgettable climax when Svengali collapses during Trilby's stage performance and her voice suddenly cracks, McGill's work left audiences literally "hypnotized." The acting was also of a very high order. Barrymore's lead performance, as the flamboyant fiend was a tour de force. Although Svengali is essentially evil, from the "whites" of his penetrating eyes, (Primitive contact lenses were used to create the eerie effect.), to his unkempt dirty beard, Barrymore injects the character with wit and pathos. Often humorous, Barrymore's Svengali is poignantly pathetic in the final death scene as he cries, "God grant me in death what you denied me in life!" Marian's Trilby is likewise a multi-faceted revelation, the perfect counterpoint to the grotesque Svengali. Innocent and childlike at the outset, we witness her maturation and inevitable corruption with a sad resignation. Her performance flawlessly captures Trilby O' Ferrell's transformation from innocent purity, to her awakening sexuality. Leo Krauth would've been proud!

John Barrymore personally selected Marian for the coveted role of the innocent milkmaid, Trilby who becomes a great singing star under the hypnotic tutelage of her malevolent music teacher, *Svengali* (Warner Bros., 1931) directed by Archie Mayo.

Marian and John Barrymore in *Svengali* (Warner Bros., 1931).

Marian followed her dynamic lead actress debut with an equally powerful performance. The still topical theme of ethics in journalism was intelligently explored in the hard-hitting, drama, *Five Star Final*, (Warner Bros., 1931), the tale of a greedy publisher (Oscar Apfel) who pressures his staff to run sensationalist stories in order to increase sales and circulation. To satisfy the boss, his hard-bitten editor (Edward G. Robinson) reluctantly resurrects the details of a decades-old murder case involving a young pregnant girl (Frances Starr) who killed her supervisor, (the father of her baby), when he refused to marry her. After being acquitted, the girl manages to start a new life as the wife of a kindly bank employee (H.B. Warner), who raises the child (Marsh) as his own, but the new publicity opens old wounds and leads to tragedy. In the film's powerful finale, the woman's grown daughter (Marsh), gun in hand, confronts those who have wrought havoc on her young life on the day of her wedding. Her emotional plea, "Why did you kill my mother?" wrings apologies and shame from the publisher, and his vicious cronies. At the fadeout, Robinson symbolically washes his hands, but cannot "wash away" what he has

Marian played a young bride whose life is shattered when unscrupulous journalists resurrect an old murder case involving her mother in director Mervyn LeRoy's uncompromising drama, *Five Star Final* (Warner Bros., 1931) costarring Edward G. Robinson, and Anthony Bushell (seen here).

Marian and Anthony Bushell in *Five Star Final* (Warner Bros., 1931).

done. The superior direction of Mervyn LeRoy, a literate screenplay by Robert Lord and Byron Morgan, and a stand-out cast headed by Robinson, Marsh, H. B. Warner, Boris Karloff, Ona Munson, and Aline MacMahon made *Five Star Final* an Academy Award nominee for Best Picture. Marian's shattering performance as young Jenny Townsend was another extraordinary achievement which inspired both critics, and audiences.

The phenomenal financial and critical success of *Svengali* inspired Warner Bros. to search out a similar vehicle for the memorable team of Barrymore and Marsh. Their selection was *The Mad Genius*, Martin Brown's play about an evil club-footed puppeteer who lives his life's desire of being a dancer through a agile young lad whom he rescues from an abusive father. The wicked Tsarakov (Barrymore) raises and trains the boy, Fedor (Donald Cook), inculcating his own desire to dance, and supervising his rise to fame. Years later, Fedor provokes the jealousy and wrath of his crippled mentor by becoming enamored of a beautiful ballerina, Nana (Marsh) which leads to tragedy and terror.

Although ultimately a box office flop, Warner Bros.' film adaptation, *The Mad Genius* (1931), was noteworthy in many respects. The steady innovative hand of gifted director, Michael Curtiz is apparent throughout, as is the technical expertise of art director, Anton Grot, who created muslin ceilings for the opulent sets a decade before the technique was said to have been invented on *Citizen Kane*. Once again, the performances of the two leads were first rate. "I think the proudest moment of my life was not when he (Barrymore) said I would do the Trilby role, but when I learned from someone else that he had said I would do for the leading role in *The Mad Genius*. . ." Marian recalled in the early 1930's.[157]

As was their custom, the brother's Warner never let their contract players gain too much confidence. They preferred to keep them off balance, unsure of their talent and utility. Since Marian had been cast in three starring roles in A-level pictures, they assigned her a supporting role in the medium budget *Road to Singapore* (1931). The female lead in the steamy tropical melodrama went to Doris Kenyon who played the bored wife of a boorish doctor (Louis Calhern), who has an affair with a notorious cad (engagingly portrayed by William Powell), and falls for him in the process. Marian's undernourished role as the sexy teenage sister of Calhern, gave her minimal opportunities.

In spite of the insignificance of her supporting role in *Road to Singapore*, by the end of 1931, Marian appeared on the fast track to superstardom. At just eighteen-years old, she had already made three important motion pictures, was named one of the W.A.M.P.A.S. (Western Association of Motion Picture Advertisers) Baby Stars of 1931, and had even merited a raise. Hollywood's elite considered her an overnight sensation, but she saw it differently.

"They called me a 'discovery' then, when I knew I wasn't. After all, I had worked in films off and on for two years. Before that — I was an extra and hoping for the big chance like every other extra."

Regarding her success, she waxed philosophical.

"Maybe I was born under a lucky star, but I'd be a fool to sit around counting on good luck to follow me forever and a day. . . Resting on

your laurels ends by resting in a rocking chair while someone else takes your place." [158]

Certainly there was little rest in store for the 5 foot 2, 102 pound, golden-haired beauty in 1932. After a thankless assignment as the foster sister/love interest of a doctor (Richard Barthelmess) in the confusing drama, *Alias the Doctor* (Warner Bros.), her home studio gave the young starlet another first rate vehicle and star-billing in the charming romantic comedy, *Beauty and the Boss* (Warner Bros., 1932), about a penniless yet brilliant young girl (Marsh) who wangles a job as private secretary to a prominent German financier (Warren William), and promptly falls in love with him. Her struggles to catch the eye of her skirt chasing employer, and keep him away from the bevy of beauties in hot pursuit, serve as the focus of the sprightly comic excercise. Miss Marsh, in a rare comic performance, was a delightful surprise as the automaton who transforms into a glamour girl to snag the man of her dreams. Her engaging performance surprised many and garnered her more laudatory reviews. Even the tough *New York Times* was singing her praises. "Without the genuinely satisfactory acting and attractive appearance of Marian Marsh, the Cinderella secretary in *Beauty and the Boss* at the Strand Theater would be difficult to go into ecstasies over . . ." gushed the reviewer. Unfortunately, Jack Warner and company appeared largely oblivious to her comic potential, preferring her as a fair damsel in distress.

"Introducing the first star of 1932" was the headline Warner Bros. publicists concocted to advertise Marian's follow-up to *Beauty and the Boss*: the dramatic, *Under Eighteen* which reteamed her with Warren William. Beneath a provocative pose of lovely Miss M. decked out in a white mink coat with diamond earrings, the ad read, "She's under eighteen . . . amazingly lovely . . . a creature of fire and emotion . . ." Sadly, despite good performances from a capable cast, the finished film did not live up to the hype, and audiences and critics were largely unenthusiastic. Marian's other 1932 films: RKO's *Sport Parade*, in which she played a charming sketch artist and Warner Bros. *Strange Justice* which had her as a honest hat check girl, were also disappointments. *Strange Justice* (Warner Bros.) would turn out to be memorable to Miss Marsh as the last picture she would make for Warner Bros.

Marian played the fast talking, super efficient secretary of a successful German financier (Warren William), who falls for her boss in the comedy, *Beauty and the Boss* (Warner Bros., 1932).

In the short span of twenty months, Marian had been working non-stop playing leads in eight motion pictures, a supporting role in another. In addition, she continued her poise, voice, and dancing instructions while fulfilling the necessary social obligations of being a star, such as premieres, parties, photo shoots, etc. It was enough to exhaust even a healthy girl of nineteen, and Marian ended up in the hospital. While recuperating, she made an important decision. Her agent informed Warner Bros. she would not return to the lot until her meager salary was tripled. This "audacity" infuriated the tight-fisted studio brass who made an important decision of their own: to allow her option to lapse, while declaring to Hollywood and the world their sweet demure young ingénue had become "difficult." [159]

While Marian was deeply disappointed by this "strange justice," she remained undeterred in her quest for recognition. She had entered films out of the necessity of contributing monetary support to her family, but in the process, had developed ambition, drive, and determination. Poise and confidence replaced a little girl's

Marian played a sketch artist romantically pursued by two best friends in *The Sport Parade* (RKO, 1932) costarring Joel McCrea and William Gargan (pictured here).

romantic notion of becoming a "movie star." Her greatest asset, as always, was an intelligent sensibility so apparent in a revealing 1935 interview conducted by noted fan magazine writer Faith Baldwin. She said,

> "I suppose I was at 'the top' for a while . . . But it was a position which I gained through influences outside of me. I knew then that I must work a long and hard time before I could maintain my foothold." [160]

Upon her recovery, the newly un-indentured Miss Marsh harbored expectations she would find quality lead roles in top drawer productions, but alas, she underestimated the closed society of the "Hollywood Boys Club" a.k.a. executives and influentials who frequently "blackballed" those whom they deemed "uncooperative." The sagacious Marian soon realized she would have to accept roles from small studios if she wanted to continue to work, but her appearances in low budget movies would do long term damage to her career.

The results of her minor studio efforts in 1933, were not altogether unpleasant, however. Such was Allied Pictures' mystery/comedy *The Eleventh Commandment* (meaning: "Thou shalt not get caught.") Based on fact, the film traced the frantic efforts of several prospective heirs to lay claim to a wealthy spinster's 50 million dollar fortune. If the convoluted mystery plot seemed aimless, the movie was rescued by good performances from Miss Marsh (as the daughter of the decedent's attorney), Theodore Von Eltz (as her fiancé), and former silent film star, Marie Prevost contributing welcome comedy relief as one of the "heirs," a bordello proprietress who masquerades as the owner of a "girls school."

For Chesterfield Studios, Marian filmed two more low budget movies: *Man of Sentiment* (1933), about a musical prodigy (Marsh) saved from becoming the mistress of a wealthy playboy when she is struck by a drunk driver, and *Notorious But Nice* (1933), the tale of a lowly clerk (Marian) in love with the upper-crust heir to a fortune (Donald Dillaway), but ending up the wife of a racketeer. The melodramatic *Daring Daughters* (Tower Pictures, 1933), directed by Christy Cabanne, gave Marian a change of pace role as the cynical, worldly-wise sister of an innocent country girl (Joan Marsh — no relation), whom she must protect from big city wolves.

Disappointed by her inability to find suitable major studio properties, in 1934, Marian accepted three European movie offers. For British International, she had heroine roles in two charming comedies: *Over the Garden Wall* (Wardour-British, 1934), with Bobby Howes, and *Love At Second Sight* a.k.a. *The Girl Thief* (Wardour-British, 1934), with former *Five Star Final* costar Anthony Bushell. For Universal's Paris office, she appeared in the romantic adventure, *The Prodigal Son* a.k.a. *The Lost Son* (1935), opposite noted German actor, director, athlete Luis Trenker. Filmed on location in the beautiful Swiss Alps, the mentally quick Miss Marsh was required to play the lead feminine role in German (a language she had never mastered). As always, she was up to the task, arising early each morning to learn her German lines. Tutors coached her in the proper inflections, and gave her the sense of the words. The result was a believable performance as a society girl attracted to an adventurer. The short, three-week shooting schedule turned out to be memorable to the 22 year-old actress. During her stay, she accompanied a hiking party in an attempt to scale the 10,000 foot Mt. Orach. One of only two people to reach the summit (her guide was the other), she triumphantly gazed out over the gorgeous Swiss countryside. It was a sight of such grandeur that it would remain indelibly etched in her memory. In the next year, she would set out on an even tougher quest, to climb back to her former position as a lead actress in grade-A Hollywood productions.

Fortified by excellent European reviews, Miss Marsh returned to Hollywood for a supporting role as the innocent sister of a hot shot insurance agent (Roger Pryor) in Universal's low-budget musical/drama *I Like It That Way* (1934). She followed with Monogram's *A Girl of the Limberlost*, (1934), one of the rare occasions when a minor studio made a special effort to elevate one of their productions to grade A status. According to publicity items, Monogram constructed fifty different sets (including an exterior swamp), to adapt Gene Stratton Porter's popular 1909 novel for the screen. Pre-production records indicate an extensive search was conducted to determine who would play the young heroine. Marian was chosen over sixty other competitors to play Elnora, a poor girl of the swamps, rejected by her mother, who blames her daughter for the death of her husband. Elnora's dramatic struggles to become educated and marry the village doctor's son (Edward Nugent) form the basis of this memorable film. Miss Marsh's charming and affecting performance proved the wisdom of her selection. It would be her favorite role, and inspire Columbia Studios to offer her a contract.[161]

After spending several months in Europe, Marian was grateful to be back home with her loving and supportive family. By 1935, the family had purchased a larger, yet modest home near the film capitol where Marian, her mother, sister, and two brothers resided. Each of her siblings was involved in the movie business, thus each had a

After her departure from Warner Bros. in 1932, Marian found good parts a scarce commodity. Among the films she made in 1933, was Universal's disappointing musical comedy, *I Like It That Way*, costarring Roger Pryor and Gloria Stuart (seen here toasting her.)

unique insight into its idiosyncrasies, and provided a well-needed support system for one another. The Krauth home was a hub of activity, full of laughter, quarrels, music, and fun. The dark-haired, refined Hariette Krauth acted as money manager, overseeing the financial resources of all of her children whose money was pooled. Marian, who was by far, the most famous, was treated no differently than the others. She was still called, "Vi," and would often be found mowing the family lawn, one of her assigned domestic duties.

In her spare moments, the active Miss Marsh often turned tomboy again. An excellent swimmer, and tennis enthusiast, she was also an expert horsewoman, and an avid skier thanks to Luis Trenker. In addition, she took great pleasure in sedentary hobbies including doll collecting, sun bathing, football (as a spectator), opera, and party going. Regarding romance, Marian preferred the company of older,

Marian, three siblings were all actors. Here she poses with brother, Anthony Edward Krauth (1912-74) who made films under the stage name Anthony Marsh.

more experienced gentleman. She told a reporter:

"I always go out with people who are older than I am . . . Young people are so — so young!" I like a man who uses words I can't use and talks a bit over my head . . . Older men are doers as well as dreamers . . ." [162]

The career of Marian Marsh received a well needed shot in the arm in 1935, when she signed a two year pact with Columbia Pictures where she would make two of her most memorable films. After roles as the daughter of a trucking company owner in the melodrama, *In Spite of Danger* (Columbia, 1935) with Chester Morris, and as a government agent looking for a million dollars worth of stolen U. S. bonds in *The Unknown Woman* (Columbia, 1935), Marian began filming the melodrama, *The Black Room* (Columbia, 1935). Originally titled *The Black Room Mystery*, this atmospheric period chiller has legitimately attained classic status. Set in 19th century Czechoslovakia, it is the story of the accursed De Berghman family whose crest reads, "I end as I began," a reflection of a prophecy that twins would begin and end the noble house, and the younger twin would slay the elder in the castle's "black room." When twins Gregor and Anton are born, their father seals up the room in hopes it will somehow prevent the inevitable, but unfortunately, the sad fate of the family comes to pass in the most astonishing of ways. The suspenseful screenplay of Henry Myers, expert direction by Roy William Neill, and Al Siegler's rich photography were among the many memorable elements of the production highlighted by Boris Karloff's compelling "performances" as the twins. Marian's role as the niece of a family friend forced to marry the evil twin, was not formidable, but she was compensated by the opportunity to wear beautiful costumes, and by the film's excellent notices which aided her quest for better parts.

Miss Marsh's follow-up was also impressive. Immediately after shooting wrapped on *The Black Room*, the famous, some would say infamous Austrian-American film director, Josef Von Sternberg chose Marian for the lead feminine role in his controversial 1935 version of Dostoyevsky's timeless classic, *Crime and Punishment* (Columbia). (It had been filmed twice previously.) Overcoming his initial opposition, Columbia had persuaded the great director to make the film as a vehicle for their new contract player, Peter Lorre, fresh from his triumph in Hitchcock's *The Man Who Knew Too Much*.

An existential detective story, *Crime and Punishment* chronicles the classic psychological struggle between a brilliant authority on crime, Roderick Raskolnikov, and wily police inspector Porfiry (Edward Arnold) who is investigating the murder of a pawnbroker (Mrs. Patrick Campbell) committed by Roderick. The extreme mental pressure of this "match of wits," eventually takes its toll on Roderick, exacerbated

In 1935, Marian had the feminine lead in Columbia's classic melodrama, *The Black Room* starring Boris Karloff as twins, one good, one evil.

by an even more formidable opponent, his re-awakened conscience. Roderick's admission of guilt and eventual surrender are largely due to the efforts of the beautiful prostitute, Sonya (Marian) who reads to him from the Bible.

Although visually exceptional, and literally jam-packed with superior acting, highlighted by the performances of Lorre, Marsh and Arnold, at the time of its release, the film received mixed reviews and was not a box office success. Some critics complained that Von Sternberg had deemphasized the novel's psychological aspects, and "converted it into a nickel-plated detective melodrama." They also made unfavorable comparisons to the more faithful French version (released concurrently), *Crime Et Chatiment* directed by Pierre Chenal and starring Pierre Blanchar.

In spite of the criticism, Marian's work in the motion picture won wide praise. Her Sonya is a beautifully realized performance, perhaps the most underrated of her career. An allegorical character, Sonya fulfills the function of Roderick's conscience even when he seems to have lost all sense of morality. In the emotional finale, she helps him see the error of his ways which saves his life. Its mixed reviews notwithstanding, the film has gradually increased its reputation over the years thanks to Von Sternberg's artful direction, striking visuals, and of course, the superb performances. Marian's fine film acting brought her once again, albeit briefly, into the Hollywood limelight. When asked about the role in 1936, Marian seemed very pleased,

"Here again was the happy combination of circumstances which made Trilby a success. Here again were merged the forces of a great director, a great star, and one of the greatest stories ever written. Of course, my Sonya was right. It had to be in that setting. I'm glad that it was good. But perhaps I can do something still better. At any rate I'm not going to stop working." [163]

Sadly, *Crime and Punishment* would be the last exceptional film of Marian's career.

Although Miss Marsh's performance opposite Peter Lorre in *Crime and Punishment* is considered among the best of her career, unfortunately, it did not lead to more substantive film offers.

Marian played the prostitute, Sonya in director Josef von Sternberg's 1935 controversial version of Dostoievsky's classic novel, *Crime and Punishment* (Columbia, 1935), costarring Peter Lorre.

In 1936, (her last year at Columbia), Marian made four medium to low-budget movies for the studio, which, although entertaining and featuring good performances, did not further her reputation or sustain her hard won momentum. The soap operatic *Lady of Secrets* should have been a winner considering its excellent cast which included Marian, Otto Kruger, Lionel Atwill, and Paramount's former grande dame, Ruth Chatterton, but even they could not make sense of a disappointing script which featured Miss Marsh as Ruth's confused daughter brought up to believe she is her younger sister. Although the snappy crime drama, *Counterfeit*, (featuring Marian as an innocent girl mixed up with crooks and killers), and the comedy, *Come Closer Folks* (which had her as the bespectacled daughter of a retailer in love with shyster salesman), had better scripts, both movies were largely ignored by elite critics who viewed second features with condescension. It was a shame as Marian was particularly charming in the latter.

CHAPTER SIX: MARIAN MARSH

Marian became friends with legendary film actress Ruth Chatterton during the filming of the soap operatic, *Lady of Secrets* (Columbia, 1936). From left to right: Ruth Chatterton, Robert Allen, Marian, and Otto Kruger.

After a minor assignment as the secretary/best girl of Ralph Bellamy in the thriller, *The Man Who Lived Twice*, in 1937, Miss Marsh departed Columbia and began freelancing. In the period 1937-1942, she would make 11 motion pictures, all modest to low budget, all but one for second-string studios. Although none advanced her career in the slightest, most had redeeming qualities, including opportunities for Marian to play a wide variety of characters.

Among her roles of this period were: the lovesick girlfriend of boxer/astrologer Joe E. Brown in the wild *When's Your Birthday* (RKO, 1937), a prison nurse in the appropriately titled, *Prison Nurse* (Republic, 1938), and murder suspects in two entertaining whodunits: *The Great Gambini* (Paramount, 1937), with Akim Tamiroff, and *Murder By Invitation* (Monogram, 1941), with Wallace Ford. Perhaps the best Marsh performance at this time was in Republic's B drama, *Youth On Parole* (1937), in which she was cast as a young girl facing the challenges of being a parolee after her incarceration for a crime

One of Marian's last films was the entertaining mystery, *The Great Gambini* (Paramount, 1937). From left to right: Marian, John Trent, William Demarest and Edward Brophy.

she did not commit. Transcending a cliched script, Marian credibly projected the heartbreak and pain the youngster endures when she meets with rejection and prejudice.

As early as the mid 1930's, Marian began expressing displeasure with the quality of her film projects, and publicly voicing her intention to quit film acting. In an interview with *Silver Screen* magazine, she raised eyebrows when she stated flatly,

"I don't intend to be an actress all my life. Five years is enough. That will enable me to make a graceful exit, and I'll only be twenty three. Young enough to travel a bit before settling down to making a husband happy." [164]

In 1937, one of Hollywood's most prominent bachelorettes became engaged to mining businessman, Albert Scott, former husband of actress Colleen Moore and several years her senior. On March 29, 1938, she wed Mr. Scott, a union lasting 21 years and producing two children: a son, Albert Parker Scott Jr. and a daughter, Catherine Mary Scott. The Scotts would divorce in 1959.

After her marriage, Marian essentially kept to the spirit of her vow when she bid adieu to moviemaking after filming PRC's tepid comedy, *House of Errors* in 1942. By then, she had been toiling on poverty row for several years, and had long since abandoned any hope of reestablishing her career and becoming a top tier actress. She told author Richard Lamparski in 1985, "I loved acting but I had become a professional because we needed the money. In 1938, I married a businessman and just drifted away from my career." [166]

In the mid 1940's, Marian Marsh enthusiastically began the second phase of her life as a full-time wife, and mother, while indulging in her passion for tennis, travel, and seeing old friends. In the 1950's, she resurrected her acting career briefly to appear in a few TV projects including a television pilot with John Forysthe, and a telefilm with Gary Merrill before officially retiring in 1959. When asked about her decision to call it quits, she said, "I found I didn't much like the work anymore . . . "

After her divorce from Scott, in September 1960, Marian married aviation pioneer/wealthy entrepreneur, Clifford Henderson. The ceremony was held on the romantic French Riviera and the honeymoon in The Netherlands. The couple made their permanent home in Palm Desert, California, which Clifford had founded in the 1940's. During the 1960's and 1970's, the happy Hendersons continued to oversee the development of the Palm Desert community, and together they established Desert Beautiful, a non-profit, volunteer organization set up to address conservation and environmental concerns in California's Coachella Valley. They also did a great deal of traveling in the United States and all over the world. [167]

Since Mr. Henderson's death in 1984 (at age 88), Marian has presided over all of his many civic, charitable, and financial interests. The grandmother of eight, as of 1998, she remains an active, very vital person, persuing her many varied causes and concerns, (including serving as director of Desert Beautiful), with the same enthusiasm and sense of purpose she displayed during her acting career. [168]

Today, as in the 1930's, there are those who dismiss actress Marian Marsh as "just another pretty face." While she certainly was a lovely woman, an attractive presence in any film, it is hard to

Marian poses for a photo at her home in 1997.

fathom their reasoning. Surely they cannot have scrutinized her superb dramatic acting in *Svengali, The Mad Genius, Five Star Final,* and *Crime and Punishment.* And most assuredly, they must have missed her flair for comedy so ably demonstrated in *Beauty and the Boss,* and *Come Closer Folks.* In these, and so many other performances, Marian Marsh utilized her innocent good looks as a basis to create credible characterizations of depth and dimension. Even though Hollywood too often wasted her talents in inferior vehicles, and she never achieved superstar status, she accepted her assignments with grace, and made the most of even the flimsiest, most ill-defined parts. In her most famous roles, she personified the perfect storybook heroine: warm, beautiful, soft spoken, sensitive, yet possessed with an inner strength which aided her in struggles with the villains and evildoers who often plagued her onscreen. It is apparent the strength of her screen heroines was born of her own. For the real Marian Marsh is possessed with the strength of character, intelligence, and sensibility she inherited from her parents.

Looking back at the life and career of this gifted actress and admirable human being, one is left echoing her sister's three word observation made over 70 years ago which has transcended the decades and continues to be reaffirmed whenever one encounters Marian Marsh in person or on film. "Isn't she beautiful!"

PART II

"AN INTERVIEW WITH MARIAN MARSH"

Reminiscing with Hollywood stars is always a treat, but a journey down memory lane with Miss Marian Marsh is an event! She impresses you from the start with her intelligence, refined eloquence, and gentle good humor. One instantly feels she is a well-grounded, deeply spiritual person, with a true sense of what is important. Her frequently poignant, sometimes humorous memories of her films, costars, and "the old times" abound in the following conversation with John Barrymore's, "Little Maid Marian."

DAN: It's such an honor to speak with you! Let me begin by asking you about your birthplace, Trinidad.

MARIAN MARSH: That's the land of the hummingbird, where the hummingbirds originated. Sailors from all over the world who stopped there would capture them and take them home. That's how the hummingbirds got around the world! It was a beautiful place! A lot of earthquakes though. My dad grew cocoa beans.

DAN: Your father was an inspirational figure to you and your family, wasn't he?

MARIAN MARSH: Oh, yes! He died so young. He caught a cold, got *pneumonia while on a business trip in Boston not long after we moved West. He loved California! He had traveled quite a lot and thought it was the best place. I've blessed him ever since, because I love California. It's a great state!*

DAN: *After living in Boston, you moved to Hollywood while still a youngster. Your sister and brothers were all involved in the movie business.*

MARIAN MARSH: Yes, the whole family. My sister, Jean made many motion pictures, and my brother Edward appeared in several war films.

DAN: *Your sister had made a name for herself as Jean Fenwick before you ever got into the business.*

MARIAN MARSH: She had made several pictures in New York on Long Island, then she worked for F. B. O. Studios.

DAN: *My research tells me she was instrumental in getting you started in films.*

MARIAN MARSH: Absolutely! She'd tell everybody about her "little sister." (laughs) She was just wonderful! In her later years, she went into business for herself successfully, selling World Book Encyclopedias. She had forty people working under her who depended on her. She would make trips all over the country.

DAN: *She was certainly a good salesman when it came to you. I read several articles relating stories of her trips to casting directors, photographers, actors, etc. on your behalf.*

MARIAN MARSH: That's all very true. She really helped me!

DAN: *The great John Barrymore became one of your mentors when he chose you for your first important film, Svengali for Warner Bros., which made you a star.*

MARIAN MARSH: No doubt about that. When he chose me for *Trilby*, it was the biggest thing in Hollywood at that time. That this girl would play opposite Barrymore!

DAN: You have said he was in one of his "good periods."

MARIAN MARSH: Yes. He wasn't drinking, was happily married to Dolores Costello. They had little children who came to the set many times. She would come with them. It was all very pleasant, very nice.

DAN: There's so much legend and so many stories attached to Mr. Barrymore. He was kind to you though, wasn't he?

MARIAN MARSH: He was wonderful! We had a very good, comfortable relationship. He was determined *Svengali* would be a good picture, which I think it turned out to be. It was nominated for Academy Awards, but not chosen. It seemed such a shame. I was hoping it would win on his account. When you think of what a handsome man he was, how wonderful he was, his acting in the early days, then in *Svengali*, he played a character role. And he played it to the hilt! (laughs)

DAN: I understand he really got "into" the part.

MARIAN MARSH: Absolutely! (laughs) He enjoyed it all, making his nose bigger, long beard, etc.

DAN: Did you ever become frightened looking into that face? When he wore those contact lenses to cover his irises, he looked demonic.

MARIAN MARSH: That was when contact lenses were first developed. After he got them in, they were hard to take out. It was quite exasperating for him. His appearance didn't bother me. I knew it was only makeup . . .

DAN: Your performance as Trilby was extraordinary. During the course of the film, we watch you transform under his spell, from *innocence to maturity. How did you prepare for the role? Did Barrymore and/or the director, Archie Mayo give you advice on how to make that transition?*

MARIAN MARSH: I remember thinking that anything as unearthly as Svengali should frighten a young person such as Trilby. That's why he could overtake or overpower — hynotize her. It's very interesting. When you get together and read the script, that's the time you learn what your attitude should be. We ran over the script many times with everyone around the table. We eventually became comfortable. Barrymore was very helpful, patient.

DAN: *Is it true Archie Mayo let you improvise?*

MARIAN MARSH: Yes, he did. He was that kind of director. He'd say, "Do what you feel is right. If I don't like it, I'll tell you so. If I don't say anything, you go ahead." He used to blow up once in a while. He was impatient. Usually it had to do with camera angles. Especially in the walking scenes when Trilby, now a great singer, walks out of the theater, and Little Billie is there, and she recognizes him for a second when he calls her name. He (Mayo) wanted it filmed a certain way. We did the scene several times, after Mayo blew up.

DAN: *There were many interesting aspects of the film. You appeared to have a nude scene in it.*

MARIAN MARSH: They didn't let me do it, you know, because I was underage. So they took a view of me and the back of another girl. She is the one that ran out. She wore a body stocking.

DAN: *According to Barrymore biographer, Alma Waters-Peters, you had some legendary visitors on the set of Svengali.*

MARIAN MARSH: That's right. Albert Einstein and Admiral Byrd. I had a picture of each of them, but I lost them. I prized the one of Admiral Byrd so. He was such a beautiful man, very handsome!

DAN: *Do you remember meeting Einstein?*

MARIAN MARSH: Yes, I met him a couple of times, once in Palm Springs. He was visiting, and I was at a hotel with my mother, sister, and brother. We were walking along Park Canyon, and I said, "My goodness, there's Albert Einstein!" (laughter) He was coming towards us with his wife. When he got to us, he hesitated. And I said, "I would like to introduce my family to you. Remember, I had met you on the set." And we shook hands, etc. The next thing I knew, he said, "Could you come in the morning? They want to take a picture of me. It would be nice to have you in the picture." (laughs) I told him, "I'd be delighted." Then his wife spoke up, "Oh he's been saying he wanted to meet a movie star, and have his picture taken with them!" So I was it!! (much laughter)

DAN: You had portraits painted of you for Svengali. Did you get to keep them?

MARIAN MARSH: Yes, I have two of them now, both oil paintings. I have one full body portrait called, "The Unfinished Portrait of Little Billie," and the other is a saintly one which is how he saw me in the film. I had another that was taken by someone. They were done by a renowned German artist. I lost a lot of things when I was an actress including a makeup box given to me by Marie Dressler.

DAN: Did you know Miss Dressler very well?

MARIAN MARSH: Oh yes! Very well. She was a great artist and actress. You could tell her what to do and you would get it exactly right. She was just a natural!

DAN: Incredibly, your second Warner Bros. film is another timeless classic, Five Star Final. In it, you worked with another great film actor, Edward G. Robinson. What are your remembrances of working with him?

MARIAN MARSH: He was very business-like. He was very into his own performance. However, when it came time to separate me out to take close-ups of my part, he was very good about giving you the cues. He felt if the actor you were acting with gave the cues, it would be *more authentic. He was so right! He was a perfectionist.*

DAN: How did you feel about making such an important film at the tender age of 17? Were you intimidated?

MARIAN MARSH: No, not at all. I had been on the stage. When you're on the stage out there all alone, there's not much that scares you after that!

DAN: I understand Robinson gave you advice on how to portray the powerful final scene. Articles say he advised you to play it, "calmly."

MARIAN MARSH: That's incorrect. He really kept out of it. He would look at me from time to time, and shake his head up and down. (laughs) We did quite a lot of rehearsing for that final scene. Everyone felt that I should make up my own mind how to play it. Aline MacMahon, who was in it, was very nice to me. When I was rehearsing that scene, she came up to me and said, "Don't give it your all in the rehearsal. Save yourself!" I've never forgotten that! I took her advice. After all, she'd been around longer than I had, and she was a very fine actress.

DAN: Well, it all worked out magnificently! Your performance was outstanding and incredibly, the film remains as topical today as when it was made.

MARIAN MARSH: You're absolutely right. I blame television for that.

DAN: Another early costar was William Powell. I know he was a particular favorite.

MARIAN MARSH: Oh, Bill Powell! He was just wonderful! Just being with Bill was wonderful! I first met Bill when I was a child. My sister was in a picture with him. Then, later, I played in Road to Singapore with him which was the first "road picture," before Bob Hope and that crowd stole the whole name. (laughs)

DAN: *What did you find so appealing about Powell?*

MARIAN MARSH: *In my book, he was a sophisticated man. He must have been sophisticated when he was born! Young girls at that time thought of him as a "man of the world," always well dressed, well groomed, and he spoke so well. He had a beautiful voice.*

DAN: *He made it look so easy on the screen.*

MARIAN MARSH: *Oh, he was like that in life. Easy going — just a delight! When anything was wrong, there was no temperament, nothing. He was just himself. He was one to follow the director.*

DAN: *Your character is infatuated with him in the movie. It was said he gave you some advice about the characterization. You thought that it might be unnatural for such a young girl to throw herself at an older gentleman.*

MARIAN MARSH: *Bill said it was natural for a young girl to like an older man, and that's a true fact! (laughs)*

DAN: *Next came another film with Barrymore,* The Mad Genius, *directed by the great Michael Curtiz who had a notorious reputation as a tough guy to get on with. Did you ever have problems with him?*

MARIAN MARSH: *He was temperamental, but no, never! I was lucky. Directors never got mad at me. They'd get mad at others, but not me. (laughs)*

DAN: *Did the volatile Mssrs. Curtiz and Barrymore get along?*

MARIAN MARSH: *They never had a battle. Michael Curtiz would flare up over "things," but it was never for long. We'd just let it roll by.*

DAN: *And Barrymore was once again pleasant to you, even giving you a special nickname.*

MARIAN MARSH: Yes, he dubbed me, "Little Maid Marian." (laughter). When he wanted me on the stage, he'd say, "Where's my Little Maid Marian?" I'd be walking in, and I'd say, "I'm coming!" (laughs)

DAN: You saw him many years later after his "excesses" had taken their toll.

MARIAN MARSH: On the dance floor at a New Years Eve party. I've never forgotten it! He was not himself. We sort of ran into one another. He was going one way, and I the other. He held on to me by my shoulder and said, "I'm not the man I used to be." I said, "I don't see any change in you whatsoever." I remember that so vividly because I felt so badly. I had never seen him out of sorts and so sad.

DAN: You did another one of my favorite Marsh films for Warner Bros. in 1932, Beauty and the Boss with Warren William. You were so charming in that movie!

MARIAN MARSH: Oh, (laughs) that is sort of a favorite of mine too! Thank you! That's so nice to hear! Warren William was a very fine man. I liked him very much! It's a shame, he died so young. He had some strange illness. He was compared a great deal to John Barrymore because of his profile.

DAN: I did an article on him a few years ago and watched the film in preparation, but I had forgotten how great you were. How did you talk so fast?

MARIAN MARSH: Oh my goodness (laughter) Just practice I guess! (laughs). With all this praise, what can this be leading to! (much laughter)

DAN: You signed with Warner Bros. twice. The first time in 1929 for a year, then you were chosen for Svengali and signed with them again? My research revealed that they worked you so hard that by 1932, you were exhausted, and decided they should be paying you more.

MARIAN MARSH: That's right. I wound up in the hospital in Santa Monica. They didn't believe I was ill. They sent their doctors to look at me. Well, it was just exhaustion!

DAN: They were notorious for working their contract players very hard!

MARIAN MARSH: In those early days, they did that with players. Some days, I would be doing two films at the same time.

DAN: After you parted company with Warner Bros., you worked in Europe with the famous German actor, adventurer, Luis Trenker on a film called, The Prodigal Son.

MARIAN MARSH: Yes. He (Trenker) was a great Swiss skier and guide who saved the lives of many people. The film was the story of a guide who gets married to a society girl, and there are problems because their lives were so different. They never bridged those differences, but scenically, the film was so beautiful!

DAN: You have a lovely story about that experience, don't you?

MARIAN MARSH: One time I was atop a mountain where we were filming. I was standing all alone, looking over at the magnificent view. I said out loud, "Oh, I wish I had a picture of this!" There was a man standing behind me who said, "You can do that." I said, "But I haven't got a camera!" He replied, "You don't need one. Come with me." So we walked right up to the edge where there was a railing. "Now, look at everything you see that you like. Then close your eyes, and think about it, and see it with your eyes closed." I practiced it. And he said, "Now you can see it whenever you want to, whenever you close your eyes." And do you know, I can! And I'm seeing it right now! Do you believe it? It's crazy, isn't it?

DAN: Yes, I do believe it, and I think it's great! It's surprising how we can train our minds.

MARIAN MARSH: Well, I've used that technique ever since with *anything beautiful. Look at it in depth, close your eyes, look again, and you've photographed it in your mind. It has a calming effect. You get very quiet.*

DAN: *I think I could use it on a daily basis. (laughter) Seriously, I bet it helped you in dealing with stressful acting situations.*

MARIAN MARSH: *Do you know what else works? Do you like to look at beautiful clouds? That's one of my best ones. If I'm feeling a little "put out" about something, I can close my eyes and say to myself, "I'll look at some clouds and calm down. (laughs) You know, you're the only person I've ever expressed that to.*

DAN: *After you returned to Hollywood, you made one of your favorite films for Monogram.*

MARIAN MARSH: *Girl of the Limberlost. I liked that so much! It was so sweet, so down to earth, all about a girl growing up in the swamps. Eddie Nugent was in that. He was such a nice young man. And wonderful Louise Dresser. We did that on location. Monogram did some nice, decent pictures.*

DAN: *Not long afterward, you did the famous, The Black Room for Columbia. I bet everyone that has ever interviewed you has asked this, so why should I be the exception. What was it like working with the great Boris Karloff, with whom you made three pictures?*

MARIAN MARSH: *Boris Karloff was a joy! A very pleasant, accommodating man — a true gentleman, and a very well-educated one. He was very easy to work with, quiet, soft spoken. To think of him playing a monster and all . . . (laughs) Well, of course, in this film, he was the two brothers, one was good and one bad.*

DAN: *What impressed me about his performance was his success at subtly shading the two characterizations to help in differentiating them.*

MARIAN MARSH: Yes! I thought he separated them very convincingly! I loved doing the film for the beautiful costumes. They were exquisite!

DAN: I know you have a very amusing story about him.

MARIAN MARSH: I visited him and his lovely wife many times. He had a lovely place. Boris had a pet pig. Well, they had invited me to dinner. His wife and I were waiting for Boris to come home. The pig was in a children's playpen, and it was quite big! As Boris drove up in his car, his wife said, "Now, watch! Watch! Be quiet!" And the pig went up and down from its two front feet to the two back! Up and down, up and down, like a big rocking chair! (much laughter) A little squeal would come out. Oh, it was so excited! Boris finally came in, and it could hear him slamming the door. By the time he got near the pig, it was screeching! Boris said, "All right! I'm coming! I'm coming!" So he climbed in the pen with the pig, and they rocked together! It was the cutest thing! Then the pig quieted down. (much laughter)

DAN: Another great Marsh classic is Crime and Punishment, a film adaptation of Dostoyevsky's masterpiece. It was directed of course, by Josef Von Sternberg, another man with a "reputation!"

MARIAN MARSH: Dreadful reputation! Let me tell you how I got the part. He was at Columbia studios at the time. I had read the book, and remarked to them that Sonya was a part I'd like to play. So, I was casually told to go see Josef Von Sternberg, the "great director." I said, "All right." So I went directly to see him. The secretary was there. She gave him my name, and I heard him say, "Oh, tell her to come in!" I remember this very well. When I walked in, he said, "Would you like to sit down?" I said, "Not particularly. I just wanted to meet you, and let you know that I'm here, and I would like to play the part of Sonya." And he said, "I'll think about it." And that was the end of that! (laughter)

DAN: Then what happened?

MARIAN MARSH: The next thing I knew, he wanted to see me through the camera. He didn't want to film anything; he just wanted to look through the camera at me. We did that, and I did a few walk-throughs, a few words, and so on.

DAN: After all of that, at least you got the part! Was he as demanding and difficult as they say?

MARIAN MARSH: Very demanding! Very temperamental! We had to do scenes over and over. Sometimes 20 takes! He just had to have it right. But do you know what he did that he was great at? He did his own lighting. I thought that was very interesting! If you run the film again, notice the lighting. He thought it added to the effect of the scene to have it lit properly.

DAN: He was what we now refer to as a "control freak."

MARIAN MARSH: He sure was! (laughter). He controlled the cameras, the lighting, the people . . . (much laughter)

DAN: My hat goes off to him. (laughs) The film is wonderful. It seems your character was it's "conscience." Peter Lorre was your costar.

MARIAN MARSH: Although he was a very fine actor, I didn't think Peter was right for the role. Why should a girl like Sonya fall in love with a man who looked like that! It should really have been played by a younger man.

DAN: He certainly gave an excellent performance however. How was he to work with? I've heard he kept to himself like Robinson.

MARIAN MARSH: Oh yes, very much so. But he was always pleasant to work with, and he worked hard at doing a good job, but if he had been more handsome, it would've been more believable.

DAN: Another interesting member of that cast was one of the grande dames of the British stage, Mrs. Patrick Campbell. I've heard she was a character.

MARIAN MARSH: *She was a real character! (laughter) She was good, and she knew she was good. That's all there was to it!*

DAN: It seems confidence is a key to any profession. How did you approach a role in general? What was your technique?

MARIAN MARSH: *I would simply try to put myself in the place of that particular person. Act the way they would act. You must really feel you ARE that person!*

DAN: In prep for an intense role such as Jennie in Five Star Final, did you ever take it home with you?

MARIAN MARSH: *I did! From the moment I started to do a part like that, it was with me all the time. You couldn't lose it! If you would lose it, and try to get it again, you couldn't. You had to be sure you kept it with you.*

DAN: I always like to ask actors who did both stage and films, which they preferred and why?

MARIAN MARSH: *The stage, because when you are on the stage, you're in charge. There's just something about it that's so good. Some nights you'd be better than other nights. You'd try to hang on to the things that made it better. I knew Alfred Lunt and Lynn Fontanne very well. I introduced myself to them while they were in Los Angeles touring. They'd seen me on the screen, and liked me very much. I went to their performances over and over. Whenever I would go backstage to see them afterward, they would say, "Did you see what we did? We left out two lines!" (laughter) They were devastated! To try and convince them, I'd say, "Well, I didn't notice it, and think how many times I've seen you! I practically know the whole play by heart, word for word." Then they'd calm down and say, "Oh, thank heavens!" (laughter)*

DAN: That's the mark of genius, to always strive for perfection.

MARIAN MARSH: *That reminds me of Fred Astaire. I was in*

London making two pictures for British International. I went to a play several times that he appeared in, in which there was a dance sequence. For some reason, they left it out one night. I looked around at the audience reaction. They didn't know. When I went backstage, Fred was walking up and down the corridor saying, "Oh, what will they think of me!" I said, "Well, I was there, and no one knew." Then, he was relieved. So I figured twice in my life I had relieved some wonderful actors!

DAN: I want to ask you about three more of your famous costars. You worked with Ruth Chatterton.

MARIAN MARSH: Oh yes! I knew her well. She was terrific! She was a pilot, you know. She flew to Cleveland for the National Air Races, and was the guest of honor. She flew her own plane in, and landed on the field there before a big crowd of a couple hundred thousand people.

DAN: How was she to work with on Lady of Secrets? She played your mother.

MARIAN MARSH: Well, I can tell you a funny story. Here I was pretty and young, and she was playing a mother for the first time. She wasn't too crazy about that! The first day we had the wedding scene, of all things. It was really in the middle of the picture, but they started with it because they had a marriage type set already built. The designer made me the most beautiful gown you could imagine. I've never seen anything like it before or since. I looked terrific in it. Well, Ruth walked off the set! She didn't like what they had made for her to wear. Everyone was aghast! So, we did other things in the meantime. The next morning, they had made another dress for her that she liked. She came back on the set and finished. (laughs)

DAN: How did she treat you after that?

MARIAN MARSH: Let me tell you the rest of the story. Well, at that time I rode a horse everyday in the morning and in the evening (for recreation). I was riding to Griffith Park one day, which was the closest *to my home. Anyway, there I was on my horse, and I spied Ruth quite a ways from me on a horse enjoying herself too. So, I thought, well, maybe I can break the ice. So I casually rode by her, and acted as if I didn't recognize her, to see what would happen. All of a sudden I heard this galloping behind me. And she came up and met me. She said, "I didn't know you rode a horse! I didn't know you liked horses!" And I said, "I can't start the day without getting on a horse." She said, "That's wonderful!" Well, from then on, we were friends! When we got back to the set the next day, it was Friday. They were talking about me working on Saturday and I said, "Oh, but that's the USC football game, and I have tickets!" So right away, she interrupted, "Let's do her scenes first, so she won't have to come on Saturday." From then on, she took care of me throughout the picture! (laughter) Isn't that cute? She was just wonderful; and acted just like a mother then!*

DAN: How about Joel McCrea with whom you made Sport Parade?

MARIAN MARSH: *Nice fellow! I liked him tremendously. We used to play volley ball in Santa Monica. He was a very good player, and that was the big game in those days. I knew his wife too, and she was wonderful. Joel was very wise financially. A director friend of his (and mine) told him to take his money and put it into real estate and suggested where, and Joel was smart enough to do it. He bought all that property along Ventura Boulevard. Oh my!!*

DAN: You stopped making films in 1942, and became a successful mother, which I would guess is as tough a job as being a movie actress.

MARIAN MARSH: *Well, yes! (laughs) I have a son and a daughter. They live in different states. I never give their names because from an early time, they've never wanted to be mentioned. They like their privacy. I can tell you that they are not in the movie business.*

DAN: You officially retired in the 1950's after you did some television.

MARIAN MARSH: Well, I'll tell you what happened. Once you've smelled the grease paint, and been around, it's always with you. I had run into Butch (Cesar) Romero one day who said, "Oh, Marian, you're still so beautiful! You should still be making pictures." I said, "Oh no! Not me." We agreed to have lunch sometime. A few weeks later, we had lunch, and as I was returning to my car, I ran into an old agent of mine. He had a television movie starting in three days and the actress was ill. He said, "You're perfect for it. Will you do it for me?" I said, "But, I have two small children." He was so desperate, I said I would, "think about it." A friend of mine was waiting for me when I got home. She advised me to do it, and she would care for the children. I agreed. The production starred Gary Merrill, the husband (at that time,) of Bette Davis.

DAN: You told me Bette visited the set one day.

MARIAN MARSH: Yes she did! (laughter) She screamed and yelled, and called me a name. (She was kidding.), and said, "How dare you get back into acting! You got out of this business once!" I told her I was just doing a friend a favor, and she calmed down. (laughter)

DAN: Was she glad to see you?

MARIAN MARSH: Oh yes! I knew her from Warner Bros. She was always carrying on. We liked one another. She was one of a kind!

DAN: You married aviation pioneer, Clifford Henderson in 1960. Tell me about him.

MARIAN MARSH: He was the founder and producer of the National Air Race, the biggest thing in the country in the 1930's. He was determined to do it. He gathered up all the famous flyers, stunt flyers, made all the arrangements, and started the first air race from Los Angeles to Cleveland.

DAN: When did you meet him?

MARIAN MARSH: I had not been married when we first met in the

1930's. Then, we met many years later. They still have the Cleveland air show, and I go every year.

DAN: He actually founded Palm Desert, California, didn't he?

MARIAN MARSH: That's right, after the second World War. He was such a fascinating man, so full of ideas! He fell in love with the desert! He bought a lot of property, got a few people together, and put up a big sign that stated, "This will be the community of your dreams." Little by little, it built up. On El Paseo, the street he drew from Highway 111, he used to have a sign that read, "El Paseo, the Fifth Avenue of the Desert." Now, there's a great big building going up there!

DAN: Tell me about the Desert Beautiful program you started, and have been involved in for many years.

MARIAN MARSH: That was after we were married in 1960. We came to the desert to live. We started it as a non-profit, all volunteer organization. We plant palm trees along the coast, and were the first to plant palms in the lower valley to Palm Springs. Another place we planted was Cathedral City.

DAN: And you're still planting! That shows not only dedication, but tenacity!

MARIAN MARSH: Yes, thirty-six years later! (laughter)

DAN: That's just another one of your many legacies.

MARIAN MARSH: You do a little of this and a little of that, and somehow it all comes together. If you want to leave something behind, plant a tree!

DAN: Well, you've left us more than just palm trees to enjoy. Now, for the ultimate cliche-ish question. How would you like to be remembered?

MARIAN MARSH: *Oh my heavens! When I used to play tennis, people would say, "Oh, you did so well!" I remember, I would say, "Well, I did my very best!" I think anything I've ever tried, I tried to do my best. That's all you can do!*

DAN: *Well, I know I speak for your legion of fans when I say, your best was mighty good!*

MARIAN MARSH: Thank you very much! You know, if you're not careful, you're going to turn my head! (much laughter) [169]

UPDATE

Marian Marsh Henderson continued to live in her home in Palm Desert, California until she died in the early hours of November 9, 2006. She was 93 years old. After a funeral Mass at Sacred Heart Catholic Church in Palm Desert, she was interred in Desert Memorial Park in Cathedral City, California. She was survived by her two children, Catherine, "Cathy," and Albert Parker Scott Jr., eight grandchildren, and seven great grandchildren. Her son, Albert, died on November 4, 2014, in Denver, Colorado. Catherine is believed to be alive and living in the southern U.S.

EXTRA

Penned by the author shortly after her death, the following tribute to Marian was published in *Classic Images* magazine. The piece, which originally included a short career summary followed by the author's personal reflections has been edited so as not to repeat aspects of Marian's career discussed in the original *Films of the Golden Age* magazine article seen above.

"A LEGACY OF BEAUTY: MARIAN MARSH"

(Originally published in *Classic Images*, January, 2007)

John Barrymore affectionately nicknamed his young costar, "Little Maid Marian." Residents of Palm Desert, California respectfully referred to their first lady as, "Marian Henderson." Vintage movie enthusiasts fondly recall her as Marian Marsh, one of the early sound era's loveliest star actresses. Today all classic film fans pause to salute one of the movie's most beautiful and affecting gentle women who died at her home in Palm Desert on November 9, 2006, age 93. I had the great good fortune to conduct a series of interviews with the unique Miss Marsh in 1998, which resulted in a 1999 *Films of the Golden Age* cover article, a 2005 Internet Movie

Database mini-biography and most importantly, a long distance friendship which I will always treasure. Looking back at the long, productive life and career of this multi-faceted woman, one is struck by her many impressive accomplishments and the legacy of beauty she leaves behind.

My opportunity to interview Marian Marsh came in 1998, as a result of a mutual friendship. One of Marian's friends, John Cavallo was also a pal of mine. When John learned of my admiration for Marian, and my interest in writing a career tribute and interview piece, he enthusiastically approached her. She kindly consented.

Have any of you ever *really* wanted to do something, and once you get the opportunity, suddenly begin to have doubts? Well, it happened to me in this case. After my initial delight in hearing the news Marian would do the interview, I became apprehensive. I'd read Gregory Mank's superb 1985 *Films in Review* article on the making of *Svengali*, and Don Leifert's excellent 1996 *Filmfax* interview with Marian on her horror films, and wasn't sure I'd be able to add anything new and substantive in my own piece. My motto has always been, if you can't write something significant or make a genuine contribution, don't do the project. This was an opportunity just too wonderful to pass up, however! You see, ever since I was a little tyke, I knew and admired Marian Marsh mainly because of her appearances in several horror/suspense classics I love, especially Warner Bros.'s *Svengali* and Columbia's wonderful *Black Room*. To me, she perfectly personified the heroine of the suspense genre. Beautifully fragile-looking, warm, soft spoken, yet possessed with an inner strength and fortitude, her onscreen heroines functioned as effective counterbalances to the villains who often menaced her on film. Resolved to unearth new information, I pressed ahead with my project.

In May 1998, I did the first of several interviews with Miss Marsh. I know it sounds phony, corny, but she was exactly as I'd I thought she'd be, ironically, similar to the characters she'd played so effectively during the 1930's. Gracious, kindly, refined, she was a real lady. I was struck immediately by her soft, well-modulated voice, a voice I don't ever recall she raised, not once in the hours we spoke then or since. And her diction, was . . . well, letter perfect. Listening to her voice on tape later, I recall thinking what a good job her original diction coach, actress Nance O'Neil had done with little Miss Marsh! I was also impressed with Marian's strength of character. Despite being a movie star and a wealthy woman, she was a well-grounded person whose thoughtful, and honest responses to my queries reflected a strong sense of the importance of family and community, and an appreciation for the great gifts life had bestowed upon her.

We covered a broad range of topics, but the bulk of our conversations centered on her peak moviemaking years from 1931-36, and the various filmmakers she worked with, her relationships with Warner Bros. and Columbia, and experiences making particular pictures. I not only asked her about her most famous costars like Barrymore, Karloff, and Powell (all of whom had been covered in previous articles), but such underrated talents as Edward G. Robinson, Warren William, Joel McCrea, and Ruth Chatterton. To my surprise and delight, she liked and admired all the above but reserved special praise for William Powell with whom she was costarred in *Road to Singapore*.

Although there was some inevitable overlap between my article/interview and the distinguished ones which preceded it, in the end, as I wrapped up my project, I felt quite positive.

Several significant quotes emerged from the sessions. Marian exhibited a certain soulful, spiritual quality which surfaced in many of her recollections. When I asked her how she dealt with the stress of film acting, she said she would often close her eyes and think of something beautiful she'd seen and photographed in her own mind. She was very passionate about many things, especially the memory of her late husband, Cliff, "a fascinating man, so full of ideas," and her beloved Desert Beautiful organization involved in a vigorous campaign against littering and over development of the Coachola Valley area. On a strictly personal note, one wonderful moment came one day when I shared my background in rehabilitation counseling with Marian. She said she could understand why I would make a good counselor because, "you're easy to talk to." I was so flattered!

When the article, *Little Maid Marian* was published in *Films of the Golden Age* (Issue #15 — Winter, 1998), I immediately sent Marian a copy. As I had hoped, the piece was very popular with the readership. Even though she'd quit making motion pictures 67 years earlier, film fans still cared. I received several congratulatory notes, but heard nothing from the person who mattered most, my subject. What if she didn't like it? Was there something contained in it she found offensive? All kinds of things began running through my mind. After a few weeks, I worked up the nerve to telephone her. I could tell right away she *did* like the article. She said she'd been busy with her various charities and hadn't had a chance to let me know. She told me she liked it so much she wanted her children and grandchildren to have copies. Later, I received two autographed photos with wonderful inscriptions.

I would speak to her many times during the next few years. She said she considered me a friend and generously volunteered to assist anytime I needed her help on a project. I took her up on the offer several times. In fact, she provided information and commentary for several of my later articles, including pieces on Nancy Carroll and Karen Morley (one of her fellow W.A.M.P. A. S. Baby Stars of 1931). Many times I telephoned her just to see how she was, and to catch up on her news.

As years passed, my *FGA* article on Marian (which was available online for a time), continued to generate interest from an intriguing mix of people. Occasionally, I would receive inquiries or complimentary letters about it. In early 2005, I was extremely pleased to receive a very kind note from Helena Wright, the curator of the Museum of History at the Smithsonian Institution in Washington D. C. Ms. Wright said she enjoyed the piece, and wondered if I would be interested in assisting a German colleague, Dieter Lorenz, who was researching a book on Alfred Krauth, a pioneer German photographer who was Marian's uncle. I was honored to help. His book, (written in German), was published in the summer of 2005. While assisting Mr. Lorenz, I noted Marian did not have a biography on the very popular, Internet Movie Database, (to my knowledge the largest collection of film information on the internet). As long as I had all my files handy, I thought it made sense to write an I.M.D.B. mini-biography on Marian.

In November, 2005, I telephoned her to inform her of the I.M.D.B. profile, the publication of the Lorenz book, and the recent Turner Classic Movies' broadcast of *Svengali*. I could tell she didn't feel particularly well, and wasn't up to one of our long conversations. She told me she'd fallen and was on the mend. I didn't keep her very long, but I do recall telling her how much classic film fans still admired her. Even the Smithsonian was interested! She seemed genuinely pleased. After approximately 15 minutes, we bid adieu. When I hung up the phone, I had a strong sense I might never hear that magnificent voice again.

During one of our interview sessions, I asked Marian how she'd like to be remembered. She replied simply, "for doing my best. I think anything I've ever tried, I tried to do my best. In the end, that's all you can do!" There is no doubt Marian Marsh did indeed do her best, often overcoming innumerable disappointments and obstacles along the way. When describing her life, beautiful seems the operable word. She certainly left me some beautiful, fond memories, but more importantly, through her many artistic contributions, philanthropic, and environmental endeavors, she has left this world a more beautiful place.[171]

CHAPTER SEVEN
"KAREN MORLEY: MAVERICK IN WHITE SATIN"

(Originally published in *Films of the Golden Age*, Spring, 2004)

The decade of flappers, easy money, and bathtub gin was almost over, and Hollywood was in turmoil. Warner Bros.'s Vitaphone process had precipitated a revolution in the moving picture industry which left studio titans scrambling to bring voices and music to the silver screen. "Out with the old, in with the new!" — was the prevailing maxim. Notable "outs" included many of the silent screen's aging superstars, forced aside for a new breed of cinematic thespians possessed with fresh acting techniques and stage-trained voices.

Among hoards of curvaceous cuties and wide-eyed dreamers vying to become the talkies' answer to Swanson and Pickford, was an exceptional 18-year-old named Mildred Linton. A reed thin wisp of a girl, with long brown hair, high cheek bones, and hooded eyes, she exuded an intellectual, slightly aristocratic air more akin to a school teacher than a movie queen. She was getting nowhere in her quest to become a film actress until one day, famed director Clarence Brown happened to hear her well-modulated speaking voice and gave her a screen test. The rest, as they say, is history. Assisted by MGM's legendary star-making machine, little Mildred became the attractive Karen Morley, one of the early sound era's most memorable leading ladies, renowned for her elegance and sophistication, her rich expressive voice, and the intelligence and intensity of her playing.

With an abundance of personal and professional assets and a precipitous start, young Miss Morley should have become a superstar, but alas, it was not to be. For beneath the delicacy of her manner, the chic sophistication of Karen's stylish satin gowns, and her perfectly coiffed hair, dwelt the heart and soul of a maverick, one who helped engineer her own decline by taking controversial political stands, and by resisting the expectations and responsibilities placed on stars by the moviemaking establishment. Hollywood's confusion on how best to utilize her unique talents exacerbated Karen's difficulties, eventually sending her career into a tailspin. By the end of the 1930's, she was being relegated to second features and supporting roles. A decade later, her movie career would end when her name appeared on Hollywood's infamous blacklist. Since then, most literary discussions of this unique artist have focused on her politics, unjustly diminishing her many accomplishments most especially memorable appearances in some of the 1930's best-loved and enduring film classics.

The third and youngest child of an impoverished farm family, the future star was born on December 12, 1909, smack dab in America's heartland, in Ottumwa, a small factory town situated amid the farms and corn fields of southeastern Iowa. At age 3, she was adopted by well-to-do realtor Walter Linton and his wife Elizabeth who named her Mildred. Almost before she could speak, little Mildred wanted to act. In a 2002 interview with the author, Karen Morley described her early artistic ambitions.

"I had designs on a career in acting from a very early age, perhaps when I began grade school. It was at this time I appeared in my first play. It was community theater in Ottumwa, Iowa. I performed throughout my formative years, seventeen plays I believe, until we moved to Los Angeles when I was sixteen . . ." [172]

In 1925, Mildred enrolled at the famed Hollywood High School. An honor student, she held fast to her artistic aspirations in spite of her parents' desire she pursue a medical career. In 1927, the youngster achieved the first of many goals, graduating H.H.S. at the top of her class. "I don't like to brag . . . Okay, I'll brag, I was class valedictorian of Hollywood High . . . After I graduated, I spent a year at U.C.L.A.," she told the author. One of her professors, actor/future film director, Irving Pichel was a source of encouragement. She confirmed Mr. Pichel's influence over her early career in 1935.

"One day, he came up to me and asked why I was wasting my time in school. He told me I ought to be in pictures. So naturally, after that, I began to wonder why I wasn't. I didn't think I had the looks to be a

film actress, but if Irving thought I had the talent, I might as well try . . . And I did. For a year and a half I tried to crash pictures . . . I registered at Central Casting for extra work . . ." [173]

Despite landing a bit role as a courtroom spectator in the 1929 Fox melodrama, *Through Different Eyes*, the newly named Karen Morley (her name derived from a character in a favorite Martha Ostenso novel, *Dark Dawn*, and from poet/novelist, Christopher Morley), had little to show for her efforts. Frustrated, she cast her artistic gaze toward the stage.

Finding work in the theater was no less difficult. At the Pasadena County Playhouse, it took Karen months to secure a walk-on and an off-stage scream. While moving props and serving as a part-time usher, she finally won the role of understudy to the lead in the melodramatic, *Ropes End*, but sadly, never got to go on stage. What might have discouraged the most dedicated young talents, never fazed the sensible, resolute Karen who utilized the time to make valuable contacts and learn all she could about her chosen profession. One of her wisest deductions was to recognize the importance of an actor's voice to their performance. She told an interviewer, honing her vocal skills was an early personal goal.

"There's a trick to listening to your own voice so that you know it, not the surface sound but the impression it makes. And the best way to learn this is to study everyday conversation. Very few people know how their voice sounds. By studied effort, you can polish your speech and eliminate many defects . . ." [174]

In 1929, Karen's stage apprenticeship finally payed off when she won the lead in P.C.P.'s production of *Fata Morgana*. Although her performance netted tepid reviews, the play attracted the attention of Jacobs and O'Brien, a talent agency who signed her, and arranged a meeting with MGM. She related the story this way.

"My real break came when I was talking to the casting director at Metro-Goldwyn-Mayer studios one day. Gaining admittance at all was something, but I wasn't getting very far trying to persuade him to make a test of me. Then, by a stroke of good fortune, Robert Montgomery

came in for his script of *Inspiration*. He asked the director if he might 'borrow' a girl to read lines to him for a test he was making for director, Clarence Brown. That was opportunity's knock at my door. I was the girl at hand and was 'loaned' to him for the test. While we were rehearsing, I was given my own test for the part of Liane in Inspiration." [175]

Impressed with her voice, (which one perceptive writer later described as, "smooth and throaty with a little catch in it, like a snag in silk"), the famed director was also taken with her manner. Not a glamour girl in the traditional sense, Karen was nevertheless able to project beauty and refinement through her attractive voice and by the confidence and poise with which she carried herself. Brown was so certain film audiences would respond to this rare young woman, he entrusted her with a key role in his next production to star MGM's golden girl, Greta Garbo.

The story of the loves of a Parisian model based on Alphonse Daudet's 1884 novel, *Sapho, Inspiration* (MGM, 1931), was a typical Garbo vehicle. Thinly-plotted and peppered with tedious dialogue (traits which marred some of her early sound films), the movie was nevertheless redeemed by Brown's deft direction, William Daniel's expert photography, a top-notch supporting cast, and of course, its charismatic star who nobly suffered her character's torments as only she could. In the small but showy role of Garbo's friend Liane, the doomed 18-year-old mistress of an aging playboy (Lewis Stone), Morley was impressive. Especially memorable was her dramatic final scene in which Liane's facial expressions convey her profound despair as the love of her life casually ends their affair. No doubt, it was on the strength of that scene which inspired MGM to sign the young lady to a long term pact in the winter of 1930, even before the film was released. Miss Morley told the author,

"Going under contract was something everybody wanted if you were not working. So naturally, I was quite thrilled. I think it was a four-year commitment at $200 a week. Once I became somewhat established, I looked forward to the expiration of the contract, as pay could then be negotiated." [176]

Miss Morley found working with the legendary Miss Garbo both fascinating and enlightening.

"Garbo was well established at the time Inspiration was shot. She didn't want anyone on the set who didn't absolutely have to be there. She was very able to think and feel in front of the camera, and made it look quite simple. I learned from watching her that being relaxed is the key to being good. Clearing the set helped her with that. She wasn't stuck up or necessarily reclusive, but that was her reputation, and I think she started to believe what she read about herself, and played it up! I never saw her have an argument on the set. Clarence Brown got out of her way. She knew what she was going to do before she came out of her trailer." [177]

Transforming ordinary mortals into supernatural entities known as movie stars was the pervue of all the big movie studios, but MGM had a star-making machine like none other. Acting, singing, and dancing lessons, photo shoots, publicity campaigns, fitness regimens, not to mention complete physical makeovers were but a few of specialized services the studio provided in order to construct a public image it could take to the bank. In Miss Morley's case, Metro-Goldwyn-Mayer's makeover included bleaching her hair blonde and putting the exceedingly slim, 5 foot 4 inch, hazel-eyed youngster on a diet of steak and potatoes to help her gain weight. Another aspect of a studio's promotion of their most promising female contract players was naming them W.A.M.P.A.S. (Western Associated Motion Picture Advertisers) Baby Stars. Karen was chosen in 1931, sharing the distinction with such future luminaries as Frances Dee, Joan Blondell, Anita Louise, and two lovely and talented Marians: Marsh and Shilling. When recently contacted by the author, the two gifted Marians recalled the honor and shed a favorable light on their fellow honoree. Miss Shilling put it this say

"As you are aware, Karen and I were W.A.M.P.A.S. sisters. My only association with her was during that period. I was a fan of hers and greatly admired her. She impressed me as a young lady of charm, dignity, and beauty. Everything about Karen seemed to reflect a mind of superior intelligence; her acting, her manner of speaking, her opinions . . . Karen was not only attractive, she was bright, brave, and

STRONG. I'd like to have known her better. . ." [178]

Miss Marsh was likewise impressed.

"What a nice person! I liked her very much. She was so stylish. I admired the way she dressed and wore her hair, and of course, her acting ability. She always appeared so mature for her years . . . We actually had two things in common. We both were W.A.M.P.A.S stars, and went to Hollywood High School." [179]

In 1931, MGM adhered to custom and introduced Karen to film audiences in small roles (mostly as jilted fiancés and long-suffering wives), in several productions including *Daybreak, The Sin of Madelon Claudet, The Cuban Love Song, Never the Twain Shall Meet,* and *Politics.* Only twice did she have better opportunities: as a glamourous spy in another of Metro's opulent "Garbo-dramas," *Mata Hari* (MGM, 1931), and on loan to RKO as the faithful secretary of a wealthy rubber magnate in *High Stakes* (1931). While making the latter, independent producer, Howard Hughes approached MGM to test Karen for a role in a gangster melodrama he planned "loosely" based on the life and times of notorious Chicago crime boss, Al Capone. After reading the hard-hitting Ben Hecht script, Karen became enthusiastic about the project, successfully lobbying MGM to try out. Luckily, her test pleased both Hughes and director Howard Hawks, so much so, they gave her a choice of two prime feminine roles. Negotiations followed which sent Karen on loan to appear as a gun moll in one of the most popular and controversial motion pictures of the 1930's, one which would make her a star.

From its inception to its final premiere, notoriety followed the production of *Scarface, The Shame of a Nation* (United Artists, 1932), the third and arguably best of the early sound era's gangster trio (which also included *Little Caesar* and *Pubic Enemy*). The controversy began with the finished script which scenarist Hecht described as a modern-day Macbeth, replete with characters based on real life criminals and action sequences literally torn from newspaper headlines. The brutal story of a mass murderer who builds a metropolitan crime empire on the bodies of all competitors only to be brought to his knees by his obsession with his own sister, Hecht patterned his

Karen played the patient fiancée of a shipping magnet's son, (Leslie Howard) who becomes involved with a Polynesian girl in *Never the Twain Shall Meet* (MGM, 1931).

anti-hero Tony Camonte on Capone whom he'd covered as a *Chicago Tribune* reporter. Real life crimes detailed in the picture included the murder of "Legs" Diamond and the St. Valentine's Day Massacre.[180] On the advice of director Hawks, Hecht threw in a psychological component: Camonte's incestuous fixation suggested by the lives of the Italian Renaissance family, the Borgias. Another controversy surrounded Hughes' selection of a talented group of youngsters to play the key roles including Morley, acclaimed New York stage actor Paul Muni (fresh from an Oscar nomination for this debut film, *The Valiant*), 36-year-old former dancer George Raft, (who had once drove a truck for bootleggers), and young ex-chorine Ann Dvorak, (a Morley friend whom she had recommended).

High drama emanated from the *Scarface* set almost daily throughout the turbulent, million dollar production (April-October, 1931). Not long after filming commenced, Hughes stunned the cast and crew by hiring several gangland criminals as consultants and four more writers (including Capone biographer, Fred Palsey), to authenticate the dialogue. Well publicized disputes and several mishaps and injuries also marred the proceedings, causing innumerable delays. Hughes' troubles intensified after filming was complete when prudish censor boards, demanded he tone down the picture's violence and sexuality. To get the film exhibited, the eccentric producer was forced to cut several key scenes, insert others, (including a prologue), AND even film an alternative ending (in which Camonte is hanged), without Hawks or Muni who refused to participate.

Hughes would be vindicated by the positive reception *Scarface* received from critics and audiences. In spite of the alterations, the movie remains a riveting motion picture; a powerful indictment of big city crime bosses which still packs a wallop thanks to Hecht's no-holds barred script, Hawks innovative direction, the groundbreaking photography of Lee Garmes, and its talented cast. Its four young leads contributed unforgettable performances against which all their subsequent work would be compared. As the sexy, ice blonde, Poppy, a power mad moll whose attachment to the ape-like Camonte is proportional to his hegemony and violent bravado, Karen was a revelation. To moviegoers familiar with her previous film work, her mature, nuanced portrayal must have come as quite a shock. Luckily, MGM was paying attention. By the time the film premiered, its young contract player had shed her ingénue image, and had been promoted to bigger and better parts, often as intelligent, no-nonsense women who use their feminine wiles to advance themselves in a male-dominated world. Miss Morley approved of the change to her screen persona and would always be grateful to Hughes for her first important film assignment. She told the author:

"I think Poppy was my favorite role . . . I always liked playing poor girls who had their sights set on something. That's the most colorful character. You can show off . . . When Howard Hughes would come to the set, people would get giddy. I don't believe we met until the picture was shooting. We went out on his boat one Sunday during the shoot. Unfortunately, I can't give you any sordid stories about him. He was a perfect gentleman . . . " [181]

As Karen had hoped, the controversial *Scarface* proved a career benchmark, which not only made her a star and changed her screen

Karen's favorite film role was the sexy, manipulative ice-blonde, Poppy in director Howard Hawks controversial melodrama, *Scarface, The Shame of a Nation* (United Artists, 1932). Here in a scene with costars Paul Muni, George Raft, and Osgood Perkins.

image, but established her credentials as a top-tier actress, initiating the brief peak period of her career (1932-35), during which she played several challenging lead roles opposite many of Hollywood's most celebrated actors. In 1932, she added nine motion pictures to her growing resume. Although none matched the excellence of *Scarface*, each had redeeming qualities including impressive performances from the ascendant Miss Morley.

Her follow-up film, the romantic mystery, *Arsene Lupin* (MGM, 1931), presented Karen with a dream opportunity to play a lighthearted lead role opposite the legendary brothers Barrymore. Although burdened with a pedestrian storyline chronicling a veteran police detective's (Lionel Barrymore) dogged efforts to nab a wily jewel thief (John Barrymore), *Lupin* was rescued by clever Bayard Veiller dialogue incomparably delivered by its three dynamic leads. Amazingly, Miss Morley (looking radiant), managed to hold her own in this elite company, contributing a scintillating performance

Spanish poster of *Scarface, The Shame of a Nation* (United Artists, 1932).
as a convicted swindler recruited by Lionel to pose as a Russian countess in order to nab the debonair crook. She falls in love with him instead. A box office winner, according to Miss Morley, *Arsene*

Lupin was as fun to make as it was to see. In a 1998 interview for Turner Classic Movies' Archival Project, she recalled the film and its memorable stars. She said the famed brothers were very kind, and referred to her as, "the actress" on the set, while they told dirty jokes she pretended not to understand.[182] Four years later, she told the author she still held the Barrymores in high esteem.

"The thing that comes most clearly to me when recalling the Barrymores, Ethel included, was they were always so entertaining. Being on the set with them was an education in itself, John, in particular. I recall him interrupting a conversation with a press agent once, to step onto the set and shoot a close-up where he had to drum up tears, which he did effortlessly. It was one take! He then stepped over and resumed his conversation with the press agent. It crossed over into the field of magic." [183]

Apparently the respect and affection Karen expressed for Hollywood's royal family was returned, for the elder Barrymore requested her as his leading lady in his next film, *Washington Masquerade* (MGM, 1932), all about the rise and fall of a folksy, Lincoln-esque politician (Lionel Barrymore). Based on a 1921 Broadway play (which also starred Lionel), the motion picture was a dramatic tour-de-force for its veteran star who created a realistic portrait of a courageous, yet flawed man. Once again, young Karen shined. Her mature performance as the ultra-chic Consuela Fairbanks, a scheming golddigger who corrupts the, "Abe Lincoln of the Senate," was as surprising as it was impressive. In a subordinate role, she made every scene count, creating a memorable characterization which at once charms and repels. Even the toughest critics cheered. "Karen Morley adds another achievement to her recent series of distinctive types," gushed *Variety*. "Here is one actress who can be a siren and still a grande dame, dealing with stereotypical characters and situations with an elegance of poise that makes them cameo-like in individuality . . ."

The versatile Karen also impressed in four other 1932 releases: as the nagging wife of a radio writer in the melodramatic, *Are You Listening* (MGM), a blackmailing vamp in the popular whodunit, *The Phantom of Crestwood* (RKO), the remorseful wife of German wrestler Wallace Beery in John Ford's *Flesh* (MGM), and as the endangered daughter of an archeologist in the delightfully camp

Karen was costarred with the famed brothers Barrymore in the comic adventure *Arsene Lupin* (MGM, 1932).

melodrama, *The Mask of Fu Manchu* (MGM), costarring Boris Karloff, Myrna Loy, and Lewis Stone. The latter, was the subject of two entertaining anecdotes she shared in her 1998 Turner Classic Movies interview. One recalled a mishap involving Karloff who fell, "flat on his face" attempting to ascend three steps because he couldn't see in his Fu Manchu costume (which included a gold mask and platform shoes!). The other involved Lewis Stone who refused director Charles Brabin's request that he jump over a pit of live alligators in a scene near the film's conclusion. When Brabin attempted to show Stone how easy it would be, one of the alligators whipped its tail and caught the director's leg, leaving a bruise from his ankle to his hip. "Lewis Stone was a smart man!" laughed Miss Morley.[184]

Fulfilling a life ambition to become a world renowned movie star must have appeared almost too good to be true to the former usher at the Pasadena County Playhouse. An MGM contract, working with Garbo and the Barrymores, great reviews in acclaimed films, what more could a girl want? In Miss Morley's case, the life of a movie star left a lot to be desired. Although deeply appreciative of her success, Karen quickly became impatient with many of the "extracurricular" responsibilities and expectations placed on studio

In full costume, Miss Morley takes a phone call during the production of *Washington Masquerade* (MGM, 1932).

contract players. To an intelligent, introspective girl who valued privacy, hated phoniness, and enjoyed contemplative time, MGM's constant demands that she do photo shoots, publicity campaigns, magazine interviews, and attend endless parties and premieres seemed unnatural and unreasonable. Perfectly willing to work 18-hour days to make a good film, Karen felt actors deserved time to

Karen won kudos for her complex portrayal of Laura Nash, an embittered young woman who has second thoughts when she and her corrupt ex-lover (Ricardo Cortez seen here), attempt to take advantage of her kindly husband in director John Ford's dramatic, *Flesh* (MGM, 1932).

themselves, and was unafraid of expressing her concerns publicly.

Her candor not only irritated her employers, but eventually, alienated certain influential columnists and writers who soon dubbed her ungrateful, uncooperative, and anti-social. Her growing problems with the Hollywood establishment were exacerbated by reports of her "standoffishness" on the sets of her films where it was said she refused to socialize with certain cast members and to genuflect at the altar of megastars. "The Girl Hollywood Can't Understand," "She Walks Alone," "Kalm, Kool, and Kollected," and "What, No

Love Life?" were but a few of the articles which reflected early press attempts to paint Karen as an aloof loner, uninterested in stardom and romance. In a 1932 magazine interview, Miss Morley tried in vain to quell the criticism. "I'm not a good mixer . . ." she candidly admitted. "You see, I was taught that friendship is a sacred thing to be carefully guarded and not cheapened by gaudy imitations. So, I don't make friends easily, even though I want people to like me."[185] Her unconventional honesty was also reflected in her opinion of romance. "From my own observations," she confided in 1931, "I'd have to say that an actress gets along better without a husband and family . . ."[186] Lamentably, Karen's conscious or unconscious failure to ingratiate herself with filmdom's influentials would have long-lasting repercussions which the gifted actress did not yet perceive.

While the outspoken Miss Morley's trademark honesty would remain forever unaltered, she'd soon have a change of heart on the subject of romance. In the fall of 1931, she became enamored of 31-year-old Charles Vidor, a Hungarian World War I veteran who emigrated to Hollywood in 1924, distinguishing himself as a film editor, screenwriter, and assistant director on a variety of Hollywood productions. A quiet man who shared Karen's keen intellect, and passion for excellence, the couple began dating shortly before filming commenced on *The Mask of Fu Manchu* slated to be Vidor's directorial debut at Metro-Goldwyn-Mayer. Apparently the relationship did not please the MGM head office. When "problems" surfaced a week into production, both the young director and the movie's leading lady, Gertrude Michael were fired and replaced by Charles Brabin and Karen Morley. The dismissal was widely interpreted as reflective of Mayer's disapproval. The romance survived and thrived, however. When engagement rumors began circulating, Louis B. Mayer flew into a tizzy, brazenly approaching Morley's parents in an attempt to prevent the nuptials. The willful Karen would have none of it. On November 5, 1932, she secretly wed Vidor in a small private ceremony at Santa Ana's Baptist Church. Years later, Karen admitted her marriage had been a mistake career-wise. "After my marriage," she said, "Mayer loaned me out on contract to make several bad movies. He held a grudge."[187]

If his majesty, "King Louis B." intended on sanctioning his defiant employee, it was not yet apparent in 1933, during which Karen was seen in two of MGM's most opulent productions. She was personal secretary to a U. S. President in *Gabriel Over the White House*, an unusual picture about a corrupt politician (Walter Huston) who, upon winning the presidency, undergoes an epiphany when he is seriously injured. Inspired by the spirit of God's messenger, he recovers and sets the country on a course of radical reform, eventually declaring martial law and dissolving Congress in order to promote world peace. Bankrolled by publisher William Randolph Hearst (who was said to have influenced its content), *Gabriel* was a box office mega-hit, thanks to the bravura acting of its star, one of the few actors who could realistically pull off such an assignment. It is a testament to Miss Morley's ability she made a strong impression in the small role of Pendie Molloy, the first person to recognize the divinity of Huston's reformation. In fact, her final scene with the dying president was so powerful it reportedly elicited audible sobs from moviegoers. Karen expressed a high regard for her costar.

"Walter Huston was a fabulous actor. I would guess that Hearst did not, as is rumored, write any speech for Huston. Rather, it's more likely Huston wanted to act something a certain way, and calmly told the director that Hearst made the suggestion." [188]

During the grueling production of *Gabriel* (filmed in only three weeks), Karen became sick. A physician visit confirmed her suspicions, she was expecting. Still feeling ill, she ignored her doctor's protestations in March 1933, to join one of the greatest casts in all Hollywood history to make another of the 1930's most beloved movies.

Whenever best lists are compiled for films of the 1930's, rarely is the opulent production of the George S. Kaufmann, Edna Ferber stage drama, *Dinner at Eight* (MGM, 1933), not included. Superbly produced by David O. Selznick, meticulously directed by George Cukor, and splendidly enacted by a dream cast, it is a grand film indeed, made grander by an impressive script. Overcoming the limitations of a large cast of megastars, scenarists Frances Marion, Herman Mankiewicz, and Donald Ogden Stewart were surprisingly successful at creating memorable, multi-dimensional parts for virtually all their primary cast. Marie Dressler's declining grande dame, Billie Burke's fluttery socialite, Wallace Beery's vulgar businessman, and Jean

Walter Huston, Karen Morley and Franchot Tone in *Gabriel Over the White House* (MGM, 1933).

Harlow's hussy with a heart were what one critic called, "definitive portrayals of their screen personas." Even the smallest roles were well written. Although Karen had only one major scene as the long-suffering wife of adulterous physician (Edmund Lowe), she had the opportunity to infuse the character with her own unique brand of grace and humanity. Working on *Dinner* proved to be a unique experience for the mother-to-be who amused herself between takes watching male crew members trying to climb into the rafters so they could look over Miss Harlow's breasts, and by using her screen husband's stethoscope to try to listen to her baby.

"Dinner At Eight was a fun picture. We all postured as though to convince the other actors that we weren't stuck up. Marie Dressler had been acting most of her life, and she told story after story, keeping us all entertained. Cukor was rumored to be temperamental, but like most of the best directors, by the time they get onto the set, the battles have been worked out." [189]

When filming was complete in May 1933, Mrs. Vidor escaped to her ocean front home in Palos Verdes where she occupied herself reading and writing poetry (one of her hobbies), while awaiting the

Edmund Lowe and Karen Morley in a scene from the all-star MGM production of *Dinner at Eight* (MGM, 1933) directed by George Cukor.

birth of her child. During the interval, the liberal actress also attended organizational meetings, becoming a member of the fledgling Screen Actors Guild, the first of many political associations (to be discussed later), which did not endear her to Hollywood power brokers. On August 26, 1933, while attending the premiere of her husband's directorial debut film, *Sensation Hunters* (Monogram, 1933), the stork came calling. A few hours later, Karen gave birth to a seven-pound baby boy, Michael Karoly Vidor in St. Vincent's hospital. Press reaction was predictable. Suddenly, several articles appeared hailing the young actress, extolling the virtues of motherhood, and insinuating her new status would forever temper her opinions and ambitions. For his part, Louis B. Mayer publicly professed elation at the news of Karen's pregnancy and motherhood. Privately, he apparently was planning to punish his intransigent employee. [190]

After four months of recuperation, Karen returned to work in January 1934, only to find her long hiatus had taken a toll on her status at her home studio. During her absence, other young talents (like Thalberg favorite, Madge Evans), had risen to prominence at MGM, and were now receiving the studio's best scripts. The sagacious Karen realized she needed a top-notch vehicle to reestablish her reputation. What she received from Mr. Mayer and company were thankless assignments in two B films: as the faithless spouse of a detective attempting to commit the perfect crime in *The Crime Doctor* (on loan to RKO, 1934), and as an orphan girl in love with her adopted mother's convict son in MGM's superficial drama *Straight Is The Way* (1934). Karen was so disappointed in the latter she chose not to renew her studio pact. She said,

"Mayer wanted to resign me, but once you became known, you didn't want to be saddled with a contract. I'm not sure it was the smartest thing to walk away from his offer. But at the time, it was quite prestigious to be out of one's contract, and have independence." [191]

Sadly, her decision to leave Hollywood's most respected studio and seek her fortune as an independent contractor would net mostly disappointing results, and hasten Karen's decline (already underway after the birth of her son). By 1938, her Cinderella story had become a fractured fairytale, and she was being relegated to second features and supporting roles.

She would have two more good years on the screen, however. In 1934, she gave an arresting performance as an unhappy wife whose divorce wreaks havoc on the emotional health of her adolescent son in RKO's *Wednesday's Child*, and followed with another of her most memorable characterizations in *Our Daily Bread* (United Artists), director King Vidor's sequel to his masterpiece, *The Crowd*. A depression-era drama detailing the tribulations of a bankrupt young couple (Karen and Tom Keene) who acquire a dilapidated farm and set up a commune in an attempt to save it from repossession, *Our*

Daily Bread almost wasn't made. Rejected by all the major studios (as left-leaning and bad box office), Vidor (no relation to Charles), was eventually forced to mortgage his personal assets and form Viking Productions to produce it, but in doing so, was obliged to limit its scope. Economically photographed (on a Tarzana golf course and on Edgar Rice Burroughs's 160-acre ranch), and employing (except for Karen), relatively unknown actors, the dedicated director/scenarist still ran up a tab in excess of $150,000 which he was unable to recoup at the box office. Vidor consoled himself with rave reviews. Although *Our Daily Bread* lacked the polish and professionalism of a big studio production, critics and discriminating moviegoers responded to its simple yet plaintiff message. At its heart, the film was a moving tribute to the human spirit, fondly remembered today for its stylistic direction, and its spectacular ditch-digging sequence: Vidor's salute to the Russian silent film, *The Earth Thirsts*. As the steadfast Mary Sims who must, not only endure the hardships of the commune, but the indignities of a straying husband, Miss Morley was at the peak of her powers, adding yet another enduring, multi-faceted performance to her impressive resume. Karen credits her director.

"King was a unique man, truly one-of-a kind, and unflappable. I was always fascinated watching how he solved problems. It was a tough shoot. As we were losing light one afternoon, while shooting the scene where over a hundred extras were digging a ditch, King tried to organize them to swing their pick axes in sync, but the fellows wouldn't maintain the rhythm. We continued the next day with the same shot, but King brought a metronome to the set, and put it in the ditch, where it couldn't be seen through the camera. One take was all it took to satisfy him . . . Later in life, he ran into a problem with his ex-wife who willed her half of their house to her dog. The dog and King had to wait each other out, though naturally, the dog didn't know it! I feel bad for gossiping, but what a trickster she was!" [192]

One of Karen's last quality movie roles came as a woman torn between love for a poor coal miner, and desire for a better life in *Black Fury* (1935), Warner Bros.' stark cinematic commentary on the harsh working conditions and corruption associated with the mining industry. Aided by a taut screenplay and an experienced cast, director Michael Curtiz pieced together an entertaining, frequently riveting film in spite of the script's grim settings and unglamorous characters. Of course, Curtiz was immeasurably aided by the high octane performance of his star Paul Muni who, by 1936, had become one of filmdom's foremost actors renowned for literally inhabiting his characters. In preparation to play the movie's lead character, the immigrant coal miner Joe Radek, Muni reportedly spent several days in an East Coast mining town researching the correct dialect. Karen found his dedication inspiring.

"Paul Muni was a joy to watch and to work with. He was the kind of actor who could entertain the crew with colorful stories until the moment the camera was rolling, then snap into the character, never missing a beat. So impressive!" [193]

Although *Black Fury* would prove a box office failure, its success with critics raised Karen's visibility and aided her rehabilitation campaign, at least temporarily. By the summer of 1935, she had signed a three-picture deal with 20th Century Fox studio, but not before defying convention and inexplicably appearing with young Mickey Rooney in the money-starved medical drama, *The Healer* a.k.a. *Little Pal* produced at Monogram, a studio notorious for grinding out second features starring actors whose careers were on the ropes.

With her filmmaking future uncertain, the unorthodox star increasingly looked homeward to find security. Although a liberated woman who viewed marriage as an equal partnership, the very feminine Karen was nonetheless a homebody who enjoyed the domesticities of being a mother and wife, and was a surprisingly outspoken defender of Hollywood marriages. In a 1937 interview, she explained her views this way.

"There are a lot of unions that go on the rocks — and many more that don't. But if there happens to be a separation in Hollywood, that old, worn out 'marriage and career argument' is dragged out by the heels again. Of course, everyone forgets the many, many happy marriages within the profession, but then maybe they don't make good gossiping. . ." [194]

Still hopeful, Karen continued her quest to reestablish her career at Fox Studios soon to become 20th Century Fox. Lamentably, Zanuck and company appeared uncertain how best to utilize their new contract player, wasting her in throwaway roles: as the faithful secretary/best girl of a timid bookkeeper in the B comedy, *$10 Raise* (Fox, 1935, Fox), a Hungarian countess in the minor league murder mystery, *Thunder in the Night* (Fox, 1935) and as the ill-fated mother of lovable moppet, Shirley Temple in the popular, *The Littlest Rebel* (Fox, 1935). The latter found the intellectual actress looking especially ill at ease as a Southern belle bedecked in hoop skirts and a blonde wig. Drawling out such memorable lines as "I reckon I better get your things together . . ." "I'll see if Rosabelle has your lunch ready . . . ," you could almost see Karen gritting her teeth, no doubt grateful when her character catches cold and dies near the film's midpoint. Despite it all, Miss Morley recalled being fascinated by her screen daughter.

"She (Temple) was so grown up for a child. She understood everything that was going on on the set and between scenes. Her mother was there all the time, but it was clear who was the boss." [195]

After a disappointing year at Fox, Karen's career rebounded briefly when she won acclaim for two supporting performances: as an airplane manufacturer in love with test pilot, Richard Dix in Columbia's action-packed adventure, *Devil's Squadron* (1936), and as a Dublin housewife widowed during the 1921 Irish Rebellion in Sam Goldwyn's moving drama, *Beloved Enemy* (United Artists). In 1937, she signed a pact with Major Studios (a Paramount subsidiary), who frittered away her hard-won momentum by poorly utilizing her in four inconsequential films: *The Last Train From Madrid, The Girl From Scotland Yard, On Such a Night,* and *The Outcast* (all made in 1937). Ironically, the poorest of them, *The Girl From Scotland Yard* is perhaps the best remembered (especially by B movie aficionados). In the title role, Karen played a secret agent/aviatrix forced into aerial battle with super villain Eduardo Ciannelli, the dastardly inventor of a death ray! To audiences below the age of 12 (and to those everlastingly entertained by death rays), Karen's over-the-top part was one to savor, but to Morley fans and moviegoers familiar with her ability, this program picture was well beneath her infinite dignity, and emblematic of a significant loss of stature.

Thurston Hall, Karen, and Lloyd Nolan in *Devil's Squadron* (Columbia, 1936).

By 1938, the handwriting was on the wall. After contracts with Fox and Paramount failed to reinvigorate her career, Karen reexamined her options. She could retire from acting and pursue her growing interest in politics and union organizing, explore some intriguing stage offers, or continue making films, doing leads in B's and character roles in A's. As she contemplated her future, she made brief film appearances in two big budget movies. In the exquisitely photographed horse-breeding epic, *Kentucky* (20th Century Fox,1938), she was back on a Civil War plantation suffering the murder of her pro-Confederate husband by a union sympathizer. In 1940, she was lured back to MGM at the behest of novelist/scenarist Aldous Huxley who'd written a part for her in his adaptation of Jane Austen's comedy of class and manners, *Pride and Prejudice* to be directed by George Cukor. Unfortunately for Karen, just prior to filming, Cukor was replaced by Robert Z. "Pop" Leonard who paired down her meaty character role until, in her words, "there was practically nothing left."[196] Still, the film was a pleasure to behold, one of the more successful film adaptations of a classic novel, enhanced by a literate script, beautiful Cedric Gibbons sets, and a splendid cast headed by MGM's new first lady, Greer Garson. One of the august group of actors assembled to breathe life into the Austen classic was Ann Rutherford, a talented dark-haired beauty who had signed with Metro-Goldwyn-Mayer in 1937, and gained fame as Mickey Rooney's long-suffering girlfriend, Polly in the popular *Andy Hardy* series. In a 2003 interview with the author, Miss Rutherford expressed fondness for both *Pride and Prejudice* and Miss Morley.

"I think it is my favorite picture I was ever in! My part wasn't that big but it drove the story . . . I tell you, when I look at it and see Mary Boland prancing down the street like a mother goose with her goslings following behind! It was inspired! It's such a crime it couldn't have been made in color, but David Selznick had gobbled up all the color film for Gone With the Wind . . . Although I did get to know Karen during the filming, I got to know her better later. . . Some years ago she went with Marsha Hunt and me to a Jane Austen Society meeting in Santa Fe. She was a joy, such a lovely lady, and a darling person. I thought she was a wonderful actress. You never saw any seams in anything she did. She said everything as though it had just come into her mind!." [197]

While making *Pride and Prejudice*, Karen was horrified by Nazi Germany's march across Europe. She told an interviewer years later, how silly the cast felt in their period costumes while Hitler conducted his murderous campaign which would soon involve the U. S. For Karen, this sad, turbulent period was made sadder by troubles in her seven-year union with Charles Vidor. It now appeared as if her heartfelt sentiments regarding marriage and career had come back to haunt her. In the summer 1940, she obtained a legal separation and took her son to New York where she appeared in three Broadway plays which, although largely unsuccessful, provided the noted film actress with good reviews and the renewed pleasure of performing before a live audience. Of the three: *The Walrus and the Carpenter* (9 performances — November, 1941), a revival of Ibsen's *Hedda Gabler* (12 performances — January, 1942), and *Little Darling* (23 performances — October, 1942), the latter, a comedy costarring Leon Ames and Barbara Bel Geddes, won the most critical praise. In fact, Karen's notices were positively glowing, even from tough critics like *New York Times*' Brooks Atkinson whose review of her portrayal appeared more a love letter than a critique.

Disappointed by her film career, in 1941, Karen accepted the first of three offers to appear on Broadway. Her initial appearance came in the comedy, *The Walrus and the Carpenter*. From left to right, Karen, director Alfred De Liagre and costar Pauline Lord discuss a scene.

Buoyed, Miss Morley returned home determined to put her personal and professional houses back in order. The first step came in January 1943, when she filed for divorce accusing her mate of "great and extreme cruelty" without specifics. A divorce decree was granted two months later in a Los Angeles Superior Court which included alimony, a property settlement, and joint custody of their son. By the time of the divorce, the talented Mr. Vidor had become an acclaimed director thanks to helming the memorable psychological thriller, *Blind Alley* (Columbia, 1939), the first of many quality motion pictures he would direct until his death in 1959. [198]

Karen played a psychotic traumatized by the murder of her betrothed on her wedding day in Columbia's atmospheric thriller, *The Unknown* (1946), costarring Jeff Donnell (seen here on the extreme right).

Resigned to her status as a character actress, 35-year-old Karen Morley finally returned to the silver screen in 1945, as a charming murderess in Republic's low budget mystery, *Jealousy*. In 1946, she signed a pact with Columbia where she gave superb performances in three better than average low budget thrillers: as the love interest of trucker Richard Dix in *The Thirteenth Hour* (1947, the 7th entry in the fondly remembered *Whistler* series), the wife of a crooked banker in the well-turned melodrama, *Framed* (1947), and notably, as a psychotic traumatized by the murder of her betrothed in the gothic murder mystery, *The Unknown* (1946). Although Karen couldn't possibly have known, the torment and persecution suffered by her character in the latter would prove a strange, ironic dress rehearsal for the trials and tribulations she'd soon endure when her political views and affiliations received intense scrutiny.

Over fifty years have passed since "blacklist" became a familiar term in the American vocabulary, but passions elicited by the word remain strong. While there is fairly broad agreement now on the unfairness and destructiveness of Hollywood's blacklist, opinions still differ widely with regard to the inquiries into communist influence in the film industry conducted by the U.S. House Special Committee on Un-American Activities, a.k.a. H.U.A.C.,which preceded it. It is not the purpose of the following brief discussion to join the unending debate, but to: 1) present a capsulized version of events leading up to and through the two sets of Hollywood H.U.A.C. hearings to better understand their impact on Miss Morley's career; and 2) to state a few conclusions a majority on both sides would not dispute. For instance, few would disagree the post World War II period (coinciding with the investigations and blacklist — 1947 to the early 1960's), was one of the film capital's darkest, a tragic, paranoia-filled time which witnessed the ruination of countless friendships, marriages, lives, and careers, and robbed the cinema of some of its most creative artists and craftsmen. The film career of Karen Morley was most certainly one of its casualties. It is important to note however, while the H.U.A.C. hearings brought Karen's movie career to an unofficial end, she was being blackballed long before anyone ever heard of the committee.

The blacklisting of Karen Morley began in the late 1930's. By then, her various rebellions (including her marriage to Vidor and motherhood), unconventional candor, and cool relations with the press had placed her out of the good graces of cinema powerbrokers who exhibited little tolerance for dissent even from the most talented actors and technicians. Karen's well-publicized political views and activities aggravated her difficulties. A liberal, stirred by injustice and the plight of the disadvantaged, by the early 1930's, Miss Morley had firmly attached herself to the Hollywood left, a large assemblage of filmmakers whose political ideologies ran the gamut. This diverse group set aside its differences temporarily during the Franklin Roosevelt presidency (1933-45), uniting to press for economic, social, and political reforms to address problems perceived as threatening American peace and prosperity. Among their causes were support for anti-Facist groups, FDR's New Deal, civil rights, and union organizing. Karen's involvement in the progressive wing of S.A.G. (Screen Actor's Guild), and active support for unionizing movie technical workers were special sore spots for Hollywood powerbrokers. She recalled her participation in a 1998 interview.

"There was a studio strike. The workers had been provoked and actors forced to cross the picket lines . . . I helped organize a small but important group of actors who tried to convince the Actor's Guild not to cross the picket lines, and although we didn't win, this attempt to keep actors on the side of the strikers cost the studios a great deal of money. And so they were mad at me . . . Hollywood had its own blacklist. I didn't need H.U.A.C. to do the trick." [199]

As her career declined, Miss Morley's interest in politics intensified. In 1944, she reportedly stated she, "found union organizing more exciting than acting," and actively promoted the production of films for the benefit of the labor movement. While World War II raged, her leftist views and activities were widely accepted, but after Roosevelt's death, and the end of the war, the political landscape experienced a sea change. Suddenly, the Communist Soviet Union (our partner during the conflict), began acting like a dedicated adversary, refusing American economic aid and installing regimes across Eastern Europe. Amid new U.S./Soviet tensions, came revelations (provided by Communist defectors), of a sophisticated underground espionage network which had infiltrated U.S. governmental agencies (during the 1930's and early1940's), and supplied the Soviets with important military and economic secrets. By painting the Democratic Party and the American Left as soft on communism, the Republicans wrested control of both houses of Congress in 1946, and immediately began hearings to address this socalled, "red menace." Their vehicle was a little known committee in Congress born in the 1930's to fight right-wing extremism.

Established in 1938, (as a result of the Black Legion disclosures), the U.S. House Special Committee on Un-American Activities (a.k.a. H.U.A.C.), became a stalwart watchdog of the American Left thanks to its chairman, anti-communist Texas Congressman Martin Dies. Seeking to expose Hollywood as a hotbed of dangerous leftwing subversives bent on utilizing films to promote 'un-American' propaganda, Dies made several fact-finding junkets to California in the early 1940's, only to be rebuffed by a united front of studio heads and personnel. His fortunes improved substantially in 1944 however, with the formation of the M.P.A. (Motion Picture Alliance for the Preservation of American Ideals), comprised of conservative producers, directors, writers, actors, etc., organized to combat "the efforts of Communist, Facist, and other totalitarian-minded groups to pervert this powerful medium (films) into an instrument for the dissemination of un-American ideals and beliefs." In March 1944, the M.P.A. sent a letter to conservative North Carolina Senator Robert Reynolds making it clear if communist hunters ever came back to the film capital, they would find a divided city with a faction willing to cooperate. In early December 1946, prominent *Chicago Tribune* publisher/FDR critic, Robert McCormick set the stage for the famous Hollywood H.U.A.C. hearings by publishing a series of articles alleging a communist takeover of the film industry. Armed with a popular mandate, some sensational press, and the M.P.A.'s implicit invitation, H.U.A.C.'s new chairman, New Jersey representative, J. Parnell Thomas made preparations for a return visit to the city of dreams determined to succeed where Dies had failed.

By May 1947, Thomas and fellow congressman John McDowell were on the West Coast conducting interviews with "friendly" witnesses (defined as those who cooperated with the committee in executive, secret sessions). In the first of many unethical acts committed by, and attributed to H.U.A.C. members, sensational tidbits were leaked to the press. In September 1947, the committee issued 43 subpoenas to filmmakers, including M.P.A. members, and suspected subversives. The public hearings conducted in Washington D.C., officially began in October with testimony from the "friendlies" (including such luminaries as Robert Montgomery, Gary Cooper, Robert Taylor, Jack Warner, and L.B. Mayer), some of whom volunteered names to the committee. Karen Morley's name came up at least once during "friendly" testimony, supplied by fellow MGM star, Robert Taylor.

By the time H.U.A.C. prepared to examine the involuntary "unfriendly" witnesses in the autumn of 1947, many Hollywood liberals had become alarmed by the hearings which they interpreted as an assault on constitutional freedoms. Backed by most newspapers and a sympathetic public, several hundred moviemakers (among them Humphrey Bogart, Lauren Bacall, John Huston, and William Wyler), formed the Committee to Protect the First Amendment (a.k.a. C.P.A.), took out ads in newspapers, and flew to Washington to show silent support for their fellow artists. On October 27, 1947, their mission turned into a public relations disaster when the first "unfriendly" witness, writer John Howard Lawson refused to answer committee questions and launched into a diatribe attacking members as "Fascists." When others testified similarly, their confrontational attitude turned press and public opinion against them and their embarrassed supporters. Newspaper editorials fastened on the witnesses' refusal to answer questions as proof they had something to hide. On November 24, 1947, Congress cited 10 "unfriendly" witnesses (a.k.a. "The Hollywood Ten"), for contempt of Congress. The next day, fifty top Hollywood executives met at New York's Waldorf Astoria, fired them, and adopted a policy that no "subversives" would be given jobs. By 1950, all ten had lost their appeals and were imprisoned. Ironically, two of them: writers Ring Lardner and Lester Cole shared a Danbury, Connecticut prison with their chief interrogator, Congressman Thomas who was convicted and sentenced to 18 months for taking kickbacks from his staff. [200]

The period between 1947-53, would be one of the most difficult and tumultuous of Karen's life. Being "named" made her virtually unemployable in paranoia-filled Hollywood. Although she did muster three more film appearances including a showy cameo as the grieving mother of a murdered child in Joseph Losey's noirish remake of the 1931 German thriller, *M* (Columbia, 1951), none were worthy of her abilities. If her professional woes weren't bad enough, in 1948, Karen made headlines when her home on Laurel Canyon Boulevard was burglarized by three gun-toting hoodlums (who were subsequently apprehended and sent to prison). Through it all, she remained strong and steadfast, bolstered by the support of her young son and a new love in her life, stage and screen actor, Lloyd Gough, whom she met during this period. A decorated World War II veteran who won a bronze star during the Normandy invasion, Gough shared Karen's passion for politics, and would soon share a spot on the blacklist alongside his wife-to-be.

Having indicted the "Hollywood Ten" in 1947, H.U.A.C. temporarily suspended its Hollywood probes and shifted attention to governmental spying. During the three-year period between the Hollywood hearings (1948-51), sensational headlines of Soviet espionage and imperialism continued to foster a climate of fear and anxiety in the U.S. The famous Alger Hiss, Rosenberg, and Fuch's spying trials, the Soviet blockade of Berlin, the communist takeover in China, and the invasion of South Korea by North Korean Communists appeared to confirm suspicions the Soviet Union and their allies were bent on world domination. Against this backdrop, came another revolutionary phase in the film industry. The advent of television and the forced divestiture of their theater chains, left studios reeling, hypersensitive to losing additional business by employing those whose politics offended segments of the public. By 1950, several underground lists had been supplied to studios filled with names of filmmakers who someone (many times without any evidence), had identified as communists, communist sympathizers (a.k.a. fellow travelers), or dupes (those who had supported communist front organizations). In 1951, an emboldened H.U.A.C. opted to refocus its attention on the cinema. Those it subpoenaed had two choices. They could produce names of alleged communists and be allowed to work, OR cite the Constitution's fifth amendment against self-incrimination. If they opted for the latter course, they would not be imprisoned, but blacklisted. According to multiple sources, at least 36 artists chose the former option, and over 200 the latter including Karen Morley.

The hearings resumed in March 1951, with the testimony of actor Larry Parks, who, in an attempt to save his livelihood, succumbed to committee pressure and named names, thus setting the precedent for future "cooperative" witnesses. Karen Morley's name came up often in early testimony. On November 13, 1952, she made her appearance before the committee. Displaying her trademark dignity and poise, the attractive blonde star took her seat beside her attorney, former Congressman Vito Marcantonio, smiling as the committee counsel examined her. Guided by her own sense of loyalty and patriotism which were offended by conduct of the hearings, she gently declined to answer questions, citing her fifth amendment right. Only once did she speak expansively when she told the committee she had attempted to use whatever influence she had to persuade the CIO-United Auto Workers to make a cartoon for use in the campaign of Franklin Roosevelt in 1944. One can only speculate what emotions filled the 42-year-old silver screen veteran when she finally emerged from the hearing. She had preserved her integrity and refused to implicate friends and coworkers, but at a high cost. "The idea that being blacklisted is heroic — forget it!" she recalled years later. "It was very ugly. It was terrible to see people fold. . ." [201]

On November 13, 1952, Miss Morley appeared before the House Un-American Activities Committee and cited her fifth amendment right against self incrimination. In doing so, she did not name names, but was blacklisted, effectively ending her film career.

Fifty years hence, historians, critics, and film fans continue to debate the true legacy of the H.U.A.C. and its hearings. Many one-sided books have painted the committee's work in blacks and whites. As in most things, the truth probably lies in between the extremes. Although it is impossible to excuse their tactics and their racism, in retrospect, the committee does deserve credit for alerting the public regarding communist espionage networks which had successfully infiltrated U. S. governmental agencies, and which left unchecked, might have posed a potential threat (as is so vividly and objectively documented in such books as *The Haunted Wood* and *Hoover and the UnAmericans: HUAC and the Red Menace*). Moreover, their unethical tactics notwithstanding, many committee members rightly felt a duty to confront this potential menace, and address the anxiety expressed by many of their constituents. [202]

Tragically, the H.U.A.C.'s record investigating Hollywood filmmakers was neither commendable *nor* successful. For all its sensational rhetoric, the committee had little to show for all the time and money spent. Certainly, it did not achieve its stated objectives, to prove the existence of dangerous Communist content in Hollywood films, and gather new information for legislation. Outside of citing a few pro-Soviet movies like *The North Star, Mission to Moscow,* and *Song of Russia* (all made to pay tribute to one of America's World War II partners), the committee failed to provide concrete evidence the movie industry had been successfully utilized by communist propagandists. In fact, the hearings made the public more aware that even though it was populated by a few professed communists, and many left-wing ideologues, Hollywood was above all else, a city of businessmen, some of the world's most successful and enthusiastic practitioners of capitalism. If the committee's intent was information gathering, the hearings were unnecessary, as the names of communists were already known, supplied by the L.A. Police Department (which had infiltrated the party in the late 1930's), and by the F.B.I. So why did the H.U.A.C. spend so much time in Hollywood? In his enlightening and exhaustive study of the psychology of the blacklist, *Naming Names*, author Victor Navasky gives the only obvious answer. "For every witness from the worlds of labor, science, the armed forces, or education, there were a dozen from the wonderful world of show biz. The committee undoubtedly enjoyed basking in the publicity glow generated by those it was interrogating." [203]

Sadly, the sole significant achievement of H.U.A.C's Hollywood investigations, besides publicity, appears to be the blacklist which would have a far-reaching negative impact on the movie industry. The stories of the shattered lives of those ruined by innuendo and accusation, the images of frightened people betraying their best friends and colleagues, the festering bitterness engendered by those caught in the H.U.A.C. web are now a familiar part of the legend of the blacklist, but only a portion of its legacy. Not so well known are some of its other affects. By pitting studio heads against their employees, the blacklist further weakened the tottering studio system which would soon collapse. Because of the blacklist, some of the cinema's most talented and experienced filmmakers were sidelined or sent packing, leaving a giant void reflected in the dearth of important, socially relevant films during the period. Another victim, according to Miss Morley, was the smart feminine lead.

"Before blacklisting there were roles of strong opinionated women. After the blacklist, studios turned to a safe topic, violence. The cult of violence began. Women were chosen for their figures and their seductive appearance. The roles were of easily frightened and passive women who were not in decision making positions." [204]

With a few exceptions, Karen Morley has largely maintained a public silence regarding the blacklist and her political activities throughout the remainder of her life. When the subjects were broached by the author in 2002, she stated the following.

"Were people trying to change the government? The answer is simple, NO. The "Hollywood Ten" laid out a blueprint for what today we call the Libertarian party. No one was attempting to prevent anyone from making their fortune or prospering as best as one was able. The idea was to keep the common man out of the poor house. Filmmakers, people in the industry, people I knew at that time were many of the smartest around. They were acting on behalf of the country to examine the possibilities. The country at the time was not defined in all the ways it is today. The motion picture industry, when it started out, naturally had no unions, and of course, it was a free-for-all. The producers didn't have to answer to anyone, and that's a recipe for disaster. When the unions were organized and implemented, it stabilized the industry. The grips, gaffers, drivers, everyone on the set, now had lives. They were able to plan, to feel security. So, as opposed to doing anything un-American, what people were doing during this period was actually, very much pro American, putting forth energy to insure the country survived and thrived." [205]

Miss Morley remained adamant in her opposition to H.U.A.C.

"People in Hollywood had the opportunity to talk, listen, and examine the state of the country and the world. The film industry had good, strong, smart men and women keeping abreast of government policies, and Uncle Sam didn't like it. And add to the fact, that a few of them, like McCarthy, thought they could become well-known politicians.

They failed miserably, but it cost a lot of people their careers." [206]

If the committee expected the actress/activist Karen Morley to suddenly retire after the ordeal, forget about politics and acting, and stay silent, they misjudged the passion and commitment she'd always brought to all of her endeavors. In 1952, the unstoppable Miss M. was back on Broadway appearing with Lloyd Gough in the comedy, *The Banker's Daughter.* In 1954, she re-entered the political arena, garnering 45,000 votes as the American Labor Party candidate for Lieutenant Governor of New York! Afterward, she remained in the "Big Apple" for several years dividing time between politics and occasional stage appearances. [207]

With the end of the blacklist in the 1960's, came new acting opportunities for both Karen and Lloyd who had married, and moved back to the West Coast. During the next two decades, Lloyd would become a popular featured player in both the mediums of television and film. By the 1960's, his wife appeared less intrigued by acting, content to support her husband's endeavors while pursuing other interests. An early proponent and researcher of alternative medicines, Karen was designing vitamin programs for cancer patients as early as 1965, and finding some success. On rare occasions, she was tempted out of semi-retirement to accept occasional acting roles on American television on such popular series as *Kung Fu* (1973), *Kojak* (1973), and *Police Woman* (1975). In 1971, she joined old friend King Vidor for an Academy of Arts and Sciences seminar on *Our Daily Bread.*

Fate would bequeath great satisfaction and sadness to Miss Morley during the latter decades of her life. On July 23, 1984, Lloyd Gough died of an aortic aneurism, ending a long and successful partnership between two individuals who shared a passion for creativity, and political activism. After his death, Karen's public appearances became rarer, largely limited to hosting screenings of *Scarface* and attending commemorative celebrations associated with some of her famous films including *Pride and Prejudice.* In 1998, she provided video-taped commentary for Turner Classic Movies Archival project, and filmed segments for televised biographies on the Barrymore family and Greta Garbo. In 1999, the San Francisco International Film Festival saluted Karen Morley as part of their ongoing series honoring, "filmmakers who have faced repression and censorship." Amidst the

The ever elegant Miss Morley posed for this photo in the 1970's.

honors, came another tragedy when in 2000, Karen's son Michael Vidor, (a successful restauranteur in the Northwest), died as a result of a traffic accident.

At the time of the *Films of the Golden Age* interview in 2002, 92-year-old Miss Morley still lived in southern California where she occasionally attended seminars and screenings of her films, as well as various conventions celebrating classic cinema. As one of the last living links to a golden age of filmmaking, she was still in demand by countless fans and film historians fascinated by her reminiscences of a time when kings and legends made the movies. At the end of her life, Miss Morley took special pride in the accomplishments of her three grandchildren: M.C. Vidor a business consultant, John Vidor a commercical director and screenwriter, and Molly Vidor, one of America's most important still-life artists. "I have three beautiful and wonderfully talented grandchildren. I know how to breed lookers," said the proud grandma. [208]

From the moment she faced the camera for her first screen test in 1929, it was apparent Karen Morley was not your average young actress seeking fame and fortune in Hollywood. Talented, exquisitely poised, with aristocratic good looks, a well modulated voice, and the wisdom to understand her own strengths and weaknesses, she was a standout. In the beginning, her uniqueness worked to her advantage as she rapidly ascended to the head of the class of up and coming young film stars. In just three years, she had amassed an impressive resume of acclaimed performances in hit films which demonstrated the breadth and range of her ability. She certainly seemed destined for greatness when things began to unravel. Ironically, some of the same qualities which had made her famous, would contribute to her undoing. In the end, she was just too intelligent and independent to accept the authority of her employers over her public and private lives, and too versatile an actress to develop an identifiable screen persona which might have prolonged her career. Of course, her politics was a factor in her decline, but contrary to popular belief, not the major factor.

For far too long, literary exposes on the life and career of this underrated star have focused primarily on the blacklist, thus devaluing her many personal and professional accomplishments. As a an artist/activist, it can be safely asserted she was a feminist trailblazer whose determination to utilize her celebrity to affect social and political change no doubt helped pave the way for many other stars who would take public stands on substantive issues. As a film actress, her achievements are impressive. A retrospective analysis of her work reveals an array of unique characterizations which will undoubtedly stand the test of time. The beguiling Sonia in *Arsene Lupin*, the resilient Mary Sims in *Our Daily Bread*, the enchantingly bitchy Consuela in *Washington Masquerade*, the conniving Poppy in *Scarface*, and the courageous,

kindly Cathleen in *Beloved Enemy* are but a few of the enduring gallery of multi-dimensional film portraits delivered with uncommon grace, intelligence, and commitment by an unforgettable maverick named Karen Morley.

UPDATE

While putting the finishing touches on the above article, news broke of the death of Karen Morley, thus making the interview contained in it the last of her life. According to press reports, she died of pneumonia at the Motion Picture and Television Hospital in Woodland Hills, California on March 8, 2003. She was 93 years old. She was cremated and her ashes scattered at sea. She was survived by her three grandchildren.

Since Miss Morley's death, much has been written about her son, Michael Karoly Vidor who passed away three years before his famous mother. It seems Michael Vidor has become almost as legendary as his famous parents, at least in the city of Portland, Oregon. Today, he is viewed as a pioneer of the restaurant scene there, having opened several noted eating places there including L' Auberge, the famed Genoa, The Wood Stove, Tanuki, and Macheesmo Mouse. Mr. Vidor's history and exploits as an entrepenuer have been covered many times during the past several years in several prominent Portland area newspapers and national magazines.

Michael's three children have continued in his and their grandparent's tradition. M.C. Vidor is a successful business consultant who is now believed to live in the northeastern, U.S. John Vidor continues to work as a producer, director, and scriptwriter. Among his achievements was producing, directing, and penning the script of *Six Days in Paradise*, a 2010 action comedy starring Michael Madsen, David Carradine, and George Kennedy. Karen's youngest grandchild, Molly, (as her proud grandmother stated), has become one of country's foremost still-life artists with several prominent showings of her acclaimed paintings throughout the Pacific Northwest and across America. [209]

CHAPTER EIGHT
"EDWARD NORRIS: BABY FACE GANGSTER"

(Two-part article originally published in *Films of the Golden Age*, Summer, 2001)

PART I

To those who appreciate the "golden age" of B movies, handsome actor Edward Norris is a significant star. Although he appeared in numerous big budget, grade-A productions at the outset of his career, he is best known today for making countless second features in the 1940's for the likes of Columbia, Universal, Monogram and PRC. To Norris, the reporter, turned starry-eyed actor who migrated to Hollywood in the early 1930's to become a great film leading man, his B-movie fate was a profound disappointment. After a promising start as an MGM contract player, his career faltered due to a combination of mismanagement, personal problems, professional mistakes, and just plain bad luck. When things did not work out as he'd hoped, however, instead of packing his bags, the tenacious Mr. Norris held on to his dream and kept making motion pictures. Movie fans are glad he did. Classic film buffs and B-movie aficionados in particular, have a soft spot in their hearts for the guy affectionately known as filmland's, "baby-faced gangster." They are in awe of his talent, and professionalism, and are grateful he left us so many first-rate performances on celluloid in a career spanning 30+ years and over 70 films. From weaklings to gangsters, from sophisticated romantic leads to tough hombres, from French Canadian trappers, to Mexican bandits, Edward Norris pursuasively played them all.

Septimus Edward Norris began life's journey on March 10, 1911, in Philadelphia. The son of socially prominent parents, his father, Richard C. Norris, was a successful gynecologist and obstetrician, and his mother, the former Grace Vogt, was the daughter of the president of the Southern Railway. The youngest of five children (two boys, and three girls), Edward, (who preferred to be addressed by his middle name), was expected to follow in his father's medical footsteps. When in his teens, his placement in the Culver Military Academy was seen as proper preparation for a career in medicine. The rebellious, restless 16-year-old Edward had other ideas however, dropping out of the Academy in 1927, to marry 18-year-old Virginia Hiller, the daughter of another prominent Philadelphia physician. [210]

Although the hasty union was doomed from the beginning, and the couple was basically separated for much of the marriage's 2 1/2 year duration, it did produce Edward Norris Jr. (born in 1929). After leaving the Academy, the child bridegroom found employment in the newspaper world as a reporter, first for *The Philadelphia Evening Bulletin*, then *The Philadelphia Ledger*. In his spare time, the good looking wavy-haired young man dabbled in acting. A 1927 trip to see his mother (now divorced), in Coronado, California, would have life-altering consequences. A chance meeting with famed director, William Wellman on a Coronado beach, led to Norris' first film work as a double for Buddy Rogers (whom he resembled), in the Academy Award winning World War I classic, *Wings* (Paramount). [211] Mesmerized by the filmmaking process, the youth became determined to make his way in the world of movies. Wellman in turn, was impressed by the brown-eyed 5 foot-11 inch tall young man's enthusiasm, and dark good looks, advising him to acquire some stage experience, and return to Hollywood.

This time, young Norris followed an elder's advice, returning to Pennsylvania, and joining two stock companies. From 1928-32, he found work in numerous stage productions and traveling shows in Pennsylvania, and along the East Coast. By early 1933, he was back in Hollywood where he located an acting job at Pasadena's Orange Grove Theater in a show called, *Doomsday Circus*. His girlfriend, a Russian ballerina, introduced young Ed to the Russian colony of actors and directors who, as a favor to her, advised him on his career. Russian-born director, Rouben Mamoulian eventually attended a performance of *Doomsday Circus*, and was impressed enough to make Norris his protégé, placing him under the part-time tutelage of Moscow Art Theater veteran actor Akim Tamiroff. [212]

In 1933, Mamoulian gave the young novice a small role in his big budget MGM epic, *Queen Christina* starring Greta Garbo. Edward's impressive work led to a long-term MGM contract at the monumental salary of $35 a week. As the studio began grooming Norris as a romantic leading man, in the period 1934-36, they introduced him to filmgoers in tiny roles in such films as *A Wicked Woman* (1934), *This Side of Heaven* (1934), *Murder in the Fleet* (1935), *Naughty Marietta* (1935), and *Small Town Girl* (1936). To showcase his ability, the studio gave Norris a showy dual role in the second installment of its acclaimed *Crime Does Not Pay* series of shorts entitled, *Alibi Racket* (MGM, 1935). It is significant to note the first short in the hit series had starred Edward's friendly rival, Robert Taylor, who had been signed by the studio just a few months after Norris, and who would soon eclipse him as the company's top young leading man.

Director Rouben Mamoulian saw potential in young Mr. Norris, and gave him a small role in his big budget epic, *Queen Christina* (MGM, 1933), starring the legendary Greta Garbo. From left to right: Garbo, Elizabeth Young, and Edward Norris.

For his first major studio assignment, MGM featured Norris in showy dual roles in *Alibi Racket* (1935), one of its popular *Crime Does Not Pay* shorts.

Edward's work in *Alibi Racket* inspired 20th Century Fox head, Darryl Zanuck to approach MGM to borrow his services for the hard-hitting crime drama, *Show Them No Mercy*. Negotiations followed which ended up netting his employers a tidy profit (They pocketed the difference between the fee paid for Norris' services and his salary.), and sending Norris on his first loan in August 1935, to join an impressive cast including Bruce Cabot, Cesar Romero, and Rochelle Hudson. Based on the famous Weyerhaeuser kidnapping, *Show Them No Mercy* (20th Century Fox, 1935), was the story of a young couple (Norris and Hudson) and their baby who are held hostage by a group of kidnappers and killers. Directed stylishly by George Marshall, the

Norris was loaned to 20th Century Fox to play a young father who, along with his wife and child are held hostage by a group of killers and kidnappers in the taut, suspenseful, *Show Them No Mercy* (20th Century Fox, 1935), costarring Rochelle Hudson.

film was riveting entertainment, successfully intermingling humor with thrills and suspense. 24-year-old Edward's performance, in his first feature-length lead role, was exceptional, netting him excellent reviews.

Understandably proud of his work, the young actor expected his employer to acknowledge his success by assigning him more substantive roles. Instead, MGM gave their prime scripts to Robert Taylor, and Franchot Tone, and Norris a walk-on in the studio's *Tough Guy* (1936), starring Jackie Cooper, a tiny 10th-billed doctor role in the medical drama, *Between Two Woman* (1937), and the lead in an *Our Gang* comedy short, *Teacher's Beau* (1935).

Increasingly disillusioned, the actor took temporary solace in his personal life. A favorite of the ladies, young Edward was a popular escort for many young Hollywood starlets. He even married beautiful young Paramount contract player, Lona Andre, but their marriage ended after only four days, a record even in Hollywood. Later, Edward would describe the Andre/Norris union as, "a publicity stunt that went too far."[213] In 1935, he met another stunning young

Paramount actress who shared many of his frustrations with Hollywood, and whose own career had been a disappointment. Her name was Ann Sheridan, and she and Norris would soon be an item. They wed in 1936. Young Edward was deeply in love with the beautiful redhead, and was influential in her move from Paramount to Warner Bros. in 1936, where she would soon become an important star.[214]

In March 1937, Norris' career reached its zenith when he was loaned to Warner Bros. at the request of director Mervyn LeRoy to costar in *They Won't Forget*, the heart-wrenching tale of the conviction and eventual lynching of a northern schoolteacher (Norris) for a murder he almost certainly did not commit. Adapted from Ward Greene's popular novel, *A Death in the Deep South*, based on Atlanta's infamous Leo Frank trial, the film pulled no punches in its indictment of intolerance, prejudice, corruption, and indifference. As the ill-fated instructor and his loyal wife, Norris and young Gloria Dickson (in her film debut), worked closely with LeRoy to create memorable characterizations. The result was one of the best, most underrated films of the 1930's, which thrilled critics and turned up on several 10 best lists including the prestigious *National Board of Review*, and *The New York Times*. Although box office receipts were curtailed by a Southern boycott, the film was successful on several levels, and was a feather in the cap of all involved especially director Mervyn LeRoy whose skill was apparent in every frame. For his superb portrayal of the doomed Robert Hale, Edward Norris won universal praise. His emotion-packed scene on the witness stand constitutes some of the film's most effective moments, and some of the best acting of his career. His excellent notices raised his visibility as an important new talent. Keenly aware of the young actor's ability and potential, 20th Century Fox, head Darryl Zanuck repeatedly attempted to purchase Norris' contract to develop him as a leading man, but MGM steadfastly refused, preferring to keep Norris around (at the unconscionable salary of $50 a week), principally as a way to keep their newly manufactured superstar, Robert Taylor from getting out of line.[215]

To say Ed Norris was deeply disappointed would be a gross understatement. After finishing an important lead in one of the years' ten best films, MGM once again relegated him to throwaway roles in such nonentities as *Bad Guy* (1937), *Mama Steps Out* (1937),

The highlight of Edward Norris' film career came in 1937, when he was loaned to Warner Bros. to play one of the leads in *They Won't Forget*, a shattering drama based on a true story. Back row from left to right: Lana Turner, Claude Rains, Allyn Joslyn. Front row: Edward Norris and Gloria Dickson.

and *Song of the City* (1937). His frustration soon transitioned into rebelliousness and depression which manifested itself in tardiness, grumbling, and excessive drinking. His complaints to "friends" soon found their way to MGM's front office, as did his burgeoning reputation as a heavy partier who appeared oblivious to professional notoriety. His beautiful and gifted wife tried in vain to temper his excesses, but she had her own career to worry about. With the October 1937, premiere of *Angels With Dirty Faces* (Warner Bros.), Miss Sheridan's professional fortunes began turning around at the very

As the northern schoolteacher, Robert Hale who is charged and convicted of murdering one of his students (Lana Turner in her screen debut), Norris received superlative reviews in *They Won't Forget* (Warner Bros., 1937).

time her husband's was on the skids. Marriage difficulties were inevitable. The couple would separate in 1938, and divorce one year later, but Edward Norris would always carry a torch for his lovely and talented ex-wife. [216]

Mired in marital and career problems, young Norris drowned his blues in a sea of self pity and booze. MGM effectively blackballed him, not only refusing to assign him new roles, but also nixing several loan agreements. In July 1938, he was finally summoned back to the studio to replace Donald Barry who bowed out of a pivotal role

Ed Norris and his wife, Ann Sheridan at a party in Hollywood during the late 1930's.

in Norman Taurog's prestigious drama, *Boys Town* weeks into filming. As adapted by Dore Schary and John Meehan, the story of Father Flanagan's valiant attempts to save troubled and homeless youths by founding the famous "Boys Town," the movie was filmed with uncommon skill by a group of accomplished technicians and an exceptional cast headed by Spencer Tracy and Mickey Rooney. Although sixth-billed, Edward's role as Rooney's convict brother who attempts to save his adolescent sibling by sending him to Flanagan, was a strong one. Norris' poise and professionalism under pressure not only added polish to the Academy Award winning film, but saved his employer thousands of dollars in costly delays after Barry's abrupt departure. His successful portrayal of escaped convict, Joe Marsh would have unforeseen consequences, however. After *Boys Town*, Norris would often be cast as shady, sinister, or morally ambiguous characters. Unlike rivals Taylor and Tone, Norris projected a certain dangerous quality under the benign surface of his good looks and the well-modulated calm of his voice — a simmering discontent if you will, which was apparent in the flash of his eyes, and arch of an eyebrow.

Despite critical accolades, *Boys Town* did little to mend Norris' tattered relationship with MGM. In 1938, a mutual agreement at last relieved him of his studio pact so he could sign with Darryl Zanuck.[217] Unfortunately, his professional fortunes would not improve with the change of employers. By the time he signed with 20th Century Fox, the studio had developed its own superstar leading man, Tyrone Power, and Norris was again relegated to second leads and character roles, or loaned to other studios.

If Norris was upset or disgruntled by his unimproved status, this time the chastened young actor kept it to himself, and 20th Century Fox obliged by keeping him busy. During his two-year association with the studio (1938-40), he made twelve film appearances, notably, as the troublemaking fiancé of Evelyn Keyes in Columbia's *The Lady in Question* (1940), as the idealistic illegitimate son of an unscrupulous publisher in *Scandal Sheet* (Columbia, 1940), a Finnish patriot in Universal's war drama, *Ski Patrol* (1940), and a doctor assisting famed bacteriologist, Paul Erlich in Warner Bros. grade-A drama, *Dr. Erlich's Magic Bullet* (1940). At 20th Century Fox, he was utilized mainly in lackluster character roles in such diverse productions as the Wyatt Earp western, *Frontier Marshal* (1939) the Ritz Brothers mystery comedy, *The Gorilla* (1939), and the dramatic *Here I Am a Stranger* (1939). Zanuck did give Norris a showy supporting role as a doomed flyer in the studio's much hyped aviatrix drama, *Tailspin* (1939), but the script and direction were weak, and the movie was a critical and box office failure. Probably Norris' best work of the 20th Century Fox period, was as the warehouse robber who sacrifices his life to save his young daughter in the low budget melodrama, *The Escape* (20th Century Fox, 1939), expertly directed by actor turned director,

Edward had a sympathetic role as the idealistic illigitemate son of an unscrupulous publisher (Otto Kruger) in Columbia's low budget drama, *Scandal Sheet* (1940), costarring Ona Munson.

Ricardo Cortez. Lamentably, Norris' excellent performance went largely unnoticed by many Hollywood elites and critics who viewed second features with condescension.

As a result of Pearl Harbor, and America's entry into World War II, 30-year-old licensed transport pilot, Edward Norris enlisted in the Air Force. He was assigned to the 7th, and later the 14th United States Air Force Training Division as a pilot instructor where he would remain throughout the war. Unlike many of his Hollywood contemporaries, Norris was able to make films during his military service.[218] In fact, the war years would be his most productive on the silver screen during which he appeared in a staggering 26 movies, all save one second features. By the time he left 20th Century Fox to freelance in 1941, Norris had reconciled himself to being a low budget movie actor. It was a cruel fate for the young man with the big dreams, but one which B movie fans continue to appreciate.

If program pictures (a.k.a. programmers, a.k.a. second features), were often burdened with low budgets, cheap sets, skeletal scripts, and excessively short shooting schedules, they had their compensations.

The poorly paid low budget movie actors could take some comfort in the creative freedom they were given by many low budget directors, and by the incredible variety of characters they had the opportunity to play. Such was the case of Edward Norris who had the chance to prove his range while making programmers for Republic, Columbia, Warner Bros., Universal, Monogram, and PRC. Although gangsters were his specialty, his characterizations ran the gamut from arch villains, to superheroes. The size of his roles varied as well, but never the dedication he brought to his film work. Between 1941-45 he appeared in such memorable low budget movies as Columbia's eerie *Crime Doctor* chiller, *Shadows in the Night* (1944), Republic's entertaining Gene Autry western, *Back in the Saddle* (1941), the wild musical farce, *Road Show* (United Artists, 1941), and the Pine/Thomas' action adventure, *I Live on Danger* (Paramount, 1942).

More prominent roles were his as the cold-blooded killer in Universal's adaptation of the Poe classic, *The Mystery of Marie Roget* (Universal,1942), a navy pilot marooned on a South Sea island in *Wings Over the Pacific* (Monogram, 1943), a mystery writer determined to clear an innocent man charged with murder in *End of the Road* (Republic, 1944), and the poor sandblaster in love with an debutante in the unpretentious comedy, *Here Comes Happiness* (Warner Bros., 1941). Of particular note for Edward Norris devotees were his memorable portrayal of a young bookie who sacrifices his life for his country in Columbia's well-paced *Sabotage Squad* (1942), and his excellent performance as the kindly young man who trades souls with a murderous gangster in Monogram's Frankenstein-ish thriller, *The Man With Two Lives* (1942, the first film in which Norris' name was placed above the title.) In his volume, *B Movies,* author Don Miller heaped praise on the latter movie, calling it a "tingly little number." He went on to describe Norris as "a steady performer usually kept under wraps, but had an opportunity here and made the most of it." [219]

By the early 1940's, the thrice-divorced Edward Norris had scaled back on his drinking, and was busy re-establishing his reputation as a ladies man. On July 19, 1942, he surprised many Hollywood insiders by marrying 21-year-old starlet, Mickey June Satterlee (the sister of Peggy Satterlee, the plaintiff in the infamous Errol Flynn rape trial), in Tempe, Arizona. Marriage #4 would have a very short

Norris played a young city slicker who becomes the owner of a ranch in Republic's *Back in the Saddle* (1941), the first of two films he made with renowned singing cowboy Gene Autry.

Mr. Norris told the author he enjoyed his role as a thrill killer in Monogram's unusual melodrama, *The Man With Two Lives* (1942), the first film in which he received star billing.

run. Just one month later, the couple separated, and were divorced in September.[220] In the months that followed, gossip columnists linked Norris with some of the screen's most glamourous women including Hedy Lamarr, Betty Hutton, and Joan Crawford. Movie magazines also featured stories of him enjoying his growing list of hobbies including hunting, fishing, airplanes, and motorcycles. His passion for the latter, led to personal friendships with many of Hollywood's biggest male stars like Clark Gable, Gary Cooper, and Randolph Scott who shared his interest.

Norris' film career began looking up in 1945, when he accepted roles in two entertaining second features for Universal: the musical comedy, *Penthouse Rhythm*, and the action adventure serial, *Jungle Queen* with young Ruth Roman. So impressed was the studio, they drew up a long term contract which might have restored some of the luster to Norris' tarnished career, but tore it up near the end of production on *Jungle Queen* when Norris was blamed for production delays and problems on the set.[221] Ever resilient, the 35-year-old actor bounced back in 1946, with three more showy low budget movie appearances: as an innocent man indicted for the murder of his wife in RKO's *The Truth About Murder*, an ill-fated blackmailer in Republic's entertaining whodunit, *Murder in the Music Hall*, and as a bloodthirsty killer in Monogram's noir thriller, *Decoy*. The latter would be one of Norris' best roles of the 1940's decade. The grim tale of a heartless woman (portrayed by British actress, Jean Gillie), and her bloody quest for buried loot, the film's fast pace, stylistic direction, ingenious photography, and exceptional acting made it a classic of the genre. Especially memorable is a scene in which she murders boyfriend Norris by running over him again and again as he attempts to change a tire. Although dutifully noting inconsistencies in the plot, critics were rightfully impressed. "It's not plausible but it doesn't have to be," said *Variety*, "For some canny direction (by Jack Bernhard), whips *Decoy* along at a jet-propelled pace so fast that the customers can't take time out for wondering." Receiving his best reviews in years, once again Ed Norris briefly envisioned bigger and better projects, but none materialized. By 1947, he was back making more programmers most of which were not without merit, but never close to re-establishing his career.

Some of his final 15 film performances (1947-55), would be

Norris found himself in trouble on the set of Universal's serial, *Jungle Queen* (1945). Disagreements and disruptions during the filming led the studio to cancel the long-term contract they had drawn up for him.

among his most interesting. He was framed for the murder of his wealthy father in the western, *Mysterious Desperado* (RKO, 1949), a love-struck French Canadian trapper in Monogram's rough and tumble action adventure, *The Wolf Hunters* (1949), and a young doctor menaced by bandits in one of Gene Autry's best latter films, *The Blazing Sun* (Columbia, 1950). Especially convincing was Norris' portrayal of a reporter who aids authorities in solving multiple crimes in the mystery, *Heartaches* (PRC, 1947), costarring the future Mrs. Norris, lovely B-movie queen, Sheila Ryan, whom he wed on March 27, 1947. His fifth and final marriage would last until 1950.[222]

That same year, Edward's friend, Warner Bros. low budget unit producer, Brian Foy hired him for small yet significant parts in a series of motion pictures. Although not top drawer productions, each was aided by expert casts, and spirited direction which elevated them to B+. As a cruel guard in the action-packed melodrama, *Inside*

The mystery, *Heartaches* (PRC, 1947) was notable to Mr. Norris, not only because it gave him a good role, but it paired him with his future bride, beautiful low budget movie actress, Sheila Ryan.

the Walls of Folsom Prison (1951), (filmed on location), a communist thug in the notorious red-baiting thriller, *I Was a Communist for the F.B.I.* (1951), and a seasoned infantry sergeant marching across Normandy in the War World II drama, *Breakthrough* (1950), Norris proved his mettle managing to stand out despite the brevity of his time onscreen. Perhaps his best film of the 1950's decade, was the exploitative yet entertaining shocker, *Highway 301*. As a member of a gang of hoods and killers, Norris won critical praise as did the film for its presentation of its subject matter from a criminal's perspective.

Unfortunately, Norris' final film work was unremarkable. He was wasted in the tiny role of a Texas farmer who dies defending the titled fortress in *The Man From Alamo* (Universal, 1953), and as a cold-blooded wife-killer in the weakly scripted, *Murder Without Tears* (Allied Artist, 1953). In 1955, actor turned first time director, Burt Lancaster hired Norris (as a last minute replacement for Ian Keith), for a small role in his frontier adventure, *The Kentuckian* (United Artists).

In the wonderful world of 1940's and 1950's Hollywood movies, bad guys always got their just desserts, including communists like Edward Norris and character actor, David MacMahon in Warner Bros.' *I Was a Communist For the F.B.I.* (1951).

It would be Norris' last motion picture. Increasingly disillusioned with moviemaking, the still youthful looking 44-year-old veteran of 70+ films decided to call it quits. He told the author:

"You had to be made of steel to withstand the disappointments and the lies. I can't tell you how many times I'd call my agent and tell him I'd been talking to a producer at a party and he'd say, 'Have your agent call me. I've got just the right part for you.' And they were lying!" [223]

He didn't quit acting however. Early on, Norris recognized the potential of television. In 1947, he made his small screen debut on a *Fireside Theater* episode, *The Phantom Rickshaw*. During the 1950's, he would do several guest starring roles on a variety of popular series including: *Adventures of Wild Bill Hickok*, *Pony Express*, and four episodes of the memorable *Perry Mason*.

Norris formally retired from show business in the early 1960's, to devote more time to his expanding list of hobbies which now included gun and classic car collections. Unlike many of his contemporaries, he was financially secure. If he had made major mistakes regarding his film career and love life, Edward Norris had also made wise decisions along the way. One of the wisest, was to invest his earnings in ocean-front real estate which would provide him with plenty of income. In 1948, he sold his home in Beverly Hills, and purchased ocean-front property in Malibu. In 1972, he bought a large ranch in northern Washington, 1 1/2 miles from the Canadian border.[224]

Three years later, his motorcycling hobby lead to a chance meeting with lovely California divorcee, Jeanne Dean. The two would soon become inseparable companions, and begin a long lasting friendship and romantic relationship Norris had been looking for all his life. During the next 18 years, they would share each others' lives, and interests, including Jeanne's passion for raising and breeding horses: prize winning Peruvian Pasos. In the decades which followed, Edward and Jeanne would win several national championships and divide their time between her Cliffside Drive home and his properties.[225]

In 1978, a firestorm destroyed Norris' Malibu home and all its contents including a Galwing Mercedes (valued in excess of $900,000), convertible sedan Mercedes, a Rolls Royce, and all his prized antique guns, not to mention a lifelong collection of irreplaceable personal and career memorabilia. It was a terrible blow to the avid hobbyist who eventually rebuilt the house and gave it to his son, Edward Jr. who moved his family (which included a wife and two children), from Baltimore. As bad as it was, the fire was minor in comparison to the two body blows Norris would suffer 15 years later. In the fall of 1993, he lost his beloved Jeanne, and in February 1994, his only son succumbed to respiratory complications and kidney failure.[226]

In 1997, Mr. Norris abandoned the Los Angeles area, and purchased an ocean-front home in northern California along with 5000 acres. Today, in 2001, he lives there with his dogs, his horses, and many grand remembrances. At 89, he still rides and enjoys traversing his land on horseback. It's a safe bet that on occasion, as he rides around his beautiful property inhaling the smog free air, he harks back to another time and place, and relives some of those disappointing yet ultimately wonderful years amid the starlit galaxy of the city of dreams. All the cinematic crime sprees, love scenes, tyrannical directors, the friendships and heartbreaks, those nights on the town with Joan Crawford, the

Two female fans meet and pose for pictures with Edward Norris (second from left), and actor, Aldo Ray (far right) in 1980.

cycling trips with his pal Clark — all unforgettable memories from a long life well lived.

A retrospective analysis of Edward Norris' film career would have to include adjectives like disappointing, unfulfilled, and unrealized. Like so many before and after him, a gifted youngster had migrated to Hollywood all full of enthusiasm and idealism only to become heartbroken, disillusioned, and outraged by the injustice, and politics so prevalent in the moviemaking world. When things began to sour (after a very promising start), the naive young Norris expressed his outrage by rebelling against the very people who had the power to make or break his career. It was a costly error. In a revealing interview with author Richard Lamparski in 1976, Mr. Norris accepted responsibility for many of his difficulties. "I've lived long enough," he said, "to see that most of what happened was my own fault. I had the wrong agent, the wrong advice, and the wrong attitude." [227]

While all that maybe true, Edward Norris can still look back on his fruitful and prodigious career with great pride. Learning from his mistakes, he redeemed himself though hard work, and perseverance. Instead of pulling up stakes when his career faltered, he held on to his dream and continued to do what he loved so much, making motion pictures. By the 1940's, he was making mostly program pictures, but still perfecting his craft. None of his latter films were nominated for Oscars, none were considered great motion pictures, but many if not most were fast-paced, and engrossing, and all were elevated by the presence of a dedicated professional actor named Edward Norris.

PART II

"CONFESSIONS OF A CINEMATIC BABY FACE GANGSTER: AN INTERVIEW WITH EDWARD NORRIS"

A combination of talent, good looks, and a stroke of good fortune landed hopeful young actor Edward Norris in the film capital in the early 1930's. His goal: to become a great romantic leading man in the world of film. Although sadly, things didn't work out as planned, and he was eventually exiled to Hollywood's poverty row, B movie aficiandos are grateful. In a career spanning 30+ years and over 70 films, the gifted actor proved his talent and versatility with credible characterizations which ran the gamut between arch villains and super heroes. Today he is best known for his villainous roles, most especially for playing gangsters.

In Part II, we hear the story from the man who lived it. In the following interview excerpts, filmdom's "baby-faced gangster" turns "states evidence," and recalls his unique life and career in his own words. At 89, still full of enthusiasm and good humor, Edward Norris relates some of the more interesting aspects of a life (on and off screen), which can best be described as remarkable.

DAN: Let me begin by thanking you so much for your time, and asking you to relate the unique story of your discovery.

EDWARD NORRIS: *I was married when I was sixteen to a debutante, a doctor's daughter. My son was born when I was 17. The marriage lasted only 2 1/2 years because I didn't have any real visible means of support. I was very young — too young! When we separated, I came out to visit my mother, now divorced and living in Coronado, California. I was on the beach in Coronado one day, when my dog got into a fight with another dog. I was pulling them apart when a man walked over and helped me. He said, "I'd like to buy your dog. I like the way he fights. I like his guts and everything about him." I said, "He's not for sale." And he said, "If you ever change your mind, here's my card. I'm staying at the Coronado Hotel now, but I'm from Hollywood." When I got home, I told my mother. She looked at the card and said, "Why, this is William Wellman, the big Hollywood director." She advised me to rethink getting rid of my dog! (laughter) So I did, and went over and told him I'd changed my mind. He wrote me out a note to his assistant, Charlie Barton and told him to send me over to Western Costume to get fitted to see if Buddy Rogers' uniform would fit me.*

DAN: So, he immediately wanted to put you in a film?

EDWARD NORRIS: *Buddy Rogers and I were lookalikes. They had to redo a scene with Clara Bow in Wings. It was the one at the Parisian Hotel with Buddy lying on the bed passed out. She comes in, takes the locket out from his tunic, and the wrong girl's picture is in it, not hers. I just had to lie on the bed, and say nothing. Wellman couldn't get Buddy because he was off doing a picture with Mary Pickford called, My Best Girl, so when he saw me, he saw an opportunity to get the picture wound up. And it changed my life!*

DAN: I bet you were a bit intimidated doing a scene with Clara Bow, who was a very big star.

EDWARD NORRIS: *Oh my god! Scared to death! She was a big star! Of course, Wings was a silent. They had music on stage to make her cry, sorrowful, soulful music. There were so many things happening. When it was over, naturally, I wanted to continue, but Wellman told me, "You need experience. The only way you're going to get it, is to go back East, and get into a stock company and learn your trade. Then come back, and I'll give you a hand." So I returned to Philadelphia, and got into stock companies there and in Cape May, New Jersey. When I came back West in 1933, I lived with five guys at the Mountain*

View Inn on Hollywood Boulevard when they had the big earthquake on my birthday, March 10, 1933. All of us went down and worked as cooks for the rescue squads.

DAN: Eventually you found work on the stage.

EDWARD NORRIS: Yes, I got a job in a show in Los Angeles called, Doomsday Circus. One night, Rouben Mamoulian came back stage and signed me to a personal contract. By this time, I was living with a ballet dancer who was being kept by a story editor at Goldwyn. Mamoulian sent me to Akim Tamiroff who was just getting started in Hollywood as a character actor after being with the Moscow Art Theater for years. He was my instructor. He had me opening a door and greeting a friend I hadn't seen 20 times. He would say, "No, you're not telling the truth. I don't believe you. Do it again." I would finally get so exasperated, I'd say, "I'm never coming back!" And he'd say, "I'll see you at ten in the morning. Don't be late." (laughter) And I was there! All the Russian colony were watching my progress. I was more or less their protégé. In the beginning, they were doing it because of my friend, Nadia, but when they saw some ability, they got interested.

DAN: You certainly had a first rate start in films.

EDWARD NORRIS: When it came time to produce Queen Christina in 1933, which Mamoulian directed, they couldn't get a leading man to play opposite Garbo because Fredric March was tied up. They tried Laurence Olivier, but he couldn't get rid of his English accent to play a Spanish nobleman. I actually made a test for the lead with Garbo because Mamoulian wanted the producers to see what the male costumes looked like before the camera in color. They put a beard on me and a moustache, long hair, everything. I was so scared that she tried to quiet me down. Of course, my inexperience, and fright showed up in the test, but the producers were interested. They ended up writing a juvenile role for me: a young man in love with Garbo's lady-in-waiting. That's what Mamoulian had wanted for me.

DAN: You've told me how scared you were during Queen Christina of both the camera and the cast.

EDWARD NORRIS: Oh yes! Mamoulian said, "I'm going to get you over this." He put me with John Gilbert and Garbo every day holding the script for them, so when they rehearsed, I was right with them. I eventually got over my fear. Being with them that much, I had no fear of anyone after that!

DAN: I must ask you the obvious. How was Miss Garbo to work with, and how did she get along with Mamoulian?

EDWARD NORRIS: She was very friendly to me, a very hardworking, thorough actress, easy to work with, just so sincere and pleasant to even the smallest people on the set. She took direction beautifully. Every now and then, she made some suggestions, but Mamoulian worked well with her. In fact, he fell in love with her.

DAN: I have to assume your appearance in a prestige picture like Queen Christina must have helped your career.

EDWARD NORRIS: Yes, MGM signed me afterwards. They signed me for five years with six-month options. Bob Taylor and I signed the same year. Eventually, they kept me on as a threat to him, so he would behave. It made me feel terrible. He was given the first Crime Does Not Pay short, and I did the second.

DAN: Did MGM groom you for stardom?

EDWARD NORRIS: Yes. They had a physical education director who kept us busy, and a dramatic coach who had us go to every play in town and write a review of it. They gave you small parts because they figured you were learning from any director you worked with. Bob Taylor and I both started at $35 a week. Gosh, the chorus girls were getting $66! I got $35 a week for Queen Christina! (laughter) It's amazing! Finally, my salary got to be $100 a week after two years. When I was loaned out, they pocketed the difference. It was pretty bad! (laughter)

DAN: In 1935, you got your first big break on loan to 20th Century Fox for a melodrama called, Show Them No Mercy.

EDWARD NORRIS: George Marshall was directing. God bless him! He was my hero, a great guy! I made a test for him, and he asked for me, saying, "I want this guy because I can do anything with him. He takes direction beautifully." So MGM said, "Go ahead, he's yours, but remember he's a greenhorn."

DAN: Do you recall any particular anecdotes from the filming?

EDWARD NORRIS: I remember Cesar Romero was playing the head gangster. During my days as a reporter, I had been assigned to cover the stage production of Show Them No Mercy, and I did an interview and story on Romero. All of a sudden, here we were in a picture together. He was basically a professional dancer and a very good one. I also remember how much he hated horses, and how funny it was they had him in the Cisco Kid series. My leading lady, Rochelle Hudson was wonderful to work with, very sincere. She was being chased around by Zanuck. One day, Zanuck's messenger came to tell her he wanted to see her after work. She said, "Tell him no, I'm going home." She was fighting that all during the production.

DAN: Your exceptional reviews for the film must have raised your hopes and expectations.

EDWARD NORRIS: Show Them No Mercy really did me a lot of good, but MGM responded by giving me bit roles. Every time I would get a good role on loan, they would give me a walk-on to reprimand me. To not appreciate what you had accomplished on another lot! It was a big comedown.

DAN: Another of your early loan outs was The Magnificent Brute with Victor McLaglen.

EDWARD NORRIS: That was my first job at Universal. McLaglen was a very nice guy, but a rebel. He had a bad attitude, and could get you into trouble by telling you not to pay attention. "Make 'em wait! To hell with them! They can't hurt ya!" he'd say. He was a heavy drinker. The film was about a steel foundry, an interesting story of hard work. I played the young leading man who falls into molten steel! (laughter) I recall doing the scene. They had a mattress for me to fall on out of the camera. That's when this guy came up to me and told me I was taking money out of his pockets. He said, "I'm the stunt man on this picture and I'm supposed to do that." Universal had let me do it to save $150!

DAN: In 1937, you did one of my all-time favorite films, They Won't Forget on loan to Warner Bros.

EDWARD NORRIS: It makes me happy to hear you say that because it was certainly something that all of us dreamed about. It was a very brave film, the best picture I ever made! It still holds up. I've shown it to several people lately, and it's amazing, even the dialogue is modern. It could be re-released today. There's a whole new generation of kids growing up now who are not familiar with it.

DAN: How did you secure such an important role?

EDWARD NORRIS: Everyone in town tested including Jimmy Stewart, Ray Milland, and Tyrone Power. I got it because Mervyn (LeRoy) could see he could change me. He said, "This guy is putty in my hands. I can do anything with him." My test turned out just as good as the scene in the picture. He told me it was the best test made.

DAN: As you know, the film was adapted from Ward Greene's novel based on the real life trial of a Jewish man in Atlanta. Did you study the Leo Frank case in preparation for the role?

EDWARD NORRIS: Oh yes! I read all about the case. As a matter of fact, the book was owned by Universal who were afraid to make it. Mervyn had to make it because his last two pictures for Warner Bros. had bombed, and Jack Warner was going to cut him off. During the filming, he was busy making a deal with MGM for his services. They Won't Forget was his last Warner Bros. picture. Ironically, he was going to MGM while I was trying to get out of my MGM contract. I was giving them some problems by then because they were stepping on me. Bob Taylor was moving real fast. I was snapping at his heels for a while, but I couldn't catch him. He was playing politics upstairs, and I wasn't. That was one of the biggest mistakes I made.

DAN: What was your impression of LeRoy and his approach to filmmaking?

EDWARD NORRIS: He had wonderful ideas, but he let actors work it out. If they couldn't, then he'd take over and show you how. The only time we had an argument on the picture was the scene where I was on the stand, telling the jury what I think. He thought I had underplayed it. He didn't want me to be humble. The line of dialogue was something like, "I'm not afraid to die, but it seems like such a waste." He wanted me to throw the dialogue at the jury, so it would make the court reporter, Allyn Joslyn say, "Oh my god, he just dug his own grave!" I didn't understand what Mervyn was trying to do. When I finally saw the rushes two days later, I realized he was right. I told him I was sorry as hell, and I'd pay for the retake. He told me I didn't have to, but asked me if I would do it his way. So we did, because I could see there was a weakness in the delivery.

DAN: I know you share my enthusiasm for your leading lady, Gloria Dickson.

EDWARD NORRIS: I liked her so much! There was a warmth and friendliness about her. It was like we had known one another all our lives. We had a wonderful rapport. She had a beautiful scene at the end of the film in which she confronted Rains and Joslyn. She was so sincere in what she did, you believed what she was saying! She was so good, she made me look good!

DAN: There's a wonderful moment in the film when they have pronounced your sentence, the camera captures a tear in your eye, and you look back at her to see that's she's ok. Then, she gets up and faces the voracious crowd.

EDWARD NORRIS: Ah yes! There was such a warmth there! LeRoy pretty much let us play our scenes the way we wanted because he could sense there was an intimacy between the two of us that worked so beautifully. He'd say, "I'm going to make another take just for safety's sake in case there's something wrong with the camera. It has nothing to do with you kids. Do it the way you just did."

DAN: *The film was a great critical success, but box office receipts were only modest.*

EDWARD NORRIS: I was so disappointed they wouldn't book it in the South. Warner Bros. thought if they could get one theater south of the Mason/Dixon line to book it, it would be railroaded out of town, and we would have gotten national publicity. But they wouldn't, because they didn't have the guts. And Warner Bros. publicity department didn't get behind it.

DAN: *A few months prior to winning your classic lead role in* They Won't Forget, *you also had the good fortune to meet your future wife, lovely Ann Sheridan. Tell me about your first date.*

EDWARD NORRIS: I took Ann to the President's Ball. Alice Faye and I were running around together at the time, and I was supposed to sit at the MGM table, and she at the 20th Century Fox. The MGM publicity department kept asking me who I was bringing. I said I had met a girl who was under contract to Paramount who had just done a very bad picture called Car 99. So, out of the clear blue sky, I called her and asked her to the ball. She said, "Who am I talking to?" I said, "Don't you remember, I met you in the lobby of this hotel in Hollywood near the Knickerbocker." And she eventually agreed to go with me. I'll never forget how astounded I was when I saw how beautiful she looked when she came down the stairs in a black outfit with that red hair!!!

DAN: *You were quite influential in her career in the beginning, weren't you?*

EDWARD NORRIS: Yes. During the time we were dating, I tried to get MGM to sign her, but they wouldn't. I was making the test for They Won't Forget at Warner Bros., and I happened to mention that we were going to be married. Warner Bros. said, "How would she like to make a test with you?" So we did, and it was a good one. She was excellent. We were living together when she made the test for Angels With Dirty Faces. I rehearsed with her prior to it. She blew up at me time and again. I got her so upset she did it perfect. I told her, "Now, do it just that way tomorrow." (laughter) The actual test was shot over my shoulder. The projectionist called the next night, and told us the old man had him run it three times.

DAN: Two questions. What was it about Ann you found so personally appealing? What was your opinion of her as an actress?

EDWARD NORRIS: She was really great! She had a wonderful sense of humor, was a great storyteller, loved limericks and jokes. She was light-hearted and down to earth, a real breath of sunshine. Everyone liked her. Annie was scared of the camera. I tried to help her get over it in every way. She finally loosened up later when she did things like I Was a Male War Bride, but back when we were married, she used to walk around the set with a bottle of coke which was really rum in a coke bottle. She was very nervous and upset. I said, "Honey, they're going to catch you." But they never did. She used to be able to drink me under the table. It was unbelievable what she could consume, and you would never know it. I think she probably got over it as time went on. I mean, who could handle all that and still do their work? I'm sure she must have quit.

DAN: Your marriage broke up in 1938, and you were divorced in 1939.

EDWARD NORRIS: I was brokenhearted when our marriage broke up. It was a tragic thing for me. My career was going down hill, while hers was going up, but we remained friends. When I was doing The Lady in Question with Rita Hayworth, Rita mentioned she was going to make a film which had been scheduled for Ann because Warner Bros. had suspended Sheridan. So I called Annie and told her what I knew, and that she better stop her agent from doing what he was doing or Warner Bros. would start borrowing Rita for all her scripts. Under the circumstances, I still tried to protect her, although she wasn't my wife anymore.

DAN: You've told me you saw her again in the early 1950's, and kept track of her up until the end of her life.

EDWARD NORRIS: When I was doing The Man From the Alamo, Ann saw me in the commissary at Universal. She through her arms around me, and gave me a big kiss in front of everybody, and made me sit down and talk with her. Everyone was trying to hear what we were saying! (laughter) Her hairdresser and I stayed friends, and she kept me informed how Ann was getting along. At the end of her life when she had the cancer during the TV series, Pistols and Petticoats, they had to carry her off and on the set. It was terrible. I wanted to be with her when she died, but she was married to Scott McKay. It broke my heart when I heard of her passing. She was such a great gal, the love of my life!

DAN: You've mentioned your career downturn and your problems with MGM. What was the nature of your difficulties?

EDWARD NORRIS: At the end of my association with the studio, we had a falling out. Every time they would send me out on loan to another studio, I'd be playing the lead role, and I'd come back, and they'd give me a walk-on part of a bellhop with one or two lines. It was degrading and broke my spirit. It was heartbreaking for an ambitious kid. I couldn't understand why I was being destroyed. I found out later, it was because they really had no investment in me at the salary I was receiving.

DAN: Did you voice your concerns?

EDWARD NORRIS: Well, I complained to Abe Lasfogle the head of the William Morris office. They were my agents. He said there was very little he could do because they had a big problem on their hands at the moment, John Barrymore. They just couldn't sober him up. Naturally, his salary was 100 times that of mine, and as a result, he commanded all their attention. I also voiced my opinion in my own home, and it was carried back to Metro by people I thought were my friends. I found out that Zanuck had tried to buy my contract twice. I finally left the William Morris Agency in 1937.

DAN: Under the circumstances, how did you land such a prominent role in a big budget, prestige picture, like Boys Town?

EDWARD NORRIS: I wasn't the first choice. Donald Barry was to have the role. When he left, they called me in to reshoot all his scenes. I made it under duress. I can remember very well when one of the casting people called me onto the set. I told them I wasn't coming back to the studio again. He said, "You've got to come. It's an emergency! You have an opportunity to clear the slate, to put yourself back on top again. This is a big moment!" I adamantly refused, but I told him I'd meet him at this bar across the street. I was drinking heavily then. He said that MGM had a black line through my name, and this would take it away. He eventually talked me into it, and asked me to come and meet the director. I had been on a two-week bender and was a mess: unshaven in a dirty old white suit. When I met Norman Taurog at the studio, he asked me if I would mind reading a part of the script. And I said, "Yes, I would. There's a lot of film on me here. What is all of this cold reading business?" I was really teed off! . . . So, he put a light on this phone booth and asked if I'd mind rehearsing this scene. I looked at it, and told him I didn't need to rehearse it. It was a phone conversation saying to the police department, there was a boy lying wounded near a church and gave the church address. Anyway, Taurog said, "Roll em!" And we did it in one take! (laughter) It was one of those times when you'd pick up a full day's work in ten minutes. After that, we did a couple other scenes. Taurog later called Mayer wondering why he was keeping me at home. He told him I had saved Metro thousands of dollars in retakes in this one day, and asked Mayer to come down and watch me the next. So they all came down. It was a scene with Spencer Tracy in which I'm telling him why I want him to take my brother to Boys Town. When we rehearsed it, Spencer played the scene on an even keel and I played it the same way, but when we shot it, he played it differently, underplaying it like he did in all of his movies. Yee gods, the scene was deadly! So I stopped right in the middle. (laughter) I remember Taurog saying, "What's the matter? Why did you stop?" (laughter) I replied, "Because Mr. Tracy rehearses it one way, and plays it another on the take." Well, all the executives walked out. They said, "Uh oh, there he goes again!!" (laughter) They didn't see the next take with me playing it way up and Spencer under the table. It turned out well. But the incident buried me with the executives.

DAN: What did Tracy do when you stopped the scene? (laughter)

EDWARD NORRIS: (laughter) He wasn't angry at all. He said, "I just hope you can get away with this. I don't think you will. They're death on that attitude of yours." I said, "As far as I'm concerned, I care about the picture not the company!"

DAN: What was your opinion of your costars Tracy and Rooney?

EDWARD NORRIS: I thought Spencer was very natural, almost to the point of dropping the scene, almost to the point that it dives. It was hard for the other actors. I enjoyed working with Mickey. He was an amazing actor who could stand outside the soundstage, telling jokes and laughing uproariously, and then turn on the tears and do a very dramatic scene.

DAN: Your reviews for Boys Town were uniformly excellent. I would assume they boosted your spirits?

EDWARD NORRIS: Yes, but after I completed the film, I left MGM. They didn't pick up my option, but I wouldn't have signed with them even if they had wanted to. I wanted to be active, not just sit on a list. So I signed with 20th Century Fox in 1938, but it was too late there. When Zanuck originally wanted to buy my contract, he had scripts ready for me like Blood and Sand. When he couldn't buy it, he developed Tyrone Power who got all the stories he had lined up for me.

DAN: A cruel twist of fate, but you did do some excellent work (mostly in character roles) in some interesting pictures during your Fox years. Let me mention a few beginning with Tailspin starring one of your old girlfriends.

EDWARD NORRIS: That was about the Powderpuff Derby. I was paired off with Nancy Kelly. My ex-love, Alice Faye was the star. What a lovely girl she was! Very shy, but a lovely person to be with. I called her, "Cuddles," and we dated for a while. We got to know each other well, and had a lot of fun. We would sit up in the balcony at the Pantages, or go out to Carpenter's Drive-in and have a hamburger. I didn't think she was the greatest actress because she had such a fear of the camera, but when she was singing, she was wonderful. I had a lot of respect for her.

DAN: What was your opinion of the film's other star, Constance Bennett, and its director, Roy Del Ruth?

EDWARD NORRIS: (laughter) Miss Bennett was pretty rough on everybody! Domineering! She was polite, but always wanted things her way. She made a lot of demands. For instance, she didn't think the gaffer was putting the right light on her. She complained a lot to show off. Del Ruth rehearsed with film. Take after take after take! We all kept wondering why. With Paul Manz doing all the airplane stunts, the film was impressive and expressive, but just didn't gel. I don't know why. They certainly took enough time! (laughter) As I recall, we were weeks late with it and Zanuck was upset, but Del Ruth just kept shooting and shooting. It drove us crazy!

DAN: Another of your Fox films was the The Gorilla starring the Ritz Brothers directed by the legendary, Allan Dwan.

EDWARD NORRIS: That one was harrowing! The brothers had a habit of taking all the good dialogue and switching it away from you to them. When they got through with the script, there was nothing left for Anita Louise and I to do. They were always calling their bookies, playing the horses. Half the time, one of them was on the phone. Dwan tried to keep a tight reign, but it was difficult. You'd prepare a scene and go to the studio, and it was gone when you got there. Scary!

DAN: You made two Grade A pictures with two big stars during this period, The Lady in Question with Rita Hayworth and Dr. Erlich's Magic Bullet with Edward G. Robinson. Any anecdotes?

EDWARD NORRIS: Rita was very nice, very quiet, seemingly aloof. The aloofness was nothing but shyness. She would just sit with her *knitting, always quiet and pleasant, but you always felt like maybe you were intruding on her inner thoughts. You'd think twice before plunking down in the chair beside her and discussing the script. Robinson basically wanted to direct Dr. Erlich. He would tell you how to do your lines. The film's director, William Dieterle, with his white gloves (laughter), was fine, but gave his cameramen and cast some impossible things to do like closing doors behind you. You had to have a third arm, and if you didn't get it right, it was all your fault. Many directors did not appreciate what actors had to do. There were certain things that were very unnatural and you looked unnatural doing them.*

DAN: *Not long after you left Fox, World War II broke out, and you enlisted in the military, yet you still continued making films.*

EDWARD NORRIS: *Yes, I was a flight instructor for the Army Air Corps during the war. I continued making films by getting someone else to fly my cadets while I was gone for ten days to two weeks to work on the B pictures I was doing. I found out what kind of scotch my c.o. liked, and I would always bring him a case. And he let me get away to do the films which kept me in walking-around money. (laughter)*

DAN: *That brings me to the subject of the B movies you began making during the war. What I admired most about you, besides your ability, was your tenacity. You kept making films even when your career was not progressing. What kept you going?*

EDWARD NORRIS: *I kept thinking that one of these days, one of the pictures would be a big hit. I kept my hope alive. I never let down, or considered giving a B picture a lesser effort. I gave them all my best. Phil Rosen was a B movie director who kept requesting me because he said I elevated his pictures. I was a fast study, and he could change the dialogue on me.*

DAN: *What was your opinion of B movies? Did you find anything artistic about the process, or was it just a way to make enough money to survive?*

EDWARD NORRIS: *I really thought some of the B pictures were better than the A's, because the B's were never boring. They moved, and the kids loved all the cops and robbers, all the action. The B picture directors were mostly action directors. Some of the B's had great stories, but unfortunately, not enough money. It's surprising how well some of them turned out though.*

DAN: Tell me about making B movies in the 1940's. The sets must have been pressure cookers!

EDWARD NORRIS: *Absolutely! (laughter) Gable and Coop both told me, "I don't know how you guys do it!" What it took them three months to do, we would do in three days. Half the time, the stand-in was sitting there watching because I wanted to rehearse. I'd often ask the director, "Can't we rehearse this while they're lighting it up?" That way we got to run the lines. The pressure was unbelievable! Every one was looking to blame someone if there were any delays. The production office didn't care how good it was as long as the picture came in on time. In a lot of cases, it worked to the actors' favor because, if the director thought you were doing it ok, he would let you do it the way you wanted to avoid delays. (laughter) There were some really excellent B movie directors like Phil Rosen, Oliver Drake, and Lew Landers. I admired their speed technique. They listened to the actors, and respected them. They would take suggestions, anything to help a scene.*

DAN: By the time you started making all the programmers, your screen image had gone through a transformation from romantic hero to villain.

EDWARD NORRIS: *Yes, they forced me into being a baby-faced gangster. I was being pulled from studio to studio doing that type of role. In the beginning, I enjoyed the gangster parts and tried to develop my own style. The villains were often times more interesting and memorable. Everyone remembers the guy they love to hate, but eventually I got upset being typecast. I wanted to do all kinds of characters and eventually, started turning the gangster roles down.*

DAN: Let me elicit your reaction and comments regarding a few

of the 26 films you made between 1941 to 1945. Let's begin with the melodramatic, I Live on Danger, a Pine Thomas production with Chester Morris and Jean Parker.

EDWARD NORRIS: *I was Jean's brother in that one, jailed on false charges. I remember Jean as a joy, easy to get along with. Chester was a hypochondriac, always on the verge of serious illness. As for Pine and Thomas, the "Dollar Bills," they were always good natured on the set. They took a great interest in guiding the film. They were very successful, and kept Paramount afloat in bad times.*

DAN: *You did one A-picture during this period, The Lady Has Plans with Ray Milland and Paulette Goddard.*

EDWARD NORRIS: *I played Milland's sidekick. The director Sidney Lanfield, had a reputation as a rough guy. The set was not a very happy place. He was always looking for somebody to blame for something. He would pick out people who were unable to talk back, like little old ladies in bit roles, and was merciless to them. He was trying to show everyone who was boss. I avoided getting into an altercation with him, but I wanted to. I just kept my cool till the job was over. Milland was very fine. I thought he was very smooth, easy going, knew his work, a real professional. Paulette was trying to have fun. She was a neighbor of mine and involved with Chaplin at the time. I liked her, but didn't think much of her as an actress. I thought she was listening to too many people.*

DAN: *In 1942, you did one of your most fondly remembered B pictures, The Man With Two Lives for Monogram.*

EDWARD NORRIS: *That was the first time I got star billing. It was an interesting story. I played the son of a wealthy businessman who changed clothes and became a leader of a gang of warehouse thieves after dark. I remember Phil Rosen, the director, really enjoyed making a movie about a leading man who was a thrill killer at night. If they had spent some money on that one, and put in a good supporting cast, it could have been a very good film.*

DAN: How about The Mystery of Marie Roget, starring Maria Montez and your good friend, Patric Knowles?

EDWARD NORRIS: *Miss Montez was very very strange! There were some complaints about her on the set, but I found her easy to get along with. I met my wonderful friend, Pat Knowles while making Marie Roget, and we were great pals from that time on. He was a very sincere man and very funny. Enid, his wife, gave up her career for him. She was doing well in London, but quit and came over here to be with him and raise their two children. She stayed with him through it all, and tried to keep him from over indulgence. He had a problem with the bottle. I remember him telling me after I quit drinking, "Don't ever think of coming back and doing a picture again. It's all changed. You can't take your car on the lot anymore. You don't have a dressing room of your own. The pressure is horrible. The glory days are gone." Pat thought his big break would come in Ivy with Joan Fontaine, but there was something very wrong with the film, and the scenes fell flat. It was too bad! He put so much hope in that one. Of course, when they're bad, the big ones can do you more harm because of all the investment. Ivy certainly had a very bad impact on Pat's career.*

DAN: Speaking of bad impacts, after Marie Roget, you did The Sultan's Daughter with the one and only Ann Corio. (laughter)

EDWARD NORRIS: *Oh boy!! (much laughter) Ann was a stripper, and had a great figure. The problem was she never learned how to act. Lindsay Parsons, who was a producer at Monogram, kept calling me in for pictures. I didn't really want to do Sultan's Daughter, but I did it for him. I wonder where Ann Corio is today?*

DAN: Maybe she's a Sultan's daughter! (much laughter) On a serious note, in 1945, after the war, you almost signed with Universal. What happened?

EDWARD NORRIS: *They had the contract all ready, but tore it up. I was doing the serial, Jungle Queen with Ruth Roman. The temperature was 102 degrees on the back lot. I was not getting along with the assistant director because there was no air conditioning in my tent on the lot. So I told him if they were not going to use me in the next shot, to call me in my dressing room (which was air conditioned), and I'd be right over. Well, he didn't like that, and turned it in to the production office. Then, another situation arose when the cameraman and his assistant asked me if I had any, "snake bite lotion," and I told them it was under my cot in my tent. So, they had a shot, and then went to lunch and drank ale. When they returned, there was a commotion. The camera fell over, and dirt got into the aperture. All this was written up as my fault. I had "sabotaged" the company! I tried to explain I wasn't pouring it down their throats, but the fact I had it in my dressing room was the factor. Some heads had to roll because the commotion held up production. So they tore up my contract. Walter Wanger had told them he would use me in his productions. I would have had a pretty good life at Universal, but it didn't work out.*

DAN: In 1946, your career experienced a resurgence when Monogram hired you for a B movie that turned out to be a minor classic, the noir thriller, Decoy.

EDWARD NORRIS: *I turned that film down three times! Each time they offered me more. I told them I didn't want to play any more gangsters! I was finished with that black hat and gun! (laughter) But finally my agent said, "Well, what do you want to do?" I told him to ask for "something ridiculous like $2,500 a week." And Monogram paid it! So I had to do it. The film turned out very well though. It had such power, it kept you right on the edge of your chair!*

DAN: Tell me about your costar, English actress, Jean Gillie.

EDWARD NORRIS: *She was very good, the protégé of Sir John Charles Thomas, the English singer. She was famous in Britain for her work on the London stage, and had married the son of Gary Cooper's producer at Warner Bros. When she came to America, she expected to be in a Cooper film, and was very disappointed Decoy was produced at a third-rate studio with an inexperienced director, and a so-called second rate B picture leading man. (laughter) Another words, I was a terrific comedown from Gary Cooper! I could understand her attitude, but as time went on, we became friends. I found* out she liked apple jack. She and I would have apple jack in the dressing room. (laughter) After the completion of Decoy, her husband arranged a screening for Jack Warner and several other important people. When Warner came to see her, she was lying in her room, blind drunk with a broken bottle of apple jack with her clothes all in disarray. Warner turned around to her father-in-law and said, "Is this the woman you want me to make a picture with?" He didn't even bother to see the film. That's how her career started and ended. She later committed suicide by jumping in the Thames River.

DAN: Let's switch gears temporarily. The early 1940's was a busy time for you both professionally and personally. Word had it you were quite the man about town, dating some very glamourous stars including Joan Crawford.

EDWARD NORRIS: We dated when she was at Warner Bros. where she had her own unit. We had met at MGM. I would take her hunting, duck shooting north of Malibu at the Wyneeme Naval Base, and then we'd spend our evenings together. We had a lot of fun. I learned a lot from her. She was the ultimate pro! She knew lighting, photography, etc. She picked her own directors, and had the gaffer trained to be where her light should be. She once told me, 'It's tougher to stay up there (to be a big star), than it is to get there.'

DAN: You didn't see any wire coat hangers, now did you? (laughter) Just kidding!

EDWARD NORRIS: No none of the stuff that was in the book. That book was one of the most outrageous things! Defaming one of the most hardworking creative artists. She was a delightful woman with a gorgeous personality, and physically immaculate. I worshipped her! I thought she was just wonderful!

DAN: The incredibly talented and volatile Betty Hutton and gorgeous Hedy Lamarr were two more of your famous women friends.

EDWARD NORRIS: Although Betty was volatile, she was a hard worker, and very successful. I can't say enough nice things about her.

She kept promising me we would do a picture together, but it never worked out. Hedy Lamarr, in contrast was a very quiet. When I would go out with her, she would want to go to places like the Sportsman's Lodge or some little diner somewhere. I used to read German nursery rhymes to her two children. She was a very devoted mother.

DAN: You dated Crawford and Lamarr at the same time which got you into some hot water, I understand! (laughter)

EDWARD NORRIS: (laughter) Yes, the press screwed that up. They said, "He's dividing his time bicycling between dressing rooms of Joan Crawford and Hedy Lamarr." That made them furious, and they both blew up. I had a terrible time! I never could patch it up with either of them. They thought I was using them for publicity. And so it goes . . .

DAN: In 1946, you finally settled down and married lovely B movie actress, Sheila Ryan, and the two of you made a murder mystery film called, Heartaches. What was it like working with your wife on a picture?

EDWARD NORRIS: It was a lot of fun. We enjoyed it. We could rehearse at home, and we'd be all set. Sheila was a real beauty, and very good actress who never got the recognition. She looked so much like Irene Dunne, they could have played older and younger sisters. They even photographed identically. She was a hard drinker during our marriage. I tried to slow it down, but they kept slipping her drinks on the set. It was a big reason her career never took off. Word travels fast. One or two phone calls and you're a dead duck! . . . We were married for three years. Her family wanted her to stay with Howard Hughes whom she had dated previously. They thought she was wasting her time with me and kept pushing her toward Hughes. When she would come back to the house in Malibu after being with her family for the weekend, I had to deprogram her. (laughter) I finally gave up. I was fighting too many odds. All my divorces were friendly though.

DAN: Let's return to your career and discuss some of your final

films. In 1950, you did The Blazing Sun, your second picture with Gene Autry of whom you had a high opinion.

EDWARD NORRIS: *I really liked Autry. He was a very nice, friendly, easy-going guy who never made himself out to be that important. He invited all of us to come over to his place after the picture was over, and had a big party in his arena.*

DAN: *That same year, you dusted off your black hat and gun once again and made a nifty little crime thriller called, Highway 301. Were the cops and robber films difficult to make with all the action sequences?*

EDWARD NORRIS: *The action sequences were difficult only if the director didn't know what he had to have. In the B's, they would often try to insert some stock footage for the long shots. That made it difficult to match it up. The pressure was always there to get it done on time. For the fight scenes, we had to have two suits alike in case one would get torn. In a lot of the little independent pictures, we had to have our own wardrobes. I remember there were a few pictures I got because I owned 48 suits! (laughter)*

DAN: *In 1955, you filmed, The Kentuckian with Burt Lancaster.*

EDWARD NORRIS: *Harold Hecht produced and Lancaster directed. I got the part as a result of an emergency. Ian Keith was doing it, and jumped inside the bottle. They had been shooting two months on location in Owensboro, Kentucky, when Lancaster called me and asked me to take over Keith's part as a gambler on the paddle wheel steamer. I told him when I was a young actor at MGM, they sent us down to see the great Ian Keith on the stage and to write a treatise on his work. I told him, "Now you're asking me to take over his job!" He told me Keith couldn't get sober, and they were all dying to get home. He asked me to do him a favor, and said he would make it up to me, arrange to have me flown in, and fitted for costumes. So I agreed, and did the role. I came to have a reputation of being a good replacement person. "If you need it fixed, Norris can fix it!" My attitude was why didn't they pick me in the first place! Why am I second choice?*

DAN: How did you like working with Burt?

EDWARD NORRIS: Lancaster and I became good friends. He was great to work with. I'll never forget the night we finished filming. He came over to my room with this beautiful blonde and big bottle of Kentucky bourbon. He said, "This is for the two of you. We'll all have breakfast together."

DAN: That was quite a bonus! (much laughter)

EDWARD NORRIS: Yes! And he gave me two box seats to the Kentucky Derby to boot! He didn't want to go. He just wanted to get home. Burt was great!

DAN: The Kentuckian would be your last film. Why did you finally give up?

EDWARD NORRIS: Well, I finally decided the strain of being called in as a replacement was just too tough. I was very bitter about the way I was being treated. I told the agency I didn't want any more of this. I said, "Obviously, I've had it, and I'll quietly retire," which I did, although I did do some TV.

DAN: How did you occupy your time after your retirement?

EDWARD NORRIS: I stayed a long time at my ranch in Washington State. I had invested my money in beach property, the smartest thing I ever did. When I sold that off, I never spent the principle, only the interest income so I could live as I wanted, have my horses, my cars, and guns.

DAN: You did take some time away from your hobbies to get romantically involved though, didn't you? (laughter)

EDWARD NORRIS: Yes. I met Jeanne Dean over an Irish setter in 1975. I was on my motorcycle on Highway 1 and saw this setter with a broken leg beside the highway. I pulled over. His leg was badly broken so I couldn't carry him on my motorcycle. I'm standing there looking *real helpless and along comes a station wagon. I flagged it down. She stopped, got out and came over. I said, "Could you take this dog to the vet?" She said, "You're Ed Norris, aren't you? I've met you before. I'm Jeanne Dean who used to ride my horse in front of your place." I told her I remembered her gorgeous red hair. She later called, and told me that the owner of the dog had been found. We were together until her death in 1993. Jeanne got me started raising Peruvian Paso Horses. She was vitally interested in them. We won just about every show we entered.*

DAN: In 1978, you suffered the loss of your invaluable collections in a fire.

EDWARD NORRIS: I was at my ranch when the Malibu beach house burned. All my cars burned including my Galwing Mercedes. It was terrible! I couldn't believe what I found. I was building a log cabin on the river at the ranch when a friend called me, and asked, "What do you want to get out of there? The black smoke is pouring down from the mountains. Ed, what do you want to get out?! You've only got a few minutes!" I said, "My dogs and my guns." I had a beautiful collection of antique silver and gold inlaid German rifles in the attic. They all burned up. He did get my dogs out, and saved my camper. He found a footlocker in which I had my valuable papers. That was it! The eucalyptus trees carry oil. It was a firestorm with 45 mile per hour winds which creates a blowtorch. The fire captain told me it was a good thing I wasn't there because I wouldn't have survived.

DAN: You eventually rebuilt the house, and gave it to your son.

EDWARD NORRIS: He lived there with his family until he died in 1994, six months after Jeanne passed away. I have two grandchildren who live in Baltimore and four great grandchildren. In 1997, I bought a place north of San Francisco on the waterfront. It is so beautiful! I've got 5,000 acres across the road where I keep my horses. I ride all over the forests and the rivers and nine miles of ocean front. My guest house looks like its sitting in the middle of the ocean. You get the feeling when you're in it, you're in a lighthouse with the waves crashing all around. It's sensational! When I found this property, I couldn't resist it.

DAN: *Wow! What a life you've lived! So many highs and lows. Many times in our conversations you've mentioned making mistakes. Looking back with a fifty year hindsight, what do you think was the biggest mistake of your career?*

EDWARD NORRIS: After I finished a big lead for Zanuck at 20th Century Fox, MGM put me in a bit role in Small Town Girl playing a college kid with a fur coat who falls down drunk with one line. After playing in a smash picture, here I am embarrassed! I eventually blew up. I shouldn't have. I should have gone along. But I felt they were pulling me down, undoing the good things I'd done. I was eventually under suspension from MGM because I fought them. Gable later told me if he had only known, he would have stopped me because one could never fight with Loewes Inc. They could and did destroy me. I wasn't smart enough to realize you had to be a politician.

DAN: *Even though you didn't become a superstar, you were hardly a failure with a career of 70+ films including some wonderful ones like Show Them No Mercy, Boys Town, and of course, They Won't Forget, not to mention all the great B's, some of which have a cult following today.*

EDWARD NORRIS: Thank you. I'm glad I came to Hollywood, and am so happy I was part of that era. It was something you couldn't do on the stage. When the show's close and the curtain comes down, that's the end of it. But some of these classic films will live on. I just lucked out to get into two or three of them. The little features were a lot of hard work. Some had good scripts and could have been big if they'd had some production money.

DAN: *Let me conclude by thanking you again for the incredible opportunity to reminisce with you and the privilege of your friendship. In all of my interviews, I always conclude with a cliche. How would you like to be remembered?*

EDWARD NORRIS: I would like to be remembered as an actor who made the little films which carried the big boring ones. Most of the ones I did were full of action, never boring. I just hope that I am remembered *as a good carpenter, a skilled craftsman who never walked through a scene because it was a B picture. I worked hard in each one to try to lift it and make the film better. If someone doesn't do their best, the camera always reveals it. You got to know what you're doing in front of the camera!* [228]

UPDATE

Mr. Norris died unexpectedly at his home in Fort Bragg, California on December 18, 2002. He was 91 years old. His death was due to accidental asphyxiation. He had lost power at his home the previous day, and apparently started a gas driven generator. He forgot, and left the generator on when he went to bed. He never woke up. His two police dogs also were found dead by his side. On June 15, 2003, a celebration of his life was held in his old home town of Malibu. There were several speakers at the service, one of whom read excerpts from the article penned by the author. Afterward, Mr. Norris' cremated remains were scattered around his old Malibu home, and on the water nearby. [229]

EXTRA

The following "extra," — is an article penned by the author to commemorate the life of Mr. Norris and the friendship between them. Originally published in *Classic Images* magazine, the precise cause of his death was not mentioned in it, because it was felt that it somehow might be misinterpreted. The article has been edited so as not to repeat career details set forth in the original Norris profile in *Films of the Golden Age* magazine seen above.

"REMEMBERING ED: EDWARD NORRIS (1911–2002)"

(Originally published in *Classic Images*, May, 2003)

Two days before Christmas, I received the incredibly sad news of the death of my friend, Edward Norris, one of classic cinema's most versatile and prolific actors who passed away on December 18, 2002, at his home in Fort Bragg, California. He was 91 years old.

Although a veteran of 70+ feature films, including many time honored, grade A classics such as *Queen Christina, Boys Town, They Won't Forget,* and *Dr. Erlich's Magic Bullet,* Norris was best known to vintage movie enthusiasts as one of the kings of low budgeters thanks to appearances in innumerable second features during the 1930's and 1940's.

I first became acquainted with Ed Norris shortly after his move to Fort Bragg, California, in 1998. I was researching an article on Gloria Dickson (his costar in *They Won't Forget*), and I had contacted him in search of anecdotes about Gloria and the film which he generously shared. When the article was published in the January 2000 issue of *Classic Images*, he telephoned to thank me for sending him a copy. We would speak often after that. Although he was 88 years old at the time, Ed had a remarkable memory. He was literally brimming with colorful stories about many of the cinema's greats and near greats whom he had known personally and/or professionally. Naturally, I was enthralled by his tales, hoping somehow, someway to convince him to share them with me in an article. When I finally worked up the courage to ask, to my surprise, he readily agreed.

Throughout the spring of 2000, we had a ongoing appointment each Friday evening at 7 p.m. to converse about his life and career. He was a film writer's ideal interview, willing and able to answer questions for as long as I wanted. Sometimes our sessions lasted in excess of 90 minutes! If Ed ever grew impatient or tired of the process, he never let on. Instead, he appeared as eager to share his memories as I was to receive and record them. All in all, I think I recorded over 13 hours of audiotape footage on Ed, far more than any other subject I've ever interviewed. In the process, I gained enormous respect and affection for him as an actor and as a man.

As an actor, I admired his talent, but even more so, his dedication and remarkable tenacity. Even when his career was not going as he'd hoped, Ed Norris kept the faith, held on to his dream, and continued to make movies, never giving less than his best. As a man, I was in awe of his kindness, honesty, and positive attitude. Throughout our many sessions, I never heard him blame anyone for his career problems. Instead, he accepted responsibility, and was unafraid of admitting his own weaknesses and mistakes.

Films of the Golden Age published my original article and interview on Ed entitled, "Baby Face Gangster" in July 2001. Not long afterward,

I received a phone call and a congratulatory note from my subject. I was, needless to say, very flattered by his praise as I knew he wasn't one to throw out compliments. As a result of the piece, he generously volunteered to aid me anytime I had a question or wanted his advice.

In the late summer of 2001, Ed suffered a stroke which necessitated a lengthy hospitalization. When I first learned of his condition, I feared the worst, but I underestimated my friend's courage and positive attitude. He proved the old adage, "You can't keep a good man down." By the fall, he was back in Fort Bragg living completely alone. Although he did have some residual speech problems, his recuperation was miraculous, particularly for a man of his age.

Shortly before Thanksgiving, 2002, I telephoned Ed to extend my holiday greetings and catch up on his news. My call came at the end of a particularly difficult day which had left me feeling down. On reflection, our conversation was important, not only because it was our last, but because it reminded me of what I admired most about Ed. He was in exceptionally good spirits, and sounded great that night. His speech difficulties had obviously improved since last we spoke. As usual, he was excited about one of his hobbies. During our previous conversation in August, he had told me he was about to drive to San Francisco to look at two classic Cadillacs which he'd found for sale in a magazine. When I inquired how he would get them home if he bought them, he told me he would worry about that when the time came! I recall being very amused. I mean, how many 91-year-olds do you know who are driving on busy freeways and out buying cars? What a guy! Naturally, one of the first questions I asked in November, was if he had purchased the cars. "Yes, both of them! They're in my barn." was his reply. He told me after he negotiated the price and made the purchase, he drove one of them home, and had the other car shipped to Fort Bragg. We both laughed. When I hung up the phone, I smiled to myself. His enthusiasm and good humor had lifted my spirits.

Our conversation was relatively brief, but in hindsight, very meaningful for underscoring Ed Norris' most remarkable quality: an incredible zest for living which he had exhibited consistently for over 91 years! And it hadn't always been easy! Having studied his life, I knew of the many disappointments, tragedies, barriers, and demons he had surmounted, ultimately emerging stronger and wiser from the experiences. Even a stroke didn't slow him down for long! To the end, he was living life on his own terms, finding new adventures, new interesting things to do, reasons to get up in the morning. While his acting talent forever etched in celluloid, will continue to impress and entertain vintage film lovers probably forever, to me, his attitude toward life is what I will remember most. His remarkable courage and unfailing will to live were truly inspiring, an example to us all. [230]

The author's invitation to Mr. Norris' memorial service on June 15, 2003.

Inscribed photo to author from Mr. Norris.

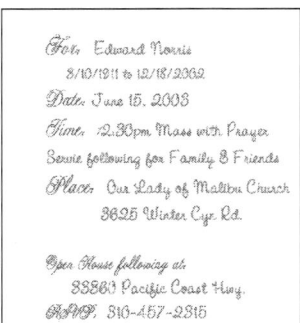

Second page of memorial invitation, June, 2003.

CHAPTER NINE
"JEAN PARKER: THE CINDERELLA GIRL"

(Two-part article originally published:
Films of the Golden Age, Summer, 1997)

PART I

Once upon a time there was a beautiful young girl who lived in a small house in a small town. Like many girls in her town, she led a simple life. She went to school each day, had an after school job, and a boyfriend her age who adored her. In her spare time, she liked to draw, to dance, and to dream. As she matured, she dreamed of being a famous artist, (for she was good at drawing), sometimes a renowned dancer. One day, a fairy godmother happened on a photo of this young lass. Magically, she transformed this lovely girl into a celebrity who mingled with the rich and famous, donned beautiful clothes, had scores of fans and admirers, and riches beyond her wildest imagination. A fable you say? Hardly. This tale is a page taken from the beginning chapters of a real case history. The heroine was the beautiful and gifted actress, Jean Parker, and the fairy godmother was a talent scout representing MGM's Louis B. Mayer who worked his "magic" molding a new movie star with a new name, heritage, and image. She was known by everyone at the studio as the "Cinderella girl."

It was a beautiful story, a rare occurrence in the cold, often cruel world of moviemaking, but too beautiful to last. Almost as quickly as he created his "Cinderella," Mayer became eager to discard her when she had the audacity to disappoint him. By letting her go, he squandered her potential to be big box office, and underestimated her skill as an actress of depth and range. The radiant young Miss Parker pressed onward however, proving her versatility in a film career lasting 35 years and over 80 films. Her roles spanned the entire range of feminine characters: from wide-eyed ingénues, to tragic heroines, from gypsies to country girls, from wisecracking amateur detectives to hard-boiled tough girls, playing each with a skill and intensity few would have imagined. Sadly, after her four-year stint at MGM, she rarely found work outside of B movies.

Born Lois Mae Green of Polish French descent on August 11, 1915, in Deer Lodge, Montana, the future film star was the daughter of a hunter and gunsmith, Louis Green and the former Melvina Burch. While only a child, Lois was adopted by the Spikard family of Pasadena due to the unemployment of her parents during the Great Depression. As a high school student in Pasadena, she demonstrated an interest in artistic endeavors: music, dance and drawing.[236]

Her junior year turned out to be a very eventful one. In order to persue her career goal of becoming a commercial artist, in 1932, 16-year-old Lois entered a poster competition to demonstrate her artistic abilities. Her entry won the contest, and as a result, her photo (in a bathing suit), appeared in a Los Angeles newspaper. MGM head, L. B. Mayer's executive secretary, Ida Koverman saw the photo and persuaded Mayer the lovely young girl had screen promise. When Koverman phoned the youngster to invite her to take a screen test, she was astonished when she replied, "I can't come tomorrow. I'm going on a hike."[237] Was this impertinence or youthful ignorance? Koverman decided it was the latter. When she finally met Lois a few days later, she liked her instantly, and explained that if the test was good, it would mean an MGM contract. Still the teen was not impressed. "I don't want a contract. I have two more years of high school to finish. I'm not an actress, I'm not beautiful," she said. The thunderstruck Koverman eventually persuaded the budding artist to do the test, and within 24 hours, MGM had a new long-term contract player, and Lois Mae Green had a new name, Jean Parker. Cinderella had emerged!

MGM immediately began grooming their new starlet, giving her acting, voice, and dance lessons and small roles in several significant 1933 MGM releases including *Divorce in the Family* with Jackie Cooper, *Gabriel Over the White House* with Walter Huston, *The Secret of Madame Blanche* with Irene Dunne, and *Storm at Daybreak* with Kay Francis. Young Jean was also cast as Princess Maria in the epic biographical drama, *Rasputin and the Empress* (MGM, 1933),

Judging from this early MGM studio photo of 16-year-old Jean, it's easy to see why L.B. Mayer's secretary thought she had movie star potential.

starring the legendary Barrymores, (the only time John, Lionel, and Ethel appeared together in a full-length feature film). All in all, she appeared in 10 films during the year, seven for MGM, and three for other studios. The loans would do much to enhance her stature.

Jean's first significant part came on loan to Columbia in Frank Capra's delightful *Lady For a Day* (1933). Costarring May Robson and Warren William, it was the tale of a fruit peddler (Robson) who receives the aid of gangsters in order to pose as a society matron to impress her young daughter (Parker) who is about to be married. Jean's ingénue role was tailor-made and her scenes with Robson were poignant. As a result of her impressive work, RKO negotiated with MGM to acquire her services for their version of the Louisa May Alcott family classic, *Little Women* (1933). Directed by George Cukor, Jean joined a stellar cast including Frances Dee, Joan Bennett and Katharine Hepburn to recreate the familiar story of the March family. Her role as the ill-fated Beth was a breakthrough, the first part to really challenge her. She described the eventful production shortly after filming wrapped.

"Playing Beth was the hardest thing I ever did. To begin with, I was scared stiff for I had no real training in acting . . . To make it harder still, I was only sixteen while the others were all over twenty-four. I was terribly shy then, and so tired from worrying, I was numb. But all the girls did everything they could to help me, particularly Miss Hepburn. She was lovely to me." [234]

The film and its cast received rave reviews. Today, *Little Women* is considered one of the best movies of the early sound period, the definitive version of Alcott's masterpiece. Parker's first lead role came as a result of her acclaimed work.

17-year-old Jean was loaned to RKO to play the tragic Beth in director George Cukor's film version of the Louisa May Alcott's classic novel, *Little Women* (1933), costarring Frances Dee on the left and Katharine Hepburn on the right.

Jean was an orphan girl abused by her stepfather played by Arthur Byron (on the right) in RKO's *Two Alone* (1934).

RKO had originally signed actress Dorothy Jordan to play the lead in the screen version of Dan Totheroh's award-winning play, *Wild Birds*. When she was forced out due to illness, director Elliott Nugent made arrangements to borrow Jean's services to play the leading role of Mazie, an orphaned teenage girl sent to live with her abusive stepfather who becomes pregnant after her involvement with a reform school escapee. Although the film retitled, *Two Alone* was at times, overly melodramatic, Jean had a showy lead role which she handled admirably.

1934 turned out to be another banner year for the budding young star who made a staggering eight motion pictures. During this time, Miss Parker often worked 18 hour days, toiling on one picture in the morning, one in the p.m. and attending acting, voice, and dancing lessons in the late evenings with no days off. It was an astonishing fete even for a teenager, but even more astounding was the fact she managed to make her varied characterizations believable under such

On loan to Fox, Jean played the gypsy, Tinka opposite Charles Boyer in the melodramatic, *Caravan* (1934).

trying circumstances. Among her more prominent 1934 portrayals was as the gypsy, Tinka, opposite Charles Boyer in Erik Charell's lavish musical drama, *Caravan* (Fox), as a crippled girl in love with an ice cream vendor in *Have a Heart* (MGM), and as the pretty pickpocket opposite George Raft in *Limehouse Blues* (Paramount). Two films were of special import. *Operator 13* (MGM), reunited Jean with director Richard Boleslawski (who had directed *Rasputin and the Empress*), and costarred her with two screen greats, Marion Davies, and Gary Cooper. An adventurous tale of Civil War spies, the film contained many exciting moments that thrilled and entertained. Critics called Jean's portrayal of a young southern belle, "splendid."

Miss Parker ended her second eventful year at MGM with an appearance in one of her most iconic films, the touchingly beautiful, *Sequoia* (MGM). Adapted from Vance Joseph Hoyt's novel, *Malibu*, the movie chronicled the curious friendship developed between a puma and a young deer when they are raised together. Directed by Chester Franklin and Edwin L Marin, and shot by cinematographer Chester Lyons on location in Sequoia National Park, production on the motion picture took two years to complete due to complications involved in filming the wildlife footage which makes up a large portion of the film. Miss Parker played Toni Marten, the young daughter of a struggling writer who finds both animals as babies, and is determined to defy nature and raise them as brothers. Although her part did not require great acting prowess, the role was especially difficult due to the often treacherous weather conditions, and because she had to handle both untrained animal costars. For her scenes with the deer and puma, the studio had men stationed outside the enclosure with rifles drawn in case anything went wrong. Another problem surfaced with censors who were not pleased with one of Jean's bathing scenes which had been filmed in the nude. Eventually, the controversial scene had to be reshot to win approval.[235] Even so, the movie was a great showcase of the soon-to-be famous Parker figure and a huge hit with critics and audiences. Andre Sennwald in *The New York Times* summed up critical reaction to the film when he called it, "profoundly touching . . . brilliant." The Parker performance was rated "excellent." Today, over 60 years later, *Sequoia* remains powerfully dramatic and affecting, as fresh as the mountain air.

The story of the unique friendship between a deer and a puma formed the basis of the heartwarming adventure drama, *Sequoia* **(MGM, 1934), filmed on location in Sequoia National Park.**

Jean's final two years at MGM (1935-36) would turn out to be as frenetic as the first two. While her training and education as an actress/star continued, she appeared in six more motion pictures during this period. These were exceedingly happy times for the auburn haired, five-foot, three-inch tall beauty who was the darling of the studio. MGM executives predicted superstardom for their ingénue.

After a well received performance as the rebellious daughter of Madie Christians in the drama, *A Wicked Woman* (MGM, 1934), Jean was paired with young Robert Taylor in the minor comic thriller *Murder in the Fleet* (MGM, 1935), then Chester Morris in the sentimental comedy *Princess O'Hara* (Universal, 1935), from the Damon Runyon story. In August 1935, she received another professional promotion when Mayer and company summoned her to travel to England to costar in the London Films' production of the satirical comedy, *The Ghost Goes West* (1935). The young star didn't need to be coaxed to join the cast of this tale of a chain-store king who buys an English castle, has it transported to America stone by stone, and picks up the ghost that haunts it in the deal. Jean had never traveled outside America, and England seemed terribly romantic. In addition, the production had other significant plusses. It had a literate Robert Sherwood screenplay, the director was the renowned, Rene Clair, and Robert Donat (Jean's favorite actor), was slated to costar.

Jean kept a diary during the five happy months of her British stay. Both the film and her experiences were among the highlights of her life. *The Ghost Goes West* which premiered in January 1936, received raves reviews. *The New York Times* called it, "an urbane, and brilliantly funny film," noting excellent acting from its leads including Jean who portrayed the confused daughter of the castle's new owner. Miss Parker was at her peak at this time, on top of the world, not only due to the film's positive reception, and but because she had fallen in love. Upon her return from Britain, she met newspaperman/freelance writer George MacDonald. It was love at first sight ending in the couple's secret elopement in Las Vegas in March 1936.[236]

The newlyweds initially planned to keep the marriage a secret, but news leaked out. On their return to Hollywood, they were surprised to learn everyone knew, and more amazed by the reception they received from Jean's bosses and "friends" at her workplace. Three years later, in 1939, Miss Parker wrote a candid and revealing article which appeared in the fan magazine *Movie Mirror* appropriately titled, "I'm an ex-Cinderella" relating the details of the couple's reception and her disillusionment with MGM.

"What a day that was! I went so eagerly, looking forward to all of the nice things people would say, the luck they would wish us. But my reception instead was a gloomy one. On everyone's face was an expression of frank disapproval . . . I began to understand that the studio was deeply displeased and upset. Marriage was the last thing they wanted for me. That a marriage — such a romantic, happy one as mine could be weighed so cold-bloodedly in Hollywood was what hurt me, scared me. Try as as I might, I couldn't see the studio's point of view, and when an opportunity came for Metro to sell my contract to Columbia, I not only agreed to the sale, but encouraged it quickly." [237]

Thus ended Jean's association with MGM and her "Cinderella phase." Unfortunately, at age 21, her movie career had already reached its zenith, and by 1937, she was already transitioning into phase #2 in which she would become a familiar face in program pictures.

After costarring with Fred MacMurray in King Vidor's entertaining Grade A western, *The Texas Rangers* (Paramount, 1936), playing a farm girl who tries to become a film actress in *The Farmer in the Dell* (RKO, 1936), and the half-breed Necia, opposite Leo Carrillo in the melodramatic, *The Barrier* (Paramount, 1937), the low budget studio, Monogram offered Jean a lead role in the adventure/drama, *Romance of the Limberlost* (1938, to costar Eric Linden). She and her new husband were encountering financial difficulties, so she agreed. She told an interviewer months later, the decision was made against the advice of her friends in the business.

"I had never made an independent picture, but I took it at once. All my friends told me that it was the worst move I could have made . . . I'd never get an A picture after that. I knew what they were saying was right, but I refused to let my pride interfere." [238]

Unfortunately, her friends were correct. During the next eight years,

Jean played an Iowa farm girl brought to Hollywood by her parents to become a movie star in the comic drama, *The Farmer in the Dell* (RKO, 1936). From left to right Esther Dale, Fred Stone and Jean in a scene from the picture.

Jean Parker would make over 40 low budget movies, never reestablishing herself as a star of major motion pictures.

In spite of her declining status, Miss Parker did make three noteworthy films during the latter 1930's, however. In 1938, she appeared to good advantage as a publisher's daughter in the homespun comedy, *The Arkansas Traveler* (Paramount). In 1939, she was third-billed to the legendary Laurel and Hardy in the very funny, *Flying Deuces* (RKO), then joined Hardy and Harry Langdon in the antebellum slapstick comedy, *Zenobia* (United Artists, 1939). Also that year, she created a mini-sensation when she traveled on a train trip from Hollywood to the Kansas premiere of Warner's epic western, *Dodge City* starring Errol Flynn. Jean was not in the cast of the film, but went along "for the ride." When the train made one of its promotional stops, a fan spotted her in one of the cars and the whispered, "Isn't that Jean Parker?" became a shout, then a roar. The crowd demanded that Jean be brought to the podium where the film's stars were giving

The low budget comedy, *Life Begins With Love* (Columbia, 1937), costarred Jean with Douglass Montgomery.

short speeches. A corridor was cleared, and Miss Parker stepped on the platform to a giant ovation. In that magic moment, Jean felt the great love that middle America had for her, and realized that common everyday Americans loved her work and identified with her characterizations. [239]

Her recent positive reviews and the much publicized train excursion briefly raised Jean's visibility. In fact, she was told that she was a contender for the plum role of Melanie in *Gone With the Wind*, but as everyone knows, she didn't get the part. In 1940, during the filming of the tender fantasy-drama, *Beyond Tomorrow* (RKO), she filed for divorce from George MacDonald. Their busy careers had often separated them for long periods, eventually dooming their union. Miss Parker would remarry twice during the 1940's: to radio news commentator Douglas Dawson (1941-43), and to foreign correspondent/ movie executive Dr. Curtis Grotter (1944-49). [240]

The 1940's decade would see Jean solidify her association with second features. The quality of her films of this period ranged from grades B to Z, but her performances were always believable. Some of her best low budget entries included *The Pittsburgh Kid* (Republic, 1941), *Hello Annapolis* (Columbia, 1942), and Universal's *Dead Man's Eyes* (1944). For Monogram, she was a telephone operator turned amateur sleuth in the delightfully wacky thrillers, *Detective Kitty O'Day* (1944), and *Adventures of Kitty O'Day* (1945). In 1941, she began a contractual relationship with co-producers, William H. Pine and William C. Thomas, appearing in a series of low-budget comic action adventures for Paramount, usually as dauntless career girls opposite Chester Morris and/or Richard Arlen. Known as the "Dollar Bills," Pine and Thomas' films were known for their economical budgets and short production schedules. Even with the obvious deficiencies, the duo's program pictures contained a certain vim and vigor, with snappy dialogue and good action scenes which proved very popular with World War II audiences. Of course, another asset was the curvy and charming Jean Parker who always brought enthusiasm, class, and conviction to even the most ill-defined parts. She would do 12 films for the production duo. Among her best known Pine/Thomas efforts were: *Flying Blind* (1941), *No Hands on the Clock* (1941), *Torpedo Boat* (1942), *I Live on Danger* (1942), *High Explosive* (1943), *One Body Too Many* (1944), and *The Navy Way* (1944). The latter film would costar her with future husband, Robert Lowery.[241]

Perhaps the finest of Jean's many program pictures during this prolific period was PRC's *Bluebeard* (1944), in which she shared top billing with veteran heavy, John Carradine. This atmospheric thriller directed by Edgar G. Ulmer, centered on a 19th century Parisian artist who strangles his models. Parker's role as the beautiful and demure Lucille, a potential victim, was a showy one which won enthusiastic notices. Today, the movie is considered a minor classic. Author Tom Weaver in his volume, *Poverty Row Horrors*, called it, "a benchmark example of style on a shoestring."[242]

Despite the popularity and redeeming qualities of many of her second features, Jean eventually grew tired of it all. She had spent eight long years toiling in programmers, and recognized her film career was clearly going nowhere. In 1945, she decided to turn her attention to legitimate theater to perfect her acting craft, appearing in off Broadway productions of *Dream Girl, Rain,* and *Born Yesterday*. In 1946, she made her Broadway debut to good reviews in the short running comedy, *Loco* (37 performances).

Chester Morris was paired with Jean in several low budget adventure films including *I Live on Danger* (Paramount, 1942), produced by the famed "Dollar Bills" a.k.a. William H Pine and William C. Thomas.

She followed with a revival of the musical comedy, *Burlesque* (1946), reprising the role of Bonny created in 1927, by young Barbara Stanwyck. Her costar was talented funny man, Bert Lahr. The show played to packed houses. Both audiences and critics were surprised by Jean's acting, singing, and dancing abilities. Apparently, all those singing and dancing lessons at MGM were finally paying dividends. Veteran character actor, Robert Weil met Miss Parker while appearing with her in *Burlesque*, initiating a 50-year friendship that endured. When asked to describe his friend, he told the author,

"Jean is a down to earth, real person, never phony, always generous and giving, and very dedicated. I had done the play, Burlesque in stock with Bert Lahr, with Eileen Heckart in the female lead. When 'Hecky' came to see me in the city, Jean came up to my dressing room to see Heckart. Jean said to Eileen, 'I'm playing a part that really belongs to you!' What a beautiful and generous thing to say!" [243]

Jean met her future husband, B movie actor, Robert Lowery (far right), while making the Pine/Thomas adventure, *The Navy Way* (Paramount, 1944), which also costarred William Henry (far left), Robert Armstrong (center).

Mr. Weil said he particularly admired the commitment Jean brought to her work.

"The last night of the show, I came into the theater early. Jean was on the stage practicing a dance step she wasn't satisfied with. That's concern and dedication!" [244]

In 1948, Miss Parker received the best reviews of her acting career when she replaced Judy Holliday as Billie Dawn, the showgirl/mistress of a crooked junk dealer in the road company version of the classic comedy, *Born Yesterday* opposite Lon Chaney Jr. The show played across the country from September 1948 until February, 1949, packing theaters in each of its stops.

In 1949, Jean returned to filmmaking when Gregory Peck asked her to appear in screenwriter, Nunnally Johnson's western, *The Gunfighter* (20th Century Fox, 1950). Originally slated to play the feminine lead, a last minute decision gave the part to Helen Westcott, and Jean the supporting role of a barroom singer who helps an

For several years Jean Parker was thought by many to have one of the best figures in Hollywood. During the war, she was one of America's top pinup girls.

aging gunslinger (Peck) to see his wife and son after a long separation. Downbeat and small scale, this adult film was a great success, and brought Jean more superb reviews. It also began the third and final phase of her motion picture career in which she played supporting roles as hardboiled, worldly women.[245]

As Billie Dawn and her junk dealing beau, Harry Brock, Jean and her longtime friend, Lon Chaney Jr. costarred in the hit road show version of the classic stage comedy, *Born Yesterday* (1948).

If her recent stage and film successes led Jean to hold out any hope of resurrecting her status as a lead film actress in grade-A productions, she would be disappointed. In 1951, she married for the fourth and final time to fellow B-movie actor and former costar, Robert Lowery. The marriage would last six years and produce Jean's only child, Robert Lowery Hanks (given his father's real name), who was born in 1952. After the birth of her son, Jean went into semi-retirement, making a few TV appearances on such series as *The Lone Wolf* (1954), *Adventures of the Falcon* (1954), *Damon Runyon Theater* (1955), and *The Red Skelton Hour* (1957) and appearing in a handful of motion pictures.[246]

In 1953, she received a call from her old friends Messrs. Pine and Thomas to appear in their upcoming 3-D Technicolor musical comedy, *Those Redheads from Seattle* for Paramount. As Liz, the tough boss of a group of "night girls" employed in a turn of the century Alaskan saloon, she was well down on the cast list in support of Rhonda Fleming and Gene Barry, but told interviewers she enjoyed making the film. One year later, in 1954, she contributed the best performance of her latter career. as Hattie, the sweetheart of a condemned killer (Edward G. Robinson) in United Artists' crime drama *Black Tuesday*. Although clearly a supporting role, her work in the picture gave filmgoers and critics another chance to see what a fine actress she was. Her reviews were uniformly excellent. The *New York Times* said she, "shined convincingly." She followed this success with the minor, but enjoyable western, *A Lawless Street* (Columbia-1955) in support of Randolph Scott and Angela Lansbury, then in 1957, supported Anthony Dexter and Sonny Tufts in the western adventure, *The Parson and the Outlaw* about the life and times of Billy the Kid. Nine years later, Jean made what would be her last feature film appearance as a town gossip in the lively western, *Apache Uprising* (Paramount-1966) starring Rory Calhoun. The film reunited her with three of her old pals and costars Richard Arlen, Lon Chaney Jr., and Johnny Mack Brown.

During the late 1950's and 1960's, Jean, (now divorced), devoted most of her time to raising her beloved son. In the 1970's, the versatile veteran actress found particular satisfaction coaching young actors sent by old studio friends to be groomed for movie roles. She said, "Sometimes I work with them on an individual basis, sometimes I

Jean had a supporting role in the western *A Lawless Street*, (Columbia, 1955). starring Randolph Scott, Angela Lansbury, and her former *The Roar of the Press* costar, Wallace Ford, pictured here.

hold classes. It's marvelous and stimulating, and I adore sharing my experience and craft." She even wrote an actor's textbook in the middle 1980's, and appeared in a series of commercials for Hollywood's First Federal Savings and Loan Association.[247] As of the writing of this article in 1997, Miss Parker lives alone in a small abode in southern California. She recently moved to be closer to her devoted son. She is a very private person who does not list her address, but speaks fondly of filmmaking and her fans.

When film historians pen their endless volumes on the movie's "golden age," the name Jean Parker is rarely if ever mentioned. Why? Despite her abilities, Jean was unable to realize her full acting potential in the cinema, eventually becoming mired in low budget productions which gave her few opportunities to showcase her talent. It is tempting to ask what went wrong. Perhaps if she had not been so eager to leave MGM, her fate might have been different. Perhaps if she had heeded her friends' advice and not initially agreed to appear in second features, she might have regained her status as a lead actress. The "what ifs" are endless.

Although she never ascended to the very top rank of stardom, when all is said and done, there was infinitely more right than wrong with the career of Jean Parker. Her 35-year career in motion pictures which produced over 80 films, can be seen as a remarkable achievement, a prolific success. Overnight, little Lois Mae Green was pulled from poverty and obscurity to become a contract player for MGM, the most prestigious studio in Hollywood. She went on to more than fulfill initial expectations, holding her own with Hollywood's finest stars, achieving lead actress status, and contributing critically acclaimed characterizations. She was at home in any type of role in any genre, but somehow many of our fondest memories of lovely Miss Parker are associated with her early ingénue/heroines. Her poignant and tragic Beth in *Little Women*, the brave and humanitarian Toni in *Sequoia*, and the charming Peggy in *The Ghost Goes West* are indelibly etched in our memories as examples of an unique artist.

Lastly, another measure of Jean's success was the adoration and devotion of her fans. Average everyday Americans related to her work and to Jean, rightly sensing she was one of them. The affection was returned. In a latter day interview, Jean spoke fondly and perceptively of her profession and its impact on the public. She said, "When anyone can give other people a few hours of escape, or enchantment, away from the ills of their work, and their own personal lives, that is a very worthwhile occupation." Enchantment, what a lovely word! What a perfect way to describe the popularity and allure of MGM 's "Cinderella girl."

PART II

"AN INTERVIEW WITH JEAN PARKER"

Early in 1996, I had the distinct pleasure of becoming acquainted with the wonderful Jean Parker. Since that time, I've spent many hours speaking with her about her career, the movies, her costars, and life. If I had to describe Miss Parker in a word, it would be one she uses frequently, delicious! What a delightful and interesting person she is, so refreshingly unpretentious, self-effacing, exuberant, and every bit as kind and thoughtful as the many heroines she played so well. She has graciously consented to let me share some of her unique memories. The following are excerpts from our conversations.

DAN: *Thank you so much for agreeing to share some your memories and unique insights with us. It was said, you got your start by making a poster.*

JEAN PARKER: Yes, I made a poster painting. It was of a gnome, a little imaginary figure. I remember my art teacher calling me on a rainy afternoon saying, "Please I want to enter this." I said, "I'm only a freshman in high school. This contest is for college students." She said, "I'm sending it!" And, I won! The actor, Keye Luke was a friend of mine and a great artist, and I won over his entry. Much later, he illustrated a book and sent it to me. I treasure it!

DAN: *Upon winning, legend has it that you got to ride in the Pasadena Tournament of Roses Parade.*

JEAN PARKER: No, I didn't ride in the parade. That was made up by the studio publicity people. I wasn't old enough to ride in the parade, or beautiful enough. There was publicity because my poster won over the college students'. I got a whole $50 for it! A newspaper photographer was sent to my home to take my picture with the poster.

DAN: *And an MGM talent scout saw you and later, the studio signed you.*

JEAN PARKER: Ida Koverman, L. B. Mayer's secretary. She was my sponsor. She liked the photo of me with my inconsequential poster.

DAN: *I want to ask you about a few of your early films and stars you worked with. One of he first films you worked on was Rasputin and the Empress, the only time the Barrymores appeared in the same feature-length film together. That must have been an experience. What were they like?*

JEAN PARKER: That was something! Lionel was the first actor I ever met when I walked on a set. I had never said a dramatic line in a high school play or anything! He was in my first scene. When we went over to rehearse it, he was so kind to me, giving helpful advice. He once said, "You have to make up your mind whether to be an artist or a dancer." He saw me "carrying on" (dancing) on the set all the time, imitating Isadora Duncan.

DAN: How about Ethel?

JEAN PARKER: She hated me, but I wasn't impressed with her either, come to think of it!

DAN: The story goes that in a certain scene, she wanted you to stand in a particular place, and when you wouldn't (obeying the director), she got mad, and called you "trash."

JEAN PARKER: Yes, it's true; she was very rude to me.

DAN: And John?

JEAN PARKER: Oh what a charmer! It kind of throws you when you have to act with an actor you have a crush on. He was so elegant, so handsome in the boots he wore in Rasputin. One day, when he was following me upstairs to makeup, he said, "Pardon me." I stopped and turned around. He said, "Maddingly beautiful ankles! Are they naturally tan like that?" I went charging up the stairs paying no attention. To call them, "maddingly beautiful" nearly killed me. I'll never forget it. (laughter)

DAN: What did he mean?

JEAN PARKER: Guess he liked the look of brown ankles when I was walking up the stairs! (much laughter)

DAN: He was probably looking up your dress! (laughter)

JEAN PARKER: He tried that later. He came into my dressing room one day. I was dressing in front of a full-length mirror. I saw him in the reflection walk up to me. All of a sudden, he reached down to my hips and pulled up my dress to my waist. There I was exposed. I turned around to slap him, but he was too fast. He ran out of the dressing room and down the hall. I was throwing things. I was furious with him. He looked back at me, and said, "Premeditary error!" (much laughter)

DAN: How was he to work with after that?

JEAN PARKER: He was always fine.

DAN: Then, you worked with the great Capra in Lady For a Day? How did that go?

JEAN PARKER: Frank Capra was just beautiful, so helpful. He used to kid me a lot. He'd come up to me and say, "Who are you today, Crawford, or Garbo?" referring to my makeup.

DAN: May Robson was your costar.

JEAN PARKER: She was a devil, and no one knew it. She was so full of fun! She came on the set one morning all wet and looking a little blue. She had been fishing for abalone.

DAN: Then came perhaps, your most famous film, Little Women. How was Miss Hepburn?

JEAN PARKER: Just gorgeous! When I told her I lacked her intensity, she told me what she needed was my relaxation. That struck me as funny because she didn't know I was half dead for not sleeping, worrying.

DAN: You certainly did some excellent films in your first three years in pictures.

JEAN PARKER: Yes, I was very lucky with Little Women, The Ghost Goes West, and Sequoia.

DAN: Another interesting film you did at this time was Operator 13. You received some wonderful reviews for that one.

JEAN PARKER: Yes, Marion Davies was so very good in that. She was just beautiful, bright, deliciously funny. Every minute was wonderful on that film. There's a scene late in the movie when she (Marion) gets married and descends a staircase. She was supposed to have tears in her eyes in that scene. I was to be at the bottom of the stairs looking up at her. She just couldn't make the tears come in the close-up. I told her, "When you come down, look at me." I was crying up a storm! (laughter). And then she cried. It was funny!

DAN: And Gary Cooper?

JEAN PARKER: He was a beautiful man, such a sweet face, wonderful, laid back, friendly. He used to tell me that when I was working, I should take time out several times a day and sit down and close my eyes. He believed in short naps.

DAN: I have to ask you, when you were at MGM, did you ever get to meet Garbo?

JEAN PARKER: Oh yes! My dressing room at MGM was next to the makeup department. I'd see her walking by frequently. I used to make sketches of her all the time, caricatures of her walking around.

DAN: Any special Garbo stories?

JEAN PARKER: When she was doing Camille with Robert Taylor, I peaked in on the set. I was standing by the door with it open just a crack. The little light alerted her that someone was watching. I immediately stepped back. Later, I peaked in again, and she motioned to me to come on in and watch. It was a lovely gesture.

DAN: How about Joan Crawford?

JEAN PARKER: A lovely person, so beautiful, always friendly. Almost everyone was nice to me. I love actors! They perform a very valuable function, helping people to lose themselves for a while.

DAN: In 1934, you did one of my favorite films, the beautiful,

Sequoia. It reminds me of some of the Disney films made many years later with the outdoor wildlife footage. That was a tough film to make, wasn't it?

JEAN PARKER: Yes. They just left us on location in Sequoia National Park. There was two-years work on that film.

DAN: You received great critical acclaim for that motion picture.

JEAN PARKER: But I didn't have that much to do except handle the animals. It was an interesting idea, a puma growing up with a deer. It was authentic when they both drank from the same waterhole at the end. The cast got together and clapped. To do that scene was thrilling!

DAN: It was remarkable to see you work so well with untrained animals.

JEAN PARKER: I used to have a way of folding the little fawn's legs together under my arms and carry him around. I could run all over the place with that little fawn. I had a way of working with the puma. I had him in my dressing room. He was brought to me when he was a baby when I first went up to Sequoia National Park. I heard him scratching around before his eyes were open.

DAN: Did he ever hurt you?

JEAN PARKER: No, never. I even did a couple of personal appearances with him to publicize the picture, one in San Francisco. I had a wide leather belt, and I had Gato with me when I entered the hotel I was to stay in. They kicked us out! (laughs) He was a wonderful cat! Leo Carrillo eventually took Gato to his ranch where he lived out the rest of his days. I visited him several times.

DAN: You told me that the censors got after you during Sequoia.

JEAN PARKER: Yes, I had an interesting scene to do where I was to dive off a cliff nude into the water, and the camera was supposed to follow me while swimming to the shore where the puma was placed.

So I dove, did the scene, was terribly proud of it, so glad I could swim that far. The puma acted beautifully, reached in with his paw, and got the fish. It was quite a scene, but the Hay's office decided that the scene could not be done nude, and it was replaced with one of me running through the woods with a black bathing suit.

DAN: Even without the nude scene, the movie showed off the famous Parker figure. Many observers said you had the best figure in Hollywood.

JEAN PARKER: Isn't that strange! I think I was terribly ordinary, not very tall. I think a great figure has to be tall like Alexis Smith. Now, there was a lady with a figure, tall, narrow shoulders, with a long neck. I thought she was beautiful.

DAN: Tell me about The Ghost Goes West which costarred you with Robert Donat.

JEAN PARKER: I had a great school girl crush on Donat. I used to hang around the set when he was doing The Count of Monte Cristo just to watch him. After I arrived in England and was on the little train to London, I received a huge bouquet of dark red roses. The card read, "Have a wonderful time, Bob." Oh, that was wonderful! He had such a sense of humor, and we had such a good time.

DAN: I imagine you were a bit intimidated working with him because he was your favorite.

JEAN PARKER: Oh, intimidated! That's putting it mildly! I was so in love with him, I shook all over all the time. He teased me because he knew I had a terrible crush on him.

DAN: Was he your favorite costar?

JEAN PARKER: Oh yes! My favorite of all. I was so mad about him that I thought to myself, "I'm going to have a son like you one of these days. And, you know what? My son looks like him a little bit.

DAN: *You loved the whole* The Ghost Goes West *experience in England, didn't you?*

JEAN PARKER: I left my heart there. I remember when I was leaving to get on the ship, Donat came with a big box wrapped beautifully. He said to unwrap it when I got to my suite. Well, when I tore off all of the wrappings, all there was in it was a little bitty card that read, "Remember??" It sounded so naughty. It was just one of his little jokes.

DAN: *Did you stay in touch with him?*

JEAN PARKER: We corresponded and exchanged music. He started my vast collection of music and music knowledge.

DAN: *He suffered all his life with asthma.*

JEAN PARKER: Awful! He called me twice from the Roosevelt Hospital in New York. That's the last time I ever heard from him. I was feeling down the other night, and I was switching TV channels, and I came across one of his early films. There he was! It was wonderful to see his face again.

DAN: *You eventually got tired of playing all those ingénues, didn't you?*

JEAN PARKER: Oh god, little Jean Parker! Oh yes! I couldn't do much else, I was so young!

DAN: *Of course, there were a few different type roles like* Caravan.

JEAN PARKER: Metro loaned me to Fox for *Caravan* with Charles Boyer. I didn't do much in it. Of all things, to cast a skinny little thing like me as a gypsy! I looked about as much like a gypsy as . . . That was the silliest thing I ever saw!

DAN: *In the late 1930's, you worked with the legendary Laurel and Hardy in* Flying Deuces. *What were they like?*

JEAN PARKER: *Darlings, just darlings! To me, they were absolutely hilarious! They couldn't move but what I wasn't falling on the floor laughing. Of course, when we got together, they planned little things to cut me up. When I was at Sardee's one night, they cooked up an act to make me laugh. They were both just wonderful. I just loved Stan. When he was ill, just before he died, he called me, and "told me off" because I had not been to see him. I wasn't able to visit him before he passed away, and it is one of my regrets. Hardy was just precious! He loved to play the piano. On the set, they had a small piano on the side, and between takes, he would go "rattling away" on it.*

DAN: **How were they to work with?**

JEAN PARKER: *Wonderful! They adlibbed a lot. They were so funny! I loved being with them because I love to laugh and entertain. What's the point of waking up in the morning if you cannot fit something humorous into your day.*

DAN: **In 1939, you went on a train trip from Hollywood to Kansas to the premiere of the film, Dodge City. Do you remember that?**

JEAN PARKER: *Oh, that was fun! A whole gang of us went to publicize that. We had a great time, Errol Flynn, etc.*

DAN: **Flynn was a great favorite of mine.**

JEAN PARKER: *I adored him! He was fun and had such a sense of humor, and a good actor! He and Donat were just fantastic. I knew him when he was married to Lili Damita, a lovely gal, very bright.*

DAN: **Then came the 1940's with all of your B-movies.**

JEAN PARKER: *I have been in some awful pictures! I think some should be smuggled out of the country like Romance of the Limberlost! (much laughter) When they didn't know what to do with a part in a film, and they needed someone who was desperately sincere, they would call me. For some strange reason, they believed everything I said! (laughter)*

DAN: *During the war years, you were under contract for Pine and Thomas.*

JEAN PARKER: *I was unofficially under contract to Paramount, and they loaned me out to Pine and Thomas' stock company along with Richard Arlen and Chester Morris. Both Pine and Thomas were nice fellows, very interested in their productions. They would visit the set and discuss things. Everyone wondered which actor, I had a crush on, Arlen or Morris. I liked them both, but not in that way.*

DAN: *Tell me about Bluebeard.*

JEAN PARKER: *That was with Carradine. I loved him. He was fun. I thought he was good-looking in that picture. His boys are good actors too.*

DAN: *But you didn't like the director, Edgar G. Ullmer though, did you?*

JEAN PARKER: *Oh I didn't! He would say, "Miss Parker, come up a little bit back!" He through his vowels around making it almost impossible to understand him. Then he'd repeat himself as if I was deaf. I was so furious! He was a fine director though, I must admit.*

DAN: *You eventually left films for the stage and Broadway in the middle 1940's.*

JEAN PARKER: *Yes, I loved it. Jed Harris' Loco, was my first play. Some of the critics said I was the "toast of Broadway." I was floored. Elaine Stritch was in Loco with me. I was pleased to know her. We had such fun together. We used to share apartments when I would come into town.*

DAN: *And you had another hit with Bert Lahr in Burlesque, singing and dancing.*

JEAN PARKER: *I hated my little tiny voice. I just couldn't stand myself. But I loved Broadway! I thought Bert and I were kind of* pathetic with the little waltz we did. I didn't feel like Bert Lahr's partner. I didn't think we looked good together.

DAN: Did you get along with him?

JEAN PARKER: We got along fine, but I understood that other people didn't like him. We would do a good show, and when we finished, I would help him take off his toupee and clean his head. That's when he would insult me, and accuse me of stealing his scenes. I didn't know if he was kidding or not.

DAN: You came back to Hollywood for The Gunfighter with Gregory Peck.

JEAN PARKER: That was great with Greg. That's quite a story. He was doing a play in La Jolla, when I came back from New York. He called me to appear in it. That led to my being cast in Gunfighter.

DAN: You originally were cast in the feminine lead.

JEAN PARKER: Yes. I was slated to play the wife and they changed it. I guess they didn't think I looked very wifely. For some strange reason, they thought I would be better as a blousy thing. I hated having my role switched.

DAN: It certainly was a good film.

JEAN PARKER: It was a great psychological western.

DAN: Then came Black Tuesday with Edward G. Robinson?

JEAN PARKER: I don't really remember a lot about that movie except the end was very Shakespearean. Everyone was shooting each other. I got a ricochet bullet! (laughter)

DAN: How was Robinson to work with?

JEAN PARKER: Delicious! You could only kiss him on one side. You know that very large mouth he had. He always had a cigar on one side, but he could kiss on the other. (laughter) I took him aside one day, and said, "Look at you. Which side am I going to make love to?" (I was his girlfriend in the picture) (much laughter)

DAN: What did he say?

JEAN PARKER: It tickled him. He certainly was not a good looking man, but was a beautiful actor. He would raise those eyes and look up, and the world opened!

DAN: Eighty films! What a legacy! What do you consider to be your finest screen performance?

JEAN PARKER: I don't think I've done anything in films that I felt was an achievement. As for my acting, the material I loved best was Born Yesterday. I love light comedy!

DAN: You did Born Yesterday with Lon Chaney Jr.

JEAN PARKER: I've so much to tell you about him. Every Wednesday, he would do the play in sign language for the deaf. That was an interesting side of him. Such a worthy person! You should be writing about him!

DAN: You're so modest. You still haven't told me which film performance you think was your best.

JEAN PARKER: I'm such a simple actress. I haven't seen most of my films. I guess I liked me in part of Little Women.

DAN: How would you like to be remembered?

JEAN PARKER: Just as a sincere actress who brought her characters to life.

DAN: You certainly are that, and so much much more! And to top it off, you have "maddeningly beautiful ankles!" (laughter) [248]

UPDATE

Jean Parker moved to the Motion Picture Country Home in Woodland Hills, California during the late 1990's. She died there from complications from a stroke on November 30, 2005. She was 90 years old. She was buried in Forest Lawn Memorial Park in Los Angeles. She was survived by her son Robert, two granddaughters, Katie and Nora Hanks, and countless fans. Her son, Robert Lowery Hanks still lives on the United States' West Coast.[249]

EXTRA

The following extra is an account of the author's friendship and experiences with Miss Parker published in *Classic Images* magazine immediately following her death. It has been edited here so as not to repeat career details mentioned in the original two part *Films of the Golden Age* article seen above.

"BONNY JEAN: REMEMBERING JEAN PARKER (1915-2005)"

(Originally published in *Classic Images*, February, 2006)

In the midst of celebrating the holiday season, classic film fans were saddened by news of the passing of one of our most beloved stars from the cinema's "golden age." Jean Parker, the lovely, brunette stage and screen veteran who appeared in grade A classics like *Little Women, Lady For a Day, The Ghost Goes West,* and *Sequoia*, and B movie gems: *Bluebeard, Beyond Tomorrow,* and *Detective Kitty O'Day* died on November 30, 2005, of complications from a stroke at the Motion Picture Country Home in Woodland Hills, California. She was 90. One of classic cinema's most attractive and prolific actresses, the popular, versatile Miss Parker's onscreen image underwent two dramatic transformations in the course of a career spanning 34 years and 80 films: from grade A ingénue, to queen of B's, to character actress. Several important things remained constant, however. In all of her films, Miss Parker never gave less than her best. Her performances were always sincere, believable, and totally professional. I had the great privilege of conducting one of the last interviews with this remarkable woman in 1996. I learned many things during our conversations, not the least of which was why bonny Jean Parker was so loved and admired both professionally and personally.

When I became acquainted with Jean Parker in 1995, she lived in a small cottage apartment in Redondo Beach, California. We had a mutual friend, the late Robert "Bobby" Weil, an acclaimed stage, screen, and television actor who'd known and admired Jean since they appeared on Broadway together in the late 1940's in *Burlesque*. A classic film enthusiast and collector, the friendly, gregarious Bobby and I had much in common. During one of our marathon chats, Bobby learned of my respect and affection for Jean, and told me he'd have her call me one of these days. To tell you the truth, I didn't really believe he would. I was mistaken!

One evening in late fall, 1995, I was sitting in front of my computer at 11:30 p.m. on a Friday night, finishing a writing project, when the telephone rang. I almost didn't answer it. It was late, and I was fatigued. I had to get up early the next day, and I'm afraid I answered in a rather unenthusiastic way. As soon as I heard the unique feminine voice ask, "May I speak to Dan?" I knew who it was! Holy Smokes! After a few awkward, star struck moments, we had a wonderful conversation mostly on the subjects of Bobby Weil and *Sequoia*, one of my all-time favorite Jean Parker films. Down to earth, witty, gracious, Jean was easy to talk to. No wonder Bobby was so fond of her! I think it says volumes about her character she would take the time to telephone a complete stranger as a favor to a friend.

I would speak to her many many times during the next few years. In early 1996, I told her I wanted to write a tribute article to her, and asked if she would consider doing an interview to accompany it. At first, she demurred. An extremely private person, Jean was not nostalgic about her films and professed little interest in rehashing the many disappointments she'd experienced in Hollywood. But I persevered, and I think I eventually wore her down. She finally acquiesced. One of the secrets of my success was occasionally mentioning some of her costars which provoked lovely memories of friendships and comradery.

After we began our formal "interview," I think she rather enjoyed the stroll down memory lane. I know, I sure did! Tales of Barrymore,

Laurel and Hardy, Coop, Flynn, and Hepburn, who could ask for more! Affectionate, funny, sometimes critical, sometimes poetic, Jean Parker's tales of Hollywood were unique and wonderful, music to this writer's ears! In the summer of 1997, excerpts from our conversations appeared (along with an in-depth career article), in *Films of the Golden Age* magazine (Issue #9). People loved it! Although the enthusiastic response was very gratifying to me, I was wise enough to know the article's popularity had much more to do with my subject than anything I did. I was merely the stenographer and organizer. It was all about Jean and her golden memories.

I remained in close contact with her for the next three years. After she moved to the Motion Picture Country Home, we spoke less frequently. When I telephoned her there, she was rarely in to take the call. Even though I always enjoyed speaking with her and catching up on her news, I was happy she wasn't sitting by the telephone. I envisioned her with her old movie buddies sitting around, socializing, exchanging remarkable memories of the "golden days." It was comforting to me.

When I learned of my friend's death, with tears in my eyes, I relived a few of our conversations and retrieved my Jean Parker file which contained a copy of the article and the entire interview. Although her reminiscences and anecdotes were as wonderful as I remembered, in hindsight, the most important, interesting thing about my experiences with Jean was not the project at all, but the chance to spend time talking to her. To me, she bore a remarkable resemblance to the heroines she played so well during the 1930's. Warm, unpretentious, amiable, and honest are all appropriate adjectives. Add artistic, talented, intelligent, and flirtatious to the list, and you have my impression of Jean the human being. Now, don't get me wrong, she wasn't Mother Teresa, just a good and decent person whom I was so proud and honored to know!

Jean was also very humble and self-effacing. As we continued to work on the project, she kept asking why I wanted to write about her. "I don't think I've done anything in films that I felt was an achievement," she said. She dismissed her legendary beauty and figure this way. "I think I was terribly ordinary, not very tall. I think a great figure has to be tall like Alexis Smith . . . I thought SHE was beautiful!" With all due respect to Miss Parker's expert opinions,

Jean Parker (1915-2005)

she was wrong on both counts. The truth is, Jean will be always be remembered for her exceptional screen performances and for her extraordinary beauty both inside and out. People knew Jean Parker was a class act way back in 1932, and they still do to this day.[250]

CHAPTER TEN
"PAULA RAYMOND: A WORKING ACTRESS"

(Two-part article originally published in *Classic Images*, February, 1997)

PART I

When 13-year-old Paula Raymond made her screen debut in 1938, as a brat in the Paramount comic drama, *Keep Smiling*, starring young Jane Withers, her first big scene called on the youngster to be the unhappy target of a bowl of mush. "It was cold and wet — that mush," she later recalled, "and they plastered me with it from head to foot. I was drenched and miserable and almost lost any desire I might have had to be an actress right then and there."[251] This rather undignified introduction to the world of making motion pictures turned out to be strangely prophetic. For during her life and long acting career, Miss Raymond would be "hit" with innumerable obstacles which might have defeated the strongest, most resilient of individuals, but not Paula! In a 30+ year acting career encompassing 25 films and innumerable television appearances, beautiful Paula Raymond used her talent, intelligence, wit, and courage to not only overcome significant professional barriers but multiple personal tragedies. She never became a superstar actress, but her story is a triumph over adversity.

The daughter of California attorney, Paul Raymond Wright, and his Irish-born wife, Marianne, the future actress was born Paula Ramona Wright in San Francisco on November 23, 1924. At age 8, while attending convent school, her mom enrolled Paula in ballet classes followed by the study of voice, music, and piano. Even at an early age, the young girl demonstrated an aptitude for the arts. An excellent singer, she sang coloratura parts in many junior opera productions including, *La Boheme*, and *Aida*. Her first experience with filmmaking came as a result of a visit to Hollywood with her mother who owned property there. During the stay, Marianne was persuaded by a friend to allow her daughter to appear in *Keep Smiling* (20th Century Fox, 1938).[252]

After receiving her primary education, Paula attended Le Conte Junior High School (Los Angeles), transferring to the legendary Hollywood High School. During her junior and senior years, she took law classes and continued to pursue her interest in the arts, appearing in several theater productions, playing leads in the Ronald Telfer Academy's *Ah Wilderness*, and *Peter Pan*. By the time she was in in her late teens, Paula had blossomed into a striking beauty. 5 ft. 6 3/4 inches tall, with light brown hair, and blue-gray-green eyes, her lovely expressive face and beautiful profile made her a natural for modeling and for the movies.

Upon graduation from high school in 1942, Paula headed for San Francisco Junior College to study law while still appearing in community theater. On October 4, 1944, she married Marine Captain Floyd Leroy Patterson, and for a time, focused her enormous energies on being the wife of a military man. Unfortunately, her husband was excessively possessive, and the union did not last. The couple would divorce two years later, after Paula gave birth to a daughter, Raeme Dorene on March 13, 1946. Left with the need to support a small child, Paula decided to move to Hollywood, and try her hand at acting and modeling. Her beauty and intelligence soon landed her modeling work with the Meade Maddick Agency.

After taking the name, Paula Raymond in 1947, she was spotted by Paramount Studios and placed under a one-year contract. "There," she told an interviewer, "I sat and did absolutely nothing . . . It was sheer torture . . ." [253] Finally, in 1948, the determined Paula (who had not yet been cast in a Paramount film), obtained a release from her studio pact, and returned to modeling. Later that year, she signed a short-term acting contract with Columbia Pictures, resulting in multiple low budget movie appearances in 1948, in such Columbia-made features as *Racing Luck* with David Bruce, *Challenge of the Range* with Charles Starrett, and *Blondie's Secret* with Penny Singleton. She was also given opportunities in the exciting and innovative new medium of television at this time. Among the first of scores of television appearances she would make in the next 20 years, were guest shots on *Your Show Time* (1949), and *The Unexpected* (1952).

One day, while working on *The Million Pound Note*, an episode of *Your Show Time*, she was observed by an MGM representative who was impressed by her performance. Word spread to the sister of George Cukor, who in turn, alerted the great director. A screen test was arranged, culminating in an MGM contract in 1949. Paula had arrived at last! In fact, she had arrived in a big way, for MGM was the most prestigious of studios. At once, they set their star-making machine in motion, grooming their contract player, and giving her roles in top notch films.

Paula's first two MGM assignments were small parts in two

important motion pictures. She played character actor, David Wayne's wealthy girlfriend in director George Cukor's delightful comedy *Adam's Rib* (1949), starring the legendary Spencer Tracy and Katharine Hepburn, then played a secretary in the adult drama *East Side, West Side* (1949), with James Mason and Barbara Stanwyck. When she had been on the lot for three months, she was approached to test for the lead feminine role in *Devil's Doorway* to star Robert Taylor. Her excellent test resulted in her joining the cast of the moving western drama, the first of multiple important, high-profile film appearances Paula would make in the period 1950-51, which enhanced her status as an up and coming young star.

A sincere attempt to rectify wrongs done to native Americans by the stereotypical way Hollywood had presented them through the years, *Devil's Doorway* (MGM, 1950), was the tale of a Native American Civil War hero (Robert Taylor) who experiences hatred and racism when he returns home after the war. Directed by Anthony Mann, the film won wide critical praise. *The New York Times* called it, "a whopping action film," giving thumbs up to Taylor's "forceful performance" in a highly unusual role. Paula's portrayal of Orrie Masters, a female attorney who tries in vain to help the Indians and maintain peace, was also hailed as "very good" by the *Times* critic.

Her second 1950 film, MGM's charming comedy-musical, *Duchess of Idaho* starring Esther Williams, Van Johnson, and John Lund, added further luster to her reputation and demonstrated her versatility. As the lovestruck secretary of a playboy/financier, fourth-billed Paula shined. Well directed by Robert Z. Leonard, a familiar romantic trifle was elevated by an a good script, opulent production numbers, and charming performances. The three top-billed stars were all hailed in various reviews, but it was Miss Raymond who stole the picture. Her portrayal of the naive and devoted Ellen Hallet, demonstrated a substantive flair for comedy. Especially effective were her scenes with Lund in which she is bumbling and awkward. One very funny moment had her hiding under a desk so Lund's girlfriend wouldn't see her. In another, she posed as his wife to scare off a woman Lund wants to dump, and ends up getting drunk. Once again, critics applauded. *The New York Times* hailed her as, "a striking brunette who is convincing as she moans 'I'm always engaged, never a bride. I must be using the wrong soap.'"

Paula played an attorney in the grim, critically acclaimed western, *Devils Doorway* (MGM, 1950), starring Robert Taylor and Marshall Thompson (seen here on the left).

Paula Raymond (left) and Esther Williams in the musical comedy, *Duchess of Idaho* (MGM, 1950).

Paula followed her impressive work in *Devil's Doorway* and *Duchess of Idaho* with another showy role as a wealthy doctor's daughter engaged to a divorced physician who still loves his ex-wife in the MGM musical comedy, *Grounds For Marriage* (1950), starring Kathryn Grayson and Van Johnson, then topped off. the productive year by being cast opposite one of Hollywood's most iconic stars. The film was the melodrama, *Crisis* and her costar would be the legendary Cary Grant.

Although ultimately a critical success, MGM's production of the taut thriller, *Crisis* (1950), starring Grant, Raymond, Jose Ferrer, and Gilbert Roland was a troubled one from beginning to end. The story of the production began in 1949, when scenarist, Richard Brooks who had penned exceptional scripts for some of the best films of the late 1940's, including *Crossfire* (RKO, 1947) and *Key Largo* (Warner Bros., 1948), was signed to a two-way contract by MGM as a writer and director. Despite this fact, Brooks had written two screenplays, but had not been allowed to direct. By the time he was assigned to adapt George Tabori's short story, *The Doubters* for the screen, Brooks had become extremely discontented at MGM. As the story goes, when he happened to see Cary Grant one day at the studio, Brooks let it be known to Grant (who had been approached to star in the film), he wanted to direct it. Grant instantly liked the man's forthright honesty, and told MGM boss Dore Schary that he wouldn't make the picture unless Brooks directed. Rather than lose Grant, MGM relented and gave Brooks the job. Of course, it turned out to be an inspired decision, as Brooks would soon become one of the studio's most acclaimed directors of such cinematic classics as *The Blackboard Jungle* (1955), and *Cat on a Hot Tin Roof* (1958).

Crisis related the story of a noted physician, (Grant) and his wife (Raymond) who, while vacationing in South America, are kidnapped by a brutal dictator (Jose Ferrer) who needs surgery for a brain tumor. The tough and cynical doctor only agrees to operate on the man if his wife is set free. Although the dictator and his allies comply with the doctor's demand, his wife is subsequently taken hostage by insurgents who make it clear to the doctor she will be killed if he does not botch the surgery. Tense and suspenseful, the film was aptly titled, not only because of its subject matter, but also due to several mishaps and crises which occurred on and off the set. During the filming, several violent arguments erupted between director Brooks and cameraman Ray June who had wanted to direct the movie himself, and resented the "green" newcomer. In their controversial book, *Cary Grant, the Lonely Heart*, writers Charles Higham and Ray Moseley related the trials of making *Crisis*.

"On the first day of shooting, there was a cumbersome difficult shot, with the camera mounted on a wheeled crane traveling on metal tracks. Brooks was nervous that June would defy him in the composition of the shot, and walked beside the crane, monitoring its every movement. Whether accidentally or deliberately, someone pushed the crane over Brook's feet. Cary came running over shouting, 'You ran over his foot! Take him to the hospital.' Brooks said, 'The hospital is next to the funeral parlor on the lot. If I leave this stage for five minutes, there'll be another director on this movie.' Cary replied, 'There is not going to be another director . . . if they throw you off the movie, I'll walk!'" [254]

Luckily nothing was broken, and Brooks returned to work on the film.

Another difficulty surfaced when Grant celebrated his 46th birthday on the set. A picture of him was taken cutting the cake with Miss Raymond. The caption in a movie magazine read, "Paula, when you invited me up for a piece, I thought . . ." Grant, (newly married to actress Betsy Drake), was furious and wanted to sue. When Paula refused to join him in the lawsuit, he became very annoyed and remained so.[255]

Despite the problems, the finished film was a critical success. Reed Porter in *The Los Angeles Mirror* called it, "a bold piece of movie adverturing." Darr Smith of *The Los Angeles Daily News* called Brook's direction, "masterful," and the acting "superlative." Today, the movie is highly regarded as a taut, well-acted thriller, a minor suspense classic. Miss Raymond's good reviews for *Crisis* were particularly ironic because the role of Helen Ferguson was not in the original script. After casting Grant, MGM insisted Brooks change the role of Ferguson's daughter (in the original story), to a love interest. Nancy Davis (Reagan), was originally slated to play the feminine lead, but when head of production, Dore Schary voiced his displeasure, she was replaced by Miss Raymond. For Paula, it was an important stroke of good luck which propelled her career. Amid difficult circumstances, she had performed admirably opposite a great star.

1951 would also be a banner year for the ambitious young actress. She followed *Crisis* with key supporting roles as a French governess in the intriguing drama, *Inside Straight* (MGM) with David Brian and Arlene Dahl, and as a suspect in a plot against President Abraham Lincoln in the melodramatic, *The Tall Target*. The latter, was a particularly strong production and is now recognized as another minor movie classic. Adapted from a George Worthington Yates story, and directed by Anthony Mann, *The Tall Target* was a tension-filled thriller about a failed attempt by Southern Radicals to assassinate the 16th President while he traveled by train from Harrisburg to Washington for his 1861 inauguration.

Although basically a piece of historical fiction, the film was well made and remains fascinating to watch thanks to well-paced direction, a taut, suspenseful script (which included several surprising twists and turns), and a superb cast headed by Dick Powell, Paula, Marshall Thompson, Adolphe Menjou, Ruby Dee, and Leif Erickson. To Miss Raymond, the role of a feisty Southern belle whose loyalty to her flawed brother (Thompson), makes her a prime suspect in the diabolical scheme, was a welcome change of pace, one which brought her more praise and attention as a top up and coming star.

From left to right: Paula Raymond, Cary Grant, and Gilbert Roland in *Crisis* (MGM, 1950), directed by Richard Brooks.

Juvenile actor, Dale Harltleben, David Brian and Paula in *Inside Straight* (MGM, 1951).

After contributing several acclaimed performances in a variety of roles and genres, Paula had every right to believe her star would continue to ascend to the heavens, but it was not to be. Instead of continuing to reward its gifted young contract player, beginning in the fall of 1951, MGM chose to squander her proven talent and momentum. Although the remaining films she was assigned in the period (1951-53), were respectable with decent production values, good casts and competent direction, after *The Tall Target*, Paula's roles while an MGM contract player were mostly minor, and inconsequential. In the comic musical, *Texas Carnival* (1951), she and her costars Esther Williams, and Howard Keel, were completely overshadowed by the zany antics of Red Skelton playing a carnival bum mistaken for an oil and cattle millionaire. The theme of small town corruption was well handled in MGM's melodramatic, *The Sellout* (1951, starring Walter Pidgeon, John Hodiak, and Raymond, but Paula's role as Pidgeon's daughter married to the city attorney (Cameron Mitchell), was not substantive.

Paula became extremely frustrated with her status at MGM after completing her lackluster part in *The Sellout*. When the studio began asking her to assist other actors with screen tests, she became convinced her employer did not have her best interests at heart.

"The last year I was there, they buried me. I didn't know what was happening . . . Later, I dated a producer from Fox who told me he had wanted me for The Steel Trap with Joseph Cotten, but when he tried to borrow me, they were pricing me out of the industry." [256]

Her frustration culminated in a confrontation with her agent, Elsie Cukor (George's sister and partner at the Lipton-Cukor Agency), whose response was to set her an appointment with MGM publicity chief, Howard Stricklyn. "I couldn't believe it. I had to go in and represent myself and that made me angry."[257] When Paula fired Ms. Cukor, it incurred the wrath of her brother, a powerful force in the industry. The unhappiness continued until 1953, when Paula was released from her contract.

Upon leaving MGM, the newly freelancing Miss Raymond still hoped she might be able to secure roles commensurate with her ability, but unfortunately, that did not happen. She did not know it yet, but her three-year stint with Metro-Goldwyn-Mayer from 1949-53, would turn out be the highlight of her film career. Although she would appear in some interesting, well made films afterward, none of the them were significant enough to establish her as a top level movie star. She came to believe studio politics and influence were key factors in her declining fortunes.

Her first motion picture as a freelance actress was a good one, however. Surely one of Paula Raymond's most famous films was *Beast From 20,000 Fathoms* (Warner Bros., 1953), the tale of death and destruction wrought on the Northeast. when a rhedosauraus (a fictional monster, part brontosaurus, part tyrannosaurus), is thawed out of its Arctic hibernation by atomic tests.

Adapted from a Ray Bradbury story, the movie was well produced and became a huge hit due to its multi-talented creators. A seasoned cast headed by Kenneth Tobey, Paula, and Cecil Kellaway, Eugene Lourie's restrained direction, and Ray Harryhausen's early stop-motion special effects were among the highlights. Historically, *Beast* is significant as the "granddaddy" of all of the post-war science created monster movies that would soon flood the market. Today, science fiction fans consider it a classic. Although her role as a paleontologist's assistant was not particularly challenging, Paula says the film generated great interest and remains a favorite of her admirers. She followed with roles as wives of law enforcement officers in two crime dramas: *City That Never Sleeps* (Republic, 1953), and *The Human Jungle* (Allied Artists, 1954). Both contained standout components (including competent scripts, direction, photography and acting), but the films and her parts in them were not significant enough to aid Paula's career.

A poor screenplay and uninspired direction defeated what Paula hoped might be her comeback film, *King Richard and the Crusaders* (Warner Bros., 1954), a lavish three million dollar epic based on Sir Walter Scott's *The Talisman* starring Laurence Harvey, George Sanders, Rex Harrison and Virginia Mayo. A huge disappointment, Scott's classic tale of medievalism was reduced to comic book simplicity. Although, once again, the movie contained admirable elements including a superb cast, Max Steiner music, and beautiful cinematography, the script defeated all the effort. Miss Raymond, looking spectacular, valiantly attempted to make something of the small, underwritten role of Queen Berengeria, but simply had too little to do except be grateful it was Virginia Mayo and not her who had to keep a straight face and utter the immortal lines, "War, War, War! That's all you think about, Dick Plantagenant!"

After the critical drubbing everyone associated with *King Richard and the Crusaders* received, Paula decided to leave filmmaking. It was a decision born of utter frustration. Between 1955 and 1958, she held down various jobs in business including insurance clerk, receptionist, construction company bookkeeper, etc, all under the name of Rae Patterson. Incredibly, no one recognized her. Why? "Cause I was given no publicity by MGM," she laughingly recalled.[258]

Hoping the "blackballing" (as she described it), had run its course, in 1958, Paula hired a new agent and set out to restart her acting career. No film offers were immediately forthcoming, but she did find work in television. Her first TV role in NBC *Matinee Theatre's* live production of *The Contingent Fee* was one of her favorites. She told the author the producers were initially reluctant to give her the opportunity.

"I was to play a Puerto Rican woman, a real character, No one would ever have cast me for such a role. I wasn't the the type . . . After they had tested all the other girls, they finally, out of courtesy, got around

Paul Christian and Paula Raymond in a scene from the iconic science fiction thriller *Beast from 20,000 Fathoms* (Warner Bros., 1953).

As the regal Queen Berengaria in *King Richard and the Crusaders* (Warner Bros., 1954).

to me. I walked in with the producer, director, everyone watching. I said, 'It's been a long time since I've done a Puerto Rican accent.' They said, 'You don't have to do an accent, Miss Raymond.' They were just accommodating me. Well of course, I did an accent, and you know what? I walked out with the role." [259]

Her role in *The Contingent Fee* would be the first of innumerable guest starring appearances she would make on television. During the period 1958-1969, she would become one of the busiest, most prominent actresses on the small screen, guesting on some of the most popular and acclaimed television series of the time including, *Peter Gunn* (1958), *Hawaiian Eye* (1959-64), *Bat Masterson* (1959-60), *One Step Beyond* (1959), *Perry Mason* (1959-64), *Bachelor Father* (1959), *77 Sunset Strip* (1959-64), *The Untouchables* (1960), *Have Gun Will Travel* (1960), *Maverick* (1961), *Death Valley Days* (1964). Ironically, it was the medium of television which would provide Paula with the opportunities to play a wide range of roles too often denied her in films. Her television success also led to lead roles in two minor films, *The Flight That Disappeared* (United Artists, 1961), and *Hand of Death* (20th Century Fox, 1962) both science fiction chillers. [260]

From 1958-69, Paula Raymond was one of the busiest actresses on the small screen, guesting on various popular, acclaimed series including *Maverick* (1961), with Jack Kelly.

Just when her career was gaining momentum, another obstacle appeared, one of the most serious of her life. On August 20, 1962, Paula was a front seat passenger in a car that sped out of control on Sunset Boulevard in Beverly Hills. She was riding home from a party with her friend, Gloria Beutel (ex-wife of actor Jack Beutel), Gloria's daughter, and a mutual friend, when Gloria lost control of the steering. The car careened into a tree, and rolled over several times. All the passengers miraculously escaped from the car with minor injuries, except Paula. She was trapped under the front seat, and the car was on fire. Two male guests at a party hosted by Dean and Jeanne Martin (taking place across the street from the accident), rushed to the scene, and pulled Paula from the car a few seconds before it blew up. She was pronounced dead on arrival at the hospital, but a neurologist (who had been called by Jeanne Martin), managed to revive her. She had sustained a skull fracture and other severe injuries. Her nose was severed from her face which necessitated plastic surgery to re-attach and stitch all of her many cuts. The plastic surgeon worked all one night. Although her looks would be essentially restored and the courageous Miss Raymond would return to work one year later, the after effects of her injuries (mainly to her nervous system), would continue to plague her. [261]

In 1963, she miraculously returned to series' TV guest shots. One episode of the popular *The Man From Uncle*, was expanded to a full-length feature film entitled, *The Spy With My Face* (MGM, 1966). In 1967, she accepted two more roles in minor films: as Countess Dracula opposite John Carradine in the campy horror thriller, *Blood of Dracula's Castle* (Crown International, 1969), and as a notorious madam in the violent western, *Five Bloody Graves* (Independent International, 1969), with Robert Dix and Scott Brady.

A decade later, in 1977, she suffered another injury which hampered her career when she tripped on a telephone cord, breaking her ankle on the set of the popular TV daytime drama, *Days of Our Lives*. The soap opera had hired her for a three-day role as a prostitute and producers were so impressed with her initial days' work, they were scrambling to write a permanent role for the actress. Sadly, the mishap and the physical impairment which followed, destroyed their plans and kept Paula from joining the cast. As always, she handled it with a sense of humor. "After all," she says laughingly, "who wants a hooker on crutches!" [262]

From left to right: Dayton Loomis, Paula Raymond and Craig Hill in *The Flight That Disappeared* (United Artists, 1961).

Alex D'Arcy and Paula Raymond played vampires in the low budget horror thriller, Blood of *Dracula's Castle* (Crown International, 1969).

From 1979-84, Paula became involved in the film distribution business for five years with the Art Greenfield Company. In 1984, her planned re-entry into films and television was interrupted yet again by physical injury when she fractured both her hips in two separate mishaps necessitating many months of recuperation. During the latter part of the 1980's, she continued to pursue her many interests and hobbies including music and poetry writing. She returned to the cinema in 1993, playing a small cameo role in the minor thriller, *Mind Twister* (American Independent Productions, 1993), but tragedy was never far away. In February 1993, she lost her beloved daughter Raeme to cancer. [263]

As of the writing of this article (1996), Miss Raymond still lives in the Hollywood home she bought 42 years ago, graciously granting occasional interviews. Of late, she has voiced interest in returning to acting in cameo roles. In August 1996, she was the guest of honor at her old alma mater, Hollywood High where a display commemorating her film and television career was unveiled in the new H.H.S. Alumni Museum. [264]

Looking back at Paula Raymond's film career, the word that comes to mind is "potential." Miss Raymond's potential to become a big star/actress was certainly great in the early part of the 1950's. From 1950-53, she achieved a big breakthrough, becoming an MGM contract player and demonstrating ability and versatility in multiple excellent, critically acclaimed motion pictures opposite some of the cinema's greatest stars, but film superstardom eluded her. Why? There is no single answer. Suffice it to say, she was too rarely given the proper vehicles to showcase her abilities, and studio politics most certainly played a significant role.

By the early 1960's, Paula had turned her attention from films to television where she had access to better scripts and opportunities. In fact, it was on TV she was able to continue to hone her acting skills and ultimately prove her overall ability, turning in excellent lead performances in a wide range of roles in countless popular projects and series' episodes. Yet, with all that in mind, film fans who have seen *Devil's Doorway, Crisis, The Tall Target,* and *Duchess of Idaho* are certainly glad that in the beginning of her acting career, the incredibly lovely Paula Raymond tried her hand at making movies, generating great charm, intelligence and adding dimension to the characters she played onscreen.

PART II

"AN INTERVIEW WITH PAULA RAYMOND"

During the last few months, I've had the pleasure and privilege of speaking to lovely Paula Raymond on several occasions about her life and career. Gracious, articulate, opinionated, and always candid, she related some of the trials and triumphs she experienced during her many years in Hollywood. As the following excerpts from our conversations illustrate, talented Paula faced life's challenges armed with great courage, intelligence, and a sense of humor.

DAN: Thank you so much for speaking to us! Your MGM movie contract came as a result of a 1949 television appearance, didn't it?

PAULA RAYMOND: Yes, I was doing a Mark Twain story, Million Pound Banknote on Story Book Theater. The second or third day of shooting, my agent, Leon Lipton showed up on the set and said he had been called by the "powers that be" on the show. They had said, "You're not going to waste this girl on television, are you?" So Leon went back to Elsie Cukor (his wife and partner), who thought they should notify her brother, George. George directed my screen test, and I was signed to a contract.

DAN: Securing an MGM contract must have been thrilling to you.

PAULA RAYMOND: No. Actually I was more needy than impressed! I wasn't even that impressed that George Cukor was directing my screen test. Basically I needed a job.

DAN: Your first picture was the wonderful Adam's Rib directed by Cukor.

PAULA RAYMOND: I'm sure that George invented that role to show me off. There was no reason for David Wayne to have a companion at that party where my character first enters. I believe that Cukor was probably introducing me to the studio. Of course, I didn't know that at the time.

DAN: I have to ask you about Tracy and Hepburn. They were such legends.

PAULA RAYMOND: Charming!

DAN: Tell me about Spencer Tracy.

PAULA RAYMOND: He was a doll! I told you about my one date with him, didn't I? Well, we had permanent dressing rooms in the same building. He was coming down from his dressing room, and I was going up to mine. He stopped me, and said, "Paula, Saturday we're giving a reception for Prince Philip of Sweden at Romanoff's. Would you do me the honor of accompanying me?" Of course, I wanted to go. But the way I was raised, a young woman does not go out with an older man alone. I don't know what was going on in Spencer's head, I'm standing there saying to myself, "How can I say yes?" I was taking forever to answer. I finally blurted out, "My mother and I would love to." So, bless his heart, he got a date for my mother, a doctor, and the four of us went to the reception! (laughter) My mother and Dr. Gage got along beautifully . . . With Spence, I was very shy. Now I'm an outgoing person, but in those days, I was a priggish prude. That's why I didn't mingle with most of the people I was working with. I just went in and did my job, and went home.

DAN: Was it apparent that he was involved with Miss Hepburn?

PAULA RAYMOND: No, if they were close, they didn't advertise.

DAN: What about the "Great Kate?"

PAULA RAYMOND: Grand, a real pro! When I say professional, that says it all. No hang-ups, no tantrums. You know your lines, you hit your spot, you ply your trade. She was great!

DAN: How did you come to be tested for Devil's Doorway?

PAULA RAYMOND: Probably George Cukor was behind that.

DAN: I understand the director Anthony Mann was not enthusiastic about you being in the film.

PAULA RAYMOND: Well, when he was testing me, that was the first time we had met, He didn't know me from Adam or Eve. He had Robert Taylor, and Louis Calhern, and all the others, and here was this nobody, that no one had heard of, Paula Raymond. So, when he was directing my test, he was giving me a helluva time. He would say, "No! No! No! Cut! Do it this way!" and then, he would say, "No! No! No! Do it that way!" and on and on. He was trying to confuse me, I guess, not knowing he was talking to an accomplished actress. I just hadn't done that much yet, and no one knew who I was. Finally, I turned to him and said, "Mr Mann, when you make up your mind how you want me to do it, I will do it that way." That shut him up, and the next take he printed. The rest is history.

DAN: What was your reaction to being cast in Devil's Doorway?

PAULA RAYMOND: I was trying to hide. I was saying to myself, thank goodness we are so far away (it was filmed in Aspen Colorado), so they can't replace me in a minute.

DAN: It was a classy picture.

PAULA RAYMOND: I've heard it was one of Bob Taylor's favorite pictures, because for once, he was able to play a different type of character. He was the charming leading man in most of his pictures.

DAN: What was your impression of Taylor?

PAULA RAYMOND: Oh, a nice guy, easy to work with. Another professional.

DAN: And Anthony Mann?

PAULA RAYMOND: He was a wonderful director. He knew how to

put a picture together. You can't take that away from him. But, oh my god, the hell he put me through!! He was after me!

DAN: You mean, he was pursuing you romantically?

PAULA RAYMOND: All the time! The crew were all making bets on the set whether he would get me into bed. He even tried to ply me with liquor. I've never been a drinker. He ordered a drink for me, a Brandy Alexander. It tasted like a spicy milkshake. One of those, and it was all I could do to eat dinner.

DAN: How did you get away from him?

PAULA RAYMOND: An MGM publicity man, Jim Campbell was always hanging around me trying to get some kind of story because I was unknown. When Tony would come up to me and say, "How about dinner tonight?" I would turn to Jim, and say, "Fine, doesn't that sound good, Jim?" (laughter) Poor Jim, always the "fifth wheel!"

DAN: You're a tricky lady, you are!

PAULA RAYMOND: It was a matter of self-preservation! (laughter)

DAN: Next came one of your personal favorite movies, Duchess of Idaho.

PAULA RAYMOND: It was my favorite of all the films I did at MGM.

DAN: I understand the director, Robert Z Leonard didn't think you were appropriate.

PAULA RAYMOND: Right — becasue he was seeing the rushes from Devil's Doorway. Of course, in that, I was playing a dramatic role. Ellen was a light part. He said, "She can't play comedy." Joe Pasternak, the producer insisted I play it against "Pop's" wishes. When I came back from Devil's Doorway, there was a rehearsal. The only part of the picture they rehearsed was the opening scene with Ellen in the night club. Well, we did the rehearsal, and when we came out, one of the screenwriters, Dorothy Cooper turned to me, and said, "Sid Fields and I wrote the script, but I wrote Ellen, and you ARE Ellen!"

DAN: Did Leonard ever warm up to you?

PAULA RAYMOND: He was a delight! He accepted me after the first rehearsal when he realized that he had the actress to play Ellen.

DAN: How was the working relationship between the principle players: Esther Williams, Van Johnson, John Lund, and you?

PAULA RAYMOND: They were all pros. I've never had a problem working with anyone except a few male egos.

DAN: And who were those egos?

PAULA RAYMOND: I'll tell you a few. They included Gene Barry, Kevin McCarthy, Ray Danton, Robert Vaughn, and Scott Brady. When I worked with Cary Grant, Dick Powell, Charles Boyer, Spencer Tracy, Robert Taylor, etc, no trace of it whatsoever!

DAN: Speaking of Cary Grant, I must ask you about Crisis. The writers Charles Higham and Ray Moseley interviewed you for their biography of Grant. In it, they stated there was a running battle between director Richard Brooks and cameraman, Ray June. Is that true?

PAULA RAYMOND: Richard Brooks did not know how to use the camera. The pressures on him were so severe. He was responsible for the screenplay as well as his directorial debut. He would yell at everybody in the cast. The first time in the history of a motion picture that a boom "accidentally" ran over a director's foot.

DAN: Brooks, who was also interviewed for the book, claimed it was not an accident.

PAULA RAYMOND: I don't really know. But I do know that the crew hated him because was he always yelling at them. He might have been forgiven, except he was able to control himself with Cary. . . When he would shout at me, I would just put my arm around his shoulder and say, "Calm down, Richard. What is it you want?" He would calm down, but it was the crew not Ray June that hated him. Ray June directed the picture pictorially. Brooks directed the actors.

DAN: *There is another interesting anecdote related in the Higham book in regard to Grant's birthday party, and a magazine article. Do you know what I mean?*

PAULA RAYMOND: Absolutely, I have the article, somewhere! (laughing)

DAN: *I'd love to see it. I understand Grant was furious, and wanted to sue.*

PAULA RAYMOND: Yes, and I talked him out of it. I asked him, "Cary, where's your sense of humor?" Everybody knew it was just for laughs. I said. "How can you sue a sense of humor?"

DAN: *He had just married Betsy Drake.*

PAULA RAYMOND: Yes. Otherwise, I might have flirted with him. (laughter)

DAN: *The Tall Target was another favorite Paula Raymond film. I thought your role was an interesting change of pace. You played a suspicious character. Do you have any recollections of the movie?*

PAULA RAYMOND: I was, once again among professionals. It all went smoothly.

DAN: *But it was directed by Anthony Mann.*

PAULA RAYMOND: This time he left me alone! He had learned his lesson! (laughter)

DAN *Perhaps your most famous film is Beast from 20,000 Fathoms.*

PAULA RAYMOND: *That film was an embarrassment to me because it was the first film I did after I left MGM. Compared to the production values of a big studio, it was embarrassing. It started as an independent film produced by Hal Chester, who had been one of the Dead End Kids. Here I was working on an independent low-budget film. Of course, the movie was later bought by Warners and it out-grossed their big 3-D production of House of Wax that year. Ray Harryhausen won an Oscar for his special effects in Beast. Later, it became an important cult film.*

DAN: **It certainly is loved by fans. Bet you still get a lot of fan mail for it.**

PAULA RAYMOND: *Oh yes! And I get pictures! In fact, I just had some reproduced for my own library. Yet, it still was embarrassing at the time, but not any more.*

DAN: **After King Richard and the Crusaders, you left acting behind.**

PAULA RAYMOND: *I was being blackballed by George Cukor for leaving his sister's agency, and was getting nowhere. I decided I'd better do something else for a living. I still had a daughter to support, so I looked in the classified ads. . . I spent three years in the business world from 1955 to 1958.*

DAN: **Then, you came back in 1958, and did TV until your auto accident in 1962.**

PAULA RAYMOND: *Yes, I was sitting in the "death seat," what I call the middle of the front seat in a car driven by Gloria Beutel (former wife of Jack), now married to Richard Bare. We were driving back from a dinner. In Beverly Hills, they have ruts going across the street for drainage, and there was water coming down from the hills. It did something to the steering. She just couldn't control the car, and we ended up hitting a tree. I didn't feel the blow. If they hadn't pulled me from that car, I would have missed coming back . . .*

DAN: **What was the extent of your injuries?**

PAULA RAYMOND : *I had no face! When your nose is gone, your face is gone. I had a skull fracture, my nervous system was destroyed, my olfactory nerves were cut. The plastic surgeon, Michael Flynn did all the work in one night, and did a beautiful job. There were pieces of skin they took off my cheek to put on my nose. There were stitches all over my face. I was told when my mother was brought to see me, she became ill. When I heard that, I thought, "What must I look like?" I asked for a mirror. When I saw myself, I said, "Thank God I never lived in my face," cause it was gone. It was full of stitches.*

DAN: I have to ask. Part of being an actor is your looks. Were you not nervous you would be permanently scarred?

PAULA RAYMOND: *Of course! It occurred to me that I would have scars all over my face, but Dr. Flynn's stitches were so fine, you don't see the scars. Anyway, I've always lived from the inside out, not the outside in, but my accident was traumatic, and disappointing.*

DAN: How many years were you laid up.

PAULA RAYMOND: *I went back to work the next year. I'm stubborn!*

DAN: And resilient! What was your rehabilitation?

PAULA RAYMOND: *It was hell coming back! Because of the damage to my nervous system, I have had to learn to control myself. If I let myself get upset, it causes nausea, so I have become a very calm person. Of course, nothing glamorous can ever happen to me without the element of the ludicrous. My bottom had caught fire before they pulled me out of the car! They treated the burn with Johnson's Baby Powder! (much laughter)*

DAN: So you came back in 1963?

PAULA RAYMOND: *Yes, I did guest appearances on Death Valley Days and Temple Houston, a series with Jeffrey Hunter and Jack Elam. I did one of the early episodes entitled, "Miss Katherine." After I finished that, I hoped I wouldn't ever have to work with Jeffrey Hunter again. He never knew his lines.*

DAN: You continued to do television work in the middle 1960's, some of the most popular series of all time.

PAULA RAYMOND: It was great! My agents were order takers. That's what they called themselves.

DAN: You also did two or three films.

PAULA RAYMOND: Yes, in 1966, Blood of Dracula's Castle, and Five Bloody Graves.

DAN: You're a woman of many talents. Tell me about some of the non-acting things you've done.

PAULA RAYMOND: Between 1969-74, I wrote special material with composer Bob Ross. I'm a lyricist as well as a musician. (pianist). We did an entire musical. It was entitled, The Reluctant Mistress, and was never produced. Bob died in 1974, and my mother in 1975, so I never did anything with the show. I would love to see Angela Lansbury do my special material songs. They are just her type of material, tongue in cheek.

DAN: In one of the short bios I read, it said that you sang coloratura parts, but then your voice deepened.

PAULA RAYMOND: Well, I lowered it. Every popular song I was trying to sing sounded like an operatic aria. One day, I was at the piano. I said, maybe I should try this Duke Ellington song an octave lower. I had a three octave range. I used to sing with Bronislau Kaper who scored Grounds of Marriage, Lili, and many other films.

DAN: Did you ever sing in a movie?

PAULA RAYMOND: Yes and no! The only time I ever sang in a film, I had to pretend I was terribly French. I did the singing voice of Hedy Lamarr in Experiment Perilous with Paul Lukas. I dubbed songs for her in my parlor voice. (laughing)

DAN: *I have that film. I'm going to have to get it out, and take a look.*

PAULA RAYMOND: *Well, when Hedy sits down and sings, that's me.*

DAN: *According to my research, you also did some directing.*

PAULA RAYMOND: *Just before my accident, I was directing. I produced, co-wrote, directed, photographed, and edited a documentary about the plight of the Southwest American Indians for the American Friends (the Quakers.) Later, I became involved in the film-distribution business with the Art Greenfield Co. from 1979 to 1984, when I started breaking my hips. (laughs)*

DAN: *You have a talent for breaking bones, don't you?*

PAULA RAYMOND: *I broke both my hips in 1984, just before I planned on going back to work, then my shoulder in 1994. The bone which was broken in my shoulder was my humerous. At the time they corrected the carpal tunnel syndrome surgically, they went into my elbow in order to release the ulna nerve, and took away my funny bone which has left me "humerless!" (much laughter)*

DAN: *Tell me about your family.*

PAULA: *I have a granddaughter in Oklahoma City, and a daughter in heaven. Raeme passed away in February 1993. It was cancer and horrible. At the end, she looked like the pictures of third world people.*

DAN: *I'm very sorry. Tell me about your granddaughter?*

PAULA RAYMOND: *Her name is Rebecca Cash Daddio, and she is a set decorator for television.*

DAN: *How do you divide your time these days?*

PAULA RAYMOND: *Poetry, music, my income properties, and fan mail.*

DAN: You once told me that you would like to return to acting.

PAULA RAYMOND: Yes, but none of the casting people know me. I would have to re-introduce myself to the industry. I'm the easiest actress in the world to direct. Just tell me what you want, and I'll do it, within limits, of course! (much laughter)

DAN: Anthony Mann found that out! Looking back at your acting career, how would you sum it up?

PAULA RAYMOND: I was a working actress! The reason I went to work as an actress was that it was the only thing I knew how to do to earn a living — and I needed a job!

UPDATE

Paula remained living in her home in West Hollywood during her last years dividing her time between her hobbies, answering fan mail, doing a variety of interviews and writing a novel to be titled, *I Was Born Right, Where Did I Go Wrong*. She died at age 79, on December 31, 2003, at the Cedar-Sinai Medical Center in Los Angeles, where she had been admitted for a respiratory ailment. She was buried in the Holy Cross Cemetery in Culver City, California. The placque on her crypt reads, "Paula Raymond, November 23, 1924–December 31, 2003, I'm Still Here. Legend Follows." She was survived by her granddaughter, Rebecca Cash Daddio who resides in the southern U.S. [266]

Paula Raymond (1924-2003).

CHAPTER ELEVEN
"ZACHARY SCOTT: A SCOUNDREL WITH STYLE"

(Originally published in *Classic Images*, March, 1998)

Was there ever a more suave and debonair 1940's movie scoundrel than Zachary Scott? Certainly none comes to mind. Even though this distinguished stage and screen actor's career encompassed a broad range of characterizations from soft-hearted weaklings to tough desperadoes, he is best remembered for his classic interpretations of elegant and charmingly deceptive villains. In the field of underhanded film malevolence, Zachary had few equals. For Scott's scoundrels were not one-dimensional ogres, but cultivated, well-heeled rogues with an intelligent wit and charm irresistible to the feminine species, silver-tongued devils if you will, whose onscreen finesse and calm exterior often masked smoldering hatreds, jealousies, and inner turmoil. In short, Zachary Scott's singular style of nasty was an experience to be savored, one which enlivened many a listless motion picture. In fact, he was so good in his treacheries, early on, he became typecast as a featured villain, stifling his development as a top ranked lead actor.

The grandson of a cattle baron, and the only son of a prominent southern surgeon, Zachary Thomson Scott Jr. was born with a proverbial "silver spoon in his mouth" on February 24, 1914, in Austin, Texas. A true "blueblood," Zachary's father was a direct descendant of George Washington's only surviving sister, Betty. A busy medical career kept Zachary Sr. away from home during his son's formative years. Thus, as a youngster, "Zach," (as he was called), commanded a good deal of attention as the only male in an all female household consisting of his mother and two sisters. In fact, he became a talented "show-off," making his stage debut at the tender age of four doing an impersonation of Chaplin at a local talent show. Although he seemed predisposed to be an entertainer, it was always "understood" that young Mr. Scott would follow in his father's footsteps, become a doctor, and join his wealthy dad's thriving medical practice.[267]

Upon graduation from high school in 1931, Zachary enrolled in medical school at the University of Texas, fully expecting to fulfill his family's wishes. Doubts soon surfaced when he became active in the college drama club and started appearing in college productions. His participation in the "Curtain Club" fostered Scott's long suppressed acting/performing ambitions. Scott told an interviewer it was at this time he became aware that his father's cherished profession was not his first love.

"I realized I was not emotionally qualified to do the things a doctor has to do. I couldn't bear to see people burdened with anxiety or to see anyone die. Since I'd been acting from the time I was in high school, I turned to that instead." [268]

Young Zachary deeply disappointed his parents when he changed his major a few months after his arrival at college. Three years later, in 1934, he boarded a cotton freighter out of New Orleans for the British Isles (as a cabin boy), determined to become an actor on the English stage.

In Great Britain, Scott eventually joined the English Repertory Company and toured London, Bristol, and Bath in various productions with an accent he described as "Australian." In the fall of 1934, he met English theater impresario Gerard Neville who gave him his first important stage role, the juvenile lead in *The Outsider* at the 17th century built Theater Royal in Bath. In 1935, he returned to the states to continue his education and to marry his best friend's former girlfriend, actress Elaine Anderson. He had met Elaine while attending the University of Texas, and carried on a steady correspondence with her during his time abroad. They were wed on Scott's twenty first birthday on February 24, 1935, at the Presbyterian Church in Dallas. After honeymooning in New York, they moved into the Virginia plantation which was the wedding gift Zachary's parents bestowed on their beloved only son.[269] Afterward, both aspiring actors returned to New York to test their wings. They spent six months in the "Big Apple," but nothing happened. After returning to Texas, both became

Zachary made his unofficial stage debut at age four as Charlie Chaplin in a local Austin talent show.

involved with the Austin Little Theater. While acting in various productions, they each held down jobs. Zachary worked for an oil refinery while teaching dramatics at a local convent school. In 1935, the Scotts became the proud parents of a daughter, Waverly. In 1938, the Lunt and Fontanne Company stopped off in Austin while on tour. Alfred Lunt and Richard Whorf (also in the troupe), were impressed with the Scotts (especially Zachary), dispatching recommendation letters to John Haggot and Laurence Langner of the Theater Guild and Westport County Playhouse.[270]

In 1940, Mr. and Mrs. Scott moved to Westport, then to New York to do revivals for The Guild. It was at this time Elaine abandoned her acting ambitions, feeling Zachary had the best chance to succeed. She would eventually become the stage manager of the prestigious Theater Guild. Zachary was, and would remain deeply touched by this unselfish act. He was soon to prove her right, landing Broadway roles in New York productions of *Ah Wilderness* (1941), and *The Damask Cheek* (1942). The latter play, which showcased Scott the anti-hero, caught the attention of Broadway producer/playwright, Edward Chodorov who selected Scott for his four-character tale of love in wartime, *Those Endearing Young Charms* (1943). Zachary contributed an excellent, critically acclaimed performance as a roguish aviator who sets out to seduce an innocent young girl. Jack Warner attended a performance of the play one night, and was so impressed, he immediately offered Scott a contract. The shrewd Zachary did not immediately sign on, holding out for more money and various perks, but in 1944, he relented, signing a seven-year pact with the brothers Warner. Although not readily apparent at the time, it was significant that Scott's performance as a charming rascal had won him his movie contract. Zach's new motion picture career required that the couple relocate to the West Coast. Again, Mrs. Scott made the sacrifice, giving up her prestigious and lucrative job stage managing such hits as *Oklahoma* to accompany her husband to the film capital in 1945.[271]

When 30-year-old Zachary Scott joined the Warner Bros. roster of players in the fall of 1944, he certainly did not fit the studio's well established mold. Sophisticated, fastidious, perfectly coiffed, impeccably dressed with gold dollars as cuff links (from his grandfather), a gold stud in his pierced left ear, and eyelashes so long and thick that makeup people had to powder them to keep from casting shadows in scenes, Scott couldn't have been more unlike the hard-edged Warner Bros. boys. The 6 foot, 1 inch tall, slim, soft-spoken, gentlemanly actor appeared more like a Ronald Colman than a Bogart, Garfield, or Cagney, but Zachary was a gregarious and friendly sort who instinctively carved a niche for himself at the studio, becoming fast friends with several Warner Bros. contract players. This was despite a rather "rocky" start after news leaked (prior to his arrival), he had signed his initial contract for considerably more money than several established Warner Bros. stars. Another clause in his lucrative pact, inserted at Scott's insistence, allowed him to do one film per year for another studio. This would become important almost immediately.

Prior to their arrival in Hollywood, the Scotts purchased a modest home just off Sunset Boulevard where he, Elaine, and 9-year-old Waverly would reside. The house would be the site of many parties and celebrations. The Scotts would soon establish themselves as a popular host couple of the Hollywood social set. The witty and intelligent Zachary was always an interesting person to be around.[272]

Scott's first Warner Bros. role was selected based on his successful Broadway performance as a villain. He was asked to grow a mustache (which would become a trademark), to play the title character in the mysterious, *The Mask of Dimitrios* (1944). The tale of a mystery writer (Peter Lorre) on the trail of a slick and evil scoundrel (Scott), the movie was a stylish and atmospheric melodrama thanks to sure-handed direction by Jean Negulesco, a literate screenplay, expert cinematography, and exceptional acting by Messrs. Lorre, Scott, and Sydney Greenstreet. Audiences and critics stood up and took note of newcomer Scott's menacing performance. His excellent reviews were a triumph for the young actor/star who proved he could handle a lead role among seasoned veterans.

Warner Bros. cast its new contract player, Scott in the lead role in his first studio production, the atmospheric melodrama, *The Mask of Dimitrios* (1944), the first of many films in which he would play villainous characters. Seen here with Faye Emerson and Eduardo Cianelli.

Scott ended his first year in the film capital with a cameo stop at the *Hollywood Canteen* (Warner Bros., 1944), an all-star wartime extravaganza. In 1945, Warner Bros. cast him in the lead in *Escape in the Desert*, the story of four Nazis who take over a gas station in the Arizona desert. Scott was to play an American flyer who happens to pass by and become involved, but problems plagued the production. According to cast member Jean Sullivan, interviewed by author Doug McClelland in his book, *Forties Film Talk*, "We filmed with Zachary Scott opposite me for months, then it was decided he was miscast and Philip Dorn replaced him."[273] Despite the setback, 1945 would be turn out to be a eventful year in the film career of Scott. He would do three films, two of which would be among his best.

The first was an adaptation of James M. Cain's novel of tortured mother love, *Mildred Pierce* (Warner Bros., 1945). An impressive cast was assembled including Scott, Jack Carson, Eve Arden and Ann Blyth to enact the tale of a self-sacrificing mother and her evil murderous daughter. To direct, came the teutonic, often brilliant Michael Curtiz who was still basking in the triumph of his great success, *Casablanca* (1942). The title role went to veteran actress, Joan Crawford, a newcomer to Warner Bros., — a top star whose career had been experiencing a downturn. Neither Jack Warner nor Curtiz were initially enthusiastic about casting Crawford, but eventually changed their minds when they realized she and the entire cast were doing extraordinary work.

A critical and box office megahit, *Mildred Pierce* turned out to be a triumph for all involved, particularly Miss Crawford who won a well-deserved Best Actress Oscar for her performance that reinvigorated her sagging career. Zachary's portrayal of Monte Beragon, the immoral, caddish, weak second husband of Mildred, was also highly regarded — netting him superb reviews and new offers. Scott followed the acclaimed *Mildred Pierce* with another roguish part as a gold digging cad opposite Faye Emerson in the minor melodrama, *Danger Signal* (Warner Bros., 1945), before exercising his option to make a film for another studio. It would be a wise career move, as it resulted in what most consider the best performance of Scott's career as the tenant farmer in *The Southerner* (United Artist, 1945). Directed by Jean Renoir (*Grand Illusion*), the movie became the great Frenchman's most critically respected American film, but it almost didn't get made.[274]

Adapted originally by Hugo Butler from the novel, *Hold Autumn in Your Hands,* the project had been difficult for Renoir to get produced primarily because studio heads saw the story of a Texas sharecropper as box office poison. After finally securing financial backing, other problems surfaced when Butler and Joel McCrea (originally slated for the lead), abruptly left due to disagreements regarding the screenplay. Renoir pressed ahead however, hiring Nunnally Johnson, then William Faulkner to assist with dialog and the southern dialect. It is widely believed that Faulkner wrote much of the finished film, but received no screen credit. Filmed in the small California town of Madera on the San Joaquin River, Scott was ultimately chosen for the title role because he was from the South. In his memoirs, *Renoir on Renoir — Interviews, Essays, and Remarks,* the great director explained his choice of Scott,

"Zachary Scott is himself a southerner . . . He knows their language; he knows their habits; and contributed a kind of exterior accuracy to the film that I found to be extremely valuable." [275]

The tale of a farmer's intense love of the land in the face of bitter adversity, *The Southerner* was typical of Renoir's emphasis on the heroics of the working class. Zachary joined an exceptional cast including Betty Field, Beulah Bondi, and J. Carrol Naish. As Sam Tucker, the sharecropper who struggles to make a life for his family, battling the wrath of nature and an antagonistic neighbor, Scott turned in a stunning performance which amply demonstrated the range and depth of his ability. *The New York Times* called the film, "a rich, unusual, and sensitive delineation of a segment of the American scene," and Scott's titled performance, "outstanding . . . at once restrained and powerful." In a 1946 interview, Scott fondly recalled the film and its eminent director.

"It was a privilege working for the great Renoir. He has the heart and brain of a genius and the simplicity of a child. Everything he feels about acting, I tried to feel . . . One day, in talking to me, Renoir expressed a philosophy that strengthened my own. 'Life is short!' he said . . . 'there isn't enough time to be bored' . . . I hope I'll never be guilty of either." [276]

Scott's most famous film role was as the immoral, irresponsibly weak Monte Beragon opposite Jack Carson and Joan Crawford in the Oscar winning drama, *Mildred Pierce* Warner Bros., 1945).

The struggles of a tenant cotton farmer and his family form the crux of the drama in Jean Renoir's *The Southerner* (United Artists, 1945) starring Zachary and Betty Field.

From left to right: Beulah Bondi, Jay Gilpin, Scott, Betty Field and Jean Vanderwilt in *The Southerner* (United Artists, 1945).

As a result of three acclaimed films, Zachary was fast becoming an important new star. Female fans were especially taken with his cultured good looks, and flooded Warner Bros. with fan letters. In 1946, *Quigley Publications* poll of exhibitors named him one of their "Stars of Tomorrow," ranking third behind Joan Leslie and Butch Jenkins. Unfortunately, at this critical juncture, Warner Bros. did not capitalize on Zachary's critical acclaim and increasing popularity by giving him roles in which would further demonstrate his acting range. In fact, quite the contrary. *The Southerner* would mark the peak of Zachary's acting career, and from here on, he would rarely be given a chance to "stretch" as an actor.

Certainly, his follow-up roles as a gangster in the minor crime thriller, *Her Kind of Man* (Warner Bros., 1946), and as a successful novelist in the drama, *Stallion Road* (Warner Bros., 1947) were unchallenging and not substantive enough to maintain his momentum. Although he fared better as the wronged husband of a woman (Ann Sheridan) who murders her lover during an extramarital affair in the mystery, *The Unfaithful* (Warner Bros., 1947), and as a young rascal who dallies with a middle-aged judge's (Spencer Tracy's) wife (Lana Turner) in the drama, *Cass Timberlane* (MGM, 1947), neither increased his reputation.

During the next two years (1948-50), Zachary continued to solidify his onscreen image as a featured cinematic rogue. Although he would have a chance to play a few leads during these years, his more substantive and colorful performances were as featured villains or lost in minor productions which were largely ignored by elite critics. A case in point was *Ruthless* (1948), produced by the B movie studio Eagle Lion. Chronicling the story of Horace Vendig (Scott) a ruthless businessman whose rise to the top of the Wall Street ladder is littered with the broken lives and the financial ruin of friends and foes alike, Scott's magnetic vampire-like portrayal might have been another triumph for the actor had it not been for the movie's disjointed script and the film's subpar production values which limited its impact.

Evil Horace seemed to be resurrected in the guise of Scott's wheelchair-bound character Max Durant in the minor romantic melodrama *Whiplash* (Warner Bros., 1948). During this period, Scott granted several interviews, publicly embracing the nefarious roles he was playing. He maintained that he preferred them, "provided that it is villainy with charm, evil with originality, and murder with music."[277] Privately, he yearned to play more diverse characters in more important assignments, conducting a vigorous campaign at Warner Bros. Although he ended up losing the role of Cody (to Bruce Bennett), in the western drama classic, *Treasure of the Sierra Madre* eventually, the campaign paid off, albeit temporarily.

While the four films Scott would make in 1949, finally gave him a well-deserved respite from villainy, three of the four were second features which likely did his career as much harm as good. His one A-level opportunity of the year came in a supporting role in the Warner Bros.' melodrama, *Flamingo Road* (1949), all about an ambitious carnival dancer (Joan Crawford) who gains social status and moves to a corrupt small southern town. Although the film was a top-notch production with a superb cast and director (Michael Curtiz), and Zachary acquitted himself well as the weak-willed Fielding Carlisle, deputy to the town's corrupt sheriff/political boss, the film's inept script and over-the-top dialogue destroyed much of its credibility. In their humorous book, *Bad Movies We Love*,

This mid-1940's photo features Elaine Scott, Waverly and Zachary posing for a photo on the set of one of one of his Warner Bros. films.

Zachary, Janis Paige and Dane Clark pose for a publicity photo to publicize the Warner Bros. melodrama, *Her Kind of Man* (Warner Bros., 1946).

authors Edward Margulies and Stephen Rebello, devote an entire chapter to *Flamingo Road*, reciting one of Crawford's speeches to deputy Zach. When asked why she ditched her job with the carnival, she replies,

"I got tired of being on the wrong end of a rabbit hunt. . . sick of moldy tents, one night stands, and greasy food, sick of people looking at me like I was cheap!" [278]

Scott deserved an Oscar nomination just for keeping a straight face.

Scott's better assignments came in three Warner Bros. second features: as a two-fisted Texan in the action-packed western, *South of St. Louis* (1949), an attorney framed for murder in the suspenseful crime thriller, *Flaxy Martin* (1949), and as a frustrated husband in the breezy farce, *One Last Fling* (1949). The latter emphasized Scott's flair for comedy, too often left unexploited by Hollywood producers.

The 1950's decade would be Scott's busiest on the silver screen, ushering in significant upheaval and change in his personal and professional lives, but sadly, his association with cinematic villainy would remain essentially unchanged. He had five film releases in 1950 alone. He was a cowardly bandit fearlessly pursued by Randolph Scott in the undistinguished Warner Bros. western, *Colt .45*, an aggressive ad man in the whimsical comedy, *Pretty Baby* (Warner Bros.), and a millionaire who becomes the victim of a deceptive vixen in RKO's big budget drama, *Born to Be Bad* co-starring Joan Fontaine, Robert Ryan, and Joan Leslie. Given its impressive cast, the latter should have been another great vehicle for Zachary, but once again, a poor screenplay defeated the best efforts of those involved, and the reviews and box office receipts were negative. In her memoirs entitled, *No Bed of Roses*, Miss Fontaine said her own performance was adversely affected by the romantic interest shown her by Howard Hughes who purchased RKO during the production, and personally cut the film. [279]

Scott's other 1950 outings were more worthy, but once again, came in lesser films. *Guilty Bystander* (Film Classics), a low budget film noir thriller gave Zachary a showy, offbeat part as a hard-drinking ex-cop searching for his kidnapped son. The film's stark, moody photography and good supporting performances aided the story of the search which takes Max, the protagonist (Scott), into the company of smugglers, shady doctors, and various other criminals and thugs. As the anguished father, Scott gave another intense riveting performance, his best since *The Southerner.* He was also very good as a father (of a young child) accused of murdering his wife in MGM's medium budget psychological melodrama, *Shadow on the Wall* costarring Ann Sothern, and young Gigi Perreau.

If Mr. Scott's films were not creating buzz in 1950, his private life was. Rumors had been circulating for two years regarding the deterioration of the Scott marriage, which both Zach and Elaine denied. They had appeared such an idyllic couple when they moved to California in 1945, so much in love with so much in common, but professional careers and the hubbub of Hollywood had a unique way of ruining the most solid union. In November 1949, Elaine filed for divorce, citing mental cruelty. Mrs. Scott claimed her husband possessed a violent temper which flared into unprovoked

Zachary Scott contributed one of the best performances of his latter career as an alcoholic ex-police detective searching for his kidnapped son in the low budget noir thriller, *Guilty Bystander* (Film Classics, 1950). Here with costar Faye Emerson.

outbursts and tantrums. As Zachary did not contest, she was granted a divorce in Santa Monica in 1950. The Scotts were granted joint custody of 14-year-old Waverly.[280] It was widely rumored that Elaine had divorced Zachary after meeting and falling madly in love with Nobel Prize winning author, John Steinbeck, whom she met at a party hosted by close friend, Ann Sothern. True or not, she married the great writer in December 1950, and remained his wife until his death in 1968.

Regardless of the circumstances, the breakup was a stunning blow to the always confident Zachary Scott, sending him into a semi-depressed state. His deteriorating psychological condition was compounded a short time later, by a freak boating accident in which he suffered severe injuries. While in a rubber craft off Topanga Canyon with fellow actor and friend John Emery, a riptide upset the light boat catapulting Zach onto a rock which knocked him unconscious. He was saved from drowning by Emery who reached him and carried him to shore. Although he recovered from his severe injuries, the mishap adversely impacted Zachary's emotional health. [281]

While in the midst of the most difficult and volatile period of his life, Scott began pouring his considerable energies into his films with mixed results. In *Secret of Convict Lake* (20th Century Fox, 1951), he joined an extraordinary cast headed by Glenn Ford in a psychological western about escaped convicts holding a group of women hostage in a small California village. Fourth-billed, Zachary managed to shine as the meanest of the gang, who wreaks havoc by attracting a neurotic (played persuasively by Ann Dvorak), who furnishes him with firearms and buried loot, but the film was weakened by substantive flaws and greeted by unenthusiastic reviews. Sadly, no one was spared who participated in the unsuccessful domestic farce, *Let's Make it Legal* (20th Century Fox, 1951), which paired Zach with screen legend Claudette Colbert. Critic Wanda Hale said, despite good intentions, the film fell flat, "due to strained farcial situations and the indifferent story." The movie's director Richard Sale, quoted in Lawrence Quirk's book, *Claudette Colbert, An Illustrated Biography*, said its failure was due to the story's weaknesses and the "insecurities of the younger cast members" which included young Marilyn Monroe in of one her early film outings. [282]

Scott's most intriguing film of 1951 was the mystery thriller, *Lightning Strikes Twice* (Warner Bros., 1951), which marked the last movie he would make under his original Warner's contract. Filled with an atmospheric moodiness, the movie's bizzare plot was made credible by an expert cast headed by Richard Todd, Mercedes McCambridge, Ruth Roman and Scott, excellent photography by Sidney Hickox, seasoned direction by King Vidor, and a surprise conclusion. Critics were unenthusuastic however, and box office receipts disappointing

While making the motion picture, lightning also struck twice in Scott's private life. In 1951, he made headlines twice by being arrested. The first event took place in a New Orleans tavern when Scott and nine others were taken into custody for violating Louisiana's segregation laws by consuming alcoholic beverages with African Americans at a black establishment. Scott, who was appearing on stage in the city, had come to the bar scouting out talent for an upcoming USO show. Charges were eventually dismissed, but not before Judge Edwin A. Babylon lectured Scott and the public, "When you're in the South, if you do go into these kinds of places, go just as spectators, don't drink." Scott later explained he had been invited to the tavern by black men, "who wore the uniform of the U. S. Navy, just back from fighting for us in Korea, and celebrating their return to the U. S. I was proud to drink with them!"[283] He probably was not so proud of his second arrest in the summer of 1951, (while on vacation in Hawaii), when he was picked up for public drunkenness. The arresting officer said Scott had been nabbed while dancing the hula barefoot outside a Honolulu saloon. When confronted, the officer said Scott became so belligerent, "it took two men to arrest him." As a result, Zachary was locked up for a few hours, then released. Although both incidents were fodder for the Hollywood gossip mill, neither prevented Scott from finding work. Finding good scripts was another matter.[284]

When he began freelancing in late autumn, 1951, the peak years of Zachary's career were clearly over. The remainder of his movies were minor affairs, pale in comparison to his previous triumphs. Scott appeared in 13 films during the period between 1952 and 1962. Only two were worthy of the best efforts he gave them. Most were low budget, foreign made motion pictures with crude scripts that gave him few if any opportunities. In 1952, he made two movies overseas. In England, he appeared with Kay Kendall in the minor adventure, *Wings of Danger*, (Hammer-Lippert, 1952), then traveled to Mexico to costar with Veronica Lake in the costumer, *Stronghold* (Lippert-Mexico, 1952). When a newspaper reporter asked Miss Lake about the latter, she called it, "a dog paying good money."[285]

Scott's personal fortunes substantially improved with his marriage to stage and screen actress Ruth Ford in June 1952. Appearing in Chicago in the comic *Bell, Book, and Candle*, Zachary took a short leave of absence to jet to New York for the nuptials. The union would be the lasting and fulfilling relationship he had longed for. The couple, along with Shelley, Miss Ford's daughter from a previous marriage (whom Scott legally adopted), would eventually take up residence at Manhattan's famous Dakota, known today as the place John Lennon was slain.[286]

During the early 1950's, Scott began his flirtation with the medium of television. With the quality of film scripts declining, Zachary took some solace in the TV material he was offered. He told interviewers he enjoyed working in television and liked the variety of the characters he was able to play. He would continue to accept work on TV up until the time of his illness. Among his major television appearances were: *Robert Montgomery Presents* (1950-55), *Viceroy Star Theater* (1954), *General Electric Summer Originals* (1956), *Lux Video Theater*, (reprising Monte in an abbreviated 'Mildred Pierce" with Virginia Bruce, 1956), *The Chevy Mystery Show* (1960), *Family Classics* (as Rochester in the production of 'Jane Eyre', 1961), *Rawhide* (1961) and *Dupont Show of the Week* (1962).[287]

He also continued to make movies, appearing as the cowardly husband of his old Warner Bros. pal, Ann Sheridan in the critically panned adventure, *Appointment in Honduras* (RKO, 1953). In 1955, he made two low budget westerns for Allied Artists: *Treasure of the Ruby Hills* with Carole Mathews, and *Shotgun* opposite Yvonne De Carlo, then reteamed with beautiful Yvonne in the ludicrous romantic adventure, *Flame of the Islands* (1955) for Republic. He followed with a third-billed part in the Robert Mitchum/Gilbert Roland minor league adventure, *Bandido* (United Artists, 1956) about Mexican rebels in 1916.

In between movie and TV projects, Zachary accepted stage offers. In April 1956, he appeared in the title role in a critically acclaimed Broadway revival of *The King and I*. Three years later, he won kudos for two other Broadway appearances in *Subway in the Sky* (1957), and *Requiem For a Nun* (1959). His wife, Ruth costarred in the latter, and also wrote the stage adaptation of the William Faulkner novel.

In 1957, Scott returned to England to appear in two of his better latter day films. He played a nasty escaped murderer who sets up an international counterfeiting ring in the melodrama, *The Counterfeit Plan* (Anglo-Amalgamated-Warner Bros., 1958), costarring Peggie Castle, then contributed an exceptional performance as a killer in the suspenseful B crime thriller, *Violent Stranger* a.k.a. *Man In the Shadow* (Anglo-British, (1957), costarring Faith Domergue. Co-producing these two motion pictures, (along with Nat Cohen and Stuart Levy), was the gifted Richard Gordon (*Fiend Without a Face, The Haunted Strangler*). When asked by the author to describe Scott and the two films, Mr. Gordon expressed admiration for his intelligent and shrewd former employee.

"I was not actually present on the sets during the productions . . . but I did have contact with Zach in London during the filming and in New York in between the two pictures. . . I liked him enormously! He had a great a sense of humor. He was a very cultured man interested in all the arts and a great conversationalist. He was also a very shrewd buisnessman . . . For Violent Stranger, Zach demanded a higher fee which was not a significant amount, but his agent was not willing to negotiate the figure. I remember asking Zach after the contract was signed, why he gave me such a rough time on this point. He laughed and said, 'I never work for the same person twice for the same price.'" [288]

Mr. Gordon told the author he recalled having to ask Scott to discard his trademark earring for his gangster role in *Counterfeit Plan*.

"He (Zach) maintained that the earring was a tradition with Greek sailors from whom his family was descended. I never checked on that story! Today it wouldn't be necessary!"

When asked his assessment of Scott as an actor, Gordon replied,

"He was underrated in Hollywood because, after a brilliant start, in Mask of Dimitrios, Warner Brothers typed him as a heavy and cast him in one similar role after another." [289]

In the late 1950's, Zachary took extended leaves from acting to spend time with his wife, daughters, and to enjoy his innumerable hobbies. A man of many interests and abilities, Scott was an expert horseman and swimmer, an avid golfer and a crack shot. Domestically, he was a gourmet cook, a successful gardener, and a collector of, (and expert on), antiques and classical music. Always a perfectionist, he achieved a self-imposed proficiency in all of these areas well above the norm. "My greatest fault," he confessed, "is I just can't sit still for long. I have to be doing something every minute."[290] Another important aspect of his personal character was a lifelong devotion to philanthropy. Throughout his many years in Hollywood, Scott was continuously involved in various charities — projects to help the poor, and excursions to entertain American troops. In press reports after World War II, his associates recalled his tireless charitable

Zachary Scott (center), played a master criminal in the British melodrama, *The Counterfeit Plan* (Anglo-Amalgamated-Warner Bros., 1957).

efforts, and how he urged his fan clubs to adopt war orphans and send food and clothing.

In 1960, Scott began his final earthly decade by appearing in the minor adventure film, *Nachez Trace* (Panarama). A year later, he signed to star in famed Spanish director Luis Bunuel's melodrama, *La Hoven* a.k.a. *The Young One* (Valiant, 1961), filmed in Mexico. The movie seemed a rather odd comeback picture for the 46-year-old star. Set on an empty island, it was the story of a sarcastic game warden (Scott) whose strange fascination and odd relationship with a young girl is disturbed by the appearance of a black musician and a preacher. Apparently meant as an allegory, Bunuel (who also wrote the screenplay), tried to make so many social statements, the film became confused and pointless, and was ultimately unsuccessful. It was a shame, because Zachary poured his heart into his performance of the Jim Crow-minded warden. He followed in 1962, with a total change of pace, as a sinister money grabber in the zany Jerry Lewis vehicle, *It's Only Money* (Paramount, 1962). Sadly, it would be his last motion picture.

In October 1963, Scott made his last Broadway appearance to mixed reviews in the satirical comedy, *Rainy Night in Newark* with Eddie Mayehoff and newcomer, Gene Hackman. In early 1965, he played a crooked jeweler opposite Gig Young in an episode of the acclaimed comic adventure series, *The Rogues*, and was looking at several scripts when he began feeling ill. He was diagnosed with a malignant brain tumor, and began radiation treatments in New York in the spring of 1965. Brain surgery followed in July, but the incurable disease had progressed too far. In August 1965, the still dapper star asked to go home to his mother's sprawling ante-bellum mansion, "Sweetbrush" in Austin, Texas. He was joined by his wife Ruth, and daughters Shelley and Waverly. (The latter, was by then Mrs. William Crawford of New York City.) On October 1, 51-year-old Zachary lapsed into a coma, and died two days later, on October 3, 1965, with his wife, mother, and daughters by his side. He was survived by Ruth, his daughters Waverly and Shelly, his mother, Sallie Masterson Scott and two sisters, Mary Scott Kleberg, and Ann Scott. He was buried in the family plot near his father in Austin Memorial Park. Obituaries and tributes abounded. Many newspapers eerily quoted the interview Zachary gave shortly after the completion of *The Southerner*. It seemed, Zachary Scott had literally lived the advice given him by his favorite director, Jean Renoir.[291]

In retrospect, Scott's movie career seems disappointing. Despite his ability and perseverance, he was unable to fulfill the great acting promise he demonstrated in his initial Hollywood films. Although he eventually proved he possessed the range and ability to handle himself admirably in any type of part, fate intervened in the guise of Jack Warner. Early on in his film career, Warner recognized Scott's ability to portray colorful villains, and began casting him as such! To be fair, Zachary Scott WAS a spectacular movie scoundrel!! He added dimension to these negative characters. Aided by his own singular wit, elegance, and style, he made them more realistic and memorable than they might have been in less talented hands. He seemed to have genuinely liked playing unsavory roles, which perhaps explains at least partially, why he was so good.

If a survey was conducted today among classic films fans to ascertain their favorite 1940's cinematic villains, Zachary Scott's name would certainly appear at or near the top of the list. Decades after his last film appearance, his fame as a movie bad guy continues to live in our memories, and is likely to survive the test of time as long as there are DVDS, and cable television. Why? As Zachary's most famous character, the ultimate elegant cad, Monte Beragon explained to Mildred Pierce, "I loaf, but in a highly decorative and charming manner."

UPDATE

In June 1967, the Austin Civic Theatre was renamed the Zachary Scott Theatre to honor the city's native son. A portrait painting of him donated by his mother, Sallie, hangs in the lobby. In 1972, as a result of a large donation from Zachary's sister, Mary, the theatre was rebuilt and expanded. Simply titled, "The Zach," it remains in operation to this day, a tribute to the actor and hometown boy.

At the time of his death, Zachary was virtually penniless. His interests in the Scott family estate (which involved oil and gas rights), was divided between his two daughters. His wife, Ruth did not appear in his will, but received his $100,000 life insurance policy. According to author Ronald Davis in his biography of Scott, *Zachary Scott, Hollywood's Sophiticated Cad*, (published in 2006), after his death, Ruth claimed she was left in financial need. Ruth told reporters Zachary had wanted their daughter Shelley to share her portion of his estate with her mother while she remained alive. When Shelley did not, relations between the pair were damaged, and never fully repaired. When Zachary's mother Sallie died in 1983, her estate was divided between her children and their heirs. The family home, "Sweetbrush" was left to the University of Texas.

Zachary's first wife, Elaine Anderson Steinbeck continued to live in the Manhattan apartment she shared with her second husband, Nobel Prize winning author, John Steinbeck after his death in 1968. As the executor of Steinbeck's estate and his greatest supporter, Elaine spent her remaining years working tirelessly to promote the great author's memory. To keep his work alive, she promoted books about him, as well as stage, film, TV, and music adaptations of his novels and short stories. She was also active in support of the Steinbeck Research Center at San Jose State University in California, and was a board member of the Bay Street Theater in Sag Harbor, New York, where she had a summer home. For decades, she had running battles with John Steinbeck's two sons (from a previous marriage), over the rights to his work. She died in Manhattan on April 27, 2003, after a long illness. She was 88 years old. She bequeathed her copyright interests to daughter, Waverly and her grandchildren. She purposely excluded Steinbeck's two sons and their heirs.

After her mother's death, Zachary and Elaine's daughter, Waverly Scott Kaffaga has continued to oversee her stepfather's (Steinbeck's) work, and consequently, has been involved in multiple new legal battles with Steinbeck's surviving son Thomas, and the heirs of his other son, John Steinbeck IV, (mostly over copyrights). In September 2017, the ongoing legal feud took a dramatic turn, when a Los Angeles federal jury awarded more than $13 million dollars (of the Steinbeck estate), to Waverly in her suit against her stepbrother and his wife. In November 2017, the Ninth Circuit Court went further, dismissing John Steinbeck's daughter-in-law and heirs' countersuit, stating they have "no right to stop movie adaptations." Waverly, now in her eighties, is believed to be living in California.

After Scott's death, his second wife, Ruth Ford Scott continued to reside at the Dakota, and to act on the stage and on television. During the 1970's, she began a romantic relationship with writer Dotson Radar, 20+ years her junior, and was a popular hostess for celebrity gatherings. Later in life, she became friends with Zachary's first wife, Elaine Steinbeck, but never repaired her relationship with her own daughter, Shelley. Ruth died on August 12, 2009, at age 98. She left her entire $8 million dollar estate (which included two art-filled apartments), to her Nepalese butler, Indra Tamang, disinheriting her daughter, her grandchild and two great-grandchildren. Her daughter, Shelley initially challenged her mother's will in court, but after receiving, "a modest settlement," told the press she was "very happy" for Mr. Tamang. Shelley Scott now lives on the West Coast.[292]

CHAPTER TWELVE
"GLORIA STUART: CHASING RAINBOWS IN DREAMLAND"

(Originally published in *Films of the Golden Age*, Spring, 2007)

Oscar night, March 23, 1998. An electric hush falls over the capacity crowd at L.A's Shrine Auditorium as actor Cuba Gooding Jr. steps to the podium. Five talented hearts begin racing as the young actor recites his canned speech and finally states his intention: to present the Oscar for best performance by an actress in a supporting role. "And the nominees are: Kim Basinger in *L.A. Confidential*, Joan Cusack in *In and Out*, Minnie Driver in *Good Will Hunting*, Julianne Moore in *Boogie Nights*, Gloria Stuart in *Titanic*." As Gooding rips open the envelope to reveal the decision of the esteemed members of the Motion Picture Academy of Arts and Sciences, each actress gazes anxiously into the camera and grips her seat, while audiences inside the auditorium and across six continents hold their collective breath!

For the ever lovely, 86-year-old screen veteran, Miss Stuart, finding out who would take home Hollywood's most prestigious prize was decidedly anticlimactic. By anyone's standard, she'd already emerged a winner with or without the golden statue. Being nominated for an Oscar for a substantive role in the most popular film of all time was a triumph, marking the successful culmination of decades of struggle for recognition as a Hollywood actress, and even more importantly, the attainment of a personal artistic goal she'd set in her youth: to do something she considered "big and great."

One wonders how many times in the days and weeks leading up to this magic moment Miss Stuart had taken time to reflect, to hark back to a time during the gloom and doom of Great Depression, when sound films were in their infancy, and a gorgeous, free-spirited young stage actress armed with a big dream had just arrived on the

Hollywood scene. Back then, Gloria's success seemed as sure as the California sunshine. Beautiful, talented, ambitious, with a camera friendly charisma and a classy low-pitched voice, she was the total package. Who knew it would take 70+ years of chasing a dream for Gloria Stuart to reach her rainbow's end!

Miss Stuart's long arduous journey to Oscar's red carpet began on July 4, 1910, not far from the Shrine Auditorium in Santa Monica, California. Born Gloria Frances Stewart, the future star was the eldest of three children of attorney Frank Stewart and his wife, postal clerk, Alice Diedrick. Of Scottish heritage, Gloria's father was said to be descended from Mary Queen of Scots. Her maternal grandfather was credited with inventing the fresco scraper utilized in road building. A beautiful, precocious child, Gloria harbored ambitions to be a performer at an early age. She recalled her first experiences as an actress in a 2006 interiew with the author.

"I don't know exactly when I first thought about being an actress. Perhaps it was when my parents built a stage in our back yard and we played prince and princess. I remember when I was in fifth grade the kids in the neighborhood would get up on the porch and sing and dance. . ." [293]

Little Gloria's comfortable middle-class childhood would be interrupted several times by family illness and calamity. Her brother, Frank was afflicted with infantile paralysis. When he was three-years-old, youngest brother Tom contracted spinal meningitis and died. In 1919, not long after being promoted to a judgeship, Gloria's father suffered severe leg injuries in a freak auto accident resulting in an infection which caused his death. Devastated personally and financially, Gloria's mother returned to her postal job, and rented the family home, moving her two children into a one bedroom cottage on a friend's lot. Despite tough times, Miss Stuart told the author her mother, Alice managed to foster her children's interest in the arts.

"Mama gave me dancing lessons from the beginning. She played music — old phonograph records a lot, and took us to the movies. Mabel Normand and Gloria Swanson were my favorites . . ." [294]

One year after her husband's untimely death, Mrs. Stewart married successful businessman, Fred Finch, and settled back into a middle-class existence, subsequently giving birth to Gloria's half-sister, Patricia Marie. By then, according to her entertaining autobiography, *I Just Kept Hoping* (co written with daughter, Sylvia), Gloria was "preoccupied" with school, her social life, and plotting a strategy for achieving her newly-minted life's ambition: to do something artistically "big and great," a pursuit which would occupy the remainder of her life.

Upon graduation from Santa Monica High School in 1927, (where she had established a reputation as a rebellious individualist), Gloria entered the University of Southern California at Berkeley majoring in Greek philosophy. While there, she became involved in the Berkeley Players. In 1929, Gloria met sculptor Gordon Newell who literally swept her off her feet. The handsome, talented son of public school teachers, Gordon shared many of Gloria's unconventional beliefs, and her passion for all things creative. Gloria's academics and finances suffered as a result of the romance. To make extra money, she found work as an artist's model, even posing in the nude. "Gloria Stuart, posing naked in a San Francisco artist's studio — me, a member of the Santa Monica haute bourgeoisie! I luxuriated in the idea . . ." [295]

The 19-year-old dropped out of college and married the penniless Newell on June 21, 1930, in an elaborate ceremony (arranged by her mother), at the Episcopal Church in Santa Monica. Possessed with big dreams of artistic success, wedding gifts, and an Essex two-seater (a gift from the Finches), the newlyweds settled into a bohemian lifestyle in a two-room apartment in beautiful Carmel, a haven for artists, writers, and musicians. Gordon found work teaching and doing various menial jobs, and Gloria landed a position writing for the local newspaper, but the couple struggled financially.

In Carmel (1930-31), Gloria honed her acting skills, appearing in a wide variety of productions at the prestigious Theater of the Golden Bough under the aegis of owner/producer Sam Kuster and director Galt Bell. Setting her sights on being a famous stage actress, Gloria quickly gained a reputation for talent and dedication. In the autumn of 1930, she attracted the attention of director/actor Morris Ankrum who offered her the role of Olivia in his production of Shakespeare's *Twelfth Night*, produced at Gilmor Brown's famed Pasadena Playhouse. [296]

In October, 1931, Ankrum returned to Carmel to direct Gloria (as Masha) in the Bough's production of Chekhov's, *The Seagull*, then asked if she'd reprise the role at Brown's private theater, the Bank Box. Although it meant a physical separation, the financially strapped Newells decided Gloria should accept the offer, and look for work in the movies. Abandoning her professed disdain for film, Gloria asked her mother to contact a family friend who knew the casting director at Paramount studios. As she bid Gordon adieu, leaving the beauty and tranquility of Carmel for the hubbub of Hollywood, Gloria couldn't possibly have known how quickly she'd achieve her goal of being in the movies, and how it would change her life forever.

On the night of her debut performance in *The Seagull*, two Hollywood casting directors were in attendance: Phil Friedman of Universal and Fred Datig of Paramount. Impressed by the girl's beauty, poise, and resonant voice, both offered screen tests. Just two days later, the radiant young neophyte had the contract she'd hoped for. In fact, she had two of them! Both Paramount and Universal claimed her. At this critical juncture, the inexperienced, confused Gloria sought the professional advise of her newly-appointed agent, but told an interviewer she received little help.

"I didn't know one studio from another. I didn't know about major and B movie studios or what their components were . . ." I didn't have to have arbitration . . . I was a free agent. But nobody told me so." [297]

Unfortunately for Gloria, the dispute landed in the hands of the Motion Picture Association with famed censor Will Hays officiating. When no agreement could be reached, a frustrated Hays reportedly suggested flipping a coin to determine who would claim Gloria's services. Much to her eventual regret, Universal won the toss. Gloria told interviewer, Tom Weaver,

"I was so innocent and so inexperienced, and very anxious to work. Paramount had Chevalier and Claudette Colbert, and Miriam Hopkins, it was a first-class studio, but I didn't know that. My agent should have given me some information about that, but she didn't." [298]

What Gloria did know was the family-run Universal was paying her double the salary Paramount offered, and more importantly, studio head Carl Laemmle Jr. enthusiastically pledged to present her in film vehicles which would showcase her ability. "I never have seen such poise, such delicate beauty, such depth, why she almost scares you," he stated in 1932. "We'll have to find some truly distinguished stories for her, in fact, the finest, because you see, nothing else would be quite fitting . . . ." [299]

Armed with Laemmle's extravagant promises, considerable natural ability and an iron determination, the newly named Gloria Stuart (her last name shortened so it would fit on a marquee), began a seven-year Universal pact in February 1932. For a time, it appeared as if Laemmle would fulfill his commitment. During her first year at Universal, Gloria made five motion pictures which established her as one of the most beautiful and talented up and coming young stars. Although she was tested for the lead and ended up playing a tiny part in the studio's "prestige" film version of the Fannie Hurst tearjerker, *Back Street* (1932), Gloria's film career really began in earnest when she was loaned to Warner Bros. for a supporting role in *Street of Women* (1932), a drama starring elegant Kay Francis. Although she looked lovely and garnered good reviews playing the daughter of an executive in love with her father's mistress' brother, Gloria did not enjoy making her film debut. She said, on the first day of production, director Archie Mayo initiated her in the "art of filmmaking," by goosing her with a buzzer.

"It was shocking to me, but everybody thought it was hilarious. That was my first five minutes on a Hollywood set. It substantiated my feeling about Hollywood, that I was slumming . . ." [300]

The young, would-be star followed with two showy supporting performances: as the girlfriend of a football star (Richard Arlen) who lets fame go to his head, in the drama, *The All American* (Universal, 1932), and as a school teacher in love with a brave air mail pilot in John Ford's riveting, stunt-filled adventure, *Air Mail* (Universal, 1932). While making the latter, she was spotted by acclaimed British-born director James Whale who asked her to appear in his upcoming film adaptation of the J. B. Priestley novel, *Benighted*, to be titled, *The*

Old Dark House (Universal, 1932). A man of impeccable taste and vision whose semi-expressionist style, use of dark humor, and thorough knowledge of the filmmaking process established him as a formidable Hollywood director, Whale was assembling a top notch group of players to film the follow-up to his mega-hit monster classic, *Frankenstein*. Gloria's cameo-like beauty, elegance, and acting skill were important factors in her selection for the coveted feminine lead. In the fall of 1932, she joined an impressive, mainly British cast headed by Charles Laughton, Raymond Massey (in their film debuts), Melvyn Douglas and Boris Karloff to enact one of the best horror comedies of all time.

The simple tale of five travelers stranded for a night at a forbidding Wales estate owned by a bizarre family, the subject matter of *Dark House* provided its director with ample opportunity to demonstrate his unique style and expertise. He did not disappoint. In his volume, *Classics of the Horror Film*, renowned film historian, William K. Everson referred to *The Old Dark House* as "the apotheosis of all Old House chillers . . . a virtual climax to such works as *The Bat, The Cat and the Canary, The Gorilla,* . . ." [301]

For young Miss Stuart, the horror classic was a breakthrough. As Margaret Waverton, the beautiful upper-crust heroine who becomes the object of the drunken butler's (Karloff) lust, Gloria was splendid. Of special note to Stuart fans, was one unforgettable scene in which glamorous Margaret nervously dons a sexy gown as religious fanatic Rebecca Femm (impeccably portrayed by British actress Eva Moore) watches and condemns from the sidelines. Although not fond of the majority of her Universal films, Miss Stuart reserves respect and affection for *Dark House*, its director, and celebrated cast. In a 2006 interview with the author, she elaborated,

"There were only two directors of taste at Universal: John Stahl, and James Whale. Whale was the best they had — very meticulous about what he wanted you to do, where to move . . . The cast of The Old Dark House were all wonderful to work with. Karloff was just great, very soft-spoken — a real English gentleman!" [302]

With Gloria's film career off to a promising start, the Newells rented a home and studio (for Gordon), in the Hollywood Hills in

CHAPTER TWELVE: GLORIA STUART

Gloria and Ralph Bellamy in director John Ford's adventure drama, *Airmail* (Universal, 1932). Photo courtesy of Richard Finegan.

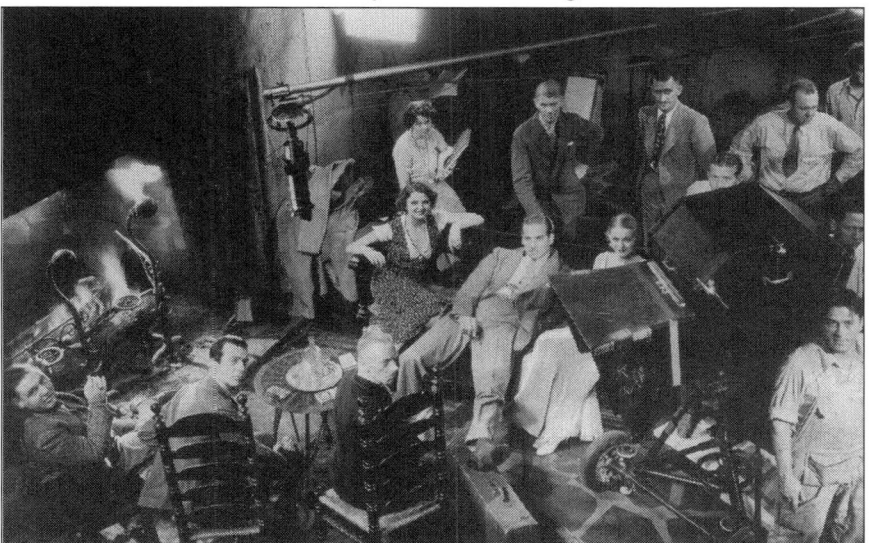

The cast and crew of Universal's *The Old Dark House* (1932), directed by James Whale (back row, second from left) paused for this publicity photo in between takes. Middle row from left to right: Lilian Bond, Melvyn Douglas, and Gloria Stuart. Front row left to right: Charles Laughton, Raymond Massey, Ernest Theisiger. Photo courtesy of Richard Finegan

Director James Whale and two assistant supervise Gloria filming an emotional scene in *The Old Dark House* (Universal, 1932). Photo courtesy of Richard Finegan.

British stage and screen actress Eva Moore and Gloria in *The Old Dark House* (Universal, 1932). Photo courtesy of Richard Finegan.

Boris Karloff and Gloria Stuart in *The Old Dark House* (Universal, 1932). Photo courtesy of Richard Finegan.

February, 1932. Gordon continued sculpting and teaching while his wife toiled long hours at the studio. Rumors of rifts between the young marrieds began almost as soon as Gordon joined his wife in Los Angeles. Gloria attempted to extinguish the speculative fires by essentially fanning the flames, sharing details of the couple's unconventional marriage (which included freedom to date others), with the conservative Hollywood press. In fact, she created a stir when she confided to one nosy reporter on their wedding night, she and Gordon vowed if ever their temperaments clashed, they would take a nuptial "vacation." To no one's surprise, in July 1933, they announced a trial separation "to save their marriage."[303]

Inspired by her friend Melvyn Douglas, Gloria became politically active, organizing actors to promote collective bargaining and better working conditions. On June 30, 1933, she became one of the founding members of the Screen Actors Guild, a dynamic organization which would change the Hollywood filmmaking process forever. Gloria told the author she remains proud of her association with the Guild.

"The hours we worked were so murderous! When I found out what a union was and understood its ideals, I took the whole bait . . . I worked very hard. We all did — on the telephone, in meetings in people's homes. In the beginning, it was all very hush-hush as we didn't want to be suspended or have our contracts cut up in little pieces, but we didn't have any difficulty signing up stars. It (S.A.G.) became so popular they all came out of the closet as union members . . . I'm proud of my part in the movement because actors are protected in their performance and their activities. They're not persecuted because they speak up and complain." [304]

Miss Stuart had little time to consider the impact of her statements or actions. After being named a W.A.M.P.A.S. (Western Association of Motion Picture Studios) Baby Star of 1933, the winsome, five-foot-five inch, hazel-eyed blonde made a mindboggling nine films in 1933, which enhanced her visibility while establishing an unfortunate pattern. Although she had feminine leads in all but one, most of her roles were clearly subordinate to the leading man's, and the vast majority were second features. At her home studio, Gloria was a girl in love with a fugitive murderer (Pat O'Brien) in the far-fetched B melodrama, *Laughter in Hell*, a commander's wife who inspires the ill-placed affections of a rebellious army recruit (Lee Tracy) in the wartime comedy drama, *Private Jones*, and notably, the daughter of the master of a sinister castle (Lionel Atwill) in the eerie low budget murder mystery, *The Secret of the Blue Room*. On loan, she was a amnesiac targeted by a murderous gangster in the minor medical melodrama, *The Girl in 419* (Paramount), the fiancé of the last man on earth (Brazilian tenor Raoul Roulien) in the fantastical musical comedy, *It's Great to Be Alive* (Fox), and the reckless headline-making daughter of a successful entrepreneur (Lionel Barrymore) in MGM's downbeat drama, *Sweepings*.

Two of Gloria's three notable 1933 releases placed her again under the tutelage of James Whale who cast her briefly, but memorably, first, as an adulterous wife murdered by her Austrian doctor husband (Paul Lukas) in the stylish courtroom melodrama, *A Kiss Before the Mirror*, then as the bewildered ex fiancé of a reckless scientist whose experiments transform him into a megalomaniacal murderer in the horror comedy, *The Invisible Man*. The latter movie, based on the H.G. Wells novel, has attained a well-deserved reputation as one of the best horror movies of all time thanks to Whales's gripping, fast paced direction, John Fulton's special effects (black velvet-clad actors filmed before black backgrounds to create "invisibility"), Arthur Edson's sensational photography, superb acting from titled villain, Claude Rains and an excellent supporting cast. Depression era filmgoers and cynical critics were equally awed. In his entertaining review of the film, *The Los Angeles Times'* Marquis Busby called it, "the most fantastic of all the bloodcurdling films. It will have your eyes sticking out on stems!" Seventy three years hence, its leading lady retains fond memories of the production, although she says its star wasn't the easiest person to work with.

"Claude Rains was a great actor, but during the filming, kept backing me into the scenery again and again . . . Whale told him to stop or we would keep doing it (the scene) again and again . . . But he tried anyway. He didn't end up giving me a hard time, because I didn't put up with it! I often regretted not talking to Bette Davis about him. I wondered how she handled him." [305]

Lionel Atwill, Paul Lukas, and Gloria Stuart take a brief break in between scenes during the production of *The Secret of the Blue Room* (Univeral, 1933). Photo courtesy of Richard Finegan.

From left to right: Paul Lukas, Lionel Atwill, Onslow Stevens, William Janney, and Gloria Stuart in the mystery, *The Secret of the Blue Room* (Universal, 1933). Photo courtesy of Richard Finegan.

Gloria admired Claude Rains as an actor, but found him difficult to work with on the set of *The Invisible Man* (Universal, 1933).

Gloria ended the productive year with a second hit movie which turned out to be more of a personal than professional triumph. Chronicling the misadventures of a kindly grocery clerk whose dreams transport him back to ancient Rome, Sam Goldwyn's million dollar musical comedy, *Roman Scandals* (United Artists), was the perfect vehicle for goggle-eyed comedian Eddie Cantor's entertaining schtick, intermingled with lavish Busby Berkeley production numbers, and melodies by the great songwriting team of Al Dubin and Harry Warren. Amid Cantor's gags, a bevy of semi-nude dancing "sweeties," and a spectacular chariot race, many excellent comic supporting performances were lost including a memorable one by the entrancing toga-clad Miss Stuart (as enslaved Princess Sylvia).

By the time she completed *Scandals*, Gloria was publicly voicing her growing displeasure with her employers and the progress of her career. Hit films were wonderful, but ambitious Gloria wanted much more.

"Working with Eddie was fun but I wanted great parts. He was very lively and charming, but very much the star. One of my great memories of Roman Scandals was one day telling Arthur I had noticed a very funny girl in the chorus.' Many years later, I realized it was Lucille Ball . . ."[306]

The "Arthur" Gloria referred to, was *Roman Scandals* scenarist, Arthur Sheekman, whom she met in between takes. According to Gloria's autobiography, their witty first encounter ended in a date resulting in one of Hollywood's longest, most satisfying love affairs. Dubbed by his friend, Groucho Marx as "the fastest wit in the West," former *Chicago Sun Times* reporter and columnist Sheekman had been lured to Hollywood by Marx in the early 1930's to draft scripts. Quickly proving himself one of the film capital's most gifted young scenarists, Sheekman co-wrote the scripts for many of the decade's most enduring comedy film classics including Marx Brothers' *Monkey Business* (Paramount, 1931), *Duck Soup* (Paramount, 1933), as well as Eddie Cantor favorites: *Roman Scandals*, and *Kid Millions* (Goldwyn, 1934). Charming, erudite, yet quiet and reserved, the mustachioed Sheekman was the perfect match for the articulate, artistically ambitious, ebullient Miss Stuart. Soon the couple were inseparable.

As Princess Sylvia in *Roman Scandals* (Goldwyn, 1933).

Even though her marriage had been over for months, Gloria was still Mrs. Gordon Newell. In May, 1934, she filed for divorce. One day after the decree was granted, Blair "Gordon" Newell married one of his art students, and two months later, (on July 29, 1934), Miss Stuart married Arthur in Agua Caliente, Mexico.[307] Although they parted ways, Gloria remained friendly with her ex-husband who eventually became one of America's foremost sculptors with work displayed across the U.S.

Personally contented, Mrs. Arthur Sheekman resolved to put her professional house in order. Increasingly disenchanted with Universal's mismanagement of her career, Gloria flirted with open rebellion when the studio signed temperamental brunette stage actress, Margaret Sullavan to a contract, gave her Miss Stuart's dressing room, and awarded her the lead in their "prestige" picture, *Only Yesterday*, a role Gloria coveted. Miss Stuart learned the news as she filmed the low budget musical drama, *I Like It That Way* (1934). She was livid, telling columnist Ruth Rankin,

"You can't be a 'yes woman' in this town and get along! . . . In two years, I've had only two really good, believable roles . . . So far, I've had the parts that ask all the questions while the person opposite me had all the answers . . ." [308]

Gloria presented her boss with an ultimatum. Either she would receive better assignments, or she'd leave Hollywood and accept an offer of employment as a journalist. According to published reports, Laemmle reiterated his commitment to Gloria, and she returned to work.

Miss Stuart's consolation "prize" for losing *Only Yesterday* was the musical drama, *Beloved* (Universal, 1934), a familial tale tracing four generations of musicians from the Civil War to the 1930's. Despite a decent budget, a good director (Victor Shertzinger), and an experienced cast (including *Only Yesterday's* leading man John Boles), the film's ponderous screenplay negated the expert efforts of all, especially Gloria who contributed a fine performance as the worshipful wife of a violinist. After its release (to mixed reviews), Laemmle reverted to form again squandering Gloria in a series of second features: as an exiled princess in love with a fast-talking journalist (Lee Tracy) in the melodrama, *I'll Tell the World* (1934), a young girl who falls under the hypnotic spell of a evil doctor (Nils Asther) in the incredible Max Marcin melodrama, *The Love Captive* (1934), and as a savvy radio programmer in the all-star musical comedy, *Gift of Gab* (1934).

For the alluring young star the only break in the tedium was being loaned to Warner Bros. for a decent, if uneventful role as Jimmy Cagney's leading lady (replacing Margaret Lindsay), in the Academy

Award nominated comic drama, *Here Comes the Navy* (1934), partially filmed aboard the ill-fated *U.S.S. Arizona*. While making *Navy*, tensions with Universal escalated once again when Gloria learned she'd lost two more important projects: *Glamour* (to Laemmle's current girlfriend, Constance Cummings), and *Little Man What Now?* (to Miss Sullavan, after Universal purchased the story for Gloria). "A fuse blew out in my brain," she later confided, "I was sick with the utter futility of my whole career and the way it was conducted."[309] Her professional woes were compounded when the studio forced her to relinquish the role of Hermia in Max Reinhardt's Hollywood Bowl production of *A Midsummer Night's Dream*. As many classic film fans know, the role was eventually played (both on stage and film), by Miss Stuart's talented second understudy, Olivia de Havilland, thus launching one of filmdom's legendary careers. Gloria told the author she was heartbroken.

"Reinhardt cast me in the role of Hermia and I was in rehearsal right up to opening night when Universal said, 'No, you can't open because we have a film for you that's starting in three or four days . . . They pulled me out! It was a major blow."[310]

Angry and dispirited, the lovely blonde actress took refuge in her social life. Renting a beautiful home in Beverly Hills, the Sheekmans became socially active, entertaining Arthur's friends and their celebrated pals. Gloria discovered she loved being a hostess. She poured all her pent up creativity into the endeavor, planning menus, designing decorations, eventually cooking. With her innate elegance and sense of style, she was a natural. Her tables were a work of art and her guest list a literal "who's who" of cinematic and literary royalty, from ace jokesters: Groucho, Benny, Jessel, to the likes of Kaufman, Chaplin, Sinclair Lewis, Dorothy Parker, and musical geniuses: Gershwin and Segovia. How could anyone remain in a bad mood while being regaled by Groucho stories or serenaded by George and Ira Gershwin? Besides, Gloria had another reason not to be depressed, she was pregnant.[311]

Incapable or unwilling to provide his unhappy contract player with the substantive roles he'd promised, in 1935, Carl Laemmle attempted to placate Gloria by upping her salary (to $1200 a week),

Increasingly unhappy with Universal film projects, Gloria was grateful when the studio loaned her services to Warner Bros. to play James Cagney's lady love in the Oscar nominated, *Here Comes the Navy* (1934).

and lending her services to other studios who presented her with pleasant if insubstantial assignments. She was especially fine as the secretary of a shipping magnate whose family causes her marital problems in Warner Bros. minor league remake of *Saturday's Children*, entitled *Maybe It's Love*, and as the lovestruck daughter of a penny-pinching millionaire in Busby Berkeley's lavish all-star musical comedy *Golddiggers of 1935* (Warner Bros.). The latter, gave Gloria another opportunity to demonstrate her comic skill, and a chance to sing a surprisingly entertaining duet with screen beau Dick Powell of the Dubin/Warren tune, "Goin Shoppin With You." Critics and audiences were impressed. One perceptive critic referred to the elegant, camera friendly actress as, "orchidaceous."

Inexplicably, Universal rewarded its "orchidacious" leading lady by attempting to cast her in *Transient Lady*, a non-descript low budget movie about a crooked roller rink. This time luck and RKO intervened and Gloria skated free. While *Laddie* (1935), RKO's adaptation of Gene Stratton Porter's caste-minded novel about a young farmer's love for a squire's daughter was not the stuff of Academy Awards, it had a good cast, a decent script, and a talented young director, George Stevens. Gloria jumped at the chance to escape Universal's B unit, but underestimated the perceptive Mr. Stevens who soon noted his leading lady's increasing girth. When confronted, Gloria denied she was expecting, but Hollywood bloodhounds caught wind of the mini-controversy. Before the film premiered, Louella Parsons announced the Sheekmans were "shopping for nursery equipment."[312] Her secret revealed, Gloria took a welcome leave of absence, utilizing the time for rest and relaxation, and to indulge in her ever expanding list of hobbies which now included eating. "After years of dieting, I ate and ate and ate. I went up to one hundred sixty odd pounds. What shall I say? I floated free." she quipped. On June 10, 1935, the Sheekmans became the proud parents of a healthy baby girl, a beloved child they named Sylvia after *Roman Scandals'* Princess Sylvia.[313]

Basking in the thrill of motherhood and dreading the thought of grinding out another long series of Universal B's, Gloria put off a return to work. "It said in my contract I had to come back in two months after the birth of a child, so I didn't lose any weight on purpose . . ." she told film historian, Tom Weaver.[314] When she finally returned, and learned Universal planned to cast her as a female Tarzan, she blew her last fuse. "I guess it was a count one, two, three. Then I really started screaming . . . I left in tears." Exasperated, she turned to her husband (newly employed by 20th Century Fox), for help. With the aid of producer Freddie Kohlmar, Arthur persuaded 20th Century Fox head, Darryl Zanuck to purchase Gloria's contract with the proviso she make two pictures a year for Universal. By

September 1935, an official agreement was reached. At last, Gloria was free of Universal's mismanagement and B-movie bondage, free to pursue her big dream, or so it seemed.

Gloria's spirits soared as she began a four-year stint with 20th Century Fox in October 1935. Zanuck welcomed her with a big publicity buildup, a suite next to his most prestigious female contract players, and a starring role opposite two of his hottest actors, but sadly, it was deja-vu over again. After a respectable start, the quality of Miss Stuart's projects quickly declined. By the end of her first year at the studio, Gloria was busy supporting Shirley Temple and/or The Ritz Brothers and churning out programmers — a mind-numbing 14 in three years!

Gloria's best 20th Century Fox opportunities came in 1936. *Professional Soldier* starring Oscar winner Victor McLaglen, Michael Whalen and popular child actor, Freddie Bartholomew, gave her a solid supporting role in a tale of intrigue and friendship involving an endangered boy king and the tough guy who protects and befriends him. As Countess Sonia (Bartholomew's caretaker), Gloria was beautifully photographed, had a lovely wardrobe, and some good scenes with screen beau, Whalen with whom she would be costarred six times. Even better, was *The Prisoner of Shark Island* which reunited the winsome blonde with *Airmail* director John Ford, in a stark, suspenseful, fact based depiction of the tragic life of Dr. Samuel Mudd, convicted of conspiring to murder President Lincoln by treating the injured John Wilkes Booth after his escape from Ford's Theater. Sentenced to life imprisonment in Fort Jefferson on "Shark Island"(in the Dry Tortugas), the film traces the degradation and torture Mudd suffers, and the valiant efforts of his wife (Stuart) to help him win a new trial and choreograph his escape. Masterfully directed, tautly scripted by Nunnally Johnson, beautifully photographed by Bert Glennon, and expertly enacted by a memorable cast (including a superb performance by Warner Baxter in the title role), *Prisoner* remains a powerful film. Its themes: the brutality of prison life (reminiscent of *I Am a Fugitive from a Chain Gang*), and injustice (prevalent in the hysteria following a national crisis), are as topical in a post 9-11 world as they were during the 1860's or in 1936. As Peggy, Dr. Mudd's brave wife, Gloria contributed a multi-dimensional portrayal, her best since *The Old Dark House*. Gentile, playful, loving in the film's early scenes, she matures into a fierce, feisty advocate for the rehabilitation of her husband's reputation, and later, a heroine who risks everything to help him escape. Critics paid homage. *Variety* called Gloria's performance "sympathetic and moving . . ." "One of the best performances of her career," proclaimed Louella Parsons. Gloria told the author she is still fond of *Shark Island*, its star, and legendary director.

"It was a wonderful film. My part wasn't very big, but interesting. I recall, there was always a lot of conversation on the set as to whether my screen husband was guilty or not. I remember reading a lot about the trial and learning about the history . . . Warner Baxter was very thorough. He knew what he was doing, and to me, that was very good. Like Claude Rains, he was completely immersed in being an actor. He carried himself as if he was a very special person which, of course, he was to his public . . . I admired John Ford, but he didn't give me much direction. He came from silents and action films, and there was always a dialogue director . . . He was very reclusive, used to put a handkerchief around his hand. To this day, I do not know what it was for." [315]

The terminally optimistic Miss Stuart thought she might finally be on the precipice of a career breakthrough when Zanuck summoned her to his office after the *Shark Island* premiere. Imagine her surprise when he informed her she would be cast in the next Shirley Temple film. "We want to build you up . . . The pictures you've made so far haven't been seen by many people. You do it." Zanuck said. Stunned and disappointed, the outspoken actress bit her tongue and soldiered on. Directed by Irving Cummings, with great songs by Buddy DeSylva and a talented cast headed by the indomitable "Curly Top," and Alice Faye, *Poor Little Rich Girl* (20th Century Fox, 1936), was, as Zanuck proclaimed, a charming grade A film seen and loved by a greater audience than any of Miss Stuart's previous pictures. Nevertheless, Gloria's small role as the love interest of Temple's widowed father, was not a worthy follow-up to *Shark Island*, and did nothing to advance her career at a critical turning point. After its release, the quality of Miss Stuart's projects declined markedly. By the time she was re-teamed with young Miss Temple two years later, (as her country cousin), in *Rebecca of Sunnybrook Farm* (20th

Gloria portayed Peggy, the wife of infamous physician Samuel Mudd (Warner Baxter) in director John Ford's acclaimed drama, *The Prisoner of Shark Island* (20th Century Fox, 1936). Photo courtesy of Richard Finegan.

Century Fox, 1938), Zanuck had long since abandoned interest in Gloria's career.

With the exception of supporting parts in the Temple films and two zany Ritz Brothers' comedies: *Life Begins at College* (1937), and *The Three Musketeers* (1939), the remainder of Gloria's tenure at 20th Century Fox was spent toiling in programmers (both for T.C.F. and other studios). Although the second features were a waste of Gloria's grade-A talent, the vast majority of her low budget films (of the

From left to right: William Demarest, Helen Westley, Shirley Temple and Gloria in *Rebecca of Sunnybrook Farm* (20th Century Fox, 1938). Photo courtesy of Richard Finegan.

period 1937-39) were fast-paced and entertaining, with intriguing premises, and snappy dialogue. Most are worth a look for no other reason than Gloria's committed performances in a wide range of roles. She was an investigative reporter involved with gangsters and G-men in the thriller, *36 Hours to Kill* (20th Century Fox, 1936), the conflicted wife of a grievously injured scientist who wishes to end his life in the engrossing right-to-die drama, *The Crime of Dr. Forbes* (20th Century Fox, 1936), a bill collector who helps a wise-cracking reporter solve a homicide in the entertaining melodrama, *Time Out For Murder* (20th Century Fox, 1938), and a pro-golfer whose jealous workaholic husband causes her marital distress in the warm-hearted comic drama, *Change of Heart* (20th Century Fox, 1938).

While many a frustrated actress turned to pills or alcohol to seek relief from professional woes, Gloria Stuart found contentment and peace in her family and a plethora of hobbies and causes. A loving husband, a beautiful toddler, a burgeoning reputation as one of Hollywood's premier hostesses, a penchant for writing poetry and gardening, and a position on the Board of Directors of S.A.G.

(1938), were all sources of joy and personal satisfaction. So happy was Gloria's marriage, she publicly moderated her much ballyhooed views on domesticity and personal freedom. "I'm going to be a wife first, an actress second, and an intellectual modern last of all," she told a columnist in 1936. Of course, being a wife first did not mean completely giving up one's individuality. In addition to her S.A.G. duties, Gloria served as chairwoman of the 6th District Democratic State Central Committee (1938), and with friend, Dorothy Parker, championed several liberal causes including the League to Aid Spanish Orphans in the Spanish Civil War, and the Anti-Nazi League.[316]

After filming her role as Queen Anne in the Ritz Brother's bizarre, burlesque version of Dumas' *The Three Musketeers* in 1939, Miss Stuart quietly completed her original seven-year contract. Neither she nor Mr. Zanuck was anxious to renew. In fact, Gloria celebrated the occasion by making a bonfire of her scripts, entrusting little Sylvia to the care of her grandmother, and setting off (with Arthur), on a spectacular pre-war trip around the world. While the couple were in France, the Nazis invaded Poland igniting the tragedy of World War II. The Sheekmans narrowly escaped the gathering storm by boarding the S.S. President Admiral which landed in New York in September 1939.[317]

If her film career appeared on life support, Gloria's thespian dreams remained alive and well. Physically refreshed from their world tour, the financially challenged Sheekmans took up residence in the 'Big Apple' where they both hoped to find success on the Broadway stage. It was not to be. Arthur came close, co-writing *Mr. Big*, a mystery comedy which opened at the Lyceum Theater in September 1941, only to close after only seven performances. Gloria struck out completely. Although she read for several Broadway roles, she was a movie actress — persona non grata in New York stage circles. Money problems eventually forced the Sheekmans to sell some of their West Coast properties, and Gloria to accept any work she could find including radio and summer theater. Between 1940-42, she won plaudits on the "straw hat circuit" (mostly on the East Coast), in several noted plays including: *The Night of January 13th* (1940, costarring Donald Brian), *Accent on Youth* (1940), *Our Town* (1940 with Thornton Wilder), *Pursuit of Happiness* (1940, with Frances Lederer), *Mr. and Mrs. North* (1941), *Curtain Going Up* (1941, with

Constance Collier and Mel Ferrer), *U.S. 90* (1941, with Warren Hull), *The Dark Tower* (1942), and *Sailor Beware* (1942, with Eric Linden).[318]

In 1943, the chastened couple returned to the West Coast, settling in Villa 12 of the famed Garden of Allah, an apartment complex built by Russian actress, Alla Nazimova as a refuge for movie stars and literary notables. A Morrocon village on Sunset Boulevard, replete with fruit trees and tropical bungalows situated around a pool shaped like the Black Sea, guests rented villas on a day to day basis allowing great freedom and flexibility at an affordable price. Among the Sheekmans' famous neighbors were humorist Robert Benchley, actor Humphrey Bogart, writers George Kaufmann and Clifford Odets. Although dispirited about her acting career, Gloria was in her element at the Garden, establishing herself as den mother to the disparate group, hosting lavish parties (1943-45), with elaborate menus and legendary guest lists. In an entertaining 2000 article penned for *The Los Angeles Times* Magazine, "Martini Time in the Garden of Allah," Gloria's daughter, Sylvia Sheekman Thompson recalled some of her parents' more memorable gatherings and her mother's devotion to them. "Dinner parties were my mother's bailiwick . . ." she said. [319]

Despite the heartbreak associated with her Hollywood career, Miss Stuart decided to re-enter films in 1943, only to be relegated once again to second features. She was the love interest of radio star Al Pearce in the Republic musical, *Here Comes Elmer* (1943), a woman threatened by the tyranny of Joseph Goebbels in Monogram's strange bio, *Enemy of Women* (1944), and the secretary of a depressed merchant who has second thoughts about suicide in *The Whistler* (1944, the first installment of the entertaining and acclaimed Columbia series directed by William Castle). After a tiny role supporting Jack Oakie and Joan Davis in the haphazard comedy, *She Wrote the Book* (Universal, 1946), 36-year-old Miss Stuart decided to retire from the screen. Arthur (now employed by Paramount), had been urging her to quit for years. "You'll never be a famous actress, Gloria. You don't have it. Give it up," he said. Gloria always chalked up his critiques to jealousy. "He didn't want me to act," she irreverently recalled in a 1999 interview. "He wanted me to be, as Groucho used to say, 'barefoot, knocked up, and in the kitchen." But by 1946, even the ever hopeful Miss Stuart was forced to read the handwriting on the wall. [320]

For the next three decades, Gloria set aside her burning desire to achieve greatness as a film actress. In 1945, the Sheekmans left the Garden, rented a Spanish-style furnished home in Laurel Canyon, and eventually purchased a larger Brentwood residence. While Arthur was busy penning treatments for such memorable films as *Blue Skies* (Paramount, 1946), *Dear Ruth* (Paramount, 1947), and *Call Me Madam* (20th Century Fox, 1953), Gloria became involved in a dizzying variety of creative endeavors: from cooking and gardening to the art of decoupage. Not surprisingly, she was good at most of the things she tried. In the late 1940's, she purchased a small antique shop on Hollywood's La Cienega Boulevard where (for 4 1/2 years), she designed and displayed her decoupage objects (furniture, lamps, etc.).

In 1954, while in Europe visiting her daughter (now a student at the Sorbonne), Gloria discovered yet another creative avenue when she toured a Parisian museum and viewed the work of Impressionist artists Monet, Manet, and Seurat. "I was so emotionally affected," she recalled in 1980, "I went back the next day and the next and

Ms. Stuart (left) played the loyal secretary of a suicidal businessman in the suspenseful, *The Whistler* (Columbia, 1944), the first entry in the entertaining film suspense series based on the classic radio show.

Gloria (far right) and husband Arthur Sheekman (center) at a Hollywood gathering in 1952.

suddenly I realized I had to paint. . ." [321] Encouraged by art teachers and academics who branded her "a true Naif" (synonym for a naive or primitive artist), Gloria painted for several years. In September 1961, 42 of her paintings (including portraits, landscapes, and still lifes), were displayed in a successful, one woman show at the prestigious Hammer Galleries in New York. It was quite an accomplishment, but was it big and great enough to compensate for her disappointing film career and quell her ambition to be a great actress? Gloria probably thought so at the time. [322]

Both Sylvia and Arthur also found happiness and success during the period. In 1955, Gloria's 19-year-old daughter fell in love with and married 30-year-old writer Eugene Thompson whose talented pen would create some of television's most memorable moments on such hit television series as *Mission Impossible* and *Columbo*. The couple would have four children. In 1958, Arthur scored what many consider his greatest success, adapting James Joyce's novel *Some Came Running* (MGM, 1958), for the screen, and in the early 1960's, won acclaim as a writer for the popular TV comedy series, *My Three Sons*. Of course, as in most families, the happiness and accomplishments were accompanied by struggles and sadness. Despite the couple's successes, the Sheekmans continued to cope with financial difficulties, and Gloria lost one of one of her greatest inspirations when her beloved mother died in 1959.[323]

More challenges lay in store in Gloria's sixth decade of life. In 1971, Arthur began having problems completing his writing assignments. Soon his erratic driving and personality changes became a major concern. A diagnosis of pre-senile dementia (a.k.a. Alzheimer's disease), was determined, eventually necessitating a full-time nurse, then hospitalization at a nursing home. Largely unaware of his condition or surroundings, he spent his final years there. His death in January 1978, left his wife deeply confused and devastated. "To me, that (Alzheimer's), is the most disastrous thing that can happen to a marriage." she said.[324]

As always, Gloria took comfort in her family, friends, and hobbies, but it wasn't enough. Gloria missed acting. She'd abandoned her career partly to please her husband, but the dream hadn't died.

"There are some people who are possessed by the need to express themselves creatively. I'm one of them. I was truly creepy crawly with ambition, dreams, what ifs . . ." [325]

After almost three decades of inactivity, Gloria telephoned her remaining movie contacts in order to give her acting dream one last shot. She would soon learn the comeback trail is a rugged, rocky road.

For 13 long years (1975-88), Gloria Stuart attempted to restart her career as a character actress on the big and small screens. Her parts ranged from bits to small, mostly inconsequential supporting roles in theatrical film releases such as: *My Favorite Year* (MGM-United Artists, 1982), *Mass Appeal* (Universal, 1984), and *Wildcats* (Warner Bros., 1986), made-for-television films including *The Legend of Lizzie Borden* (1975), *Irwin Allen's Adventures of a Queen* (1975), *Flood* (1976), *In the Glitter Palace* (1977), *Merlene of the Movies* (1981), and *Shootdown* (1986), and series guest starring roles on *The Waltons*, and *Murder She Wrote*. Although she had fun, lent class and credibility to the productions, and garnered some good notices, by 1988, she began to lose patience. Distracted by a new romance and competing creative endeavors, Gloria set aside her acting ambitions for a second time.

In 1983, 73-year-old Gloria found two new loves: Ward Ritchie and the art of printing. The proprietor of the famed Laguna Verde Imprenta, award-winning master printer and graphic designer, Ritchie was one of the intellectuals Gloria knew in the early 1930's as Mrs. Gordon Newell. Now a widower, the two reconnected when Ward sent the actress one of his books following the death of a mutual friend. After their first date, they rarely left each other's side. Tied by affection and mutual interests (notably a love for books), they encouraged and influenced one another artistically. Inspired by Ritchie, Gloria purchased her own printing press (housed in her garage), and found great satisfaction and acclaim designing, illustrating, and printing handmaid collectors' books of poetry and art which eventually were housed in the Victoria and Albert Museum in London, the Getty Center in Brentwood, and the Library of Congress special collections. Among her significant achievements: *Portrait by the Artist, Don Bacchardy*, a book featuring art and commentary by the famous portrait painter. In January 1996, Ward Ritchie died at age 92. Although their 13-year relationship had suffered recent setbacks, his passing left another void which would not easily be filled, not even by Gloria's family and myriad of interests.[326]

At a personal and professional low point, when others might have given up, 85-year-old Gloria Stuart forged ahead, and fate rewarded her. Four months after Ward's death, she received a telephone message from Lightstorm Entertainment, the production company of acclaimed director, James Cameron (*Terminator, Terminator II*). Currently casting his next blockbuster, *Titanic*, a romantic drama set aboard the doomed ocean liner, Cameron was looking for a veteran star to play the significant supporting role of Rose Calvert, an elderly Titanic survivor who in 1996, details her tragic love affair with a poor artist against the backdrop of the disaster. After consulting her friend, famed casting director, Marvin Paige, Gloria returned the call. The next day, she met with Cameron's own casting director, who gave her a copy of the script. After a meeting with Cameron, Gloria realized the significance of the opportunity. "Old Rose in the *Titanic* script grabbed me instantly," she remembered. "I knew that evening the role I had wanted, and waited for all these many years had arrived! . . ." On July 9, 1996, Gloria received the news. Old Rose was hers! Her reaction was a mixture of elation, determination, and not a little anxiety. "I felt Old Rose was my last chance to prove I could be a first-ranked actress."[327]

Much has been written and produced on the making of James Cameron's *Titanic* (Paramount-20th Century Fox, 1997), including documentaries, books, and filmed interviews. Suffice it to say, the most expensive film ever made was a spectacle on the grandest of scales. Inspired by Robert Ballard's famed 1987 National Geographic documentary on the Titanic wreckage, director, producer, writer Cameron spared no expense in making his film authentic, from constructing a special studio in Rosarito, Mexico, building a 90% scale model of the vessel which floated in a 17 million gallon water tank, to duplicating interiors and furnishings from original designs, and filming (to spectacular affect), the actual wreckage: inventing and utilizing a special underwater 35 mm. camera in a titanium case mounted on the Russian submersible Mir 1. State of the art special effects, elaborate period costumes, and an exceptional cast headed by Leonardo Di Caprio, Kate Winslet, and Kathy Bates added further dimension.[328]

On July 17, 1996, Gloria flew to Nova Scotia to film her scenes on a Halifax sound stage and aboard the Russian ship, Academik Keldysh. Although her screen time was relatively short, her role as 101-year-old Rose (the elderly counterpart of Kate Winslet — a character reportedly based on noted Ojai artist, Beatrice Wood), was pivotal, with several important close-ups and vital voice overs: narration which framed the motion picture and voiced its social commentary. Initially anxious about "connecting with the lens," Gloria became more confident as she viewed the daily rushes and realized she was effectively communicating with the camera, "filling the screen only with my eyes." Gloria told the author, producer/director Cameron instantly recognized her contribution when he examined her footage.

"He said two things I will always always treasure. First, he said I was looking for a Lillian Gish performance, and I got it. If I had known Old Rose was going to be so good, I would have written more for her!" [329]

Cameron was still working on his epic in July 1997, when the film was scheduled for release. Mired in costly delays, speculation ran rampant the film might well turn out as disastrous as the catastrophe it was depicting. Many important sequences were re-filmed by the meticulous director including Gloria's key final scene (in which she throws the famed Heart of the Ocean blue diamond into the Atlantic, thus returning it to the *Titanic*). It took 14 hours of tedious takes and retakes to film the simple nonspeaking sequence, but Gloria didn't mind. She had only admiration for the man who'd breathed new life into her acting career. "James Cameron is a true Renaissance man," she told Stephen Smith in *The L. A. Times* (1997). "He's a scientist who's won two Academy Awards for invention, he's a writer, director, producer. . ." [330]

Titanic premiered at last in December 1997. A combination of epic disaster, romantic love story, and social critique, it was met with rave reviews. "It is flawlessly crafted, intelligently constructed, strongly acted, and spellbinding," said critic Roger Ebert. Audiences were likewise impressed. In just two weeks, the film grossed over 100 million, and was firmly ensconced at #1 at the box office for four months! By the end of its long run, worldwide box receipts exceeded 1.8 billion, making *Titanic* the most successful motion picture of its time: a big and great achievement if ever there was one! Gloria was jubilant! "At 86, I was going to achieve my theatrical goal. How nutty can life be?" [331]

The exhilaration was tinged with disappointment, however. A big chunk of her role (roughly 50%), had been excised from the final print. Although a let down, the veteran actress eventually took it in stride.

"Cameron was so simpatico. A couple of times he said to me, 'Here comes our Academy Award actress.' Then, the film was cut so. I said to him, 'There goes my award!' He said, 'Gloria, we did everything we could, but nobody's going to sit more than 5 hours in a theater. The theater owners can't turn a film around which runs longer. I wasn't the only one cut. Everyone was. What is the saying, 'the face on the cutting room floor?' It was all our faces: Kate's, Leonardo's, everyone's!" [332]

In spite of the cuts, Gloria's affecting narration and bravura

At 86 years old, Gloria (center) won America's hearts and an Oscar nomination as old Rose in director/producer, James Cameron's blockbuster, *Titanic* (Paramount/20th Century Fox, 1997) which featured an all star cast including Bill Paxton (left) and Suzy Amis (right).

on-camera performance retained power. Funny, irreverent, yet poignant and sad, Old Rose was unforgettable! Her close-ups are a revelation. Mirrored in her eyes, audiences see a composite reflection of the joy, fear, anger, and pain so effectively depicted throughout the picture.

The enormous success of the film sparked a renewed interest in Miss Stuart's acting career, and fueled speculation she might well be candidate for major motion picture awards. From December 1997 to February 1998, as part of a massive television and print media blitz, Gloria did innumerable important TV and newspaper interviews, addressing her role in *Titanic* and all aspects of her life and career.

While caught up in the whirlwind, Miss Stuart began receiving the recognition so long denied her. A Golden Globe nomination from the Hollywood Foreign Press Association was followed by one from the Screen Actor's Guild and A. M. P. A. S. (Academy of Motion Picture Arts and Sciences), all for best supporting actress of 1997. Although she lost the Golden Globe to *L.A. Confidential's* Kim Basinger, Gloria was heartened and a bit surprised to receive two standing ovations from S.A.G., one accompanied by a tribute documentary and a special "Actor" for her work in support of the Guild, and the other for winning best supporting actress, sharing the honor with Miss Basinger. After her S.A.G. win, oddsmakers gave Gloria a good shot at besting Basinger for the ultimate prize: the Oscar. Gloria's friends continually massaged her confidence, so much so, the ever hopeful Miss Stuart began to believe them. "I wanted the nomination very very much, as much as you can want anything — and of course, I said that would be enough, but it wasn't enough." she told Turner Classic Movies in an Archival Project interview. [333]

Cuba Gooding tore open the envelope. "And the Oscar goes to. . ." Gooding looked at the envelope, paused, smiled, "Kim Basinger in *L. A. Confidential.*" Looking lovely in an Escada-created blue satin gown adorned by a spectacular 15 carat, 20 million dollar blue diamond by Harry Winston, a composed Gloria Stuart led the applause for her rival. It was difficult to lose the Academy Award, but in her heart, Gloria knew *Titanic* had made her a big winner. "I felt euphoric that night," she told *People* magazine. "It was what I had always wished for and finally achieved." In 2006, she told the author how gratified she felt by the recognition.

"I must say, achieving my acting ambition involved a great deal of crying time for so long . . . I certainly watched the stars come and go over the years and envied the ones who had good roles. Watching the Academy Awards every year had always been a bitter trip for me for many reasons, but mainly because I always knew I could have been there. . ." [334]

Miss Stuart did not rest on her laurels. *Titanic* had given her acting career a new lease on life, and she was determined to utilize it. Despite a severe arthritic condition (exacerbated by a fall suffered in 1996), and a notable aversion to playing "sweet, loyal, old grandmas," the youthful, energetic star continued to work. Her post-*Titanic* credits included a variety of theatrical films and television movies and series all featuring her as witty, plucky characters, not unlike the actress playing them. She was Kate Capshaw's feisty, eccentric grandmother in Dreamworks' quirky romantic comedy, *The Love Letter* (Dream Works, 1999), a sassy, profane bag lady in Wim Wenders' noir thriller, *The Million Dollar Hotel* (Lions Gate Films, 2000), the peppery mother of covert C.I.A. agent, Dyan Cannon in the charming TV comedy, *My Mother the Spy* (2000), and a 112-year-old survivor of the American Civil War in *Murder She Wrote: The Last Free Man* (TV-2001). Among her series appearances were guest starring roles in *The Invisible Man* (2001), *Touched By An Angel* (2001), *General Hospital* (two appearances 2002, 2003), and *Miracles* (2003). As of 2006, Gloria's last acting performance was a small role in Wim Wenders production, *Land of Plenty* (I. F. C. Films, 2004), an evocative drama about kinship and healing.

Since 1997, Miss Stuart has also contributed insightful commentary to several important historical and film-related documentaries including *The Titanic Chronicles* (1999) (in which she and other actors read excerpts from the Senate testimony of Titanic survivors), *Humphrey Bogart, You Must Remember This* (1997), *Universal Horror* (1998), *Forever Hollywood* (1999), *The World of Gods and Monsters: A Journey with James Whale* (1999), *I Used to Be in Pictures* (2000), and *Hollywood Legends* (2004). In 1999, the veteran actress dusted off her diaries, and with a major assist from her gifted daughter (the noted author of over a dozen bestselling cooking and gardening books), shared her exceptional life story in the appropriately titled autobiography, *I Just Kept Hoping*, and one year later, marked the 90th anniversary of her birth, by receiving her star on the Hollywood Walk of Fame accompanied by her attractive family. As of the writing of this article, at 96, Gloria is still a force to be reckoned with. As feisty, generous, and creative as ever, she is currently designing, and printing a book on Oriental butterfly kites and no doubt planning the next mountain she can climb. If her past history is any judge, there is little doubt the unsinkable Gloria Stuart will accomplish whatever dream she has in mind, no matter how hopeless or impossible it may appear.

In retrospect, acclaimed film and stage actress, gourmet cook, legendary hostess, noted oil painter, distinguished book designer and printer, pioneer union and social activist, AND one of the world's foremost dreamers, Gloria Stuart has amassed an amazing resume of significant accomplishments during her long, extraordinary life. Her secret: early on she set an ambitious goal for herself, and with self-confidence, boundless energy, determination, and talent, doggedly pursued it through thick and thin, through rejection, disappointment, and heartache. She never became a film superstar, but her acting triumph in *Titanic* at age 86 is a testament to her artistic dream and to the indomitable can-do spirit which has characterized her life.

Despite all she's achieved, to many, this inimitable woman's most important legacy is not one of her fine film performances or beautiful works of art, but the life lessons contained in her story. In the months immediately following the release of *Titanic*, Miss Stuart was bombarded with letters from seniors lauding her film work and relating how her achievements so late in life had impacted their lives. "I've received so many letters mostly from women saying, 'You've helped me so much,'" Gloria said in 1999, "When I saw you at 89 doing movies and everything, I decided I'd get out of my chair and do something. . ." [335] At the end of her remarkable lifelong quest to become a great film actress, it appears as if Gloria Stuart has become a great inspiration, not only to seniors, but to all who dare to dream!

UPDATE

For the remainder of her life, Gloria Stuart continued to create, entertain, and inspire, regaling interviewers and the public with her tales of Hollywood and all the legendary people she had known and/or worked with. At the time of our interview in January, 2006, at 96, she was extremely sharp, witty, articulate and occasionally, feisty, and opinionated. A breast cancer survivor, in 2005, Gloria was diagnosed with lung cancer, but continued on as before. On June 19, 2010, the Screen Actors Guild honored Miss Stuart by presenting her with the Ralph Morgan Award at a luncheon in her honor. A couple of weeks later, on July 1, 2010, Miss Stuart added another impressive accomplishment to her incredible resume when she celebrated a century of life. In commemoration of the occasion, the Academy of Motion Picture Arts and Sciences hosted a special party for her on July 21, 2010, which it called, "A Centennial Celebration with Gloria Stuart." Hosted by movie writer and critic, Leonard Maltin at the Samuel Goldwyn Theater, the occasion was marked by several film clips, speeches, and conversations with Gloria. Among the 1000 people who attended, were Gloria's family, and many old friends, former coworkers and admirers including director James Cameron, Francis Fisher, and Suzy Amis from *Titanic*, and

CHAPTER TWELVE: GLORIA STUART

After she read the above article/interview, the author received this autographed photo of his subject.

classic film actresses, Carla Laemmle, Ann Rutherford, and Anne Jeffries. Looking increasing frail, but still lovely, the indominable Gloria was there to greet the celebrants, hear the presentations and help blow out the candles on her enormous cake. By all accounts, it was a memorable occasion and a fitting tribute. Gloria Stuart died at her West Los Angeles home of respiratory failure roughly two months later, on September 26, 2010. Her daughter, Sylvia said her mother had largely ignored the lung cancer diagnosis she received five years earlier. "She also was a breast cancer survivor, but she just paid no attention to illness. She was a very strong woman and had other fish to fry." Gloria was survived by her daughter Sylvia Thompson Sheekman, four grandchildren, and several great grandchildren. She was cremated, and her ashes were presented to her family. [336]

Part 2
The Films

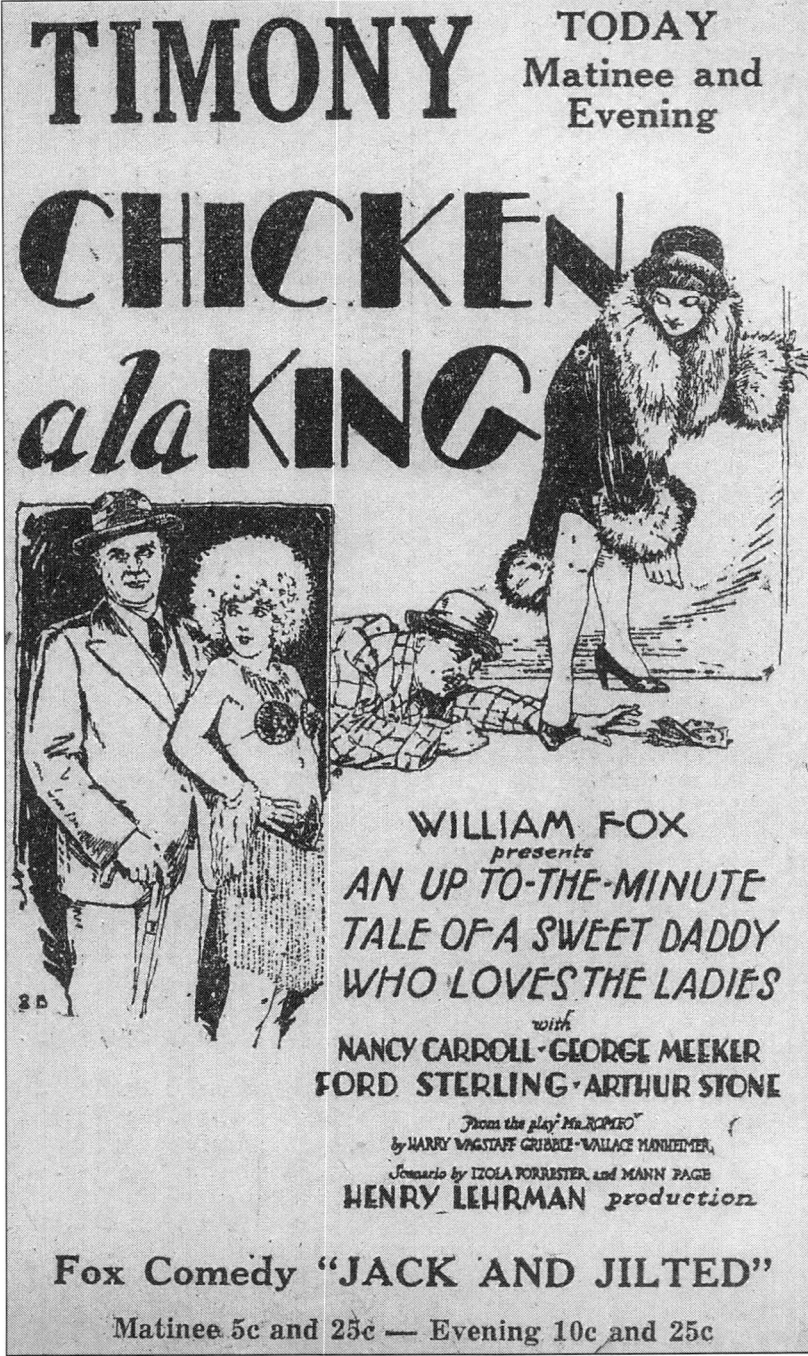

THE FILMS OF NANCY CARROLL

LADIES MUST DRESS (1927)
FOX FILM CORPORATION
DIRECTOR: VICTOR HEERMAN
CAST: VIRGINIA VALLI, LAWRENCE GRAY, TOM COOLEY, NANCY CARROLL, EARLE FOXE, WILIAM TOOKER

ABIE'S IRISH ROSE (1928)
PARAMOUNT
DIRECTOR: VICTOR FLEMING
CAST: NANCY CARROLL, CHARLES "BUDDY" ROGERS, JEAN HERSHOLT, BERNARD GORCY, IDA KRAMER

EASY COME, EASY GO (1928)
PARAMOUNT PICTURES
DIRECTOR: FRANK TUTTLE
CAST: NANCY CARROLL, RICHARD DIX, CHARLES SELLON, FRANK CURRIER, GUY OLIVER

CHICKEN A LA KING (1928)
FOX FILM CORPORATION
DIRECTOR: HENRY LEHRMAN
CAST: NANCY CARROLL, GEORGE MEEKER, FORD STERLING, ARTHUR STONE, FRANCES LEE

THE WATER HOLE (1928)
PARAMOUNT PICTURES
DIRECTOR: R. RICHARD JONES
CAST: NANCY CARROLL, JACK HOLT, JOHN BOLES, MONTAGUE SHAW, ANN CHRISTY, JACK PERRIN

Manhattan Cocktail (1928)
PARAMOUNT PICTURES
DIRECTOR: DOROTHY ARZNER
CAST: RICHARD ARLEN, NANCY CARROLL, DANNY O'SHEA, PAUL LUKAS, LILYAN TASHMAN

The Shopworn Angel (1928)
PARAMOUNT PICTURES
DIRECTOR: RICHARD WALLACE
CAST: NANCY CARROLL, GARY COOPER, PAUL LUKAS, ROSCOE KARNS, EMMETT KING, BEN WOODRUFF

Wolf of Wall Street (1929)
PARAMOUNT PICTURES
DIRECTOR: ROWLAND V. LEE
CAST: GEORGE BANCROFT, BACLANOVA, NANCY CARROLL, PAUL LUKAS, ARTHUR RANKIN, BRANDON HURST

Sin Sister (1929)
FOX FILM CORPORATION
DIRECTOR: CHARLES KLEIN
CAST: NANCY CARROLL, LAWRENCE GRAY, JOSEPHINE DUNN, MYRTLE STEDMAN, ANDERS RANDOLF

Close Harmony (1929)
PARAMOUNT PICTURES
DIRECTOR: JOHN CROMWELL, EDWARD SUTHERLAND
CAST: CHARLES "BUDDY" ROGERS, NANCY CARROLL, RICHARD "SKEETS" GALLAGHER, JACK OAKIE

Dance of Life (1929)
PARAMOUNT PICTURES
DIRECTOR: JOHN CROMWELL
CAST: HAL SKELLY, NANCY CARROLL, RALPH THEADORE, DOROTHY REVIER, MAY BOLEY, OSCAR LEVANT

ILLUSION (1929)
PARAMOUNT PICTURES
DIRECTOR: LOTHAR MENDES
CAST: CHARLES "BUDDY" ROGERS, NANCY CARROLL, JUNE COLLYER, KAY FRANCIS, REGIS TOOMEY

SWEETIE (1929)
PARAMOUNT PICTURES
DIRECTOR: FRANK TUTTLE
CAST: NANCY CARROLL, JACK OAKIE, WILLIAM AUSTIN, HELEN KANE, STUART ERWIN, CHARLES SELLON

PARAMOUNT ON PARADE (1930)
PARAMOUNT PICTURES
DIRECTOR: MULTIPLE DIRECTORS INCLUDING ERNEST LUBITSCH, EDMUND GOULDING AND DOROTHY ARZNER.
CAST: ALL STAR CAST INCLUDING GARY COOPER, MAURICE CHEVALIER, NANCY CARROLL, CLARA BOW

DANGEROUS PARADISE (1930)
PARAMOUNT PICTURES
DIRECTOR: WILLIAM WELLMAN
CAST: NANCY CARROLL, RICHARD ARLEN, WARNER OLAND, FRANCIS MCDONALD, DOROTHEA WOLBERT

HONEY (1930)
PARAMOUNT PICTURES
DIRECTOR: WESLEY RUGGLES
CAST: NANCY CARROLL, STANLEY SMITH, RICHARD "SKEETS" GALLAGHER, LILLIAN ROTH, MITZI GREEN

THE DEVIL'S HOLIDAY (1930)
PARAMOUNT PICTURES
DIRECTOR: EDMUND GOULDING
CAST: NANCY CARROLL, PHILLIPS HOLMES, JAMES KIRKWOOD, HOWARD BOSWORTH, ZASU PITTS

Laughter (1930)
Paramount Pictures
Director: Harry D'Abbadie D'Arrast
Cast: Nancy Carroll, Fredric March, Frank Morgan, Glenn Anders, Diane Ellis

Follow Thru (1930)
Paramount Pictures
Directors: Lawrence Schwab, Lloyd Corrigan
Cast: Charles "Buddy" Rogers, Nancy Carroll, Zelma O'Neill, Jack Haley, Eugene Pallette

Stolen Heaven (1931)
Paramount Pictures
Director: George Abbott
Cast: Nancy Carroll, Phillips Holmes, Louis Calhern, Edward Keane, Guy Kibbee

The Night Angel (1931)
Paramount Pictures
Director: Edmund Goulding
Cast: Nancy Carroll, Fredric March, Phoebe Foster, Alison Skipworth, Alan Hale

Personal Maid (1931)
Paramount Pictures
Director: Monta Bell
Cast: Nancy Carroll, Pat O'Brien, Gene Raymond, Mary Boland, George Fawcett

Wayward (1932)
Paramount Pictures
Director: Edward Sloman
Cast: Nancy Carroll, Richard Arlen, Pauline Frederick, John Litel, Margalo Gillmore

Broken Lullaby (1932)
Paramount Pictures
Director: Ernst Lubitsch
Cast: Nancy Carroll, Phillips Holmes, Lionel Barrymore, Tom Douglas, ZaSu Pitts

The Scarlet Dawn (1932)
Warner Bros.
Director: William Dieterle
Cast: Douglas Fairbanks Jr., Nancy Carroll, Lilyan Tashman, Guy Kibbee, Sheila Terry

Hot Saturday (1932)
Paramount Pictures
Director: William Seiter
Cast: Nancy Carroll, Cary Grant, Randolph Scott, Edward Woods, Lillian Bond

Under-Cover Man (1932)
Paramount Pictures
Director: James Flood
Cast: George Raft, Nancy Carroll, Roscoe Karns, Gregory Ratoff, Lew Cody, Noel Francis

Child of Manhattan (1933)
Columbia Pictures
Director: Edward Buzzell
Cast: Nancy Carroll, John Boles, Clara Blandick, Jane Darwell, Betty Grable

The Woman Accused (1933)
Paramount Pictures
Director: Paul Sloane
Cast: Nancy Carroll, Cary Grant, John Halliday, Irving Pichel, Louis Calhern

The Kiss Before the Mirror (1933)
Universal Pictures
Director: James Whale
Cast: Nancy Carroll, Frank Morgan, Paul Lukas, Gloria Stuart, Jean Dixon, Walter Pidgeon

I Love That Man (1933)
Paramount Pictures
Director: Harry Joe Brown
Cast: Edmund Lowe, Nancy Carroll, Lew Cody, Robert Armstrong, Warren Hymer

Springtime For Henry (1934)
Fox Film Corporation
Director: Frank Tuttle
Cast: Otto Kruger, Nancy Carroll, Nigel Bruce, Heather Angel, Herbert Mundin, Arthur Hoyt

Transatlantic Merry-Go-Round (1934)
Reliance Pictures/United Artists
Director: Ben Stoloff
Cast: Gene Raymond, Nancy Carroll, Jack Benny, Sydney Howard, Mitzi Green, Sid Silvers

Jealousy (1934)
Columbia Pictures
Director: Roy William Neill
Cast: Nancy Carroll, George Murphy, Donald Cook, Raymond Walburn, Inez Courtney

I'll Love You Always (1935)
Columbia Pictures
Director: Leo Bulgakov
Cast: Nancy Carroll, George Murphy, Raymond Walburn, Arthur Hohl, Jean Dixon

After the Dance (1935)
Columbia Pictures
Director: Leo Bulgakov
Cast: Nancy Carroll, George Murphy, Thelma Todd, Jack LaRue, Arthur Hohl, Thurston Hall

Atlantic Adventure (1935)
Columbia Pictures
Director: Albert S. Rogell
Cast: Nancy Carroll, Lloyd Nolan, Harry Langdon, Arthur Hohl, E.E. Clive, Dwight Frye

That Certain Age (1938)
Universal Pictures
Director: Edward Ludwig
Cast: Deanna Durbin, Melvyn Douglas, Jackie Cooper, Irene Rich, Nancy Carroll, Jackie Searle

There Goes My Heart (1938)
United Artists
Director: Norman Z. McLeod
Cast: Fredric March, Virginia Bruce, Patsy Kelly, Alan Mowbray, Nancy Carroll, Arthur Lake

THE FILMS OF GLORIA DICKSON

They Won't Forget (1937)
Warner Bros.
Director: Mervyn LeRoy
Cast: Claude Rains, Allyn Joslyn, Gloria Dickson, Edward Norris, Otto Kruger

Talent Scout (1937)
Warner Bros.
Director: William Clemens
Cast: Donald Woods, Jeanne Madden, Fred Lawrence, Charles Halton, Gloria Dickson (bit)

Gold Diggers in Paris (1938)
Warner Bros.
Director: Ray Enright
Cast: Rudy Vallee, Rosemary Lane, Hugh Herbert, Allen Jenkins, Gloria Dickson, Fritz Feld

Racket Busters (1938)
Warner Bros.
Director: Lloyd Bacon
Cast: Humphrey Bogart, George Brent, Gloria Dickson, Allen Jenkins, Walter Abel

Secrets of an Actress (1938)
Warner Bros.
Director: William Keighley
Cast: Kay Francis, George Brent, Ian Hunter, Gloria Dickson, Penny Singleton

Heart of the North (1938)
Warner Bros.
Director: Lewis Seiler
Cast: Dick Foran, Gloria Dickson, Gale Page, Allen Jenkins, Patric Knowles

They Made Me a Criminal (1939)
Warner Bros.
Director: Busby Berkeley
Cast: John Garfield, Claude Rains, Ann Sheridan, May Robson, Gloria Dickson, Ward Bond

Waterfront (1939)
Warner Bros.
Director: Terry O. Morse
Cast: Gloria Dickson, Dennis Morgan, Marie Wilson, Sheila Bromley, Frank Faylen

The Cowboy Quarterback (1939)
WARNER BROS.
DIRECTOR: NOEL M. SMITH
CAST: BERT WHEELER, MARIE WILSON, GLORIA DICKSON, WILLIAM DEMAREST, EDDIE FOY JR.

No Place to Go (1939)
WARNER BROS.
DIRECTOR: TERRY O. MORSE
CAST: DENNIS MORGAN, GLORIA DICKSON, FRED STONE, SONNY BUPP, ALDRICH BOWKER

On Your Toes (1939)
WARNER BROS.
DIRECTOR: RAY ENRIGHT
CAST: VERA ZORINA, EDDIE ALBERT, ALAN HALE, FRANK McHUGH, GLORIA DICKSON

Private Detective (1939)
WARNER BROS.
DIRECTOR: NOEL M. SMITH
CAST: JANE WYMAN, DICK FORAN, GLORIA DICKSON, MAXIE ROSENBLOOM

King of the Lumberjacks (1940)
WARNER BROS.
DIRECTOR: WILLIAM CLEMENS
CAST: JOHN PAYNE, GLORIA DICKSON, STANLEY FIELDS, JOE SAWYER, VICTOR KILIAN

Tear Gas Squad (1940)
WARNER BROS.
DIRECTOR: TERRY O. MORSE
CAST: DENNIS MORGAN, JOHN PAYNE, GLORIA DICKSON, GEORGE REEVES, FRANK WILCOX

I Want a Divorce (1940)
Paramount Pictures
Director: Ralph Murphy
Cast: Joan Blondell, Dick Powell, Gloria Dickson, Frank Fay, Jessie Ralph

This Thing Called Love (1940)
Columbia Pictures
Director: Alexander Hall
Cast: Rosalind Russell, Melvyn Douglas, Binnie Barnes, Gloria Dickson

The Big Boss (1941)
Columbia Pictures
Director: Charles Barton
Cast: Otto Kruger, Gloria Dickson, John Litel, Don Beddoe, Robert Fiske

Mercy Island (1941)
Republic Pictures
Director: William Morgan
Cast: Ray Middleton, Gloria Dickson, Otto Kruger, Donald Douglas

The Affairs of Jimmy Valentine (1942)
Republic Pictures
Director: Bernard Vorhaus
Cast: Dennis O'Keefe, Ruth Terry, Gloria Dickson, George E. Stone, Roscoe Ates

Power of the Press (1943)
Columbia Pictures
Director: Lew Landers
Cast: Gloria Dickson, Guy Kibbee, Otto Kruger, Lee Phelps, Lee Tracy

Lady of Burlesque **(1943)**
United Artists
Director: William A. Wellman
Cast: Barbara Stanwyck, Michael O'Shea, J. Edward Bromberg, Iris Adrian, Gloria Dickson

The Crime Doctor's Strangest Case **(1943)**
Columbia Pictures
Director: Eugene Forde
Cast: Warner Baxter, Lynn Merrick, Gloria Dickson, Barton MacLane, Jerome Cowan

Rationing **(1944)**
MGM
Director: Willis Goldbeck
Cast: Wallace Beery, Marjorie Main, Donald Meek, Dorothy Morris, Gloria Dickson

THE FILMS OF CLAIRE DODD

Our Blushing Brides **(1930)**
MGM
Director: Harry Beaumont
Cast: Robert Montgomery, Joan Crawford, Anita Page, Claire Dodd (uncredited)

Whoopie **(1930)**
Sam Goldwyn/United Artists
Director: Thornton Freelan
Cast: Eddie Cantor, Ethel Shutta, Paul Gregory, Marian Marsh, Claire Dodd (uncredited)

Up Pops the Devil **(1931)**
Paramount Pictures
Director: A. Edward Sutherland
Cast: Richard "Skeets" Gallagher, Norman Foster, Carole Lombard, Claire Dodd (uncredited)

The Lawyer's Secret (1931)
PARAMOUNT PICTURES
DIRECTORS: LOUIS J. GASNIER, MAX MARCIN
CAST: CLIVE BROOK, CHARLES "BUDDY" ROGERS, RICHARD ARLEN, FAY WRAY, CLAIRE DODD (UNCREDITED)

Confessions of a Co-Ed (1931)
PARAMOUNT PICTURES
DIRECTORS: DUDLEY MURPHY, DAVID BURTON
CAST: PHILLIPS HOLMES, SYLVIA SIDNEY, NORMAN FOSTER, CLAUDIA DELL, CLAIRE DODD (UNCREDITED)

The Secret Call (1931)
PARAMOUNT PICTURES
DIRECTOR: STUART WALKER
CAST: RICHARD ARLEN, PEGGY SHANNON, CHARLES TROWBRIDGE, CLAIRE DODD

An American Tragedy (1931)
PARAMOUNT PICTURES
DIRECTOR: JOSEF VON STERNBERG
CAST: PHILLIPS HOLMES, SYLVIA SIDNEY, FRANCES DEE, IRVING PICHEL, CLAIRE DODD (UNCREDITED)

The Road to Reno (1931)
PARAMOUNT PICTURES
DIRECTOR: RICHARD WALLACE
CAST: LILYAN TASHMAN, CHARLES "BUDDY" ROGERS, PEGGY SHANNON, CLAIRE DODD (UNCREDITED)

Girls About Town (1931)
PARAMOUNT PICTURES
DIRECTOR: GEORGE CUKOR
CAST: KAY FRANCIS, JOEL MCCREA, LILYAN TASHMAN, ALAN DINEHART, CLAIRE DODD (UNCREDITED)

Working Girls **(1931)**
Paramount Pictures
Director: Dorothy Arzner
Cast: Judith Wood, Dorothy Hall, Charles "Buddy"
   Rogers, Claire Dodd (uncredited)

Under Eighteen **(1931)**
Warner Bros.
Director: Archie Mayo
Cast: Warren William, Marian Marsh, Anita Page,
   Regis Toomey, Claire Dodd (uncredited)

Two Kinds of Women **(1932)**
Paramount Pictures
Director: William C. DeMille
Cast: Miriam Hopkins, Phillips Holmes, Wynne Gibson,
   Claire Dodd (uncredited)

Alias the Doctor **(1932)**
First National Pictures
Directors: Michael Curtiz, Lloyd Bacon
Cast: Richard Barthelmess, Marian Marsh,
   Norman Foster, Claire Dodd (uncredited)

Dancers in the Dark **(1932)**
Paramount Pictures
Director: David Burton
Cast: Miriam Hopkins, Jack Oakie, George Raft,
   Eugene Pallette, Claire Dodd (uncredited)

The Broken Wing **(1932)**
Paramount Pictures
Director: Lloyd Corrigan
Cast: Lupe Velez, Leo Carrillo, Melvyn Douglas,
   George Barbier, Claire Dodd

This Is the Night (1932)
PARAMOUNT PICTURES
DIRECTOR: FRANK TUTTLE
CAST: LILY DAMITA, CARY GRANT, CHARLIE RUGGLES, ROLAND YOUNG, CLAIRE DODD (UNCREDITED)

Man Wanted (1932)
WARNER BROS.
DIRECTOR: WILLIAM DIETERLE
CAST: KAY FRANCIS, DAVID MANNERS, UNA MERKEL, ANDY DEVINE, CLAIRE DODD

Guilty as Hell (1932)
PARAMOUNT PICTURES
DIRECTOR: ERLE C. KENTON
CAST: EDMUND LOWE, VICTOR MCLAGLEN, RICHARD ARLEN, CLAIRE DODD (UNCREDITED)

Crooner (1932)
WARNER BROS.
DIRECTOR: LLOYD BACON
CAST: DAVID MANNERS, ANN DVORAK, KEN MURRAY, J. CARROL NAISH, CLAIRE DODD

Lawyer Man (1932)
WARNER BROS.
DIRECTOR: WILLIAM DIETERLE
CAST: WILLIAM POWELL, JOAN BLONDELL, DAVID LANDAU, HELEN VINSON, CLAIRE DODD, ALLEN JENKINS

The Match King (1932)
WARNER BROS.
DIRECTOR: HOWARD BRETHERTON
CAST: WARREN WILLIAM, LILY DAMITA, GLENDA FARRELL, JULIETTE COMPTON, CLAIRE DODD

Parachute Jumper (1933)
Warner Bros.
Director: Alfred E. Green
Cast: Douglas Fairbanks Jr., Bette Davis, Frank McHugh, Claire Dodd, Leo Carrillo

Hard to Handle (1933)
Warner Bros.
Director: Mervyn LeRoy
Cast: James Cagney, Mary Brian, Allen Jenkins, Ruth Donnelly, Claire Dodd

Blondie Johnson (1933)
Warner Bros.
Director: Ray Enright
Cast: Joan Blondell, Chester Morris, Allen Jenkins, Earle Foxe, Claire Dodd

Elmer the Great (1933)
Warner Bros.
Director: Mervyn LeRoy
Cast: Joe E. Brown, Patricia Ellis, Claire Dodd, Frank McHugh, Preston Foster

Ex-Lady (1933)
Warner Bros.
Director: Robert Florey
Cast: Gene Raymond, Bette Davis, Frank McHugh, Monroe Owsley, Claire Dodd

Ann Carver's Profession (1933)
Columbia Pictures
Director: Edward Buzzell
Cast: Fay Wray, Gene Raymond, Claire Dodd, Arthur Pierson, Frank Albertson

Footlight Parade (1933)
Warner Bros.
Director: Lloyd Bacon
Cast: James Cagney, Joan Blondell, Ruby Keeler, Dick Powell, Frank McHugh, Claire Dodd

My Woman (1933)
Columbia Pictures
Director: Victor Schertzinger
Cast: Helen Twelvetrees, Victor Jory, Wallace Ford, Claire Dodd, Hobart Cavanaugh

Massacre (1934)
Warner Bros.
Director: Alan Crosland
Cast: Richard Barthelmess, Ann Dvorak, Dudley Digges, Claire Dodd, Henry O'Neill

Gambling Lady (1934)
Warner Bros.
Director: Archie Mayo
Cast: Barbara Stanwyck, Joel McCrea, Pat O'Brien, Claire Dodd, C. Aubrey Smith

Journal of a Crime (1934)
First National Pictures
Director: William Keighley
Cast: Ruth Chatterton, Adolphe Menjou, Claire Dodd, George Barbier, Noel Madison

Smarty (1934)
Warner Bros.
Director: Robert Florey
Cast: Joan Blondell, Warren William, Edward Everett Horton, Frank McHugh, Claire Dodd

The Personality Kid (1934)
Warner Bros.
Director: Alan Crosland
Cast: Pat O'Brien, Glenda Farrell, Claire Dodd, Robert Glecker, Henry O'Neill

I Sell Anything (1934)
Warner Bros.
Director: Robert Florey
Cast: Pat O'Brien, Ann Dvorak, Claire Dodd, Roscoe Karns, Hobart Cavanaugh

Secret of the Chateau (1934)
Universal Pictures
Director: Richard Thorpe
Cast: Claire Dodd, Alice White, Osgood Perkins, Jack LaRue, George E. Stone

Babbitt (1934)
Warner Bros.
Director: William Keighley
Cast: Guy Kibbee, Aline MacMahon, Claire Dodd, Maxine Doyle, Minor Watson

Roberta (1935)
RKO Radio Pictures
Director: William A. Seiter
Cast: Irene Dunne, Randolph Scott, Fred Astaire, Ginger Rogers, Helen Westley, Claire Dodd

The Case of the Curious Bride (1935)
Warner Bros.
Director: Michael Curtiz
Cast: Warren William, Margaret Lindsay, Donald Woods, Claire Dodd, Allen Jenkins

The Glass Key **(1935)**
PARAMOUNT PICTURES
DIRECTOR: FRANK TUTTLE
CAST: GEORGE RAFT, EDWARD ARNOLD, CLAIRE DODD,
 RAY MILLAND

Don't Bet on Blondes **(1935)**
WARNER BROS.
DIRECTOR: ROBERT FLOREY
CAST: WARREN WILLIAM, CLAIRE DODD, GUY KIBBEE,
 WILLIAM GARGAN, ERROL FLYNN

The Goose and the Gander **(1935)**
WARNER BROS.
DIRECTOR: ALFTED E. GREEN
CAST: KAY FRANCIS, GEORGE BRENT, GENEVIEVE TOBIN,
 JOHN ELDREDGE, CLAIRE DODD

The Payoff **(1935)**
WARNER BROS.
DIRECTOR: ROBERT FLOREY
CAST: JAMES DUNN, CLAIRE DODD, PATRICIA ELLIS,
 ALAN DINEHART, JOSEPH CREHAN

The Singing Kid **(1936)**
WARNER BROS.
DIRECTORS: WILLIAM KEIGHLEY, BUSBY BERKELEY
CAST: AL JOLSON, SYBIL JASON, BEVERLY ROBERTS, LYLE TALBOT,
 CLAIRE DODD

Navy Born **(1936)**
REPUBLIC PICTURES
DIRECTOR: NATE WATT
CAST: WILLIAM GARGAN, CLAIRE DODD, DOUGLAS FOWLEY,
 DOROTHY TREE, GEORGE IRVING

Murder By an Aristocrat **(1936)**
Warner Bros.
Director: Frank MacDonald
Cast: Lyle Talbot, Marguerite Churchill, Claire Dodd,
    John Eldredge, Gordon Elliott

Two Against the World* a.k.a. *One Fatal Hour **(1936)**
Warner Bros.
Director: William McGann
Cast: Humphrey Bogart, Beverly Roberts, Linda Perry,
    Henry O'Neill, Claire Dodd

The Case of the Velvet Claws **(1936)**
Warner Bros.
Director: William Clemens
Cast: Warren William, Claire Dodd, Winifred Shaw,
    Gordon Elliott, Addison Richards

The Women Men Marry **(1937)**
MGM
Director: Errol Taggart
Cast: George Murphy, Josephine Hutchinson, Claire Dodd,
    Sidney Blackmer

Romance in the Dark **(1938)**
Paramount Picures
Director: H. C. Potter
Cast: Gladys Swarthout, John Boles, John Barrymore,
    Claire Dodd, Fritz Feld

Fast Company **(1938)**
MGM
Director: Edward Buzzell
Cast: Melvyn Douglas, Florence Rice, Claire Dodd,
    Louis Calhern, George Zucco

Three Loves Has Nancy (1938)
MGM
DIRECTOR: RICHARD THORPE
CAST: JANET GAYNOR, ROBERT MONTGOMERY, FRANCHOT TONE, GUY KIBBE, CLAIRE DODD

Charlie Chan in Honolulu (1938)
20TH CENTURY FOX PICTURES
DIRECTOR: H. BRUCE HUMBERSTONE
CAST: SIDNEY TOLER, SEN YUNG, PHYLLIS BROOKS, EDDIE COLLINS, CLAIRE DODD

Woman Doctor (1939)
REPUBLIC PICTURES
DIRECTOR: SIDNEY SALKOW
CAST: FRIEDA INESCOURT, HENRY WILCOXON, CLAIRE DODD, SYBIL JASON, CORA WITHERSPOON

Slightly Honorable (1939)
UNITED ARTISTS
DIRECTOR: TAY GARNETT
CAST: PAT O'BRIEN, EDWARD ARNOLD, BRODERICK CRAWFORD, RUTH TERRY, CLAIRE DODD

If I Had My Way (1940)
UNIVERSAL PICTURES
DIRECTOR: DAVID BUTLER
CAST: BING CROSBY, GLORIA JEAN, CHARLES WINNINGER, ALLYN JOSLYN, CLAIRE DODD

The Black Cat (1941)
UNIVERSAL PICTURES
DIRECTOR: ALBERT S. ROGELL
CAST: BASIL RATHBONE, HUGH HERBERT, ANNE GWYNNE, BELA LUGOSI, CLAIRE DODD

In the Navy (1941)
Universal Pictures
Director: Arthur Lubin
Cast: Budd Abbott, Lou Costello, Dick Powell,
   Claire Dodd, The Andrews Sisters

Don Winslow of the Navy (1942) (serial)
Universal Pictures
Directors: Ford Beebe, Ray Taylor
Cast: Don Terry, Walter Sande, John Litel,
   Samuel S. Hinds, Claire Dodd

The Mad Doctor of Market Street (1942)
Universal Pictures
Director: Joseph H. Lewis
Cast: Lionel Atwill, Una Merkel, Claire Dodd,
   Nat Pendleton, Anne Nagel, Hardie Albright

Mississippi Gambler a.k.a. *Danger On the River* (1942)
Universal Pictures
Director: John Rawlins
Cast: Kent Taylor, Frances Langford, John Litel,
   Shemp Howard, Claire Dodd

The Daring Young Man (1942)
Columbia Pictures
Director: Frank R. Strayer
Cast: Joe E. Brown, Marguerite Chapman, William Wright,
   Roger Clark, Claire Dodd

THE FILMS OF RICHARD GREENE

Sing As We Go (1934)
Ealing Studios-British
Director: Basil Dean
Cast: Gracie Fields, John Loder, Dorothy Hyson,
   Richard Greene (uncredited)

Four Men and a Prayer (1938)
20th Century Fox
Director: John Ford
Cast: Loretta Young, Richard Greene, George Sanders, David Niven, C. Aubrey Smith

My Lucky Star (1938)
20th Century Fox
Director: Roy Del Ruth
Cast: Sonja Henie, Richard Greene, Cesar Romero, Joan Davis, Buddy Ebsen, Arthur Treacher

Submarine Patrol (1938)
20th Century Fox
Director: John Ford
Cast: Richard Greene, Nancy Kelly, Preston Foster, George Bancroft, Warren Hymer

Kentucky (1938)
20th Century Fox
Director: David Butler
Cast: Loretta Young, Richard Greene, Walter Brennan, Karen Morley, Moroni Olsen

The Little Princess (1939)
20th Century Fox
Director: Walter Lang
Cast: Shirley Temple, Richard Greene, Anita Louise, Ian Hunter, Arthur Treacher

The Hound of the Baskervilles (1939)
20th Century Fox
Director: Sidney Lanfield
Cast: Basil Rathbone, Nigel Bruce, Richard Greene, Wendy Barrie, Lionel Atwill

Stanley and Livingstone (1939)
20th Century Fox
Directors: Henry King, Otto Brower
Cast: Spencer Tracy, Nancy Kelly, Richard Greene, Walter Brennan, Charles Coburn

Here I Am a Stranger (1939)
20th Century Fox
Director: Roy Del Ruth
Cast: Richard Greene, Richard Dix, Brenda Joyce, Roland Young, Gladys George

Little Old New York (1940)
20th Century Fox
Director: Henry King
Cast: Alice Faye, Fred MacMurray, Richard Greene, Brenda Joyce, Andy Devine, Fritz Feld

I Was an Adventuress **(1940)**
20TH CENTURY FOX
DIRECTOR: GREGORY RATOFF
CAST: VERA ZORINA, RICHARD GREENE, ERICH VON STROHEIM, PETER LORRE, SIG RUMAN

Flying Fortress **(1942)**
WARNER BROS. — BRITISH
DIRECTOR: WALTER FORDE
CAST: RICHARD GREENE, CARLA LEHMANN, BETTY STOCKFIELD, SIDNEY KING

Unpublished Story **(1942)**
TWO CITIES FILMS — BRITISH
DIRECTOR: HAROLD FRENCH
CAST: RICHARD GREENE, VALERIE HOBSON, BASIL RADFORD, ROLAND CULVER, MILES MALLESON

Yellow Canary **(1943)**
RKO RADIO PICTURES — BRITISH
DIRECTOR: HERBERT WILCOX
CAST: ANNA NEAGLE, RICHARD GREENE, ALBERT LIEVEN, LUCIE MANNHEIM, NOVA PILBEAM

Don't Take It to Heart **(1944)**
TWO CITIES — BRITISH
DIRECTOR: JEFFREY DELL
CAST: RICHARD GREENE, ALFRED DRAYTON, PATRICIA MEDINA, MOORE MARRIOTT, JOAN HICKSON

Showtime **(1946)**
EMBASSY PICTURES — BRITISH
DIRECTORS: GEORGE KING, LEONTINE SAGAN
CAST: RICHARD GREENE, ANN TODD, PETER GRAVES, HAZEL COURT, MORLAND GRAHAM

Forever Amber **(1947)**
20th Century Fox
Directors: Otto Preminger, John M. Stahl
Cast: Linda Darnell, Cornel Wilde, Richard Greene, George Sanders, Jessica Tandy

The Fighting O'Flynn **(1949)**
Universal Pictures
Director: Arthur Pierson
Cast: Douglas Fairbanks Jr., Helena Carter, Richard Greene, Patricia Medina, Arthur Shields

The Fan **(1949)**
20th Century Fox
Director: Otto Preminger
Cast: Jeanne Crain, Madeleine Carroll, George Sanders, Richard Greene, Martita Hunt

If This Be Sin a.k.a. That Dangerous Age **(1949)**
London Films — British
Director: Gregory Ratoff
Cast: Myrna Loy, Roger Livesey, Peggy Cummins, Richard Greene, Elizabeth Allan

Now Barabbas **(1949)**
Warner Bros. — British
Director: Gordon Parry
Cast: Richard Greene, Cedric Hardwicke, Kathleen Harrision, Richard Burton

The Desert Hawk **(1950)**
Universal Pictures
Director: Frederick de Cordova
Cast: Yvonne DeCarlo, Richard Greene, Jackie Gleason, George Macready, Rock Hudson

Operation X **(1950)**
LONDON FILMS — BRITISH
DIRECTOR: GREGORY RATOFF
CAST: EDWARD G. ROBINSON, PEGGIE CUMMINS,
   RICHARD GREENE, NORA SWINBRUNE, FINLAY CURRIE

Shadow of the Eagle **(1950)**
VALIANT FILMS — BRITISH
DIRECTOR: SIDNEY SALKOW
CAST: RICHARD GREENE, VALENTINA CORTESE, GRETA GYNT,
   BINNIE BARNES, HUGH FRENCH

The Rival of the Empress
A.K.A. ***La rivate dell'imperatrice*** **(1951)**
SCALERA FILMS — BRITISH-ITALIAN
DIRECTORS: JACOPO COMIN, SIDNEY SALKOW
CAST: RICHARD GREENE, VALENTINA CORTESE, GRETA GYNT,
   ISA POLA, HUGH FRENCH

Lorna Doone **(1951)**
COLUMBIA PICTURES
DIRECTOR: PHIL KARLSON
CAST: BARBARA HALE, RICHARD GREENE, CARL BENTON REID,
   WILLIAM BISHOP, RON RANDELL

The Black Castle **(1952)**
UNIVERSAL PICTURES
DIRECTOR: NATHAN H. JURAN
CAST: RICHARD GREENE, BORIS KARLOFF, STEPHEN MCNALLY,
   RITA CORDAY, LON CHANEY JR.

Rogue's March **(1953)**
MGM
DIRECTOR: ALLAN DAVIS
CAST: PETER LAWFORD, RICHARD GREENE, JANICE RULE,
   LEO G. CARROLL, JOHN ABBOTT, PATRICK AHERNE

Bandits of Corsica **(1953)**
United Artists
Director: Ray Nazzaro
Cast: Richard Greene, Paula Raymond, Raymond Burr, Dona Drake, Lee Van Cleef

Contraband Spain **(1955)**
Associated British-Pathe — British
Directors: Lawrence Huntington, Julio Salvado
Cast: Richard Greene, Anouk Aimee, Michael Dennison, Jose Nieto, Alfonso Estela

Beyond the Curtain **(1960)**
Martin Films Ltd. — J. Arthur Rank Film Distributors — British
Director: Compton Bennett
Cast: Richard Greene, Eva Bartok, Marius Goring, Lucie Mannheim, Andree Melly

Sword of Sherwood Forest **(1960)**
Hammer Films — British
Director: Terence Fisher
Cast: Richard Greene, Peter Cushing, Niall MacGinnis, Sarah Branch, Nigel Green

Island of the Lost **(1967)**
Paramount Pictures
Director: John Florea
Cast: Richard Greene, Luke Halpin, Sheilah Wells, Irene Tsu, Robin Mattson

The Blood of Fu Manchu **(1967)**
Tower of London Productions — British
Director: Jesus Franco
Cast: Christopher Lee, Richard Greene, Howard Marion-Crawford, Shirley Eaton, Maria Rohm

***The Castle of Fu Manchu* (1969)**
Tower of London Films — British
Director: Jesus Franco
Cast: Christopher Lee, Richard Greene, Howard Marion-Crawford, Gunther Stoll, Rosalba Neri

***Tales from the Crypt* (1972)**
Amicus Productions — British
Director: Freddie Francis
Cast: Ralph Richardson, Joan Collins, Peter Cushing, Ian Hendry, Richard Greene, Nigel Patrick

THE FILMS OF JOHN HODIAK

***Stranger in Town* (1943)**
MGM
Director: Roy Rowland
Cast: Frank Morgan, Richard Carlson, Jean Rogers, Porter Hall, John Hodiak

***I Dood It* (1943)**
MGM
Director: Vincent Minnelli
Cast: Red Skelton, Eleanor Powell, Richard Ainley, Lena Horne, Patricia Dane, John Hodiak

***Swing Shift Maisie* (1943)**
MGM
Director: Norman Z. McLeod
Cast: Ann Sothern, James Craig, Jean Rogers, Connie Gilchrist, John Qualen, John Hodiak

***Song of Russia* (1943)**
MGM
Director: Gregory Ratoff
Cast: Robert Taylor, Jean Peters, John Hodiak, Robert Benchley, Felix Bressart

Lifeboat **(1944)**
20th Century Fox
Director: Alfred Hitchcock
Cast: Tallulah Bankhead, William Bendix, Walter Slezak, Mary Anderson, John Hodiak

Marriage is a Private Affair **(1944)**
MGM
Director: Robert Z. Leonard
Cast: Lana Turner, James Craig, John Hodiak, Frances Gifford, Hugh Marlowe, Natalie Schafer

Sunday Dinner For a Soldier **(1944)**
20th Century Fox
Director: Lloyd Bacon
Cast: Anne Baxter, John Hodiak, Charles Winninger, Anne Revere, Chill Wills

***A Bell For Adano* (1945)**
20th Century Fox
Director: Henry King
Cast: John Hodiak, Gene Tierney, William Bendix, Glenn Langan, Richard Conte, Roy Roberts

The Harvey Girls **(1946)**
MGM
Director: George Sidney
Cast: Judy Garland, John Hodiak, Ray Bolger, Angela Lansbury, Virginia O'Brien

Somewhere in the Night **(1946)**
20th Century Fox
Director: Joseph L. Mankiewicz
Cast: John Hodiak, Nancy Guild, Lloyd Nolan, Richard Conte, Josephine Hutchinson

Two Smart People (1946)
MGM
DIRECTOR: JULES DASSIN
CAST: LUCILLE BALL, JOHN HODIAK, LLOYD NOLAN, HUGO HAAS, LENORE ULRIC, LLOYD CORRIGAN

Desert Fury (1947)
PARAMOUNT PICTURES
DIRECTOR: LEWIS ALLEN
CAST: BURT LANCASTER, LIZABETH SCOTT, MARY ASTOR, JOHN HODIAK, CHRISTINE MILLER, JAMES FLAVIN

The Arnello Affair (1947)
MGM
DIRECTOR: ARCH OBOLER
CAST: JOHN HODIAK, GEORGE MURPHY, FRANCES GIFFORD, DEAN STOCKWELL, EVE ARDEN

Love From a Stranger (1947)
EAGLE LION
DIRECTOR: RICHARD WHORF
CAST: SYLVIA SIDNEY, JOHN HODIAK, JOHN HOWARD, ISOBEL ELSOM, ERNEST COSSART

Homecoming (1948)
MGM
DIRECTOR: MERVYN LeROY
CAST: CLARK GABLE, LANA TURNER, JOHN HODIAK, ANNE BAXTER, RAY COLLINS, GLADYS COOPER

Command Decision (1948)
MGM
DIRECTOR: SAM WOOD
CAST: CLARK GABLE, WALTER PIDGEON, VAN JOHNSON, BRIAN DONLEVY, JOHN HODIAK

The Bribe **(1949)**
MGM
DIRECTOR: ROBERT Z. LEONARD
CAST: ROBERT TAYLOR, AVA GARDNER, CHARLES LAUGHTON, VINCENT PRICE, JOHN HODIAK

Battleground **(1949)**
MGM
DIRECTOR: WILLIAM WELLMAN
CAST: VAN JOHNSON, JOHN HODIAK, RICARDO MONTALBAN, GEORGE MURPHY, DON TAYLOR

Malaya **(1949)**
MGM
DIRECTOR: RICHARD THORPE
CAST: SPENCER TRACY, JAMES STEWART, SYDNEY GREENSTREET, VALENTINA CORTESA, JOHN HODIAK

Ambush **(1949)**
MGM
DIRECTOR: SAM WOOD
CAST: ROBERT TAYLOR, JOHN HODIAK, ARLENE DAHL, DON TAYLOR, JEAN HAGEN, LEON AMES

A Lady Without Passport **(1950)**
MGM
DIRECTOR: JOSEPH H. LEWIS
CAST: HEDY LAMARR, JOHN HODIAK, JAMES CRAIG, GEORGE MACREADY, STEVEN GERAY

The Miniver Story **(1950)**
MGM
DIRECTOR: H. C. POTTER
CAST: GREER GARSON, WALTER PIDGEON, JOHN HODIAK, LEO GENN, CATHY O'DONNELL

Night Into Morning (1951)
MGM
DIRECTOR: FLETCHER MARKLE
CAST: RAY MILLAND, JOHN HODIAK, NANCY DAVIS, LEWIS STONE, JEAN HAGEN, ROSEMARY DeCAMP

The People Against O'Hara (1951)
MGM
DIRECTOR: JOHN STURGES
CAST: SPENCER TRACY, PAT O'BRIEN, DIANA LYNN, JOHN HODIAK, JAMES ARNESS, ANN DORAN

Across the Wide Missouri (1951)
MGM
DIRECTOR: WILLIAM WELLMAN
CAST: CLARK GABLE, RICARDO MONTALBAN, JOHN HODIAK, ADOLPHE MENJOU, J. CARROL NAISH

The Sellout (1951)
MGM
DIRECTOR: GERALD MAYER
CAST: WALTER PIDGEON, JOHN HODIAK, AUDREY TOTTER, PAULA RAYMOND, THOMAS GOMEZ

Battle Zone (1952)
ALLIED ARTISTS
DIRECTOR: LESLEY SELANDER
CAST: JOHN HODIAK, LINDA CRISTAL, STEPHEN McNALLY, MARTIN MILNER, RICHARD EMORY

Ambush at Tomahawk Gap *(1953)*
COLUMBIA PICTURES
DIRECTOR: FRED F. SEARS
CAST: JOHN HODIAK, JOHN DEREK, DAVID BRIAN, MARIE ELENA MARQUES, RAY TEAL

Conquest of Cochise (1953)
COLUMBIA PICTURES
DIRECTOR: WILLIAM CASTLE
CAST: JOHN HODIAK, ROBERT STACK, JOY PAGE, RICO ALANIZ

Mission Over Korea (1953)
COLUMBIA PICTURES
DIRECTOR: FRED F. SEARS
CAST: JOHN HODIAK, JOHN DEREK, AUDREY TOTTER, MAUREEN O'SULLIVAN, HARVEY LEMBECK

Dragonfly Squadron (1954)
ALLIED ARTISTS
DIRECTOR: LESLEY SELANDER
CAST: JOHN HODIAK, BARBARA BRITTON, BRUCE BENNETT, JESS BARKER, CHUCK CONNORS

Trial (1955)
MGM
DIRECTOR: MARK ROBSON
CAST: GLENN FORD, DOROTHY McGUIRE, ARTHUR KENNEDY, JOHN HODIAK, KATY JURADO

On the Threshold of Space (1956)
20TH CENTURY FOX
DIRECTOR: ROBERT D. WEBB
CAST: GUY MADISON, VIRGINIA LEITH, JOHN HODIAK, DEAN JAGGER, WARREN STEVENS

THE FILMS OF MARIAN MARSH

BILLED AS MARILYN MORGAN

Whoopie (1930)
GOLDWYN-UNITED ARTISTS
DIRECTOR: THORNTON FREELAN
CAST: EDDIE CANTOR, ETHEL SHUTTA, PAUL GREGORY, MARILYN MORGAN

Hell's Angels **(1930)**
CADDO COMPANY-UNITED ARTISTS
DIRECTOR: HOWARD HUGHES
CAST: BEN LYON, JAMES HALL, JEAN HARLOW, JOHN DARROW,
   LUCIEN PRIVAL, MARILYN MORGAN

Where Canaries Sing Bass **(1931) (SHORT)**
RKO-PATHE
DIRECTOR: GEORGE GREEN
CAST: JAMES GLEASON, HARRY GRIBBON, IVAN LINOV,
   MARILYN MORGAN

Slow Poison **(1931) (SHORT)**
RKO-PATHE
DIRECTOR: HARRY SWEET
CAST: JAME GLEASON, HARRY GRIBBON, MAE BUSCH,
   TOM KENNEDY, MARILYN MORGAN

Doomed to Win (1931) (SHORT)
RKO-PATHE
DIRECTOR: GEORGE GREEN
CAST: JAMES GLEASON, RUSSELL GLEASON, OLIVE COOPER,
   JACK PENNICK, MARILYN MORGAN

BILLED AS MARIAN MARSH:

Svengali **(1931)**
WARNER BROS.
DIRECTOR: ARCHIE MAYO
CAST: JOHN BARRYMORE, MARIAN MARSH, LUIS ALBERNI,
   LUMSDEN HARE, DONALD CRISP

Five Star Final **(1931)**
FIRST NATIONAL
DIRECTOR: MERVYN LEROY
CAST: EDWARD G. ROBINSON, MARIAN MARSH, H. B. WARNER,
   ANTHONY BUSHELL, FRANCES STARR

The Road to Singapore (1931)
Warner Bros.
Director: Alfred E. Green
Cast: William Powell, Doris Kenyon, Marian Marsh, Louis Calhern, Alison Skipworth

The Mad Genius (1931)
Warner Bros.
Director: Michael Curtiz
Cast: John Barrymore, Marian Marsh, Donald Cook, Carmel Myers, Luis Alberni

Under Eighteen (1932)
Warner Bros.
Director: Archie Mayo
Cast: Marian Marsh, Regis Toomey, Warren William, Anita Page, Emma Dunn, Joyce Compton

Alias the Doctor (1932)
First National Pictures
Director: Lloyd Bacon
Cast: Richard Barthelmess, Marian Marsh, Norman Foster, Lucille LaVerne, Adrienne Dore

Beauty and the Boss (1932)
Warner Bros.
Director: Roy Del Ruth
Cast: Marian Marsh, Warren William, Charles Butterworth, David Manners, Mary Doran

Strange Justice (1932)
RKO Radio Pictures
Director: Victor Schertzinger
Cast: Marian Marsh, Reginald Denny, Richard Bennett, Norman Foster, Irving Pichel

The Sport Parade (1932)
RKO Radio Pictures
Director: Dudley Murphy
Cast: Joel McCrea, William Gargan, Marian Marsh, Walter Catlett, Richard "Skeets" Gallagher

The Eleventh Commandment (1933)
Allied Pictures
Director: George Medford
Cast: Marian Marsh, Theodore Von Eltz, Alan Hale, Marie Prevost, Ethel Wales

Daring Daughters (1933)
Capitol Films
Director: Christy Cabanne
Cast: Marian Marsh, Kenneth Thompson, Joan Marsh, Bert Roach, Allen Vincent, Lita Chevret

Notorious But Nice (1933)
Chesterfield
Director: Richard Thorpe
Cast: Marian Marsh, Betty Compson, Donald Dillaway, Rochelle Hudson, John St. Polis

Man of Sentiment (1933)
Chesterfield
Director: Richard Thorpe
Cast: Marian Marsh, Owen Moore, William Bakewell, Christian Rub, Edmund Breese

Over the Garden Wall (1934)
Wardour-British
Director: John Daumery
Cast: Bobby Howes, Marian Marsh, Margaret Bannerman, Viola Lyel

Love at Second Sight (1934)
WARDOUR-BRITISH
DIRECTOR: PAUL MERZBACH
CAST: MARIAN MARSH, ANTHONY BUSHELL, CLAUDE HULBERT, JOAN GARDNER, STANLEY HOLLOWAY

I Like it That Way (1934)
UNIVERSAL PICTURES
DIRECTORS: CHANDLER SPRAGUE, JOSEPH SANTLEY
CAST: GLORIA STUART, ROGER PRYOR, MARIAN MARSH, SHIRLEY GREY, LUCILLE GLEASON, NOEL MADISON

Girl of the Limberlost (1934)
MONOGRAM
DIRECTOR: W. CHRISTY CABANNE
CAST: MARIAN MARSH, LOUISE DRESSER, RALPH MORGAN, HENRY B. WALTHALL, EDWARD NUGENT

The Prodigal Son (1935)
UNIVERSAL PICTURES
DIRECTOR: LUIS TRENKER
CAST: LUIS TRENKER, MARIAN MARSH

In Spite of Danger (1935)
COLUMBIA PICTURES
DIRECTOR: LAMBERT HILLYER
CAST: WALLACE FORD, MARIAN MARSH, ARTHUR HOHL, CHARLEY GRAPEWIN, CHARLES MIDDLETON

The Unknown Woman (1935)
COLUMBIA PICTURES
DIRECTOR: ALBERT ROGELL
CAST: RICHARD CROMWELL, MARIAN MARSH, DOUGLAS DUMBRILLE, HENRY ARMETTA, ARTHUR HOHL

The Black Room (1935)
COLUMBIA PICTURES
DIRECTOR: ROY WILLIAM NEILL
CAST: BORIS KARLOFF, MARIAN MARSH, ROBERT ALLEN,
    KATHERINE DE MILLE, THURSTON HALL

Crime and Punishment (1935)
COLUMBIA PICTURES
DIRECTOR: JOSEF VON STERNBERG
CAST: PETER LORRE, MARIAN MARSH, TALA BIRELL,
    ELIZABETH RISDON, MRS. PATRICK CAMPBELL

Lady of Secrets (1936)
COLUMBIA PICTURES
DIRECTOR: MARION GERIN
CAST: RUTH CHATTERTON, OTTO KRUGER, LIONEL ATWILL,
    MARIAN MARSH, LLOYD NOLAN, ROBERT ALLEN

Counterfeit (1936)
COLUMBIA PICTURES
DIRECTOR: ERLE C. KENTON
CAST: CHESTER MORRIS, MARGOT GRAHAME, MARIAN MARSH, LLOYD NOLAN, CLAUDE GILLINGWATER

The Man Who Lived Twice (1936)
COLUMBIA PICTURES
DIRECTOR: HARRY LACHMAN
CAST: RALPH BELLAMY, MARIAN MARSH, THURSTON HALL, ISABEL JEWELL, NANA BRYANT, WARD BOND

Come Closer Folks (1936)
COLUMBIA PICTURES
DIRECTOR: D. ROSS LEDERMAN
CAST: JAMES DUNN, MARIAN MARSH, WYNNE GIBSON, HERMAN BING, GENE LOCKHART

When's Your Birthday? (1937)
RKO RADIO PICTURES
DIRECTOR: HARRY BEAUMONT
CAST: JOE E. BROWN, MARIAN MARSH, FRED KEATING, EDGAR KENNEDY, MAUDE EBURNE

The Great Gambini (1937)
PARAMOUNT PICTURES
DIRECTOR: CHARLES VIDOR
CAST: AKIM TAMIROFF, MARIAN MARSH, JOHN TRENT, GENEVIEVE TOBIN, REGINALD DENNY

Youth On Parole (1937)
REPUBLIC PICTURES
DIRECTOR: PHIL ROSEN
CAST: MARIAN MARSH, GORDON OLIVER, MARGARET DUMONT, PEGGY SHANNON, MILES MANDER

Saturday's Heroes (1937)
RKO Radio Pictures
Director: Edward Lilly
Cast: Van Heflin, Marian Marsh, Richard Lane,
    Alan Bruce, Minor Watson, Willie Best

The Girl Thief (1938)
Radius-Wardour-British
Director: Paul Merxbach
Cast: Marian Marsh, Anthony Bushell, Claude Hillbert,
    Ralph Ince, Stanley Holloway

Prison Nurse (1938)
Repbublic Pictures
Director: James Cruze
Cast: Henry Wilcoxon, Marian Marsh, Bernadene Hayes,
    Ben Weldon, John Arledge

A Desperate Adventure (1938)
Republic Pictures
Director: John H. Auer
Cast: Ramon Novarro, Marian Marsh, Margaret Tallichet,
    Eric Blore, Andrew Tombes

Missing Daughters (1939)
Columbia Pictures
Director: C. C. Coleman
Cast: Richard Arlen, Rochelle Hudson, Marian Marsh,
    Isabel Jewell, Dick Wessell

Fugitive From a Prison Camp (1940)
Columbia Pictures
Director: Lewis D. Collins
Cast: Jack Holt, Marian Marsh, Robert Barrat,
    Phillip Terry, Dennis Moore, Jack LaRue

Murder By Invitation (1941)
Monogram
Director: Phil Rosen
Cast: Wallace Ford, Marian Marsh, Sarah Padden, Gavin Gordon, Minerva Urecal

The Gentleman From Dixie (1941)
Monogram
Director: Al Herman
Cast: Jack LaRue, Marian Marsh, Clarence Muse, Robert Kellard, Mary Ruth

The House of Errors (1942)
PRC
Director: Bernard B. Ray
Cast: Harry Langdon, Marian Marsh, Ray Walker, Betty Blythe, Guy Kingsford

THE FILMS OF KAREN MORLEY

Thru Different Eyes (1929)
Fox Film Corporation
Director: John Blystone
Cast: Mary Duncan, Edmund Lowe, Warner Baxter, Sylvia Sidney, Karen Morley (uncredited).

Strangers May Kiss (1931)
MGM
Director: George Fitzmaurice
Cast: Norma Shearer, Robert Montgomery, Marjorie Rambeau, Karen Morley (uncredited).

Daybreak (1931)
MGM
Director: Jacques Feyder
Cast: Ramon Novarro, Helen Chandler, Jean Hersholt, C. Aubrey Smith, Karen Morley

Politics (1931)
MGM
Director: Charles Reisner
Cast: Marie Dressler, Polly Moran, Roscoe Ates,
    Karen Morley, William Bakewell

The Sin of Madelon Claudet (1931)
MGM
Director: Edgar Selwyn
Cast: Helen Hayes, Lewis Stone, Neil Hamilton,
    Robert Young, Jean Hersholt, Karen Morley.

Never the Twain Shall Meet (1931)
MGM
Director: W.S. VanDyke
Cast: Leslie Howard, Conchita Montenegro,
    C. Aubrey Smith, Karen Morley

Mata Hari (1931)
MGM
Director: George Fitzmaurice
Cast: Greta Garbo, Ramon Novarro, Lionel Barrymore,
    Lewis Stone, Karen Morley

Inspiration (1931)
MGM
Director: Clarence Brown
Cast: Greta Garbo, Robert Montgomery, Lewis Stone,
    Marjorie Rambeau, Karen Morley

High Stakes (1931)
RKO Radio Pictures
Director: Lowell Sherman.
Cast: Lowell Sherman, Mae Murray, Edward Martindel,
    Leyland Hodgson, Karen Morley

Cuban Love Song (1931)
MGM
Director: W. S. VanDyke
Cast: Lawrence Tibbett, Lupe Velez, Ernest Torrence, Jimmy Durante, Karen Morley

Arsene Lupin (1932)
MGM
Director: Jack Conway
Cast: John Barrymore, Lionel Barrymore, Karen Morley, John Miljan, Tully Marshall

Scarface (1932)
United Artists
Director: Howard Hawks
Cast: Paul Muni, Ann Dvorak, Karen Morley, Osgood Perkins, Boris Karloff, George Raft

Are You Listening? (1932)
MGM
Director: Harry Beaumont
Cast: William Haines, Madge Evans, Anita Page, Karen Morley, Neil Hamilton, Wallace Ford

Washington Masquerade (1932)
MGM
Director: Charles Brabin
Cast: Lionel Barrymore, Karen Morley, Diane Sinclair, Nils Asther, Reginald Barlow

Downstairs (1932)
MGM
Director: Monta Bell
Cast: John Gilbert, Paul Lukas, Virginia Bruce, Hedda Hopper, Karen Morley (uncredited)

The Phantom of Crestwood (1932)
RKO Radio Pictures
Director: J. Walter Rubin
Cast: Karen Morley, Ricardo Cortez, H. B. Warner, Pauline Frederick, Aileen Pringle.

The Mask of Fu Manchu (1932)
MGM
Director: Charles Brabin
Cast: Boris Karloff, Lewis Stone, Karen Morley, Charles Starrett, Myrna Loy, Jean Hersholt

Man About Town (1932)
Fox Film Corporation
Director: John Francis Dillon
Cast: Warner Baxter, Karen Morley, Conway Tearle, Leni Stengel, Lawrence Grant

Flesh (1932)
MGM
Director: John Ford
Cast: Wallace Beery, Karen Morley, Ricardo Cortez, Jean Hersholt, John Miljan, Vince Barnett

Gabriel Over the White House (1933)
MGM
Director: Gregory La Cava
Cast: Walter Huston, Arthur Byron, Karen Morley, Franchot Tone, Dickie Moore

Dinner At Eight (1933)
MGM
Director: George Cukor
Cast: Marie Dressler, John Barrymore, Wallace Beery, Jean Harlow, Lionel Barrymore

Our Daily Bread **(1934)**
INDEPENDENT
DIRECTOR: KING VIDOR
CAST: KAREN MORLEY, TOM KEENE, JOHN QUALEN, BARBARA PEPPER, ADDISON RICHARDS

Wednesday's Child **(1934)**
RKO RADIO PICTURES
DIRECTOR: JOHN S. ROBERTSON
CAST: FRANKIE THOMAS, EDWARD ARNOLD, KAREN MORLEY, SHIRLEY GREY, ROBERT SHAYNE

Straight Is the Way **(1934)**
MGM
DIRECTOR: PAUL SLOANE
CAST: FRANCHOT TONE, MAY ROBSON, KAREN MORLEY, GLADYS GEORGE, NAT PENDLETON

The Crime Doctor **(1934)**
RKO RADIO PICTURES
DIRECTOR: JOHN ROBERTSON
CAST: OTTO KRUGER, KAREN MORLEY, NILS ASTHER, JUDITH WOOD, WILLIAM FRAWLEY, DONALD CRISP

The Healer A.K.A. ***Little Pal*** **(1935)**
MONOGRAM
DIRECTOR: REGINALD BARKER
CAST: RALPH BELLAMY, KAREN MORLEY, MICKEY ROONEY, JUDITH ALLEN, ROBERT MCWADE

Black Fury **(1935)**
WARNER BROS.
DIRECTOR: MICHAEL CURTIZ
CAST: PAUL MUNI, KAREN MORLEY, WILLIAM GARGAN, BARTON MACLANE, J. CARROLL NAISH

Thunder In the Night (1935)
FOX FILM CORPORATION
DIRECTOR: GEORGE ARCHAINBAUD
CAST: EDMUND LOWE, KAREN MORLEY, PAUL CAVANAUGH,
 UNA O'CONNOR, GENE LOCKHART

$10 Raise (1935)
FOX FILM CORPORATION
DIRECTOR: GEORGE MARSHALL
CAST: EDWARD EVERETT HORTON, KAREN MORLEY,
 ALAN DINEHART, GLEN BOLES, BERTON CHURCHILL,

The Littlest Rebel (1935)
FOX FILM CORPORATION
DIRECTOR: DAVID BUTLER
CAST: SHIRLEY TEMPLE, JOHN BOLES, JACK HOLT, KAREN MORLEY
 BILL ROBINSON, GUINN WILLIAMS

Devil's Squadron (1936)
COLUMBIA PICTURES
DIRECTOR: ERLE C. KENTON
CAST: RICHARD DIX, KAREN MORLEY, LLOYD NOLAN,
 SHIRLEY ROSS, HENRY MOLLISON

Beloved Enemy (1936)
GOLDWYN/UNITED ARTISTS
DIRECTOR: H. C. POTTER
CAST: MERLE OBERON, BRIAN AHERNE, KAREN MORLEY,
 JEROME COWAN, DAVID NIVEN

Last Train from Madrid (1937)
PARAMOUNT PICTURES
DIRECTOR: JAMES HOGAN
CAST: DOROTHY LAMOUR, LEW AYRES, GILBERT ROLAND,
 KAREN MORLEY, LIONEL ATWILL

The Girl From Scotland Yard (1937)
PARAMOUNT PICTURES
DIRECTOR: ROBERT VIGNOLA
CAST: KAREN MORLEY, ROBERT BALDWIN, EDUARDO CIANNELLI, MILLI MONTI, LLOYD CRANE

The Outcast (1937)
PARAMOUNT PICTURES
DIRECTOR: ROBERT FLOREY
CAST: WARREN WILLIAM, KAREN MORLEY, LEWIS STONE, RICHARD CARLE, JACKIE MORAN

On Such a Night (1937)
PARAMOUNT PICTURES
DIRECTOR: E.A. DUPONT
CAST: GRANT RICHARDS, KAREN MORLEY, ROSCOE KARNS, EDUARDO CIANNELLI, MILLI MONTI

Kentucky (1938)
20TH CENTURY FOX
DIRECTOR: DAVID BUTLER.
CAST: LORETTA YOUNG, RICHARD GREENE, WALTER BRENNAN, DOUGLAS DUMBRILLE, KAREN MORLEY

Pride and Prejudice (1940)
MGM
DIRECTOR: ROBERT Z. LEONARD
CAST: GREER GARSON, LAURENCE OLIVIER, MARY BOLAND, EDNA MAY OLIVER, KAREN MORLEY

Jealousy (1945)
REPUBLIC PICTURES
DIRECTOR: GUSTAV MACHATY
CAST: JOHN LODER, JANE RANDOLPH, KAREN MORLEY, NILS ASTHER, HUGO HAAS, HOLMES HERBERT

The Unknown (1946)
COLUMBIA PICTURES
DIRECTOR: HENRY LEVIN
CAST: KAREN MORLEY, JIM BANNON, JEFF DONNELL, ROBERT SCOTT, ROBERT WILCOX, JAMES BELL

The Thirteenth Hour (1947)
COLUMBIA PICTURES
DIRECTOR: WILLIAM CLEMENS
CAST: RICHARD DIX, KAREN MORLEY, MARK DENNIS, JOHN KELLOGG, REGIS TOOMEY, JIM BANNON

Framed (1947)
Columbia Pictures
Director: Richard Wallace
Cast: Glenn Ford, Janis Carter, Barry Sullivan,
    Edgar Buchanan, Karen Morley

Samson and Delilah (1949)
Paramount Pictures
Director: Cecil B. DeMille
Cast: Hedy Lamarr, Victor Mature, George Sanders,
    Angela Lansbury, Karen Morley (uncredited)

M (1951)
Columbia Pictures
Director: Joseph Losey
Cast: David Wayne, Howard Da Silva, Luther Adler,
    Martin Gabel, Karen Morley

Born to the Saddle (1953)
Astor Pictures
Director: William Beaudine
Cast: Chuck Courtney, Donald Woods, Leif Erickson,
    Karen Morley, Rand Brooks

THE FILMS OF EDWARD NORRIS

Queen Christina (1933)
MGM
Director: Rouben Mamoulian
Cast: Greta Garbo, John Gilbert, Lewis Stone,
    Akim Tamiroff, Edward Norris (uncredited)

Coming Out Party (1934)
Fox Film Corporation
Director: John Blystone
Cast: Frances Dee, Gene Raymond, Alison Skipworth,
    Nigel Bruce, Edward Norris (bit)

A Wicked Woman **(1934)**
MGM
DIRECTOR: CHARLES BRABIN
CAST: MADY CHRISTIANS, CHARLES BICKFORD, JEAN PARKER, BETTY FURNESS, EDWARD NORRIS (BIT)

This Side of Heaven **(1934)**
MGM
DIRECTOR: WILLIAM K. HOWARD
CAST: LIONEL BARRYMORE, FAY BAINTER, MAE CLARKE, TOM BROWN, MARY CARLISLE, E. NORRIS (BIT)

Alibi Racket **(1935) (SHORT)**
MGM
DIRECTOR: GEORGE B. SEITZ
CAST: EDWARD NORRIS

Murder in the Fleet **(1935)**
MGM
DIRECTOR: EDWARD SEDGWICK
CAST: ROBERT TAYLOR, JEAN PARKER, TED HEALY, UNA MERKEL, JEAN HERSHOLT, EDWARD NORRIS (BIT)

One New York Night **(1935)**
MGM
DIRECTOR: JACK CONWAY
CAST: FRANCHOT TONE, CONRAD NAGEL, STEFFI DUNA, CHARLES STARRETT, EDWARD NORRIS (BIT)

Naughty Marietta **(1935)**
MGM
DIRECTOR: W. S. VAN DYKE
CAST: JEANNETTE MACDONALD, NELSON EDDY, FRANK MORGAN, ELSA LANCHESTER, EDWARD NORRIS (BIT)

Show Them No Mercy **(1935)**
Fox Film Corporation
Director: George Marshall
Cast: Rochelle Hudson, Cesar Romero, Bruce Cabot, Edward Norris, Warren Hymer

The Perfect Tribute **(1935) (short)**
MGM
Director: Edward Sloman
Cast: Charles "Chic" Sale, Walter Brennan, Claude King, Edward Norris, Oscar Apfel

Mad Love **(1935)**
MGM
Director: Karl Freund
Cast: Peter Lorre, Colin Clive, Frances Drake, Ted Healy, Sarah Haden, Edward Norris (bit)

Society Doctor **(1935)**
MGM
Director: George B. Seitz
Cast: Chester Morris, Virginia Bruce, Robert Taylor, Billie Burke, Edward Norris (bit)

Wagon Trail **(1935)**
Ajax Films
Director: Harry Fraser
Cast: Harry Carey, Gertrude Messenger, Edward Norris, Earl Dwire, John Elliott

Teacher's Beau **(1935) (short)**
Roach-MGM
Director: Gus Meins
Cast: Spanky MacFarland, Scott Beckett, Carl "Alfalfa" Switzer, Edward Norris

Tough Guy **(1936)**
MGM
DIRECTOR: CHESTER FRANKLIN
CAST: JACKIE COOPER, JOSEPH CALLEIA, JEAN HERSHOLT,
    MISCHA AUER, EDWARD NORRIS

Small Town Girl **(1936)**
MGM
DIRECTOR: WILLIAM WELLMAN
CAST: ROBERT TAYLOR, JANET GAYNOR, BINNIE BARNES,
    LEWIS STONE, EDWARD NORRIS (BIT)

The Magnificent Brute **(1936)**
UNIVERSAL PICTURES
DIRECTOR: JOHN C. BLYSTONE
CAST: VICTOR MCLAGLEN, WILLIAM HALL, BINNIE BARNES,
    JEAN DIXON, EDWARD NORRIS

Bad Guy **(1937)**
MGM
DIRECTOR: EDWARD CAHN
CAST: BRUCE CABOT, VIRGINIA GREY, EDWARD NORRIS,
    CHARLEY GRAPEWIN, CLIFF EDWARDS

Between Two Women **(1937)**
MGM
DIRECTOR: GEORGE B. SEITZ
CAST: FRANCHOT TONE, MAUREEN O'SULLIVAN, VIRGINIA BRUCE,
    EDWARD NORRIS, CLIFF EDWARDS

Mama Steps Out **(1937)**
MGM
DIRECTOR: GEORGE B. SEITZ
CAST: ALICE BRADY, GUY KIBBEE, BETTY FURNESS,
    DENNIS MORGAN, EDWARD NORRIS

Song of the City (1937)
MGM
DIRECTOR: ERROL TAGGART
CAST: MARGARET LINDSAY, JEFFREY DEAN (DEAN JAGGER),
　　　J. CARROL NAISH, EDWARD NORRIS

They Won't Forget (1937)
WARNER BROS.
DIRECTOR: MERVYN LeROY
CAST: CLAUDE RAINS, GLORIA DICKSON, ALLYN JOSLYN,
　　　EDWARD NORRIS, OTTO KRUGER

Boy's Town (1938)
MGM
DIRECTOR: NORMAN TAUROG
CAST: SPENCER TRACY, MICKEY ROONEY, HENRY HULL,
　　　GENE REYNOLDS, EDWARD NORRIS

On Trial (1939)
WARNER BROS.
DIRECTOR: TERRY MORSE
CAST: JOHN LITEL, MARGARET LINDSAY, EDWARD NORRIS,
　　　JANET CHAPMAN, JAMES STEPHENSON

The Escape (1939)
20TH CENTURY FOX
DIRECTOR: RICARDO CORTEZ
CAST: KANE RICHMOND, AMANDA DUFF, JUNE GALE,
　　　EDWARD NORRIS, HENRY ARMETTA, FRANK REICHER

Frontier Marshal (1939)
20TH CENTURY FOX
DIRECTOR: ALLAN DWAN
CAST: RANDOLPH SCOTT, NANCY KELLY, CESAR ROMERO,
　　　BINNIE BARNES, EDWARD NORRIS

The Gorilla (1939)
20TH CENTURY FOX
DIRECTOR: ALLAN DWAN
CAST: THE RITZ BROTHERS, ANITA LOUISE, PATSY KELLY, BELA LUGOSI, LIONEL ATWILL, EDWARD NORRIS

Newsboy's Home (1939)
UNIVERSAL PICTURES
DIRECTOR: HAROLD YOUNG
CAST: JACKIE COOPER, EDMUND LOWE, WENDY BARRIE, EDWARD NORRIS, SAMUEL S. HINDS

Tail Spin (1939)
20TH CENTURY FOX
DIRECTOR: ROY DEL RUTH
CAST: ALICE FAYE, CONSTANCE BENNETT, NANCY KELLY, JOAN DAVIS, JUNE GALE, EDWARD NORRIS

Here I Am a Stranger (1939)
20TH CENTURY FOX
DIRECTOR: ROY DEL RUTH
CAST: RICHARD GREENE, RICHARD DIX, BRENDA JOYCE, GLADYS GEORGE, EDWARD NORRIS

The Lady in Question (1940)
COLUMBIA PICTURES
DIRECTOR: CHARLES VIDOR
CAST: BRIAN AHERNE, RITA HAYWORTH, GLENN FORD, IRENE RICH, EVELYN KEYES, EDWARD NORRIS

Scandal Sheet (1940)
COLUMBIA PICTURES
DIRECTOR: NICK GRINDE
CAST: ONA MUNSON, OTTO KRUGER, EDWARD NORRIS, JOHN DILSON, DON BEDDOE

Ski Patrol (1940)
Universal Pictures
Director: Lew Landers
Cast: Philip Dorn, Luli Deste, Stanley Fields,
    Samuel S. Hinds, Edward Norris

Dr. Erlich's Magic Bullet (1940)
Warner Bros.
Director: William Dieterle
Cast: Edward G. Robinson, Ruth Gordon, Otto Kruger,
    Donald Crisp, Edward Norris

Angels With Broken Wings (1941)
Republic Pictures
Director: Bernard Vorhaus
Cast: Binnie Barnes, Gilbert Roland, Mary Lee,
    Billy Gilbert, Edward Norris, Jane Frazee

Back in the Saddle (1941)
Republic Pictures
Director: Lew Landers
Cast: Gene Autry, Smiley Burnette, Mary Lee,
    Edward Norris, Jacqueline Wells (Julie Bishop)

Doctor's Don't Tell (1941)
Republic Pictures
Director: Jacques Tourneur
Cast: John Beal, Florence Rice, Edward Norris,
    Ward Bond, Douglas Fowley, Grady Sutton

Here Comes Happiness (1941)
Warner Bros.
Director: Noel Smith
Cast: Edward Norris, Mildred Coles, Richard Ainley,
    Russell Hicks, Marjorie Gateson

Road Show (1941)
UNITED ARTISTS
DIRECTOR: HAL ROACH
CAST: ADOLPHE MENJOU, CAROLE LANDIS, JOHN HUBBARD, PATSY KELLY, EDWARD NORRIS

Close Call for Ellery Queen (1942)
COLUMBIA PICTURES
DIRECTOR: JAMES HOGAN
CAST: WILLIAM GARGAN, MARGARET LINDSAY, RALPH MORGAN, EDWARD NORRIS, CHARLEY GRAPEWIN

The Great Impersonation (1942)
UNIVERSAL PICTURES
DIRECTOR: JOHN RAWLINS
CAST: RALPH BELLAMY, EVELYN ANKERS, EDWARD NORRIS, AUBREY MATHER, HENRY DANIELL

I Live On Danger (1942)
PARAMOUNT PICTURES
DIRECTOR: SAM WHITE
CAST: CHESTER MORRIS, JEAN PARKER, ELIZABETH RISDON, EDWARD NORRIS, DICK PURCELL

The Lady Has Plans (1942)
PARAMOUNT PICTURES
DIRECTOR: SIDNEY LANFIELD
CAST: PAULETTE GODDARD, RAY MILLAND, ROLAND YOUNG, ALBERT DEKKER, EDWARD NORRIS

The Man With Two Lives (1942)
MONOGRAM
DIRECTOR: PHIL ROSEN
CAST: EDWARD NORRIS, FREDRICK BURTON, ADDISON RICHARDS, EDWARD KEANE, HUGH SOTHERN

Sabotage Squad **(1942)**
Columbia Pictures
Director: Lew Landers
Cast: Bruce Bennett, Kay Harris, Edward Norris, Sidney Blackmer, Don Beddoe

The Mystery of Marie Roget **(1942)**
Universal Pictures
Director: Phil Rosen
Cast: Patric Knowles, Nell O'Day, Maria Montez, Maria Ouspenskaya, Edward Norris

The Sultan's Daughter **(1943)**
Monogram
Director: Arthur Dreifuss
Cast: Ann Corio, Charles Butterworth, Tim Ryan, Irene Ryan, Edward Norris

Mug Town **(1943)**
Universal Pictures
Director: Ray Taylor
Cast: Billy Halop, Huntz Hall, Gabriel Dell, Bernard Punsley, Edward Norris

No Place For a Lady **(1943)**
Columbia Pictures
Director: James Hogan
Cast: William Gargan, Margaret Lindsay, Phyllis Brooks, Dick Purcell, Edward Norris

Sing a Jingle **(1943)**
Universal Pictures
Director: Edward C. Lilley
Cast: Allan Jones, June Vincent, Edward Norris, Betty Kean, Gus Schilling

Wings Over the Pacific **(1943)**
Monogram
Director: Phil Rosen
Cast: Inez Cooper, Edward Norris, Allan Scott, Montagu Love, Robert Armstrong

You Can't Beat the Law **(1943)**
Monogram
Director: Phil Rosen
Cast: Edward Norris, Joan Woodbury, Jack LaRue, Milburn Stone, Robert Homans

Career Girl **(1944)**
PRC
Director: Wallace W. Fox
Cast: Frances Langford, Edward Norris, Iris Adrian, Craig Woods

End of the Road **(1944)**
Republic Pictures
Director: George Blair
Cast: Edward Norris, John Abbott, June Storey, Jonathan Hale, Pierre Watkin

Men on Her Mind **(1944)**
PRC
Director: Wallace W. Fox
Cast: Mary Beth Hughes, Edward Norris, Ted North, Luis Alberni, Alan Edwards

Night Club Girl **(1944)**
Universal Pictures
Director: Edward F. Cline
Cast: Vivian Austin, Billy Dunn, Edward Norris, Maxie Rosenbloom

Shadows in the Night (1944)
Columbia Pictures
Director: Eugene Forde
Cast: Warner Baxter, Nina Foch, George Zucco, Minor Watson, Edward Norris

The Singing Sheriff (1944)
Universal Pictures
Director: Leslie Goodwins
Cast: Bob Crosby, Fay McKenzie, Fuzzy Knight, Iris Adrian, Samuel S. Hinds, Edward Norris

Penthouse Rhythm (1945)
Universal Pictures
Director: Edward F. Cline
Cast: Jimmy Dodd, Bobby Worth, Louis Da Pron, Judy Clark, Edward Norris

Jungle Queen (1945) (serial)
Universal Pictures
Directors; Ray Taylor, Lewis D. Collins
Cast: Edward Norris, Eddie Quillan, Douglas Dumbrille, Ruth Roman, Tala Birell

Decoy (1946)
Monogram
Director: Bernard Brandt
Cast: Jean Gillie, Edward Norris, Robert Armstrong, Herbert Rudley, Sheldon Leonard

Murder in the Music Hall (1946)
Republic Pictures
Director: John English
Cast: Vera Hruba Ralston, William Marshall, Helen Walker, Ann Rutherford, Edward Norris

THE TRUTH ABOUT MURDER (1946)
RKO Pictures
Director: Lew Landers
Cast: Morgan Conway, Bonita Granville, Rita Corday, Don Douglas, Edward Norris

HEARTACHES (1947)
PRC
Director: Basil Wrangell
Cast: Sheila Ryan, Edward Norris, Chill Wills, James Seay, Frank Orth

TRAPPED BY BOSTON BLACKIE (1948)
Columbia Pictures
Director: Seymour Friedman
Cast: Chester Morris, June Vincent, Richard Lane, Edward Norris, George E. Stone

FORGOTTEN WOMEN (1949)
Monogram
Director: William Beaudine
Cast: Elyse Knox, Edward Norris, Robert Shayne, Veda Ann Borg, Noel Neill

THE MYSTERIOUS DESPERADO (1949)
RKO Pictures
Director: Lesley Selander
Cast: Tim Holt, Richard Martin, Edward Norris, Frank Wilcox, Robert Livingstone

THE WOLF HUNTERS (1949)
Monogram
Director: Budd Boetticher
Cast: Kirby Grant, Jan Clayton, Helen Parrish, Edward Norris, Ted Hecht

The Blazing Sun **(1950)**
COLUMBIA PICTURES
DIRECTOR: JOHN ENGLISH
CAST: GENE AUTRY, LYNN ROBERTS, PAT BUTTRAM,
   ANNE GWYNNE, EDWARD NORRIS, KENNE DUNCAN

Highway 301 **(1950)**
WARNER BROS.
DIRECTOR: ANDREW L. STONE
CAST: STEVE COCHRAN, VIRGINIA GREY, ROBERT WEBBER,
   RICHARD EGAN, EDWARD NORRIS

Killer Shark **(1950)**
MONOGRAM
DIRECTOR: BUDD BOETTICHER
CAST: RODDY McDOWELL, LAURETTE LUEZ, ROLAND WINTERS,
   EDWARD NORRIS, DICK MOORE

Surrender **(1950)**
REPUBLIC PICTURES
DIRECTOR: ALLAN DWAN
CAST: VERA RALSTON, JOHN CARROLL, WALTER BRENNAN,
   FRANCIS LEDERER, EDWARD NORRIS

Breakthrough **(1950)**
WARNER BROS.
DIRECTOR: LEWIS SEILER
CAST: DAVID BRIAN, JOHN AGAR, FRANK LOVEJOY, PAUL PICERNI,
   EDWARD NORRIS

Inside the Walls of Folsom Prison **(1951)**
WARNER BROS.
DIRECTOR: CRANE WILBUR
CAST: DAVID BRIAN, STEVE COCHRAN, TED DE CORSIA,
   DOROTHY HART, EDWARD NORRIS

I Was a Communist for the F.B.I. (1951)
WARNER BROS.
DIRECTOR: GORDON DOUGLAS
CAST: FRANK LOVEJOY, DOROTHY HART, PHILIP CAREY,
　　EDWARD NORRIS, JAMES MILLICAN

Murder Without Tears (1953)
ALLIED ARTISTS
DIRECTOR: WILLIAM BEAUDINE
CAST: CRAIG STEVENS, JOYCE HOLDEN, RICHARD BENEDICT,
　　EDWARD NORRIS, TOM HUBBARD

The Man From the Alamo (1953)
UNIVERSAL PICTURES
DIRECTOR: BUDD BOETTICHER
CAST: GLENN FORD, JULIE ADAMS, VICTOR JORY, HUGH O'BRIAN,
　　CHILL WILLS, EDWARD NORRIS

The Kentuckian (1955)
UNITED ARTISTS
DIRECTOR: BURT LANCASTER
CAST: BURT LANCASTER, DIANNE FOSTER, JOHN MCINTIRE,
　　UNA MERKEL, EDWARD NORRIS

THE FILMS OF JEAN PARKER

Divorce in the Family (1932)
MGM
DIRECTOR: CHARLES REISNER
CAST: JACKIE COOPER, CONRAD NAGEL, LEWIS STONE,
　　LOIS WILSON, JEAN PARKER, LOUISE BEAVERS

Rasputin and the Empress (1932)
MGM
DIRECTORS: RICHARD BOLESLAWKI, CHARLES BRABIN
CAST: JOHN BARRYMORE, LIONEL BARRYMORE, ETHEL
　　BARRYMORE, RALPH MORGAN, JEAN PARKER

The Secret of Madame Blanche **(1933)**
MGM
DIRECTOR: CHARLES BRABIN
CAST: IRENE DUNNE, LIONEL ATWILL, PHILLIPS HOLMES, UNA MERKEL, JEAN PARKER, DOUGLAS WALTON

Gabriel Over the White House **(1933)**
MGM
DIRECTOR: GREGORY LA CAVA
CAST: WALTER HUSTON, FRANCHOT TONE, KAREN MORLEY, ARTHUR BYRON, DICKIE MOORE, JEAN PARKER

Made on Broadway **(1933)**
MGM
DIRECTOR: HARRY BEAUMONT
CAST: ROBERT MONTGOMERY, MADGE EVANS, SALLY EILERS, C. HENRY GORDON, JEAN PARKER

What Price Innocence? **(1933)**
COLUMBIA PICTURES
DIRECTOR: WILLARD MACK
CAST: JEAN PARKER, MINNA GOMBELL, WILLARD MACK, BETTY GRABLE, BRYANT WASHBURN

Storm at Daybreak **(1933)**
MGM
DIRECTOR: RICHARD BOLESLAWSKI
CAST: KAY FRANCIS, WALTER HUSTON, NILS ASTHER, PHILLIPS HOLMES, JEAN PARKER

Lady For a Day **(1933)**
COLUMBIA PICTURES
DIRECTOR: FRANK CAPRA
CAST: MAY ROBSON, WARREN WILLIAM, GUY KIBBE, GLENDA FARRELL, NED SPARKS, JEAN PARKER

Little Women **(1933)**
RKO Radio Pictures
Director: George Cukor
Cast: Katharine Hepburn, Joan Bennett, Jean Parker,
 Frances Dee, Paul Lukas, Edna May Oliver

You Can't Buy Everything **(1934)**
MGM
Director: Charles Reisner
Cast: May Robson, Jean Parker, Lewis Stone, Mary Forbes,
 William Bakewell, Reginald Mason

Two Alone **(1934)**
RKO Radio Pictures
Director: Elliott Nugent
Cast: Jean Parker, ZaSu Pitts, Beulah Bondi, Tom Brown,
 Arthur Byron, Nydia Westman

Caravan **(1934)**
Fox Film Corporation
Director: Erik Charell
Cast: Charles Boyer, Loretta Young, Jean Parker,
 Phillips Holmes, Louise Fazenda

Lazy River **(1934)**
MGM
Director: George B. Seitz
Cast: Jean Parker, Robert Young, Ted Healy,
 Nat Pendleton, C. Henry Gordon

Operator 13 **(1934)**
MGM
Director: Richard Boleslawski
Cast: Marion Davies, Gary Cooper, Jean Parker,
 Katharine Alexander, Ted Healy

Have a Heart (1934)
MGM
DIRECTOR: DAVID BUTLER
CAST: JEAN PARKER, JAMES DUNN, UNA MERKEL, STU ERWIN, WILLARD ROBERTSON, SAMUEL S. HINDS

A Wicked Woman (1934)
MGM
DIRECTOR: CHARLES BRABIN
CAST: MADY CHRISTIANS, JEAN PARKER, CHARLES BICKFORD, BETTY FURNESS, ROBERT TAYLOR

Limehouse Blues (1934)
PARAMOUNT PICTURES
DIRECTOR: ALEXANDER HALL
CAST: GEORGE RAFT, JEAN PARKER, ANNA MAY WONG, KENT TAYLOR, BILLY BEVAN

Sequoia (1934)
MGM
DIRECTOR: CHESTER FRANKLIN
CAST: JEAN PARKER, RUSSELL HARDIE, SAMUEL S. HINDS, PAUL HURST,

Princess O'Hara (1935)
UNIVERSAL PICTURES
DIRECTOR: DAVID BURTON
CAST: JEAN PARKER, CHESTER MORRIS, LEON ERROL, VINCE BARNETT, HENRY ARMETTA, VERNA HILLIE

Murder in the Fleet (1935)
MGM
DIRECTOR: EDWARD SEDGWICK
CAST: ROBERT TAYLOR, JEAN PARKER, UNA MERKEL, TED HEALY, JEAN HERSHOLT, NAT PENDLETON

The Ghost Goes West **(1935)**
UNITED ARTISTS
DIRECTOR: RENE CLAIR
CAST: ROBERT DONAT, JEAN PARKER, EUGENE PALLETTE,
   ELSA LANCHESTER, RALPH BUNKER

The Farmer in the Dell **(1936)**
RKO RADIO PICTURES
DIRECTOR: BEN HOLMES
CAST: FRED STONE, JEAN PARKER, ESTHER DALE, MORONI OLSEN,
   FRANK ALBERTSON, LUCILLE BALL

The Texas Rangers **(1936)**
PARAMOUNT PICTURES
DIRECTOR: KING VIDOR
CAST: FRED MACMURRAY, JACK OAKIE, JEAN PARKER,
   LLOYD NOLAN, EDWARD ELLIS

The Barrier **(1937)**
PARAMOUNT PICTURES
DIRECTOR: LESLEY SELANDER
CAST: LEO CARRILLO, JEAN PARKER, JAMES ELLISON,
   OTTO KRUGER, ANDY CLYDE, J. M. KERRIGAN

Life Begins with Love **(1937)**
COLUMBIA PICTURES
DIRECTOR: RAY McCAREY
CAST: JEAN PARKER, EDITH FELLOWS, DOUGLASS MONTGOMERY,
   LUMSDEN HARE, AUBREY MATHER

Penitentiary **(1938)**
COLUMBIA PICTURES
DIRECTOR: JOHN BRAHM
CAST: WALTER CONNOLLY, JOHN HOWARD, JEAN PARKER,
   ROBERT BARRAT, BESS FLOWERS

Romance of the Limberlost **(1938)**
Monogram
Director: William Nigh
Cast: Jean Parker, Eric Linden, Marjorie Main,
   Edward Pauley, Betty Blythe, Sarah Padden

The Arkansas Traveler **(1938)**
Paramount Pictures
Director: Alfred Santell
Cast: Bob Burns, Jean Parker, Fay Bainter, John Beal,
   Lyle Talbot, Dickie Moore

Romance of the Redwoods **(1939)**
Columbia Pictures
Director: Charles Vidor
Cast: Charles Bickford, Jean Parker, Al Bridge,
   Gordon Oliver, Ann Shoemaker, Lloyd Hughes

Zenobia **(1939)**
United Artists
Director: Gordon Douglas
Cast: Oliver Hardy, Harry Langdon, Billie Burke,
   Alice Brady, Jean Parker, James Ellison

She Married a Cop **(1939)**
Republic Pictures
Director: Sidney Salkow
Cast: Phil Regan, Jean Parker, Jerome Cowan,
   Dorothea Kent, Benny Baker, Barnett Parker

Flight at Midnight **(1939)**
Republic Pictures
Director: Sidney Salkow
Cast: Phil Regan, Jean Parker, Noah Beery Jr.,
   Robert Armstrong, Harlan Briggs

Parents on Trial (1939)
COLUMBIA PICTURES
DIRECTOR: SAM NELSON
CAST: JEAN PARKER, JOHNNY DOWNS, LINDA PERRY

The Flying Deuces (1939)
RKO RADIO PICTURES
DIRECTOR: A. EDWARD SUTHERLAND
CAST: STAN LAUREL, OLIVER HARDY, JEAN PARKER,
    REGINALD GARDINER, CHARLES MIDDLETON

Knights of the Range (1940)
PARAMOUNT PICTURES
DIRECTOR: LESLEY SELANDER
CAST: RUSSELL HAYDEN, VICTOR JORY, JEAN PARKER,
    MORRIS ANKRUM, ETHEL WALES

Son of the Navy (1940)
MONOGRAM
DIRECTOR: WILLIAM NIGH
CAST: JAMES DUNN, JEAN PARKER, MARTIN SPELLMAN,
    WILLIAM ROYLE, SELMER JACKSON

Beyond Tomorrow (1940)
RKO RADIO PICTURES
DIRECTOR: A. EDWARD SUTHERLAND
CAST: HARRY CAREY, C. AUBREY SMITH, CHARLES WINNINGER,
    MARIA OUSPENSKAYA, JEAN PARKER

Young America Flies (1940) (SHORT)
WARNER BROS.
DIRECTOR: B. REEVES EASON
CAST: JEAN PARKER, DONALD WOODS, WILLIAM LUNDIGAN,
    HENRY O'NEILL, SUSAN PETERS

Roar of the Press (1941)
Monogram
Director: Phil Rosen
Cast: Wallace Ford, Jean Parker, Jed Prouty, Suzanne Kaaren, Robert Fraser

Power Dive (1941)
Paramount Pictures
Director: James P. Hogan
Cast: Richard Arlen, Jean Parker, Helen Mack, Roger Pryor, Cliff Edwards

The Pittsburgh Kid (1941)
Republic Pictures
Director: Jack Townley
Cast: Billy Conn, Jean Parker, Dick Purcell, Alan Baxter, Veda Ann Borg, Jonathan Hale

Flying Blind (1941)
Paramount Pictures
Director: Frank McDonald
Cast: Richard Arlen, Jean Parker, Nils Asther, Marie Wilson, Roger Pryor, Eddie Quillan

No Hands on the Clock (1941)
Paramount Pictures
Director: Frank McDonald
Cast: Chester Morris, Jean Parker, Rose Hobart, Dick Purcell, Astrid Allwyn, Rod Cameron

Torpedo Boat (1942)
Paramount Pictures
Director: John Rawlins
Cast: Richard Arlen, Jean Parker, Mary Carlisle, Phil Terry, Dick Purcell, William Haade

The Girl from Alaska (1942)
REPUBLIC PICTURES
DIRECTOR: NICK GRINDE
CAST: RAY MIDDLETON, JEAN PARKER, JEROME COWAN, ROBERT H. BARRAT, FRANCIS MCDONALD

Hello, Annapolis (1942)
COLUMBIA PICTURES
DIRECTOR: CHARLES BARTON
CAST: TOM BROWN, JEAN PARKER, LARRY PARKS, PHIL BROWN, JOSEPH CREHAN, THURSTON HALL

I Live on Danger (1942)
PARAMOUNT PICTURES
DIRECTOR: SAM WHITE
CAST: CHESTER MORRIS, JEAN PARKER, ELISABETH RISDON, EDWARD NORRIS, DICK PURCELL

Hi, Neighbor (1942)
REPUBLIC PICTURES
DIRECTOR: CHARLES LAMONT
CAST: JEAN PARKER, JOHN ARCHER, JANET BEECHER, MARILYN HARE, BILL SHIRLEY

Tomorrow We Live (1942)
PRC
DIRECTOR: EDGAR G. ULMER
CAST: RICARDO CORTEZ, JEAN PARKER, EMMETT LYNN, WILLIAM MARSHALL, ROSANNE STEVENS

Wrecking Crew (1942)
PARAMOUNT PICTURES
DIRECTOR: FRANK MCDONALD
CAST: CHESTER MORRIS, RICHARD ARLEN, JEAN PARKER, JOE SAWYER, ESTHER DALE, EVELYN BRENT

The Traitor Within **(1942)**
REPUBLIC PICTURES
DIRECTOR: FRANK MCDONALD
CAST: DONALD M. BARRY, JEAN PARKER, GEORGE CLEVELAND, RALPH MORGAN, BRADLEY PAGE

High Explosive **(1943)**
PARAMOUNT PICTURES
DIRECTOR: FRANK MCDONALD
CAST: CHESTER MORRIS, JEAN PARKER, BARRY SULLIVAN, RAND BROOKS, DICK PURCELL

Alaska Highway **(1943)**
PARAMOUNT PICTURES
DIRECTOR: FRANK MCDONALD
CAST: RICHARD ARLEN, JEAN PARKER, RALPH SANFORD, WILLIAM HENRY, JOE SAWYER, EDDIE QUILLAN

Minesweeper **(1943)**
PARAMOUNT PICTURES
DIRECTOR: WILLIAM BERKE
CAST: RICHARD ARLEN, JEAN PARKER, RUSSELL HAYDEN, GUINN WILLIAMS, EMMA DUNN

The Deerslayer **(1943)**
REPUBLIC PICTURES
DIRECTOR: LEW LANDERS
CAST: BRUCE KELLOGG, JEAN PARKER, LARRY PARKS, WANDA MCKAY, YVONNE DECARLO

The Navy Way **(1944)**
PARAMOUNT PICTURES
DIRECTOR: WILLIAM BERKE
CAST: ROBERT LOWERY, JEAN PARKER, BILL HENRY, ROSCOE KARNS, ROBERT ARMSTRONG

Lady in the Death House **(1944)**
REPUBLIC PICTURES
DIRECTOR: STEVE SEKELY
CAST: JEAN PARKER, LIONEL ATWILL, DOUGLAS FOWLEY, MARCIA MAE JONES, ROBERT MIDDLEMASS

Detective Kitty O'Day **(1944)**
MONOGRAM
DIRECTOR: WILLIAM BEAUDINE
CAST: JEAN PARKER, PETER COOKSON, TIM RYAN, VEDA ANN BORG, EDWARD GARGAN

Oh, What a Night! **(1944)**
MONOGRAM
DIRECTOR: WILLIAM BEAUDINE
CAST: EDMUND LOWE, MARJORIE RAMBEAU, JEAN PARKER, PIERRE WATKIN, ALAN DINEHART

One Body Too Many **(1944)**
PARAMOUNT PICTURES
DIRECTOR: FRANK MCDONALD
CAST: JACK HALEY, JEAN PARKER, BELA LUGOSI, BERNARD NEDELL, BLANCHE YURKA, DOUGLAS FOWLEY

Dead Man's Eyes **(1944)**
UNIVERSAL PICTURES
DIRECTOR: REGINALD LEBORG
CAST: LON CHANEY JR., JEAN PARKER, PAUL KELLY, THOMAS GOMEZ, JONATHAN HALE

Bluebeard **(1944)**
PRC
DIRECTOR: EDGAR G. ULMER
CAST: JOHN CARRADINE, JEAN PARKER, NILS ASTHER, LUDWIG STOSSEL, TEALA LORING

***Adventures of Kitty O'Day* (1945)**
MONOGRAM
DIRECTOR: WILLIAM BEAUDINE
CAST: JEAN PARKER, PETER COOKSON, TIM RYAN, LORNA GRAY, RALPH SANFORD, JAN WILEY

***Rolling Home* (1946)**
AFFLIATED PRODUCTIONS — SCREEN GUILD
DIRECTOR: WILLIAM BERKE
CAST: JEAN PARKER, RUSSELL HAYDEN, PAMELA BLAKE, RAYMOND HATTON, JONATHAN HALE

***The Gunfighter* (1950)**
20TH CENTURY FOX
DIRECTOR: HENRY KING
CAST: GREGORY PECK, HELEN WESTCOTT, MILLARD MITCHELL, JEAN PARKER, KARL MALDEN, SKIP HOMEIER

***Toughest Man in Arizona* (1952)**
REPUBLIC PICTURES
DIRECTOR: R.G. SPRINGSTEEN
CAST: VAUGHN MONROE, JAON LESLIE, EDGAR BUCHANAN, VICTOR JORY, JEAN PARKER, HARRY MORGAN

***Those Redheads from Seattle* (1953)**
PARAMOUNT PICTURES
DIRECTOR: LEWIS R. FOSTER
CAST: RHONDA FLEMING, GENE BARRY, AGNES MOOREHEAD, GUY MITCHELL, JOHN KELLOGG, J. PARKER

***Black Tuesday* (1954)**
UNITED ARTISTS
DIRECTOR: HUGO FREGONESE
CAST: EDWARD G. ROBINSON, JEAN PARKER, PETER GRAVES, MILBURN STONE, WARREN STEVENS

A Lawless Street **(1955)**
COLUMBIA PICTURES
DIRECTOR: JOSEPH H. LEWIS
CAST: RANDOLPH SCOTT, ANGELA LANSBURY, WARNER ANDERSON,
   JEAN PARKER, WALLACE FORD

The Parson and the Outlaw **(1957)**
COLUMBIA PICTURES
DIRECTOR: OLIVER DRAKE
CAST: ANTHONY DEXTER, CHARLES "BUDDY" ROGERS,
   JEAN PARKER, SONNY TUFTS, ROBERT LOWERY

Apache Uprising **(1965)**
PARAMOUNT PICTURES
DIRECTOR: R. G. SPRINGSTEEN
CAST: RORY CALHOUN, CORRINE CALVET, JOHN RUSSELL,
   LON CHANEY JR., RICHARD ARLEN, JEAN PARKER

THE FILMS OF PAULA RAYMOND

Keep Smiling **(1938)**
20TH CENTURY FOX
DIRECTOR: HERBERT L. LEEDS
CAST: JANE WITHERS, GLORIA STUART, HENRY WILCOXON,
   HELEN WESTLEY, PAULA RAYMOND (UNCREDITED)

Variety Girl **(1947)**
PARAMOUNT PICTURES
DIRECTOR: GEORGE MARSHALL
CAST: MARY HATCHER, OLGA SAN JUAN, DEFOREST KELLEY,
   PAULA RAYMOND (UNCREDITED)

Powder River Gunfire **(1948)** **(SHORT)**
UNIVERSAL PICTURES
DIRECTOR: HAROLD MOORE
CAST: KENNE DUNCAN, ROYAL RAYMOND, DONALD DOUGLAS,
   PAULA RAYMOND

Night Has a Thousand Eyes (1948)
PARAMOUNT PICTURES
DIRECTOR: JOHN FARROW
CAST: EDWARD G. ROBINSON, GAIL RUSSELL, JOHN LUND, VIRGINIA BRUCE, P. RAYMOND (UNCREDITED)

Rusty Leads the Way (1948)
COLUMBIA PICTURES
DIRECTOR: WILL JASON
CAST: TED DONALDSON, SHARYN MOFFETT, ANN DORAN, JOHN LITEL, PAULA RAYMOND

Sealed Verdict (1948)
PARAMOUNT PICTURES
DIRECTOR: LEWIS ALLEN
CAST: RAY MILLAND, FLORENCE MARLY, JOHN HOYT, BRODERICK CRAWFORD, PAULA RAYMOND

Racing Luck (1948)
COLUMBIA PICTURES
DIRECTOR: WILLIAM BERKE
CAST: GLORIA HENRY, STANLEY CLEMENTS, DAVID BRUCE, PAULA RAYMOND, DOOLEY WILSON

Blondie's Secret (1948)
COLUMBIA PICTURES
DIRECTOR: EDWARD BERNDS
CAST: PENNY SINGLETON, ARTHUR LAKE, LARRY SIMMS, JEROME COWAN, PAULA RAYMOND (UNCREDITED)

Challenge of the Range (1949)
COLUMBIA PICTURES
DIRECTOR: RAY NAZZARO
CAST: CHARLES STARRETT, PAULA RAYMOND, BILLY HALOP, STEVE DARRELL, SMILEY BURNETTE

ADAM'S RIB (1949)
MGM
DIRECTOR: GEORGE CUKOR
CAST: SPENCER TRACY, KATHARINE HEPBURN, JUDY HOLLIDAY, PAULA RAYMOND (UNCREDITED)

HOLIDAY AFFAIR (1949)
RKO RADIO PICTURES
DIRECTOR: DON HARTMAN
CAST: ROBERT MITCHUM, JANET LEIGH, WENDELL COREY, GRIFF BARNETT, P. RAYMOND (UNCREDITED)

EAST SIDE, WEST SIDE (1949)
MGM
DIRECTOR: MERVYN LeROY
CAST: BARBARA STANWYCK, JAMES MASON, VAN HEFLIN, AVA GARDNER, P. RAYMOND (UNCREDITED)

CRISIS (1950)
MGM
DIRECTOR: RICHARD BROOKS
CAST: CARY GRANT, JOSE FERRER, PAULA RAYMOND, SIGNE HASSO, RAMON NOVARRO, LEON AMES

DUCHESS OF IDAHO (1950)
MGM
DIRECTOR: ROBERT Z. LEONARD
CAST: ESTHER WILLIAMS, VAN JOHNSON, JOHN LUND, PAULA RAYMOND, CLINTON SUNDBERG

DEVIL'S DOORWAY (1950)
MGM
DIRECTOR: ANTHONY MANN
CAST: ROBERT TAYLOR, LOUIS CALHERN, PAULA RAYMOND, MARSHALL THOMPSON, JAMES MITCHELL

Grounds For Marriage (1951)
MGM
DIRECTOR: ROBERT Z. LEONARD
CAST: VAN JOHNSON, KATHRYN GRAYSON, PAULA RAYMOND, BARRY SULLIVAN, LEWIS STONE

Inside Straight (1951)
MGM
DIRECTOR: GERALD MAYER
CAST: DAVID BRIAN, ARLENE DAHL, BARRY SULLIVAN, MERCEDES MCCAMBRIDGE, PAULA RAYMOND

The Tall Target (1951)
MGM
DIRECTOR: ANTHONY MANN
CAST: DICK POWELL, PAULA RAYMOND, ADOLPHE MENJOU, RUBY DEE, LEIF ERICKSON

Texas Carnival (1951)
MGM
DIRECTOR: CHARLES WALTERS
CAST: ESTHER WILLIAMS, RED SKELTON, HOWARD KEEL, ANN MILLER, PAULA RAYMOND, KEENAN WYNN

The Sellout (1952)
MGM
DIRECTOR: GERALD MAYER
CAST: WALTER PIDGEON, JOHN HODIAK, AUDREY TOTTER, PAULA RAYMOND, KARL MALDEN

Bandits Of Corsica (1953)
UNITED ARTISTS
DIRECTOR: RAY NAZZARO
CAST: RICHARD GREENE, PAULA RAYMOND, RAYMOND BURR, DONA DRAKE, LEE VAN CLEEF

The Story of Three Loves (1953)
MGM
Directors: Vincente Minnelli, Gottfried Reinhardt
Cast: Pier Angeli, Ethel Barrymore, Leslie Caron,
   Kirk Douglas, Paula Raymond (uncredited)

City That Never Sleeps (1953)
Republic Pictures
Director: John H. Auer
Cast: Gig Young, Mala Powers, William Talman,
   Edward Arnold, Paula Raymond, Chill Wills

The Beast from 20,000 Fathoms (1953)
Warner Bros.
Director: Eugene Lourie
Cast: Kenneth Tobey, Paula Raymond, Cecil Kellaway,
   Donald Woods, Steve Brodie

King Richard and the Crusaders (1954)
Warner Bros.
Director: David Butler
Cast: Rex Harrison, Virginia Mayo, George Sanders,
   Laurence Harvey, Paula Raymond

The Human Jungle (1954)
Allied Artists
Director: Joseph M. Newman
Cast: Gary Merrill, Jan Sterling, Regis Toomey,
   Chuck Connors, Paula Raymond

The Gun That Won the West (1955)
Columbia Pictures
Director: William Castle
Cast: Dennis Morgan, Paula Raymond, Richard Denning,
   Chris O'Brien, Robert Bice

Flight That Disappeared (1961)
United Artists
Director: Reginald Le Borg
Cast: Craig Hill, Paula Raymond, Dayton Lummis, Harvey Stephens, Addison Richards

Hand of Death (1962)
20th Century Fox
Director: Gene Nelson
Cast: John Agar, Paula Raymond, Stephen Dunne, Roy Gordon, Joe Besser

Blood of Dracula's Castle (1969)
Crown International Pictures — Columbia
Directors: Al Adamson, Jean Hewitt
Cast: John Carradine, Paula Raymond, Alexander D'Arcy, Robert Dix, Jennifer Bishop

Five Bloody Graves (1969)
Independent-International Pictures
Director: Al Adamson
Cast: Robert Dix, Scott Brady, Jim Davis, John Carradine, Paula Raymond

Mind Twister (1993)
American Independent Productions
Director: Fred Olen Ray
Cast: Telly Savalas, Erika Nann, Gary Hudson, Richard Roundtree, Paula Raymond

THE FILMS OF ZACHARY SCOTT

The Mask of Dimitrios (1944)
Warner Bros.
Director: Jean Negulesco
Cast: Sydney Greenstreet, Zachary Scott, Faye Emerson, Peter Lorre, Victor Francen

Hollywood Canteen (1944)
WARNER BROS.
DIRECTOR: DELMER DAVES
CAST: ALL-STAR CAST

Danger Signal (1945)
WARNER BROS.
DIRECTOR: ROBERT FLOREY
CAST: FAYE EMERSON, ZACHARY SCOTT, BRUCE BENNETT,
   MONA FREEMAN, JOHN RIDGELY

The Southerner (1945)
UNITED ARTISTS
DIRECTOR: JEAN RENOIR
CAST: ZACHARY SCOTT, BETTY FIELD, BEULAH BONDI,
   PERCY KILBRIDE, BLANCHE YURKA, J. CARROL NAISH

Mildred Pierce (1945)
WARNER BROS.
DIRECTOR: MICHAEL CURTIZ
CAST: JOAN CRAWFORD, JACK CARSON, ANN BLYTH,
   ZACHARY SCOTT, EVE ARDEN, BRUCE BENNETT

Her Kind of Man (1946)
WARNER BROS.
DIRECTOR: FREDERICK DE CORDOVA
CAST: DANE CLARK, JANIS PAIGE, ZACHARY SCOTT,
   FAYE EMERSON, GEORGE TOBIAS

Cass Timberlane (1947)
MGM
DIRECTOR: GEORGE SIDNEY
CAST: SPENCER TRACY, LANA TURNER, ZACHARY SCOTT,
   TOM DRAKE, MARY ASTOR, MARGARET LINDSAY

Stallion Road **(1947)**
WARNER BROS.
DIRECTOR: JAMES V. KERN
CAST: RONALD REAGAN, ALEXIS SMITH, ZACHARY SCOTT, PEGGY KNUDSON, HARRY DAVENPORT

The Unfaithful **(1947)**
WARNER BROS.
DIRECTOR: VINCENT SHERMAN
CAST: ANN SHERIDAN, LEW AYRES, ZACHARY SCOTT, EVE ARDEN, JEROME COWAN, STEVEN GERAY

Ruthless **(1948)**
EAGLE-LION
DIRECTOR: EDGAR G. ULMER
CAST: ZACHARY SCOTT, LOUIS HAYWARD, DIANA LYNN, SYDNEY GREENSTREET, MARTHA VICKERS

Whiplash **(1948)**
WARNER BROS.
DIRECTOR: LEWIS SEILER
CAST: DANE CLARK, ALEXIS SMITH, ZACHARY SCOTT, EVE ARDEN, JEFFREY LYNN, S. Z. SAKALL

Flamingo Road **(1949)**
WARNER BROS.
DIRECTOR: MICHAEL CURTIZ
CAST: JOAN CRAWFORD, ZACHARY SCOTT, SYDNEY GREENSTREET, DAVID BRIAN, GLADYS GEORGE

Flaxy Martin **(1949)**
WARNER BROS.
DIRECTOR: RICHARD BARE
CAST: VIRGINIA MAYO, ZACHARY SCOTT, DOROTHY MALONE, TOM D'ANDREA, DOUGLAS FOWLEY

One Last Fling (1949)
WARNER BROS.
DIRECTOR: PETER GODFREY
CAST: ALEXIS SMITH, ZACHARY SCOTT, DOUGLAS KENNEDY, ANN DORAN, VEDA ANN BORG

South of St. Louis (1949)
WARNER BROS.
DIRECTOR: RAY ENRIGHT
CAST: JOEL McCREA, ALEXIS SMITH, ZACHARY SCOTT, DOROTHY MALONE, DOUGLAS KENNEDY

Born to be Bad (1950)
RKO RADIO PICTURES
DIRECTOR: NICHOLAS RAY
CAST: JOAN FONTAINE, ROBERT RYAN, ZACHARY SCOTT, JOAN LESLIE, MEL FERRER, KATHLEEN HOWARD

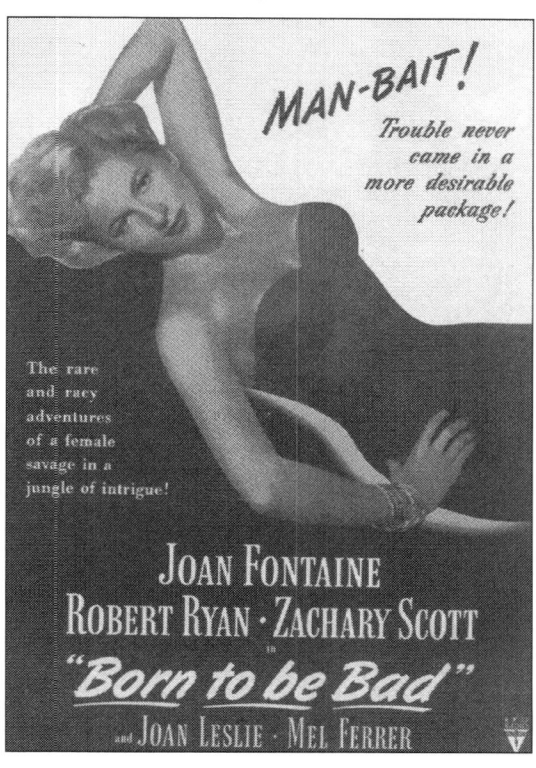

Guilty Bystander (1950)
Film Classics
Director: Joseph Lerner
Cast: Zachary Scott, Faye Emerson, Mary Boland, Sam Levene, Kay Medford

Colt .45 (1950)
Warner Bros.
Director: Edwin L. Marin
Cast: Randolph Scott, Ruth Roman, Zachary Scott, Lloyd Bridges, Alan Hale

Shadow on the Wall (1950)
MGM
Director: Patrick Jackson
Cast: Ann Sothern, Zachary Scott, Gigi Perreau, Nancy Davis, Kristine Miller, John McIntire

Pretty Baby (1950)
Warner Bros.
Director: Bretaigne Windust
Cast: Dennis Morgan, Betsy Drake, Zachary Scott, Edmund Gwenn, William Frawley

Let's Make it Legal (1951)
20th Century Fox
Director: Richard Sale
Cast: Claudette Colbert, MacDonald Carey, Zachary Scott, Barbara Bates, Robert Wagner

Lightning Strikes Twice (1951)
Warner Bros.
Director: King Vidor
Cast: Richard Todd, Ruth Roman, Mercedes McCambridge, Zachary Scott, Darryl Hickman

The Secret of Convict Lake (1951)
20th Century Fox
Director: Michael Gordon
Cast: Glenn Ford, Gene Tierney, Ethel Barrymore,
 Zachary Scott, Ann Dvorak, Barbara Bates

Dead on Course a.k.a. ***Wings of Danger*** (1952)
Hammer-Lippert (British)
Director: Terence Fisher
Cast: Zachary Scott, Robert Beatty, Kay Kendall,
 Colin Tapley, Arthur Lane, Diane Cilento

Stronghold (1952)
Lippert-Mexico
Director: Steve Sekely
Cast: Veronica Lake, Zachary Scott, Arturo de Cordova

Appointment in Honduras (1953)
RKO Radio Pictures
Director: Jacques Tourneur
Cast: Glenn Ford, Ann Sheridan, Zachary Scott,
 Rudolfo Acosta, Jack Elam

Flame of the Islands (1955)
Republic Pictures
Director: Edward Ludwig
Cast: Yvonne DeCarlo, Howard Duff, Zachary Scott,
 Kurt Kaszner, James Arness

Shotgun (1955)
Allied Artists
Director: Lesley Selander
Cast: Sterling Hayden, Yvonne DeCarlo, Zachary Scott,
 Guy Prescott, Robert Wilke

The Treasure of Ruby Hills (1955)
Allied Artists
Director: Frank McDonald
Cast: Zachary Scott, Carole Matthews, Barton MacLane, Dick Foran, Lola Albright

Bandido (1956)
United Artists
Director: Richard Fleischer
Cast: Robert Mitchum, Ursula Theiss, Gilbert Roland, Zachary Scott, Rodolfo Acosta

Flight Into Danger (1956) (TV)
Canadian Broadcasting Company
Director: Gabriel Axel
Cast: James Doohan, Corrine Conley, Kate Reid, Zachary Scott

The Violent Stranger (1957)
Merton-Park, Anglo-British
Director: Montgomery Tully
Cast: Zachary Scott, Faith Domergue, Peter Illing, Faith Brook, Gordon Jackson

The Counterfeit Plan (1958)
Anglo-Amalgamated-Warner Bros.—British
Director: Montgomery Tully
Cast: Zachary Scott, Peggie Castle, Mervyn Johns, Sydney Tapler, Lee Paterson

Natchez Trace (1960)
Panarama Films
Director: Alan Crosland Jr.
Cast: Zachary Scott, William Campbell, Marcia Henderson, Irene James, Kenne Duncan

The Young One **(1961)**
Produccione-Olmeca-Vallad-Vitalite, Mexican
Director: Luis Bunuel
Cast: Zachary Scott, Kay Meersman, Bernie Hamilton,
    Claudio Brook

It's Only Money **(1962)**
Paramount Pictures
Director: Frank Tashlin
Cast: Jerry Lewis, Zachary Scott, Joan O'Brien,
    Mae Questel, Jessie White, Barbara Pepper

THE FILMS OF GLORIA STUART

Street of Women **(1932)**
Warner Bros.
Director: Archie Mayo
Cast: Kay Francis, Alan Dinehart, Marjorie Gateson,
    Roland Young, Gloria Stuart

Back Street **(1932)**
Universal Pictures
Director: John Stahl
Cast: Irene Dunne, John Boles, June Clyde,
    George Meeker, ZaSu Pitts, Gloria Stuart

The All American **(1932)**
Universal Pictures
Director: Russell Mack
Cast: Richard Arlen, Andy Devine, Gloria Stuart,
    James Gleason, Preston Foster

The Old Dark House **(1932)**
Universal Pictures
Director: James Whale
Cast: Boris Karloff, Melvyn Douglas, Charles Laughton,
    Gloria Stuart, Lillian Bond

Airmail (1932)
Universal Pictures
Director: John Ford
Cast: Ralph Bellamy, Pat O'Brien, Gloria Stuart Lillian Bond, Russell Hopton

Laughter in Hell (1933)
Universal Pictures
Director: Edward L. Cahn
Cast: Pat O'Brien, Tom Conlon, Merna Kennedy, Berton Churchill, Gloria Stuart

Sweepings (1933)
RKO Radio Pictures
Director: John Cromwell
Cast: Lionel Barrymore, Alan Dinehart, Eric Linden, William Gargan, Gloria Stuart

Private Jones (1933)
UNIVERSAL PICTURES
DIRECTOR: RUSSELL MACK
CAST: LEE TRACY, DONALD WOODS, GLORIA STUART, SHIRLEY GREY, EMMA DUNN, WALTER CATLETT

The Kiss Before the Mirror (1933)
UNIVERSAL PICTURES
DIRECTOR: JAMES WHALE
CAST: NANCY CARROLL, FRANK MORGAN, PAUL LUKAS, GLORIA STUART, JEAN DIXON, WALTER PIDGEON

The Girl in 419 (1933)
PARAMOUNT PICTURES
DIRECTOR: GEORGE SOMNES
CAST: JAMES DUNN, GLORIA STUART, DAVID MANNERS, WILLIAM HARRIGAN, SHIRLEY GREY, JACK LaRUE

It's Great to Be Alive **(1933)**
Fox Film Corporation
Director: Alfred Werker
Cast: Raul Roulien, Gloria Stuart, Edna May Oliver, Joan Marsh, Dorothy Burgess

Secret of the Blue Room **(1933)**
Universal Pictures
Director: Kurt Neumann
Cast: Lionel Atwill, Gloria Stuart, Paul Lukas, Edward Arnold, Onslow Stevens

The Invisible Man **(1933)**
Universal Pictures
Director: James Whale
Cast: Claude Rains, Gloria Stuart, William Harrigan, Henry Travers, Una O'Connor

Roman Scandals **(1933)**
United Artists
Director: Frank Tuttle
Cast: Eddie Cantor, Ruth Etting, Gloria Stuart, David Manners, Veree Teasdale

Beloved **(1934)**
Universal Pictures
Director: Victor Schertzinger
Cast: John Boles, Gloria Stuart, Albert Conti, Dorothy Peterson, Morgan Farley

I Like It That Way **(1934)**
Universal Pictures
Director: Harry Lachman
Cast: Gloria Stuart, Roger Pryor, Marian Marsh, Shirley Grey, Lucille Gleason, Noel Madison

I'll Tell the World (1934)
UNIVERSAL PICTURES
DIRECTOR: EDWARD SEDGWICK
CAST: LEE TRACY, GLORIA STUART, ROGER PRYOR,
 ONSLOW STEVENS, ALEC B. FRANCIS, LAWRENCE GRANT

The Love Captive (1934)
UNIVERSAL PICTURES
DIRECTOR: MAX MARCIN
CAST: NILS ASTHER, GLORIA STUART, PAUL KELLY,
 ALAN DINEHART, ADDISON RICHARDS, JOHN WRAY

Here Comes the Navy (1934)
WARNER BROS.
DIRECTOR: LLOYD BACON
CAST: JAMES CAGNEY, PAT O'BRIEN, GLORIA STUART,
 FRANK MCHUGH, DOROTHY TREE, ROBERT BARRAT

Gift of Gab (1934)
UNIVERSAL PICTURES
DIRECTOR: KARL FREUND
CAST: EDMUND LOWE, GLORIA STUART, RUTH ETTING,
 PHIL BAKER, ETHEL WATERS, ALICE WHITE

Maybe It's Love (1935)
WARNER BROS.
DIRECTOR: WILLIAM MCGANN
CAST: GLORIA STUART, ROSS ALEXANDER, HELEN LOWELL,
 RUTH DONNELLY, FRANK MCHUGH

Golddiggers of 1935 (1935)
WARNER BROS.
DIRECTOR: BUSBY BERKELEY
CAST: DICK POWELL, GLORIA STUART, ADOLPHE MENJOU,
 GLENDA FARRELL, GRANT MITCHELL, ALICE BRADY

Laddie **(1935)**
RKO Radio Pictures
Director: George Stevens
Cast: John Beal Gloria Stuart, Virginia Weidler, Charlotte Henry, Donald Crisp, Gloria Shea

Professional Soldier **(1935)**
20th Century Fox
Director: Tay Garnett
Cast: Victor McLaglen, Freddie Bartholomew, Gloria Stuart, Michael Whalen

The Prisoner of Shark Island **(1936)**
20th Century Fox
Director: John Ford
Cast: Warner Baxter, Gloria Stuart, Joyce Kay, Claude Gillingwater, John Carradine

The Crime of Dr. Forbes **(1936)**
20th Century Fox
Director: George Marshall
Cast: Gloria Stuart, Robert Kent, Henry Armetta, J. Edward Bromberg, Sara Haden

Poor Little Rich Girl **(1936)**
20th Century Fox
Director: Irving Cummings
Cast: Shirley Temple, Alice Faye, Gloria Stuart, Jack Haley, Michael Whalen, Sara Haden

36 Hours to Kill **(1936)**
20th Century Fox
Director: Eugene Forde
Cast: Brian Donlevy, Gloria Stuart, Douglas Fowley, Isabel Jewell, Warren Hymer

The Girl on the Front Page (1936)
Universal Pictures
Director: Harry Beaumont
Cast: Edmund Lowe, Gloria Stuart, Reginald Owen,
   David Oliver, Spring Byington

Wanted Jane Turner (1936)
RKO Radio Pictures
Director: Edward Killy
Cast: Lee Tracy, Gloria Stuart, Judith Blake,
   Barbara Pepper, Willard Robertson

The Lady Escapes (1937)
20th Century Fox
Director: Eugene Forde
Cast: Gloria Stuart, Michael Whalen, George Sanders,
   Cora Witherspoon, Don Alvarado

Girl Overboard (1937)
Universal Pictures
Director: Sidney Salkow
Cast: Gloria Stuart, Walter Pidgeon, Billy Burrud,
   Hobart Cavanaugh, Sidney Blackmer

Life Begins in College (1937)
20th Century Fox
Director: William A. Seiter
Cast: The Ritz Brothers, Joan Davis, Tony Martin,
   Gloria Stuart, Fred Stone, Nat Pendleton

Change of Heart (1938)
20th Century Fox
Director: James Tinling
Cast: Gloria Stuart, Michael Whalen, Lyle Talbot,
   Jane Darwell

Rebecca of Sunnybrook Farm **(1938)**
20TH CENTURY FOX
DIRECTOR: ALLAN DWAN
CAST: SHIRLEY TEMPLE, RANDOLPH SCOTT, JACK HALEY,
    GLORIA STUART, PHYLLIS BROOKS

Island in the Sky **(1938)**
20TH CENTURY FOX
DIRECTOR: HERBERT I. LEEDS
CAST: GLORIA STUART, MICHAEL WHALEN, PAUL KELLY,
    ROBERT KELLARD, JUNE STOREY, PAUL HURST

Keep Smiling **(1938)**
20TH CENTURY FOX
DIRECTOR: HERBERT I. LEEDS
CAST: JANE WITHERS, GLORIA STUART, HENRY WILCOXON,
    HELEN WESTLEY, JED PROUTY

Time Out for Murder **(1938)**
20TH CENTURY FOX
DIRECTOR: H. BRUCE HUMBERSTONE
CAST: GLORIA STUART, MICHAEL WHALEN, CHICK CHANDLER,
    DOUGLAS FOWLEY, JEAN ROGERS

The Lady Objects **(1938)**
COLUMBIA PICTURES
DIRECTOR: ERLE C. KENTON
CAST: LANNY ROSS, GLORIA STUART JOAN MARSH,
    PIERRE WATKIN, ROBERT PAIGE, ANN DORAN

Winner Take All **(1939)**
20TH CENTURY FOX
DIRECTOR: OTTO BROWER
CAST: TONY MARTIN, GLORIA STUART, HENRY ARMETTA,
    SLIM SUMMERVILLE, KANE RICHMOND

The Three Musketeers (1939)
20th Century Fox
Director: Allan Dwan
Cast: Don Ameche, The Ritz Brothers, Binnie Barnes, Lionel Atwill, Gloria Stuart

It Could Happen to You (1939)
20th Century Fox
Director: Alfred Werker
Cast: Stuart Erwin, Gloria Stuart, Raymond Walburn, Douglas Fowley, Paul Hurst

Here Comes Elmer (1943)
Republic Pictures
Director: Joseph Santley
Cast: Al Pearce, Dale Evans, Frank Albertson, Gloria Stuart, Wally Vernon, Luis Alberni

The Whistler (1944)
Columbia Pictures
Director: William Castle
Cast: Richard Dix, J. Carroll Naish, Gloria Stuart, Alan Dinehart, Joan Woodbury, Cy Kendall

Enemy of Women a.k.a. *The Mad Lover* (1944)
Monogram
Diector: Alfred Zeisler
Cast: Claudia Drake, Paul Andor, Donald Woods, H. B. Warner, Gloria Stuart

She Wrote the Book (1946)
Universal Pictures
Director: Charles Lamont
Cast: Joan Davis, Jack Oakie, Mischa Auer, Kriby Grant, John Litel, Gloria Stuart

The Legend of Lizzie Borden (TV) (1975)
Director: Paul Wendkos
Cast: Elizabeth Montgomery, Fionnuala Flannagan, Ed Flanders, Gloria Stuart

Adventures of the Queen (TV) (1975)
Director: David L. Rich
Cast: Robert Stack, David Hedison, Ralph Bellamy, Bradford Dillman, Sorell Booke, G. Stuart

Flood (TV) (1976)
Director: Earl Bellamy
Cast: Robert Culp, Martin Milner, Barbara Hershey, Richard Basehart, Carol Lynley, G. Stuart

In the Glitter Palace (TV) (1977)
Director: Robert Butler
Cast: Chad Everett, Barbara Hershey, Anthony Zerbe, Howard Duff, Gloria Stuart

Best Place to Be (TV) (1979)
Director: David Miller
Cast: Donna Reed, Efrem Zimbalist Jr., Mildred Dunnock, Betty White, Gloria Stuart

The Incredible Journey of Dr. Meg Laurel (TV) (1979)
Director: Guy Green
Cast: Lindsay Wagner, Jane Wyman, Dorothy McGuire, Andrew Duggan, Gloria Stuart

The Two Worlds of Jennie Logan (TV) (1979)
Director: Frank DeFelitta
Cast: Lindsay Wagner, Marc Singer, Alan Feinstein, Linda Gray, Gloria Stuart

MERLENE OF THE MOVIES (TV) (1981)
DIRECTOR: NANCY MALONE
CAST: GLORIA STUART, AMANDA THOMPSON,
 BENJAMIN THOMPSON

THE VIOLATION OF SARAH MCDAVID (TV) (1981)
DIRECTOR: JOHN L. MOXEY
CAST: PATTY DUKE, NED BEATTY, JAMES SLOYAN, ALLY SHEEDY,
 GLORIA STUART

MY FAVORITE YEAR (1982)
MGM-UNITED ARTISTS
DIRECTOR: RICHARD BENJAMIN
CAST: PETER O'TOOLE, MARK LINN-BAKER, JESSICA HARPER,
 JOSEPH BOLOGNA, BILL MACY, G. STUART

MASS APPEAL (1984)
UNIVERSAL PICTURES
DIRECTOR: GLENN JORDAN
CAST: JACK LEMMON, ZELJKO IVANCK, CHARLES DURNING,
 LOUISE LATHAM, GLORIA STUART

WILDCATS (1986)
WARNER BROS.
DIRECTOR: MICHAEL RITCHIE
CAST: GOLDIE HAWN, SWOOZIE KURTZ, ROBYN LIVELY,
 JAMES KEACH, GLORIA STUART

SHOOTDOWN (TV) (1986)
DIRECTOR: MICHAEL PRESSMAN
CAST: ANGELA LANSBURY, GEORGE COE, KYLE SECOR,
 MOLLY HAGAN, GLORIA STUART

TITANIC (1997)
PARAMOUNT PICTURES/20TH CENTURY FOX
DIRECTOR: JAMES CAMERON
CAST: LEONARDO DICAPRIO, KATE WINSLET, KATHY BATES,
 FRANCES FISHER, GLORIA STUART

The Titanic Chronicles **(TV) (1999)**
DIRECTOR: EMMETT JAMES
CAST: ERIC BRAEDEN, TIM CURRY, BERNARD HILL,
   DAVID MCCALLUM, GLORIA STUART

The Love Letter **(1999)**
DREAM WORKS
DIRECTOR: PETER CHAN
CAST: KATE CAPSHAW, BLYTHE DANNER, TOM EVERETT SCOTT,
   TOM SELLECK, GLORIA STUART

My Mother the Spy **(TV) (2000)**
DIRECTOR: ELODIE KEENE
CAST: DYAN CANNON, JAYNE BROOK, KEVIN KILNER,
   DAVID PALFFY, GLORIA STUART

The Million Dollar Hotel **(2000)**
ICON ENTERTAINMENT, LIONS GATE FILMS
DIRECTOR: WIM WENDERS
CAST: MEL GIBSON, JEREMY DAVIES, MILLA JOVOVICH,
   JIMMY SMITS, GLORIA STUART

Murder, She Wrote: The Last Free Man **(TV) (2001)**
DIRECTOR: ANTHONY PULLEN SHAW
CAST: ANGELA LANSBURY, PHYLICIA RASHAD, MICHAEL JACE,
   GLORIA STUART

Land of Plenty **(2004)**
EMOTION PICTURES, I.F.C. FILMS
DIRECTOR: WIM WENDERS
CAST: MICHELLE WILLIAMS, JOHN DIEHL, SHAUN TOUB,
   BURT YOUNG, GLORIA STUART

SELECTED BIBLIOGRAPHY

BOOKS

American Film Institute Catalog of Motion Pictures Produced in the United States, Feature Films, 1931–1940. Berkeley: University of California Press, 1999.

American Film Institute Catalog of Motion Pictures Produced in the United States, Feature Films, 1941–1950. Berkeley: University of California Press, 1999.

American Film Institute Catalog of Motion Pictures Produced in the United States, Feature Films, 1951–1960. Berkeley: University of California Press, 1999.

Behlmer, Rudy. *Inside Warner Brothers (1935-1951).* New York: Simon & Schuster, 1987.

Cocchi, John. *Second Features.* Bethesda, MD: Carol Publishing, 1991.

Cotten, Joseph. *Variety Will Get you Somewhere.* San Francisco: Mercury House Inc., 1987.

Eames, John Douglas. *The Paramount Story.* Portland: Octopus Books Limited, 1985.

Everson, William K. *Classics of the Horror Film.* New York: Citadel, 1995.

Davis, Ronald. *Zachary Scott, Hollywood's Sophisticated Cad.* Jackson: University Press of Mississippi, 2006.

Fontaine, Joan. *No Bed of Roses.* New York: William Morrow & Company, 1978.

Geist, Kenneth. *People Will Talk, The Life and Films of Joseph L. Maniewwicz.* Boston: Da Capo Press, 1983.

Higham, Charles & Roy Moseley. *Cary Grant, The Lonely Heart*, New York: Harcourt Brace Jovanovich, 1989.

Juran, Robert A. *Old Familiar Faces.* Movie Memories Publishing, 1995.

Katz, Ephraim. *The Film Encyclopedia, 3rd Edition.* New York: Harper Collins, 1998.

Lamparski, Richard. *Whatever Became Of . . . ?* First Series, New York: Bantam Books, 1976.

Lamparski, Richard. *Whatever Became Of . . . ?* Fifth Series, New York: Bantam Books, 1976.

Lamparski, Richard. *Whatever Became of . . . ?* Tenth Series, New York: Crown Publishing, 1986.

Lamparski, Richard. *Whatever Became of . . . ?* Eleventh Series, New York: Crown Publishing, 1989.

Larkin, Rochelle. *Hail, Columbia.* New York: Arlington House, 1975.

Lasky, Betty. *RKO The Biggest Little Major Of Them All.* Jacksonville: Roundtable Publishing, 1989.

Liebman, Ron. *The WAMPAS Baby Stars*. Jefferson, NC: McFarland & Company, 2000.

Magers, Boyd & Michael G. Fitzgerald. *Western Women*. Jefferson, NC: McFarland & Company, 1999.

Maltin, Leonard. *Leonard Maltin's Classic Movie Guide. Third Edition*. New York: Penguin Books, 2015.

Mank, Gregory William. *Hollywood Cauldron*. Jefferson, NC: McFarland & Company, 1994.

Margulies, Edward & Stephen Rebello, *Bad Movies We Love*, New York: Penguin Books, 1993.

McClelland, Doug. *Forties Film Talk*. Jefferson NC: McFarland & Company, 1992.

Miller, Don. *B Movies*. New York: Ballantine Books, 1973.

Morella, Joe & Edward Epstein. *Lana*. Berkeley, California: Berkeley Publishing, 1989.

Nash, Jay Robert & Stanley Ralph Ross. *The Motion Picture Guide*. Canterbury, UK: Cinebooks, 1986.

Navasky, Victor S. *Naming Names*. New York: Penguin Books, 1980.

Nemcek, Paul. *The Films of Nancy Carroll*. New York: Lyle Stuart Inc., 1969.

Osborne, Robert. *Academy Awards Illustrated*. Hollywood: Marvin Miller Enterprises, 1965.

Parish, James Robert. *Actors' Television Credits 1950–1972*. Metuchen, NJ: Scarecrow Press, 1973.

Parish, James Robert & Ronald L. Bowers. *The MGM Stock Company: The Golden Era.* New Rochelle, NY: Arlington House, 1974.

Parish, James Robert & Michael R. Pitts. *The Great Science Fiction Pictures.* Lanham, MD: Scarecrow Press, 1977.

Parish, James Robert & William T. Leonard. *Hollywood Players, The Thirties.* Carlstadt, NJ: Rainbow Books, 1976.

Prindle, David F. *The Politics of Glamour, Ideology and Democracy in The Screen Actor's Guild.* Madison, Wisconsin: University of Wisconsin Press, 1988.

Quinlan, David. *The Film Lover's Companion, 4th Edition.* Secaucus, NJ: Carol Publishing Group.

Quirk, Lawrence. *Claudette Colbert: An Illustrated Biography.* New York: Crown Publishers, 1985.

Ragan, David. *Who's Who in Hollywood 1900–1976.* New York: Arlington House, 1976.

Robertson, James C. *The Casablanca Man, The Cinema of Michael Curtiz.* New York: Routledge, 1994.

Schickel, Richard. *The Men Who Made the Movies.* New York: Atheneum, 1975.

Schuster, Mel. *Motion Picture Performers: A Bibliography of Magazine and Periodical Articles, 1900–1969.* Metuchen, New Jersey: Scarecrow Press Inc., 1971.

Schuster, Mel. *Motion Picture Performers: A Bibliography of Magazine and Periodical Articles Supplement No.1, 1970–1974.* Metuchen, New Jersey: Scarecrow Press Inc., 1976.

Shipman, David. *The Great Movie Stars, The Golden Years*. Boston: De Capo Press, 1979.

Stuart, Gloria & Sylvia Thompson, *I Just Kept Hoping*. New York: Little, Brown and Company, 1999.

Terrace, Vincent. *The Complete Encyclopedia of Television Programs 1947–1976*. Cranbury, NJ: A.S. Barnes & Company, 1976.

Thomas, Tony & Aubrey Solomon. *The Films of Twentieth Century Fox*. New York: Citadel Press, 1979.

Tuska, Jon. *The Detective in Hollywood*. New York: Doubleday & Company, 1978.

Weaver, Tom. *Poverty Row Horrors*. Jefferson, NC: McFarland & Company Inc., 1993.

Weaver, Tom. *It Came From Weaver Five*. Jefferson, NC: McFarland & Company, 1996.

Weinstein, Allen & Alexander Vassiliev. *The Haunted Wood: Soviet Espionage in America — The Stalin Era*, New York: Modern Library, 2000.

Wellman, William Jr. *Wild Bill Wellman*. New York: Pantheon, 2015.

Westmore, Frank & Muriel Davidson. *The Westmores of Hollywood*. Philadelphia: Lippincott, 1976.

Wollstein, Hans J. *Vixens, Floozies and Molls*. Jefferson, NC: McFarland & Company, 1999.

ARTICLES

Anker, Jerry. "Paula Raymond." *Hollywood High School Celebrity Museum flyer*, August, 1996.

Asher, J. "The Name is Zack." *Photoplay*, March, 1946.

Baily, Tom W. "Manhattan Nancy." *Screenland*, 1928.

Baldwin, Faith. "Self Made Marian." *Modern Screen*, 1931.

Baldwin, Faith. "The Truth About Nancy Carroll." *Modern Screen*, April, 1931.

Barnes, Bart. "Oscar-Winner Anne Baxter Is Dead at 62." *Washington Post*, December 13, 1985.

Baxter, Anne. "How Could I Be So Wrong." *Modern Screen*, August, 1949.

Benjamin, George. "Hit Hollywood Early." *Modern Screen*, 1935.

Bloch, Judy. "Karen Morley, The Unvanquished — Silencing the Voice of an Ever-Political Femme Fatale." *San Francisco Film Festival flyer*, 1999

Burke, Randolph Carroll. "Hollywood's Happiness Girl." *Picturegoer Weekly*, November, 1931.

Carroll, Nancy. "Hoofing to Fame with Nancy Carroll, Part I." *Screen Secrets*, January, 1929.

Carroll, Nancy. "Hoofing to Fame with Nancy Carroll, Part II." *Screen Secrets*, February, 1929.

Cassa, Anthony. "Zachary Scott, Superior Scoundrel." *Hollywood Studio*, September, 1982.

Corbin, Elinor. "The Littlest Rebel." *Photoplay*, November, 1929.

Crowe, Harry J. "She Learned About Women From Them." *New Movie Magazine*, October, 1931.

Darnton, Charles. "She'd Rather Work Than Eat!" *Modern Screen*, July, 1935.

Dillon, Frank. "She's Not Afraid." *Modern Screen*, 1938.

Dolven, Frank. "Ann Sheridan Deserved a Brighter Star." *Big Reel*, July, 1995.

Dora, Albert. "Dangerous at Seventeen." *Movie Mirror*, 1931, pg. 125.

Drier, Hans. "The House That Zach Built." *Photoplay*, September, 1949.

Ergenbright, Eric. "She Started Something." *Play*, 1932.

Fidler, James M. "The Past, The Present, and The Future of Jean Parker." *Screenland*, March, 1934.

Fox, Margalit. "Marian Marsh, 93, Petite Star of 'Svengali' Dies." *New York Times*, November, 2006.

Franchey, John. "Villains With Vitamins." *Motion Picture*, 1944.

Grayson, Charles. "Kalm, Kool, and Collected — that's Karen." *Motion Picture*, November, 1932.

Guggenheimer, Paul. "One Hundred Years of John Hodiak." *Pittsburgh Gazette*, April 16, 2014.

Hall, Bob. "Buy Buy Blues." *Photoplay*, 1942.

Hamilton, S. "Sketch, Edward Norris." *Photoplay*, January.

Harmetz, Aljean and Robert Berkvist. "Gloria Stuart, an Actress Rediscovered Late, Dies at 100." *New York Times*, September 27, 2010.

Hartley, Katherine. "She Used to Be Demure!" *Photoplay*, 1939.

Heacock, Francis. "It's All a Plot." *Modern Movies*, 1947.

Hopper, Hedda. "It Takes Guts." *Modern Screen*, August, 1945.

Howe, Herb. "Family Bachelor." *Photoplay*, March, 1946.

Hoyt, Caroline Somers. "How 'Sequoia' Was Made." *Modern Screen*, June, 1935.

Jones, C. "Afraid of Love." *Silver Screen*, February, 1932.

Kent, J. "Her Return to the Screen." *Movie Classic*, February, 1936.

King, Susan. "Classic Hollywood: The Academy Salutes Gloria Stuart." *Los Angeles Times*, July 21, 2010.

King, Susan. "The Latest Bloomer in Hollywood." *Los Angeles Times*, September 14, 1999.

Lathem, Maude, "Trying Too Hard to Please." *Picture Play*, July, 1935.

Lee, S. "Hollywood's New Heart Breaker." *Screen Book*, August, 1938.

Leifert, Don. "Marian Marsh, From Barrymore's Boudoir to Karloff's Black Room." *Filmfax*, January/February, 1996.

Madson, Elaine. "Gloria Stuart, One Glorious Rose." *Venice*, December 1997.

Mank, Gregory. "Marian Marsh Recalls Filming 'Svengali' With Barrymore." *Films in Review*, December, 1985, pg. 580.

McKegg, William. "Soft Iron Hand." *Photoplay*, October, 1933.

McLellan, Dennis. "Gloria Stuart dies at 100; 'Titanic' actress." *Los Angeles Times*, September 27, 2010.

McClellan, Dennis. "Paula Raymond, MGM Leading Lady in '50's, Prolific TV Actress." *Los Angeles Times*, January 10, 2004.

Michaels, Joan. "Hollywood's New Stop, Look, and Sigh Man." *Screenland*, 1944.

Morehouse, Ward. "Nancy Carroll Renews Career in Touring Play." *New York Times*, 1963.

Morley, Karen. "Karen Morley Reveals Her Story." *Film Pictorial*, March 16, 1935.

Oettinger, Malcolm H. "The Claire Dodd Mystery." *Picture Play*, March, 1935.

Oliver, Myrna. "Karen Morley, 93: Star of 1930's Films Was Blacklisted in '50's." *Los Angeles Times*, April 23, 2003.

Parker, Jean. "I'm An Ex-Cinderella." *Movie Mirror*, April, 1939.

Parsons, Louella. "Miss Medina Asks Divorce." *Los Angeles Herald-Examiner*, June 21, 1951.

Peck, Stacey. "Gloria Stuart Q & A." *Los Angeles Times*, April 13, 1980.

Proctor, Kay. "They Thought They Would Keep Their Marriage a Secret." *Photoplay*, July, 1936.

Rankin, Ruth. "And Gloria Was Burned Up." *New Movie Magazine*, May, 1934.

Rankin, Ruth. "No, the Animals Weren't Trained." *Shadow Play*, February, 1935.

Reisman-Cooper, Barbara. "She's Queen of the World." *Modern Maturity*, March, 1999.

Roarke, Mary. "Jean Parker, 90, Had More than 70 Films, Including 'Little Women, The Gunfighter." *Los Angeles Times*, December 10, 2005.

Simonson, Robert. "Jean Parker, Stage and Film Actress, Is Dead at 90." *Playbill*, December 13, 2005.

Smith, Jewel. "Hollywood's Newest Cinderella." *Play Magazine*, 1931.

Smith, Steven. "Back in Bloom." *Los Angeles Times*, December 20, 1997.

Smithson, E.J. "The Luckiest Girl in Hollywood." *Picture Play*, 1938.

Springer, John. "Nancy Carroll." *Films in Review*, April, 1956.

Springer, John. "Nancy Carroll: Film Star of the Talkies." *The Entertainers*, 1964.

Squire, Nancy Winslow. "Sentimental Gentleman." *Modern Screen*, March, 1946.

Thompson, Sylvia. "Martini Time in the Garden of Allah." *Los Angeles Times*, November 5, 2000.

Tollefson, Rodika. "Genetic Creativity: Belfair Bead Artist's Talents Have Deep Roots." *Kitsap Sun*, January 6, 2010.

Vallance, Tom. "Paula Raymond Obituary." *The Independent*, January 9, 2004.

Van Neste, Dan. "Bonny Jean, Remembering Jean Parker (1915–2005)." *Classic Images*, February, 2006.

Van Neste, Dan. "A Legacy of Beauty." *Classic Images*, January, 2007.

Van Neste, Dan. "Remembering Ed — Edward Norris 1911-2002." *Classic Images*, May, 2003.

Wade, Jack. "The Ham from Hamtramck." *Modern Screen*, February, 1945.

Whitely Fletcher, Adele. "An Open Letter to Nancy Carroll." *Modern Screen*, 1931.

Whitely Fletcher, Adele. "What's Going to Happen to Nancy?" *Modern Screen*, March, 1932.

Wilson, Dixie. "Girl of the Month." *Good Housekeeping*, August, 1937.

ONLINE RESOURCES

American Film Institute Database — http://wwwafi.com/members/catalog/
American Silent Feature Film Survival Database — Library of Congress — https://www.loc.gov/
Ancestry.com — http://www.ancestry.com/
Classic Images — http://www.classicimages.com/
The Coloradoan website — http://.Coloradoan.com/
Family History Library, L.D. S. Church — http://www.familysearch.org/
Find a Grave website — https://www.findagrave.com/
Filmreference.com — http://www.filmreference.com/
Garbo Forever website — http://www.garbofoever.com/
Glamour Girls of the Silver Screen — http://www.glamourgirlsofsilverscreen.com/

Hollywood Reporter website —
   http://www.hollywoodreporter.com/
Hollywood Walk of Fame website —
   http://www.walkoffame.com/
Internet Broadway Database — http://www.ibdb.com/
Internet Movie Database — http://www.imdb.com/
Immortal Ephemera — http://www.immortalephemera.com/
Jerry Haedinges' Vintage Radio Logs —
   http://www.otrsite.com/radiolog/
Joancrawfordbest.com — http://www.joancrawfordbest.com/
Legendary Greta Garbo website —
   http://legendarygretagarbo.com/
Library of Congress websites — http://www.loc.gov/library-digital.html
Los Angeles Times website — http://latimes.com/
Media History Digital Library — http://mediahistoryproject.org/
New York Times website — https://www.nytimes.com/
NBC Los Angeles Website — http://www.NBClosangeles.com/
Nitrateville website — http://www.nitrateville.com/
Official Greta Garbo website — http://www.gretagarbo.com/
Old Time Radio website — http://www.otr.net/
Pittsburgh Post-Gazette website — http://www.post-gazette.com/
Pre-code.com — http://www.pre.code.com/
Radio Goldindex — http://www.radiogoldindex.com/
Self Styled Siren Blog — http://selfstyledsiren.blogspot.com/
Silent Era website — http://silentera.com/
Silent Film website — www.silentfilm.org/
Smithsonian Magazine website —
   http://www.smithsonianmag.com/
Turner Classic Movies website — http://www.tcm.com/
TV.com website — http://www.tv.com/
Variety website — http://www.variety.com/

END NOTES

CHAPTER ONE — "NANCY CARROLL: ONE OF THE FIGHTING IRISH"

[1] Patricia Kirkland Bevan taped interview with Dan Van Neste, May 2000.

[2] Carroll, Nancy. "Hoofing to Fame with Nancy Carroll, Part I," *Screen Secrets*, January 1929, pg 21.

[3] Carroll, Nancy. "Hoofing to Fame with Nancy Carroll, Part I." *Screen Secrets*, January 1929, pg. 22.

[4] Carroll, Nancy. "Hoofing to Fame with Nancy Carroll, Part I." *Screen Secrets*, January 1929, pg. 22.

[5] Carroll, Nancy. "Hoofing to Fame with Nancy Carroll, Part I." *Screen Secrets*, January 1929, pg. 22.

[6] Carroll, Nancy. "Hoofing to Fame with Nancy Carroll, Part I." *Screen Secrets*, January 1929, pg. 63; and Corbin, Elinor. "The Littlest Rebel," *Photoplay*, November 1929, pg. 63.

[7] Carroll, Nancy. "Hoofing to Fame with Nancy Carroll, Part I." *Screen Secrets*, January 1929, pg. 63; and Corbin Elinor. "The Littlest Rebel." *Photoplay*, November 1929, pg. 63

[8] Carroll, Nancy. "Hoofing to Fame with Nancy Carroll, Part I," *Screen Secrets*, January 1929; and Corbin, Elinor. "The Littlest Rebel," *Photoplay*, November 1929, pg. 63.

[9] Patricia Kirkland Bevan taped interview with Dan Van Neste, May 2000.

[10] Carroll, Nancy. "Hoofing to Fame with Nancy Carroll, Part II." *Screen Secrets*, February, 1929.

[11] Baily, Tom W. "Manhattan Nancy." *Screenland*, 1928, pgs. 99-100; and Springer, John. "Nancy Carroll." *Films in Review*, April 1956.

[12] Baily, Tom W. "Manhattan Nancy." *Screenland*, 1928 pgs. 99-100; and Springer, John, "Nancy Carroll." *Films in Review*, April, 1956.

[13] Burke, Randolph Carroll. "Hollywood's Happiness Girl." *Picturegoer Weekly*, November 1931, pgs. 11-12.

[14] Nemcek, Paul. *The Films of Nancy Carroll*. New York: Lyle Stuart Inc., c. 1969, pg. 23.

[15] Burke, Randolph Carroll. "Hollywood's Happiness Girl." *Picturegoer Weekly*, November 1931, pgs. 11-12.

[16] Osborne, Robert. *Academy Awards Illustrated*. Hollywood: Marvin Miller Enterprises, c. 1965, pg. 27.

[17] McKegg, William. "Soft Iron Hand." *Photoplay*, October 1933, pg. 68.

[18] David Chierichetti Taped Interview with Dan Van Neste, May 2000.

[19] Whitely Fletcher, Adele. "An Open Letter to Nancy Carroll." *Modern Screen*, 1931.

[20] Baldwin, Faith. "The Truth About Nancy Carroll." *Modern Screen*, April 1931, pg. 98.

[21] Patricia Kirkland Bevan taped interview with Dan Van Neste, May 2000.

[22] Springer, John. "Film Star of the Talkies." *The Entertainers*, 1964, pg. 61.

[23] Nemcek, Paul. *The Films of Nancy Carroll.* New York: Lyle Stuart Inc., c. 1969, pg. 18.

[24] David Chierichetti taped interview with Dan Van Neste, May 2000.

[25] Whitely Fletcher, Adele. "What's Going to Happen to Nancy?" *Modern Screen*, March 1932, pg. 121.

[26] Patricia Kirkland Bevan taped interview with Dan Van Neste, June 2000.

[27] McKegg, William. "Soft Iron Hand." *Photoplay*, October 1933, pg. 72.

[28] Patricia Kirkland Bevan taped interview with Dan Van Neste, June 2000.

[29] Nemcek, Paul, *The Films of Nancy Carroll.* New York: Lyle Stuart Inc., c. 1969, pg. 32.

[30] Patricia Kirkland Bevan taped interview with Dan Van Neste, June 2000.

[31] Springer, John. "Nancy Carroll." *Films in Review*, April 1956.

[32] John Springer taped interview with Dan Van Neste, May 2000.

[33] Nemcek, Paul, *The Films of Nancy Carroll.* New York: Lyle Stuart Inc., c. 1969, pg. 32.

[34] John Springer taped interview with Dan Van Neste, May 2000.

[35] Springer, John. "Nancy Carroll." *Films in Review*, April 1956.

[36] Don Bevan taped interview with Dan Van Neste, June 2000.

[37] Don & Patricia Kirkland Bevan taped interview with Dan Van Neste, June 2000.

[38] Morehouse, Ward. "Nancy Carroll Renews Career in Touring Play." *New York Times*, 1963.

[39] Will Hutchins taped interviews with Dan Van Neste, May 2000.

[40] *Los Angeles Times* obituary for Nancy Carroll, August 11, 1965.

[41] Patricia Kirkland Bevan taped interview with Dan Van Neste, May 2000.

[42] John Springer taped interview with Dan Van Neste, May 2000.

[43] John Springer taped interview with Dan Van Neste, May 2000.

[44] Don Bevan taped interview with Dan Van Neste, June 2000.

[45] Suzanne Benedetto online interview with Dan Van Neste, June 2000.

[46] Sources for the information contained in the "Update" section for Nancy Carroll include the following: Gussownov, Mel. "John Springer, 85, Hollywood Publicist, Dies." *New York Times*, November 1, 2001; and "Obituary — John Springer, Press Agent to an Illustrious Array of Entertainers." *Los Angeles Times*, November 2, 2001; Letter from Donald Bevan to Dan Van Neste, dated October 26, 2000 on the death of Patricia Kirkland; and Weber, Bruce. "Obituary — Donald Bevan, 93, Sardi's Artist and 'Stalag 17' Writer Dies." *New York Times*, June 30, 2013, pg. B8; and "Obituary — Donald Bevan, Caricaturist

and 'Stalag 17' Playwright Dies at 93." *Variety*, July 5, 2013; and Wagner, Laura. "Obituary for David Chierichetti." *Classic Images*, January 2017.

[47] John Springer taped interview with Dan Van Neste, May 23, 2000.

CHAPTER TWO — "GLORIA DICKSON: WE WON'T FORGET"

[48] Wilson, Dixie. "Girl of the Month." *Good Housekeeping*, August 1937, pg. 38.

[49] Dillon, Frank. "She's Not Afraid." *Modern Screen*, 1938, pg 17.

[50] Smithson, E.J. "The Luckiest Girl in Hollywood." *Picture Play*, 1938, pg. 34; and "Round-Up of Youth." *Photoplay*, January 1938, pg. 79.

[51] Wilson, Dixie. "Girl of the Month." *Good Housekeeping*, August 1937, pg. 38.

[52] Edward Norris taped interview with Dan Van Neste, August 30, 1999, August 31, 1999.

[53] "The Life Story of Gloria Dickson." *Picture Show*, December 1940, pg. 16.

[54] "Sketch." *Modern Screen*, November 1937, pg. 75; and Smithson, E.J. "The Luckiest Girl in Hollywood." *Screenland*, 1938, pg. 68.

[55] Wilson, Dixie. "Girl of the Month." *Good Housekeeping*, August 1937, pg. 38.

[56] Vincent Sherman taped interview with Dan Van Neste, September 1999.

[57] Smithson, E.J. "The Luckiest Girl in Hollywood." *Picture Play*, 1938, pg. 68.

58 Vincent Sherman taped interview with Dan Van Neste, September 1999.

59 Westmore, Frank & Muriel Davidson. *The Westmores of Hollywood.* Philadelphia: Lippincott, c. 1976.

60 "Actress Ends Marriage." *Los Angeles Examiner*, June 16, 1940.

61 "Gloria Dickson." *World of Yesterday*, June 1980, pgs 4, 5, 6.

62 Miller, Don. *B Movies.* New York: Ballantine Books, c. 1973, pg. 265.

63 "Miss Dickson Asks Divorce." *Los Angeles Examiner*, April 19, 1944.

64 "Gloria Dickson Perishes in Hillside Home Fire." *Los Angeles Times*, April 12, 1945, pg. 1.

65 "Actress Gloria Dickson Burns to Death." *Los Angeles Examiner*, April 11, 1945, pgs. 1,5.

66 "Gloria Dickson of Films Dies in L.A. Home Fire." *Los Angeles Times*, April 11, 1945, pgs. 1-2.

67 "Gloria Dickson's Mother Visits Scene of Death." *Los Angeles Examiner*, April 12, 1945.

68 http://www.findagrave.com/

69 Note in Gloria Dickson's files at the A.M.P.A.S./Margaret Herrick Library in Los Angeles.

70 Wilson, Dixie. "Girl of the Month." *Good Housekeeping*, August 1937, pgs. 38-39.

71 http://www.findagrave.com/; and http://www.ancestry.com/

[72] http://www.glamourgirlsofthesilverscreen.com/

[73] Sources for the information contained in the "Update" section for Gloria Dickson include the following: McClellan, Dennis. "Obituaries — Vincent Sherman, 99; Director for Warner Bros. in 1940's." *Los Angeles Times*, June 20, 2006; and Bervist, Robert. "Vincent Sherman Studio-Era Hollywood Director Dies at 99." *New York Times*, June 21, 2006; and Bernstein, Adam. "Obituary — Director Vincent Sherman." *Washington Post*, June 22, 2006.

CHAPTER THREE — "CLAIRE DODD: DIMPLED AND DANGEROUS"

[74] John Cooper taped interviews with Dan Van Neste May 9 & May 10, 2011.

[75] John Cooper taped interview with Dan Van Neste, May 9, 2011.

[76] Claire's marriage to John Milton Strauss is covered in multiple sources including: Wollstein, Hans J. *Vixens, Floozies and Molls*. Jefferson, NC: McFarland & Company, c. 1999, pg. 74; and Warner Brothers Studio Biography in Claire's file at the A.M.P.A.S./Margaret Herrick Library in Los Angeles; and March, 5, 1938 article in the *Los Angeles Examiner*, "Says Broker Called Her 'Stupid.'"

[77] Oettinger, Malcolm H. "The Claire Dodd Mystery." *Picture Play*, March 1935, pg. 77.

[78] John Cooper taped interview with Dan Van Neste, May 9, 2011.

[79] John Cooper taped interview with Dan Van Neste, May 9, 2011.

[80] Oettinger, Malcolm H. "The Claire Dodd Mystery." *Picture Play*, March 1935, pg. 77.

81 Sybil Jason written interview with Dan Van Neste, June 2011.

82 John Cooper taped interview with Dan Van Neste, May 9, 2011.

83 John Cooper taped interview with Dan Van Neste, May 9, 2011.

84 John Cooper taped interview with Dan Van Neste, May 9, 2011.

85 John Cooper taped interview with Dan Van Neste, May 9, 2011.

86 John Cooper taped interview with Dan Van Neste, May 9, 2011.

87 John Cooper taped interview with Dan Van Neste, May 9, 2011.

88 Claire Dodd's death was covered in several short obituary pieces in multiple newspapers and magazines, the most prominent being: *New York Times*, November 25, 1973, *Los Angeles Times*, November 22, 1973, and *Los Angeles Herald Examiner*, November 26, 1973.

89 John Cooper taped interview with Dan Van Neste, May 9, 2011.

90 Sources for the information contained in the "Update" section for Claire Dodd include the following: Brand Cooper interview with Dan Van Neste, October, 2018.

CHAPTER FOUR — "RICHARD GREENE: SWASHBUCKLER WITH A DOUBLE-EDGED SWORD"

91 Parish, James Robert & William Leonard. "Richard Greene." *Hollywood Players, The Thirties*. Carlstadt, N.J.: Rainbow Books, c. 1976, pg. 269; and 20th Century Fox Studio Biography, 1947, pg. 10.

92 Parish, James Robert & William Leonard. "Richard Greene." *Hollywood Players, The Thirties*. Carlstadt, N.J.: Rainbow Books, c. 1976, pg. 266.

[93] Parish, James Robert & William Leonard. "Richard Greene." *Hollywood Players, The Thirties*. Carlstadt, N.J.: Rainbow Books, c. 1976, pg. 269; and Columbia Studio Biography, 1960, pg.1.

[94] Parish, James Robert & William Leonard. "Richard Greene." *Hollywood Players, The Thirties*. Carlstadt, N.J.: Rainbow Books, c. 1976, pg. 269.

[95] Lee, S. "Hollywood's New Heart Breaker." *Screen Book*, August 1938, pg. 24.

[96] 20th Century Fox Studio Biography, 1947, pg. 11.

[97] 20th Century Fox Studio Biography, 1947, pg. 11.

[98] Parish, James Robert & William Leonard. "Richard Greene." *Hollywood Players, The Thirties*. Carlstadt, N.J.: Rainbow Books, c. 1976, pg. 270; and 20th Century Fox Studio Biography, 1947, pg. 11.

[99] 20th Century Fox Studio Biography, 1947, pg. 11.

[100] 20th Century Fox Studio Biography, 1947, pg. 11.

[101] Parsons, Louella. "Miss Medina Asks Divorce." *Los Angeles Herald-Examiner*, June 21, 1951, Section 1, pg. 5; and "Film Star Richard Greene Turned Cold to Her Charms, Wife Testifies." *Los Angeles Herald-Examiner*, June 25, 1951.

[102] Cotten, Joseph. *Variety Will Get you Somewhere*. San Francisco: Mercury House Inc., c. 1987, pg. 87.

[103] "The British Hopalong." *TV Guide*, July 1956, pg. 8.

[104] Paula Raymond taped interview with Dan Van Neste, May 15, 1997.

[105] Parish, James Robert. *Actors Television Credits (1950-1972)*, Metachen, NJ: Scarecrow Press, 1973, pgs. 335-336.

[106] The TV series *The Adventures of Robin Hood* is covered in detail in several books and articles including: Parish, James Robert & William Leonard. "Richard Greene." *Hollywood Players, The Thirties*. Carlstadt, N.J.: Rainbow Books, c. 1976, pgs. 266-273; and Columbia Studio Biography, 1960; and *London Times* Obituary "Richard Greene." June 3, 1985.

[107] Several obituary articles claimed Mr. Greene and his second wife, Ms. Summers-Greene were divorced in 1980, while others claim they were separated.

[108] "Obituary — Richard Greene Star of Film and Television." *London Times*, June 3, 1985, pg. 12; and "Obituary — Richard Greene, Actor in Film and Television." *New York Times*, June 6, 1985, pg. B1; and "Obituary — TV's Robin Hood Dies." *Los Angeles Times*, June 2, 1985, pg. B5; and "Obituary — Richard Greene." *Variety*, June 5, 1985, pg. 93.

[109] Sources for the information contained in the "Update" section for Richard Greene include the following. Nancy Oakes von Hoyningen-Huene's death was covered in various newspapers around the world including *The New York Times* who printed a short Obituary on Jaunary 21, 2005. The Roosevelt-Garcia marriage was covered in detail by *The New York Times*, and *The Boston Globe*, including: Lasky, Margeauz, "Lady Garcia, Jack Roosevelt." *New York Times*, September 18, 2010. Patricia Leigh-Wood's activities to restore and renovate the historical Bahamian estate of her grandfather and her various charity and cultural work has received widespread coverage in several newspapers and magazines including *The Portland Magazine*, and *The Bahamas Weekly*.

CHAPTER FIVE — "JOHN HODIAK: THE HERO FROM HAMTRAMCK"

[110] "John Hodiak Dies From Heart Attack." *New York Times*, October 19, 1955.

[111] Guggenheimer, Paul. "One Hundred Years of John Hodiak." *Pittsburgh Gazette*, April 16, 2014; and Howe, Herb. "Family Bachelor," *Photoplay*, March 1946, pg. 75.

[112] Howe, Herb. "Family Bachelor." *Photoplay*, March 1946, pg. 75.

[113] Wade, Jack. "The Ham from Hamtramck." *Modern Screen*, February,1945, pg. 87.

[114] Howe, Herb. "Family Bachelor." *Photoplay*, March 1946, pg. 75.

[115] 1946 MGM Studio Biography found in the John Hodiak file in Margaret Herrick Library.

[116] 1946 MGM Studio Biography found in the John Hodiak file in Margaret Herrick Library; and Parish, James Robert & Ronald L. Bowers. *The MGM Stock Company: The Golden Era*. New Rochelle, NY: Arlington House, c. 1974, pg. 351.

[117] Howe, Herb. "Family Bachelor." *Photoplay*, March 1946, pg. 75.

[118] Hopper, Hedda. "It Takes Guts." *Modern Screen*, August 1945, pgs. 88-89; and Parish, James Robert & Ronald L. Bowers. *The MGM Stock Company: The Golden Era*. New Rochelle, NY: Arlington House, c. 1974, pg. 352.

[119] Morella, Joe & Edward Epstein. *Lana*. Berkeley, California: Berkeley Publishing, c. 1989, pg. 77.

[120] Wade, Jack. "The Ham from Hamtramck." *Modern Screen*, February 1945, pg. 86.

[121] Howe, Herb. "Family Bachelor." *Photoplay*, March 1946, pg. 75.

[122] Baxter, Anne. "How Could I Be So Wrong." *Modern Screen*, August 1949, pg. 92.

123 Hodiak, John. "The Role I Liked Best." *Saturday Evening Post*, June 28, 1947.

124 Howe, Herb. "Family Bachelor." *Photoplay*, March 1946, pg. 75.

125 Weiler, A. H. "Journey to a Star." *New York Times*, July 8, 1945.

126 Geist, Kenneth. *Pictures Will Talk, The Life and Films of Joseph L. Mankiewicz*. Boston: Da Capo Press, c. 1983.

127 Josephine Hutchinson letter to Dan Van Neste dated January 30, 1998.

128 "John Hodiak." *Americana Annual*, 1956, pg.328.

129 Baxter, Anne. "How Could I Be So Wrong." *Modern Screen*, August 1949, pg. 92.

130 Parsons, Louella. "John Is No Hodiakaccident." *Chicago Daily Tribune*, January 12, 1947.

131 Squire, Nancy Winslow. "Sentimental Gentleman." *Modern Screen*, March 1946, pg. 115.

132 Baxter, Anne. "How Could I Be So Wrong." *Modern Screen*, August 1949, pg. 92.

133 John Wiegman taped interview with Dan Van Neste dated October 1997.

134 Wellman, William Jr. *Wild Bill Wellman*. New York: Pantheon, c. 2015, pg. 442.

135 Paula Raymond taped interview with Dan Van Neste dated February 27, 1998.

136 Baxter, Anne. "How Could I Be So Wrong." *Modern Screen*, August 1949, pg. 92.

137 Squire, Nancy Winslow. "Sentimental Gentleman." *Modern Screen*, March 1946, pg. 70.

138 Reid, Louis. "How to Lose a Husband." *Silver Screen*, January 1953, pg. 70.

139 Parsons, Louella. "John Is No Hodiakaccident." *Chicago Daily Tribune*, January 12, 1947.

140 "Actor John Hodiak Victim of Sudden Heart Attack — Star Left H.A.F. B Just 10 Days Ago After Scenes Here." *Alamogordo Daily News*, October 19, 1955, pg. 1.

141 John Hodiak's sudden death was covered extensively in newspapers, magazines, and various obituary items, most notably in *Los Angeles Herald Examiner*, October 20, 1955; and "John Hodiak Dies Suddenly of Heart Attack." *Los Angeles Times*, October 20, 1955; and "Actor John Hodiak Victim of Sudden Heart Attack — Star Left H.A.F. B Just 10 Days Ago After Scenes Here." *Alamogordo Daily News*, October 19, 1955, pg. 1.

142 John Wiegman taped interview with Dan Van Neste, dated October 1997.

143 Josephine Hutchinson letter to Dan Van Neste dated January 30, 1998.

144 20th Century Fox studio biography, September 13, 1943.

145 "John Hodiak Left No Will." *New York Times*, November 3, 1955; and "Anne Baxter Will Claim Rights to Hodiak Estate." *Hollywood Citizen News*, April 21, 1956; and "Hodiak Parents Granted Home." *Hollywood Citizen News*, May 29, 1956.

146 Sources for the information contained in the "Update" section for John Hodiak include the following articles. Barnes, Bart. "Oscar-Winner Anne Baxter Is Dead at 62." *Washington Post*, December 13, 1985; and "Anne Baxter Dies at 62, 8 Days After

Her Stroke." *Los Angeles Times*, December 12, 1985; and Vallance, Tom. "Obituary, Josephine Hutchinson, *Independent*, June 13, 1998; and "Obituary — Josephine Hutchinson, 94, Movie Actress." *New York Times*, June 19, 1998; and Tollefson, Rodika. "Genetic Creativity: Belfair Bead Artist's Talents Have Deep Roots." *Kitsap Sun*, January 6, 2010; and "Aliquippa Native Had Successful Stage and Screen Career." *Aliquippa Times*, (Pennsylvania), January 21, 2013; and Katrina Hodiak Lunore's profile in https://www.linkedin/

CHAPTER SIX — "MARIAN MARSH: LITTLE MAID MARIAN"

[147] Benjamin, George. "Hit Hollywood Early." *Modern Screen*, 1935, pg. 35.

[148] Smith, Jewel. "Hollywood's Newest Cinderella." *Play Magazine*, 1931, pg. 107.

[149] Benjamin, George. "Hit Hollywood Early." *Modern Screen*, 1935, pg. 77.

[150] Benjamin, George. "Hit Hollywood Early." *Modern Screen*, 1935, pg. 77.

[151] Dora, Albert. "Dangerous at Seventeen." *Movie Mirror*, 1931, pg. 125.

[152] Columbia Pictures Biography, June 1936; and Benjamin, George. "Hit Hollywood Early." *Modern Screen*, 1935, pg. 77; and Leifert, Don. "Marian Marsh, From Barrymore's Boudoir to Karloff's Black Room." *Filmfax*, January/February 1996.

[153] Baldwin, Faith. "Self Made Marian." *Modern Screen*, 1931, pg. 122; and Leifert, Don. "Marian Marsh, From Barrymore's Boudoir to Karloff's Black Room." *Filmfax*, January/February, 1996.pg. 122.

[154] Mank, Gregory. "Marian Marsh Recalls Filming 'Svengali' With Barrymore." *Films in Review*, December 1985, pg. 580.

[155] Mank, Gregory. "Marian Marsh Recalls Filming 'Svengali' With Barrymore." *Films in Review*, December 1985, pg. 580.

[156] Mank, Gregory. "Marian Marsh Recalls Filming 'Svengali' With Barrymore." *Films in Review*, December 1985, pg. 581.

[157] Crowe, Harry J. "She Learned About Women From Them." *New Movie Magazine*, October 1931, pg. 55.

[158] Benjamin, George. "Hit Hollywood Early." *Modern Screen*, 1935, pgs. 35-36.

[159] Benjamin, George. "Hit Hollywood Early." *Modern Screen*, 1935, pg. 77.

[160] Kent, J. "Her Return to the Screen." *Movie Classic*, February 1936.

[161] Marian Marsh taped interview with Dan Van Neste May 28, 1998.

[162] "Marian Marsh Back From Trip." *Los Angeles Examiner*, May 29, 1931.

[163] "Her Star Moves Back to the Heights." *Hollywood*, February 1936.

[164] Jones, C. "Afraid of Love." *Silver Screen*, February 1932, pg. 20.

[165] "Marsh Marries." *Los Angeles Times*, March 30, 1938.

[166] Lamparski, Richard, *Whatever Became of . . . ?* Tenth Series, New York: Crown Publishing, 1986, pg. 117.

[167] Lamparski, Richard, *Whatever Became of . . . ?* Tenth Series, New York: Crown Publishing, 1986, pg. 117.

168 Marian Marsh taped interview with Dan Van Neste dated June 11, 1998.

169 Marian Marsh taped interviews with Dan Van Neste dated May 28-29, 1998, June 11, 1998, *Films of the Golden Age*, Winter 1998, pgs. 20-37.

170 Sources for the information contained in the "Update" section for Marian Marsh included the following. Obituary articles were published in most major newspapers across the U.S. and around the world. They include: Fox, Margalit. "Marain Marsh, 93, Petite Star of 'Svengali' Dies." *New York Times*, November 11, 2006; and McLellan, Dennis. "Marian Marsh Henderson, 93; '30s Actress Starred in 'Svengali' *Los Angeles Times*, November 13, 2006 and Bernstein, Adam. "Obituary — '30's Movie Heroine, Marian Marsh; Opposite Barrymore, Karloff." *Washington Post*, November 13, 2006. Information was also taken from the following tribute articles: "Marian Marsh." *The Guardian*, January 22, 2007; and Mayer, Alicia. "Marian Marsh — Chocolate Exec's Doll-faced Daughter." https://www.hollywoodessays.com/, August 26, 2012. More facts on the family of Marian Marsh can be found on https://www.ancestry.com/; and https://www.findagrave.com/. Albert Parker Scott Jr.'s death was covered in an obituary item: "Albert Parker Scott Jr." *Coloradoan*, November 6, 2014.

171 Van Neste, Dan. "A Legacy of Beauty." *Classic Images*, January 2007, pgs. 26-27.

CHAPTER SEVEN — "KAREN MORLEY: MAVERICK IN WHITE SATIN"

172 Karen Morley interview with Dan Van Neste, August 2002.

173 Morley, Karen. "Karen Morley Reveals Her Story." *Film Pictorial*, March 16, 1935, pg. 10.

[174] Lathem, Maude. "Trying Too Hard to Please." *Picture Play*, July 1935, pg. 56.

[175] Morley, Karen. "Karen Morley Reveals Her Story." *Film Pictorial*, March 16, 1935, pg. 11.

[176] Karen Morley interview with Dan Van Neste, August 2002.

[177] Karen Morley interview with Dan Van Neste, August 2002.

[178] Marian Schilling written interview with Dan Van Neste, July 2002.

[179] Marian Marsh taped interview with Dan Van Neste, July 9, 2002.

[180] *American Film Institute of Motion Pictures Produced in the United States, Feature Films, 1931–1940.* Berkeley: University of California Press, c. 1999.

[181] Karen Morley interview with Dan Van Neste, August 2002.

[182] Karen Morley taped interview for Turner Classic Movies Archival Project. Tapes stored at the University of Georgia, Atlanta, 1998.

[183] Karen Morley interview with Dan Van Neste, August 2002.

[184] Karen Morley taped interview for Turner Classic Movies Archival Project. Tapes stored at the University of Georgia, Atlanta, 1998.

[185] "She Walks Alone." *Picture Play*, 1932.

[186] Grayson, Charles. "Kalm, Kool, and Kollected — that's Karen." *Motion Picture*, November 1932, pgs. 86-87.

[187] Karen Morley taped interview for Turner Classic Movies Archival Project. Tapes stored at the University of Georgia, Atlanta, 1998; and Karen Morley taped and written interviews

with Dan Van Neste, October 29, 1999, November 2, 1999, August 2002.

[188] Karen Morley interview with Dan Van Neste, August 2002.

[189] Karen Morley interview with Dan Van Neste, August 2002.

[190] "Karen Morley Gives Birth." *Los Angeles Times*, August 27, 1933.

[191] Karen Morley taped interview for Turner Classic Movies Archival Project. Tapes stored at the University of Georgia, Atlanta, 1998; and Karen Morley interview with Dan Van Neste, August 2002.

[192] Karen Morley interview with Dan Van Neste, August 2002.

[193] Karen Morley interview with Dan Van Neste, August 2002.

[194] Paramount Studio Biography dated January 29, 1937 found in Karen Morley files at the Margaret Herrick Library, Los Angeles.

[195] Karen Morley interview with Dan Van Neste, August 2002.

[196] Karen Morley taped interviews with Dan Van Neste, October 29, 1999, November 2, 1999.

[197] Ann Rutherford taped interview with Dan Van Neste, September 1, 1999.

[198] "Karen Morley Divorce." *Los Angeles Examiner*, March 3, 1943.

[199] Bloch, Judy. "Karen Morley, The Unvanquished — Silencing the Voice of an Ever-Political Femme Fatale." *San Francisco Film Festival flyer*, 1999, pg. 115.

[200] Accounts of the background, and the history of House Un-American Activities Committees' investigations, and the resulting

blacklist were taken from many sources. The primary ones include three books each with a different perspective: Navasky, Victor S. *Naming Names*. New York: Penguin Books, c. 1980; and Weinstein, Allen & Alexander Vassiliev. *The Haunted Wood: Soviet Espionage in America — The Stalin Era*, New York: Modern Library, c. 2000; and Prindle, David F. *The Politics of Glamour, Ideology and Democracy in The Screen Actor's Guild*, Madison, Wisconsin: University of Wisconsin Press, c. 1988.

[201] "Morley to Testify." *Hollywood Reporter*, November 1951; and Bloch, Judy. "Karen Morley, The Unvanquished — Silencing the Voice of an Ever-Political Femme Fatale." *San Francisco Film Festival* flyer, 1999, pg. 115.

[202] Navasky, Victor S. *Naming Names*. New York: Penguin Books, c. 1980; and Weinstein, Allen & Alexander Vassiliev. *The Haunted Wood: Soviet Espionage in America — The Stalin Era*, New York: Modern Library, c. 2000; and Prindle, David F. *The Politics of Glamour, Ideology and Democracy in The Screen Actor's Guild*, Madison, Wisconsin: University of Wisconsin Press, c. 1988.

[203] Navasky, Victor S. *Naming Names*. New York: Penguin Books, c. 1980, pg. xiv.

[204] Bloch, Judy. "Karen Morley, The Unvanquished — Silencing the Voice of an Ever-Political Femme Fatale." *San Francisco Film Festival flyer*, 1999, pg. 115.

[205] Karen Morley interview with Dan Van Neste, November 2002.

[206] Karen Morley interview with Dan Van Neste, November, August 2002.

[207] Lamparski, Richard. *Whatever Became of . . . ?* Eleventh Series, New York: Crown Publishing, c. 1989.

208 Karen Morley interview with Dan Van Neste, November/August, 2002.

209 Sources for the information contained in the "Update" section for Karen Morley include the following articles. Miss Morley's death was covered in obituary pieces across the country. The most prominent would include: Oliver, Myrna. "Karen Morley, 93; Star of 1930s Films, Was Blacklisted in '50's Dies." *Los Angeles Times*, March 8, 2003; and "Karen Morley, 93, A Movie Star Until a Congressional Hearing." *New York Times*, April 27, 2003; and Bergen, Ronald. "Obituary — Karen Morley." *The Guardian*, April 20, 2003; and http://www.findagrave.com/. Karen's family information was found in several newspaper and magazine articles. Michael Karoly's legendary career as a restauranteur was covered in: "In the '70s and '80, This Prolific Portland Restauranteur Redefined 'Fine Dining.'" *Portland Monthly*, August 15, 2016; and Sarasohn, David. "The Life and Times of Genoa, 1971-2008." *The Oregonian*, November 19, 2008; and "Can Macheezmo Mouse Make a Comeback? New Owners Hope So." *The Oregonian*, August 19, 2013; and "List of the State of Oregon Luminaries." The Oregonian, 2013. Information on John B. Vidor was taken primarily from http://www.imdb.com/. Molly Vidor's artistic career has been covered extensively in the Portland, Oregon area including in the following articles: "Portland Artists Featured in Upcoming Exhibit." *East Oregonian*, July 1, 2017; and "Molly Vidor Profile." State of Oregon Arts Commission list, 2013; and "Dark: A Show to Winter." Exhibition of the work of Prominent Portland Artists including Molly Vidor, February 5-March 12, 2010, *The Oregonian*. In addition, Miss Vidor has discussed her work and life in several interviews mainly in Portland, Oregon radio and television stations.

CHAPTER EIGHT — "EDWARD NORRIS: BABY FACE GANGSTER"

210 Hamilton, S. "Sketch, Edward Norris." *Photoplay*, January, 1938, pg. 69; and 1936 MGM Studio Biography from files on

Edward Norris in Margaret Herrick Library in Los Angeles, California; and Edward Norris taped interviews with Dan Van Neste, August, 30, 1999, February 25, 2000, March 3, 2000, March 10, 2000, March 17, 2000.

[211] Hamilton, S. "Sketch, Edward Norris." *Photoplay*, January 1938, pg. 69; and 1946 RKO Studio Biography from Edward Norris files at Margaret Herrick Library in Los Angeles.

[212] 1936 MGM Studio Biography from files on Edward Norris in Margaret Herrick Library, Los Angeles, California; and Edward Norris taped interviews with Dan Van Neste, August, 30, 1999, February 25, 2000, March 3, 2000, March 10, 2000, March 17, 2000.

[213] Edward Norris taped interviews with Dan Van Neste, August, 30, 1999, February 25, 2000, March 3, 2000, March 10, 2000, March 17, 2000.

[214] Dolven, Frank. "Ann Sheridan Deserved a Brighter Star." *Big Reel*, July 1995, pg. 156.

[215] 1946 RKO Studio Biography from files on Edward Norris in Margaret Herrick Library in Los Angeles, California; and Edward Norris taped interviews with Dan Van Neste, August, 30, 1999, February 25, 2000, March 3, 2000, March 10, 2000, March 17, 2000.

[216] Dolven, Frank. "Ann Sheridan Deserved a Brighter Star." *Big Reel*, July 1995. Pg. 156; and Edward Norris taped interview with Dan Van Neste, March 17, 2000.

[217] *Los Angeles Examiner* item, November 1938; and 1946 RKO Studio Biography from files on Edward Norris in Margaret Herrick Library in Los Angeles, California.

[218] 1946 RKO Studio Biography from files on Edward Norris in Margaret Herrick Library in Los Angeles, California.

[219] Miller, Don. *B Movies*. New York: Ballantine Books, c. 1973, pg. 277.

[220] Edward Norris taped interview with Dan Van Neste August 20, 2000.

[221] Edward Norris taped interview with Dan Van Neste March 10, 2000.

[222] *Los Angeles Examiner* item, March 29, 1947; and Edward Norris taped interview with Dan Van Neste March 10, 2000.

[223] Edward Norris taped interview with Dan Van Neste March 17, 2000.

[224] 1946 RKO Studio Biography from files on Edward Norris in Margaret Herrick Library in Los Angeles, California; and Edward Norris taped interview with Dan Van Neste, March 17, 2000.

[225] Edward Norris taped interview with Dan Van Neste, February 25, 2000.

[226] Edward Norris taped interviews with Dan Van Neste, March 10, 2000, March 17, 2000.

[227] Lamparski, Richard. *Whatever Became Of . . . ?* First Series, New York: Bantam Books, c. 1976, pg. 154.

[228] Edward Norris taped interviews with Dan Van Neste, August, 30, 1999, February 25, 2000, March 3, 2000, March 10, 2000, March 17, 2000, August 20, 2000.

[229] Sources for the information contained in the "Update" for Edward Norris would include a note dated December 21, 2002 from Mr. Norris' daughter-in-law Nancy Norris informing me of his death and the cause. Mr. Norris' death was covered in various newspapers and Hollywood magazines and journals on

both the East and West Coasts including *The Los Angeles Times, The New York Times, The Malibu Times, Classic Images,* etc. His memorial service was covered by an article in *The Malibu Times* on June 11, 2003.

[230] Van Neste, Dan. "Remembering Ed — Edward Norris 1911–2002," *Classic Images*, May 2003, pgs. 26-27.

CHAPTER NINE — "JEAN PARKER: THE CINDERELLA GIRL"

[231] Parker, Jean. "I'm An Ex-Cinderella." *Movie Mirror*, April 1939, pg. 32.

[232] Fidler, James M. "The Past, The Present, and The Future of Jean Parker." *Screenland*, March 1934, pg. 93.

[233] Fidler, James M. "The Past, The Present, and The Future of Jean Parker." *Screenland*, March 1934, pg. 93.

[234] Darnton, Charles. "She'd Rather Work Than Eat." *Modern Screen*, July 1935, pg. 49.

[235] Hoyt, Caroline Somers. "How 'Sequoia' Was Made." *Modern Screen*, June 1935, pg. 96; and Jean Parker taped interview with Dan Van Neste, August 1, 1996; and Rankin, Ruth. "No, the Animals Weren't Trained." *Shadow Play*, February 1935.

[236] Proctor, Kay. "They Thought They Would Keep Their Marriage a Secret." *Photoplay*, July 1936, pg. 54.

[237] Parker, Jean. "I'm An Ex-Cinderella." *Movie Mirror*, April 1939, pg. 89.

[238] Parker, Jean. "I'm An Ex-Cinderella." *Movie Mirror*, April 1939, pg. 90.

[239] Hartley, Katherine. "She Used to Be Demure." *Photoplay*, 1939, pg. 23; and Heacock, Francis. "It's All a Plot." Modern Movies, 1947.

[240] Paramount Studio Biography dated March 13, 1953 found in Jean Parker files in Margaret Herrick Library, Los Angeles, California.

[241] Hall, Bob. "Buy Buy Blues." *Photoplay*, 1942. pgs 50-51.

[242] Weaver, Tom. *Poverty Row Horrors*. Jefferson, NC: McFarland & Company Inc., c. 1993, pg. 183.

[243] Robert Weil taped interview with Dan Van Neste, September 1996.

[244] Robert Weil taped interview with Dan Van Neste, September 1996.

[245] Paramount Studio Biography dated March 13, 1953 found in Jean Parker files in Margaret Herrick Library, Los Angeles, California; and Jean Parker taped interview with Dan Van Neste December 20, 1996.

[246] Ragan, David. *Who's Who in Hollywood 1900–1976*. New Rochelle, New York: Arlington House, c. 1976, pgs. 345-346; and Lamparski, Richard. *Whatever Became of . . . ?* Fifth Series, New York: Bantam Books, c. 1976, pgs. 107-108.

[247] Ragan, David. *Who's Who in Hollywood 1900–1976*. New Rochelle, New York: Arlington House, c. 1976, pgs. 345-346; and Lamparski, Richard. *Whatever Became of . . . ?* Fifth Series, New York: Bantam Books, c. 1976, pgs. 107-108.

[248] Jean Parker taped interviews with Dan Van Neste, January 9, 1996, August 1, 1996, December 20, 1996, January 18, 1997, January 25, 1997.

[249] Sources for the information contained in the "Update" section for Jean Parker include the following obituaries: "Jean Parker, Movie Actress, Is Dead at 90." *New York Times*, December, 13, 2005; and "Rourke, Mary. "Jean Parker, 90; Actress Had More Than 70 Film Credits, Including 'Little Women,' 'The Gunfighter.'" *Los Angeles Times*, December 10, 2005; and Simonson, Robert. "Jean Parker, Stage and Film Actress, Is Dead at 90." *Playbill*, December 13, 2005; and Bergen, Ronald. "Jean Parker." *The Guardian*, December 12, 2005. Also, information was culled from Jean's son, Robert Lowery Hanks, and the website: http;//glamourgirlsofthesilverscreen.com/

[250] Van Neste, Dan. "Bonny Jean, Remembering Jean Parker (1915-2005)." *Classic Images*, February 2006, pgs. 68-71.

CHAPTER TEN — "PAULA RAYMOND: A WORKING ACTRESS"

[251] 1954 McFadden & Eddy Agency Biography of Paula Raymond contained in her file at Margaret Herrick Library, Los Angeles, California, pg. 3.

[252] 1954 McFadden & Eddy Agency Biography of Paula Raymond contained in her file at Margaret Herrick Library, Los Angeles, California, pg. 3.

[253] 1954 McFadden & Eddy Agency Biography of Paula Raymond contained in her file at Margaret Herrick Library, Los Angeles, California, pg. 4.

[254] Higham, Charles & Roy Moseley. *Cary Grant, The Lonely Heart.* San Diego, California: Harcourt Brace Jovanovich, c. 1989, pg. 202.

[255] Higham, Charles & Roy Moseley. *Cary Grant, The Lonely Heart.* San Diego, California: Harcourt Brace Jovanovich, c. 1989, pg. 202, 203.

256 Paula Raymond taped interviews with Dan Van Neste, September 5, 1996, September 28, 1996, October 19, 1996.

257 Paula Raymond taped interviews with Dan Van Neste, September 5, 1996, September 28, 1996, October 19, 1996.

258 Paula Raymond taped interviews with Dan Van Neste, September 5, 1996, September 28, 1996, October 19, 1996.

259 Paula Raymond taped interview with Dan Van Neste, September 28, 1996.

260 Vallance, Tom. "Paula Raymond Obituary." *The Independent*, January 9, 2004.

261 McClellan, Dennis. "Paula Raymond, MGM Leading Lady in '50's, Prolific TV Actress." *Los Angeles Times*, January 10, 2004.

262 Paula Raymond taped interview with Dan Van Neste, September 28, 1996.

263 Paula Raymond taped interview with Dan Van Neste dated October 19, 1996.

264 Anker, Jerry. "Unveiling of Paula Raymond display at Hollywood High School Celebrity Museum." August, 1996.

265 Paula Raymond taped interviews with Dan Van Neste, August 1, 1996, September 5, 1996, September 28, 1996, October 12, 1996, October 19, 1996.

266 Sources for the information contained in the "Update" for Paula Raymond include the following: Bergen, Ronald. "Obituary- Paula Raymond." *The Guardian*, January 14, 2004; and Vallance, Tom. "Obituary — Paula Raymond." *The Independent*, January 9, 2004; and McLellan, Dennis. "Paula Raymond, 79 Dies; and "MGM Leading lady in '50's, Prolific TV Actress." *Los Angeles Times*, January 10, 2004.

CHAPTER ELEVEN — "ZACHARY SCOTT: A SCOUNDREL WITH STYLE"

[267] Michaels, Joan. "Hollywood's New Stop, Look, and Sigh Man." *Screenland*, 1944, pg. 34.

[268] Scott, Zachary. "My First Kiss." *Photoplay*, September 1946.

[269] 1947 Warner Brothers Studio Biography in Zachary Scott file in Margaret Herrick Library, Los Angeles, California, pg. 3.

[270] Michaels, Joan. "Hollywood's New Stop, Look, and Sigh Man." *Screenland*, 1944, pg. 98.

[271] Asher, J. "The Name is Zack." *Photoplay*, March 1946, pgs. 57.

[272] Drier, Hans. "The House That Zach Built." *Photoplay*, September 1949, pg. 52.

[273] McClelland, Doug. *Forties Film Talk.* Jefferson, NC: McFarland & Company, c. 1992, pg. 356.

[274] Robertson, James C. *The Casablanca Man, The Cinema of Michael Curtiz*, New York: Routledge, c. 1994, pgs. 87-92.

[275] Renoir, Jean. *Renoir on Renoir, Interviews, Essays, and Remarks.* Cambridge, United Kingdom: Cambridge University Press, c. 1990, pg. 219.

[276] Asher, J. "The Name is Zack." *Photoplay*, March 1946, pgs. 76.

[277] Franchey, John. "Villains With Vitamins." *Motion Picture*, 1944, pg. 113.

[278] Margulies, Edward & Stephen Rebello, *Bad Movies We Love*, New York: Penguin Books, c. 1993, pg. 75.

279 Fontaine, Joan. *No Bed of Roses*. New York: William Morrow & Company, c. 1978.

280 Parsons, Louella. "And Now Divorce." *Los Angeles Herald-Examiner*, November 14, 1949.

281 Parsons, Louella. "Zachary Scott Saved From Drowning at Sea." *Los Angeles Herald-Examiner*, November 30, 1949.

282 Quirk, Lawrence. *Claudette Colbert: An Illustrated Biography*. New York: Crown Publishers, c. 1985, pg. 110.

283 "Scott, 10 Others Freed in Court." *Los Angeles Times*, February 1951, pg. 16.

284 "Hula Jails Zachary Scott." *Los Angeles Times*, July 12, 1951.

285 Cassa, Anthony. "Zachary Scott, Superior Scoundrel." *Hollywood Studio*, September 1982, pg.35.

286 Louella Parsons. "Zachary Scott Weds Sunday." *Los Angeles Herald Examiner*, June 25, 1952; and Cassa, Anthony. "Zachary Scott, Superior Scoundrel." *Hollywood Studio*, September 1982, pg.35.

287 Parish, James Robert. *Actors' Television Credits 1950–1972*. Metuchen, NJ: Scarecrow Press, c. 1973, pgs. 734-735.

288 Richard Gordon taped and written interviews with Dan Van Neste, September 1997.

289 Richard Gordon taped and written interviews with Dan Van Neste, September 1997.

290 Franchey, John. "Villains With Vitamins." *Motion Picture*, 1944, pg. 113.

[291] Obituaries of varying lengths were posted across the country and the world including "Zachary Scott Dies of Cancer." *Los Angeles Herald-Examiner*, October 4, 1965; and "Zachary Scott is Dead at 51." *San Francisco Chronicle*; and "Tumor Fatal to Zachary Scott." *Los Angeles Times* October 4, 1965.

[292] Sources for the information contained in the Update section for Zachary Scott include various articles and books. The information regarding the Zach theater, family history, deaths is contained in: Davis, Ronald. *Zachary Scott, Hollywood's Sophisticated Cad*. Jackson: University Press of Mississippi, c. 2006. The deaths and legal wranglings of Elaine Anderson Steinbeck, Waverly Scott Kaffaga, Shelley Scott and Ruth Ford, etc. are covered in the following pieces: "Obituary — Elaine Steinbeck, B'way Stage Manager, wife of John Steinbeck." *Variety*, April 29, 2003; and Nemy, Enid. "Elaine Steinbeck, 88, Author's Widow Dies." *New York Times*, April 29, 2003; and "Waverly Scott Kaffaga, as Executor of the Estate of Elaine Anderson Steinbeck, David Scott Farber, Anderson Farber Runkle, Jebel Kaffaga, Bahar Kaffaga, and Jean Anderson Boone vs. Thomas Steinbeck and Black Smythe," U.S. Court of Appeals, Second Circuit, http://www.findlaw.com/ August 13, 2008; and Simonson, Robert. "Ruth Ford, Actress and Salon Hostess, Dead at 98." *Playbill*, August 17, 2009; and Usborne, David. "I Leave It All to My Butler, the Dying Wish of Reclusive Star.' *Independent*, May 12, 2010; and Cullins, Ashley. "John Steinbeck's Stepdaughter Awarded $13 M by Jury in Heirs' Fight." *The Hollywood Reporter*, September 5, 2017; and Schwab, Michael. "John Steinbeck's stepdaughter wins $13 Million in Lawsuit over his Literary Estate." *Los Angeles Times*, September 7, 2017. According to a piece posted on http://www.courthousenews.com/ on November 17, 2017, regarding the latter suit, The Ninth Circuit Court also ruled that Steinbeck's son's heirs and his daughter-in-law have no right to stop movie adaptations of his literary work.

CHAPTER TWELVE — "GLORIA STUART: CHASING RAINBOWS IN DREAMLAND"

[293] Gloria Stuart taped interviews with Dan Van Neste, January, 14, 2006, January 15, 2006.

[294] Gloria Stuart taped interview with Dan Van Neste, January, 14, 2006.

[295] Stuart, Gloria & Sylvia Thompson, *I Just Kept Hoping*. New York: Little, Brown and Company, c. 1999, pg. 25.

[296] Ergenbright, Eric. "She Started Something." *Play*, 1932, pg. 21.

[297] Stuart, Gloria & Sylvia Thompson. *I Just Kept Hoping*. New York: Little, Brown and Company, c. 1999, pgs. 28-29; and Parish, James Robert & William Leonard. *Hollywood Players, The Thirties*. Carlstadt, N.J.: Rainbow Books, c. 1976, pg. 496-497.

[298] Weaver, Tom. *It Came From Weaver Five*. Jefferson, NC: McFarland & Company, c. 1996, pg. 315.

[299] Parish, James Robert & William Leonard. *Hollywood Players, The Thirties*. Carlstadt, N.J.: Rainbow Books, c. 1976, pg. 497.

[300] Stuart, Gloria & Sylvia Thompson. *I Just Kept Hoping*. New York: Little, Brown and Company, c. 1999, pg. 42.

[301] Everson, William K. *Classics of the Horror Film*. New York: Citadel, c. 1995, pg.81.

[302] Gloria Stuart taped interview with Dan Van Neste, January, 14, 2006.

[303] Keleher, Leroy. "Fourth of July Girl." *Picture Play*, August 1932, pg. 41.

[304] Gloria Stuart taped interview with Dan Van Neste, January, 14, 2006.

[305] Gloria Stuart taped interview with Dan Van Neste, January, 14, 2006.

[306] Gloria Stuart taped interview with Dan Van Neste, January, 14, 2006.

[307] "Gloria Stuart, Film Actor to Marry Writer." *Los Angeles Examiner*, July 26, 1934; and "Gloria Stuart, Ex-Mate Marries His Art Student." *Los Angeles Times*, May 20, 1934; and Parish, James Robert. *Hollywood Players, The Thirties*. Carlstadt, N.J.: Rainbow Books, c. 1976, pg. 497.

[308] Rankin, Ruth. "And Gloria Was Burned Up." *New Movie Magazine*, May 1934, pg. 35.

[309] Rankin, Ruth. "And Gloria Was Burned Up." *New Movie Magazine*, May 1934, pg. 35.

[310] Gloria Stuart taped interview with Dan Van Neste, January 14, 2006.

[311] Stuart, Gloria, & Sylvia Thompson. *I Just Kept Hoping*. New York: Little, Brown and Company, c. 1999, pgs. 69-70.

[312] Louella Parsons *Los Angeles Examiner* column, January 21, 1935.

[313] Carroll, Harrison. *Los Angeles Evening Herald Express* article, July 2, 1935.

[314] Weaver, Tom. *It Came From Weaver Five*. Jefferson, NC: McFarland & Company, c. 1996, pg. 323.

[315] Gloria Stuart taped interview with Dan Van Neste, January, 14, 2006.

316 Madson, Elaine. "Gloria Stuart, One Glorious Rose." *Venice*, December 1997, pg. 24; and Stuart, Gloria & Sylvia Thompson. *I Just Kept Hoping*. New York: Little, Brown and Company, c. 1999, pgs. 44-45.

317 Stuart, Gloria, & Sylvia Thompson. *I Just Kept Hoping*. New York: Little, Brown and Company, c. 1999, pgs. 92-110.

318 Stuart, Gloria, & Sylvia Thompson. *I Just Kept Hoping*. New York: Little, Brown and Company, c. 1999, pgs. 128-129.

319 Thompson, Sylvia. "Martini Time in the Garden of Allah." *Los Angeles Times*, November 5, 2000, pg. 38.

320 King, Susan. "The Latest Bloomer in Hollywood." *Los Angeles Times*, September 14, 1999, pg. F-9.

321 Peck, Stacey. "Gloria Stuart Q & A." *Los Angeles Times*, April 13, 1980, pg. 30.

322 "Gloria Stuart," *Films in Review*, October 1961.

323 Stuart, Gloria, & Sylvia Thompson. *I Just Kept Hoping*. New York: Little, Brown and Company, c. 1999, pgs. 180-181, 306.

324 King, Susan. "The Latest Bloomer in Hollywood." *Los Angeles Times*, September 14, 1999, pg. F-9.

325 Stuart, Gloria, & Sylvia Thompson. *I Just Kept Hoping*. New York: Little, Brown and Company, c. 1999, pg. 167.

326 Reisman-Cooper, Barbara. "She's Queen of the World." *Modern Maturity*, March, 1999; and Reismann-Cooper, Barbara. *Biblio*, January 1999, pg. 28.

327 Smith, Steven. "Back in Bloom." *Los Angeles Times*, December 20, 1997, pg. F-8.

328 Stuart, Gloria, & Sylvia Thompson. *I Just Kept Hoping*. New York: Little, Brown and Company, c. 1999, pgs. 252-294.

329 Gloria Stuart taped interview with Dan Van Neste, January, 14, 2006.

330 Smith, Steven. "Back in Bloom." *Los Angeles Times*, December 20, 1997, pg. F-8.

331 Stuart, Gloria, & Sylvia Thompson. *I Just Kept Hoping*. New York: Little, Brown and Company, c. 1999, pg. 271.

332 Gloria Stuart taped interview with Dan Van Neste, January, 14, 2006.

333 Gloria Stuart taped interview with Turner Classic Movies Archival Project, University of Georgia, Atlanta, circa 1997.

334 Gloria Stuart taped interview with Dan Van Neste, January, 15, 2006; and "Where Are They Now?" *People*, April 10, 2000.

335 King, Susan. "The Latest Bloomer in Hollywood." *Los Angeles Times*, September 14, 1999, pg. F-1.

336 Sources for the information contained in the "Update" for Gloria Stuart include several articles. Among them are: King, Susan. "Classic Hollywood: The Academy Salutes Gloria Stuart." *Los Angeles Times*, July 21, 2010; and Painter, Alysia Gray Painter. "Centennial Celebration with Gloria Stuart." http://www.nbclosangeles.com/ Gloria's death was reported around the world. Articles included: McLellan, Dennis. "Gloria Stuart Dies at 100; 'Titanic" Actress." *Los Angeles Times*, September 27, 2010; and Harmetz, Aljean and Robert Berkvistsept. "Gloria Stuart, an Actress Rediscovered Late, Dies at 100." *New York Times*, September 27, 2010; and Kilday, Gregg. "'Titanic's' Gloria Stuart Dies at 100." *Hollywood Reporter*, September 27, 2010; and Hulzack, Sarah. "Gloria Stuart, Actress in 'Titanic' Dies at 100" *Washington Post*, September 27, 2010.

PHOTO CREDITS

All reasonable effort has been made to trace the copyright holders of the photos featured in this book, but if any have been overlooked, the author and publisher will gladly remove them.

All Paramount & Republic photos © Paramount Pictures. All Rights Reserved

All RKO photos © RKO Pictures LLC. All Rights Reserved

All Warner Bros/First National photos © Warner Bros. Entertainment Inc. Co. All Rights Reserved

All Columbia photos c. Columbia Pictures/Sony Entertainment. All Rights Reserved

All MGM photos © Metro-Goldwyn-Mayer Studios Inc. All Rights Reserved

All 20th Century-Fox photos © 20th Century-Fox Film Corporation All Rights Reserved

The remaining photos are from the author's personal collection unless so noted.

ABOUT THE AUTHOR

A native of Michigan, Dan Van Neste was a nationally known recording artist and a rehabilitation counselor prior to becoming an author and biographer. During the last three decades, he has penned over 50 major classic movie-related articles for various magazines, newspapers and film journals. Best known for his star profiles in *Classic Images* and *Films of the Golden Age*, his work has merited seven cover stories and often included original interviews with vintage filmmakers. His acclaimed books include: *The Whistler: Stepping Into the Shadows* (BearManor Media, 2011), a salute to the influential, groundbreaking suspense film series produced by Columbia Pictures (1944-48), and *The Magnificent Heel: The Life and Films of Ricardo Cortez*, (BearManor Media, 2017), a complete biography and filmography of the versatile, prolific and charismatic stage, film, and television actor. The latter book was named to multiple best film books of 2017 lists, and was a nominee for 2018 Richard Wall Memorial Award given by the Theater Library Association. For more information visit http://.danvanneste.com/

INDEX

A

Abbott & Costello – 95
Abbott, George – 41, 96
Abie's Irish Rose (1928) – 18, 413
Accent on Youth (stage) – 397
Across the Wide Missouri (1951) – 142, 445
Adam's Rib (1949) – 326, 339-340
Adrian, Iris – 71
Adventures of Kitty O'Day (1945) – 300, 488
Adventures of Robin Hood, The (TV) – 103, 117-118, 118p
Adventures of Wild Bill Hickok, The (TV) – 257
Affairs of Jimmy Valentine, The (1942) – 69, 422
After the Dance (1935) – 35, 419
Ah Wilderness (stage) – 305
Airmail (1932) – 379, 381p, 393, 502, 503
Alaska Highway (1943) – 486
Alberni, Luis – 156
Alcott, Louisa May – 292
Aldrich Family, The (TV) – 38
Alias the Doctor (1932) – 81, 162, 425, 449
Alibi Racket (short) (1935) – 243, 244, 244p, 465
All About Eve (1950) – 143
All American, The (1932) – 379, 501
Allen, Robert – 173p
Ambush (1949) – 141, 444
Ambush at Tomahawk Gap (1953) – 144, 445
American Tragedy, An (1931) – 424
Ames, Leon – 224
Amis, Suzy – 405p, 408
Anderson, Lindsay – 117
Anderson-Steinbeck, Elaine – 354-356, 357, 363p, 364-365, 372-373
Andre, Lona – 245
Andrew Sisters, The – 95
Angels With Broken Wings (1941) – 470
Angels With Dirty Faces (1938) – 247, 268
Ankrum, Morris – 377
Ann Carver's Profession (1933) – 85, 86p, 427
Apache Uprising (1965) – 305, 489
Apfel, Oscar – 158

Appointment in Honduras (1953) – 368, 499
Arden, Eve – 358
Are You Listening? (1932) – 211, 458
Arkansas Traveler, The (1938) – 298, 482
Arlen, Richard – 24, 30, 41, 50, 300, 305, 316
Armstrong, Robert – 302
Arnello Affair, The (1947) – 136, 443
Arnold, Edward – 94p, 169, 170
Arsene Lupin (1932) – 209-211, 212p, 237, 458
Arthur, Jean – 48
Arzner, Dorothy – 18
Astaire, Fred – 89p, 95, 189-190
Asther, Nils – 389
Astor, Mary – 136
Atlantic Adventure (1935) – 35, 419
Atwill, Lionel – 95, 108p, 172, 384, 385p, 386p
Austen, Jane – 223, 224
Autry, Gene – 252, 253p, 255, 280

B

Babbitt (1934) – 89, 429
Babylon, Edwin A. – 366
Bacall, Lauren – 229
Bachelor Father (TV) – 335
Bachelor, Stephanie – 71
Back in the Saddle (1941) – 252, 253p, 470
Back Street (1932) – 379, 501
Bad Guy (1937) 246, 467
Baer, Abel – 23
Balanchine, George – 65

Ball, Lucille – 133, 387
Ballard, Robert – 403
Bandido (1956) – 368, 500
Bandits of Corsica (1953) – 115, 439, 492
Banker's Daughter, The (stage) – 235
Bankhead, Tallulah – 127, 128, 129p, 130p
Bare, Richard – 345
Barrier, The (1937) – 297, 481
Barry, Donald – 248, 250, 270
Barry, Gene – 305, 343
Barrymore, Ethel – 291, 308-309
Barrymore, John – 152, 155, 156, 157, 157p, 158p, 160-161, 177, 178-180, 183-184, 195, 197, 209-211, 212p, 235, 269, 291, 309-310, 321
Barrymore, Lionel – 30, 112, 209-211, 212p, 235, 291, 308-309, 384
Barthelmess, Richard – 162
Bartholomew, Freddie – 393
Barton, Charles – 261
Basinger, Kim – 375, 405, 406
Bat Masterson (TV) – 335
Bates, Kathy – 403
Battle Zone (1952) – 142, 445
Battleground (1949) 123, 139, 140p, 444
Baxter, Anne – 128, 130, 134-135, 136, 138p, 139-140, 142-143, 144, 147-148, 150
Baxter, Warner – 71, 72p, 393-394, 395p
Beast from 20,000 Fathoms, The (1953) – 332-333, 334p, 344-345, 493

Beauty and the Boss (1932) – 162, 163p, 176, 184, 449
Beery, Wallace – 73, 73p, 211, 216
Bel Geddes, Barbara – 40, 224
Belcher, Ernest – 154
Bell For Adano, A (1945) – 123, 130, 132p, 441
Bell, Book, and Candle (stage) – 307
Bell, Galt – 377
Bellamy, Ralph – 173, 381p
Beloved (1934) – 389, 504
Beloved Enemy (1936) – 222, 238, 461
Benchley, Robert – 398
Bendix, William – 41-42, 43p, 52, 127, 129p, 130
Benedetto, Suzanne – 45, 46
Bennett, Bruce – 362
Bennett, Constance – 272
Bennett, Joan – 292
Benny, Jack – 34, 340
Berkeley, Busby – 387, 391
Bernhard, Jack – 254
Best Place to Be (TV) – 510
Between Two Women (1937) – 245, 467
Beutel, Gloria – 336, 345
Beutel, Jack – 336
Bevan, Donald – 38, 40-44, 46
Bevan, Patricia Kirkland – 13-14, 17, 27, 32-34, 36-39, 39p, 41-44, 46
Beyond the Curtain (1960) – 119, 439
Beyond Tomorrow (1940) – 299, 319, 483
Big Boss, The (1941) – 69, 422
Black Castle, The (1952) – 115, 116, 116p, 438

Black Cat, The (1941) – 95, 432
Black Fury (1935) – 220-221, 460
Black Room, The (1935) – 169, 170p, 186-187, 196, 453, 453p
Black Tuesday (1954) – 305, 317, 488
Blackboard Jungle, The (1955) – 328
Blanchar, Pierre – 170
Blazing Sun, The (1950) – 255, 280, 476
Blind Alley (1939) – 225
Blondell, Joan – 66, 78, 84, 86, 88p, 205
Blondie Johnson (1933) – 78, 85, 427
Blondie's Secret (1948) – 325, 490
Blood and Sand (1941) – 271
Blood of Dracula's Castle (1969) – 336, 337p, 347, 494
Blood of Fu Manchu, The (1968) – 120, 439
Blue Gardenia, The (1953) – 143
Blue Skies (1946) – 399
Bluebeard (1944) – 300, 316, 319, 487
Blyth, Ann – 358
Bogart, Humphrey – 62, 92p, 95, 229, 356, 398
Boles, John – 389
Boleslawski, Richard – 294
Bolger, Ray – 134
Bond, Lillian – 381p
Bondi, Beulah – 359, 361p
Born to Be Bad (1950) – 364, 497, 497p
Born to the Saddle (1953) – 464
Born Yesterday (stage) – 300, 302, 304p, 318

Bow, Clara – 261
Boyer, Charles – 294, 294p, 314, 343
Boys Town (1938) – 248-250, 270-271, 283, 285, 468
Brabin, Charles – 212, 215
Bradbury, Ray – 332
Brady, Scott – 336, 343
Brando, Marlon – 142
Breakthrough (1950) – 256, 476
Brennan, Walter – 105
Brent, George – 62
Brian, David – 330, 331p
Brian, Donald – 397
Bribe, The (1949) – 138, 444
Broadway Bill (1934) – 34, 48
Broadway Melody, The (1929) – 20
Brodie, Steve – 141
Broken Lullabye a.k.a *The Man I Killed* (1932) – 29-30, 31p, 49, 417
Broken Wing (1932) – 83, 425
Bromberg, J. Edward – 71
Brook, Clive – 81
Brooks, Louise – 50
Brooks, Richard – 328-330, 343-344
Brophy, Edward – 174p
Brown, Clarence – 204-205
Brown, Joe E. – 85, 95, 173
Brown, Johnny Mack – 305
Brown, Lou – 23
Bruce, David – 325
Bruce, Nigel – 107
Bruce, Virginia – 36, 368
Bruckner, Wilbur – 124
Bunuel, Luis – 370
Burch, Melvina – 290
Burlesque (play) – 21, 301, 316-317
Burroughs, Edgar Rice – 220

Burton, Richard – 46
Bushell, Anthony – 159p, 160p, 165
Butler, Hugo – 359
Byrd, Admiral Richard – 180

C

Cabanne, Christy – 165
Cabot, Bruce – 244
Cagney, James – 84, 85, 88p, 88p, 95, 356, 389, 391p
Cain, James M. – 358
Caine Mutiny Court Martial, The (stage) – 123, 145-146
Calhern, Louis – 27, 161, 341
Calhoun, Rory – 305
Call Me Madam (1953) – 399
Cameron, James – 402-406, 408
Camille (1936) – 311
Campbell, Mrs. Patrick – 169, 188-189
Cannon, Dyan – 407
Cantor, Eddie – 154, 387
Capone, Al – 206
Capra, Frank – 48, 210
Capshaw, Kate – 406
Captain Scarlett (1953) – 115
Caravan (1934) – 294, 294p, 314, 479
Career Girl (1944) – 473
Carewe, Arthur Edmund – 155
Carradine, David – 239
Carradine, John – 300, 316
Carrillo, Leo – 312
Carroll, Nancy – 12-53, 12p, 16p, 19p, 21p, 23p, 24p, 25p, 26p, 29p, 30p, 31p, 33p, 35p, 37p, 39p, 198, 413-419

Carson, Jack – 358, 360
Casablanca (1942) – 358
Case of the Curious Bride, The (1935) – 91-92, 429
Case of the Velvet Claws, The (1936) – 91-92, 431
Cass Timberlane (1947) – 361-362, 495
Castle of Fu Manchu, The (1969) – 440
Castle, Peggie – 368
Castle, William – 398
Cat on a Hot Tin Roof (1958) – 328
Cavallo, John – 196
Challenge of the Range (1949) – 325, 490
Chaney, Lon Jr. – 116p, 302, 304p, 305, 318
Change of Heart (1938) – 396, 507
Chaplin, Charles – 275, 355, 390
Charlie Chan in Honolulu (1938) – 93, 432
Charrell, Eric – 294
Chase, The (stage) – 142
Chatterton, Ruth – 172, 173p, 190-191, 197
Chester, Hal – 345
Chevalier, Maurice – 378
Chevy Mystery Show (TV) – 368
Chicago (play) – 17
Chicken A-La-King (1928) – 18, 412p, 413
Chierichetti, David – 27, 30, 46, 50
Child of Manhattan (1933) – 32, 49, 417
Chodorov, Edward – 356
Christian, Paul – 334
Christians, Mady – 296

Ciannelli, Eduardo – 222, 357p
Cindy (stage) – 42
Citizen Kane (1941) – 161
City That Never Sleeps (1953) – 333, 493
Clair, Rene – 296
Clare, Sidney – 34
Clark, Dane – 363
Close Call for Ellery Queen (1942) – 471
Close Harmony (1929) – 20-21, 23, 48, 414
Cohen, Nat – 368
Colbert, Claudette – 62, 366, 378
Cole, Lester – 230
Collier, Constance – 398
Colman, Ronald – 356
Colt 45 (1950) – 364, 498
Columbo (TV) – 400
Come Closer Folks (1936) – 172, 176, 454
Coming Out Party (1934) – 464
Command Decision (1948) – 138, 443
Confessions of a Co-Ed (1931) – 424
Conquest of Cochise (1953) – 144, 145p, 446
Contraband Spain (1955) – 115, 439
Cook, Donald – 160
Cooper, Austene – 97, 101
Cooper, Brand – 97, 101
Cooper, Dorothy – 343
Cooper, Gary – 20, 44, 46, 229, 254, 274, 277, 294, 311, 321
Cooper, H. Brand – 95, 97, 98p
Cooper, Jackie – 245, 290
Cooper, John – 79, 81-82, 87, 95, 97, 98-100, 101

Cooper, Peter – 97, 101
Coots, M. Fred – 20
Corday, Paula – 115, 116p, 120
Corio, Ann – 72, 276
Cortez, Ricardo – 214p, 251
Costello, Dolores – 156, 179
Cotton, Joseph – 114, 332
Count of Monte Cristo, The (1934) – 313
Counterfeit (1936) – 172, 454
Counterfeit Plan, The (1958) – 368-369, 370p
Cowboy Quarterback, The (1939) – 65, 421
Craven, John – 38
Crawford, Joan – 16, 46, 80, 254, 258, 278, 279, 311, 358, 360p, 362-363
Crime and Punishment (1935) – 169-171, 171p, 172p, 176, 187-189, 453
Crime Doctor, The (1934) – 219, 460
Crime Doctor's Strangest Case, The (1943) – 71, 72p, 423
Crime Et Chatiment (1935) – 170
Crime of Dr. Forbes, The (1936) – 396, 506
Crisis (1950) – 328-330, 330p, 338, 343-344, 491
Crisp, Donald – 156
Cromwell, John – 20
Cronyn, Hume – 128, 129p
Crooner (1932) – 83, 426
Crosby, Bing – 95, 96p
Crossfire (1947) – 328
Crowd, The (1928) – 219
Cuban Love Song (1931) – 206, 458
Cukor, Elsie – 332, 339

Cukor, George – 216-217, 223, 292, 325-326, 339-340, 341, 345
Cummings, Irving – 394
Cummins, Peggy – 113
Curtain Going Up (stage) – 397
Curtis, Tony – 40
Curtiz, Michael – 161, 183, 221, 358, 362
Cusack, Joan – 375

D

D'Arcy, Alex – 337p
D'Arrast, Harry D'Abbadie – 25
Daddio, Rebecca Cash – 348, 350
Dahl, Arlene – 141, 330
Dale, Esther – 298p
Damask Cheek (stage) – 356
Damita, Lili – 315
Damon Runyon Theater (TV) – 305
Dance of Life (1929) – 21-22, 414
Danger Signal (1945) – 358, 495
Dangerous Island (1967) – 120
Dangerous Paradise (1930) – 22, 24p, 415
Danton, Ray – 343
Darcel, Denise – 140p
Daring Daughters (1933) – 451
Daring Young Man, The (1942) – 95, 433
Darnell, Linda – 113
Datig, Fred – 378
Daudet, Alphonse – 204
Davidson, Muriel – 66
Davies, Marion – 294, 311
Davis, Bette – 65, 84, 98-100, 192, 385
Davis, Joan – 398

Davis, Lou – 20
Davis, Nancy – 329
Davis, Ronald – 372
Dawson, Douglas – 299
Daybreak (1931) – 206, 456
Days of Our Lives (TV) – 33
De Carlo, Yvonne – 368
De Grass, Robert – 71
De Havilland, Olivia – 390
De Maurier, George – 155
De Sylva, Buddy – 23, 394
Dead End Kids – 62, 64p
Dead Man's Eyes (1944) – 300, 487
Dean, Jeanne – 258, 281-282
Deanna Durbin – 36
Dear Ruth (1947) – 399
Death Valley Days (TV) – 335, 346
Decoy (1946) – 254, 277-278, 474
Dee, Frances – 205, 292, 292p
Dee, Ruby – 230
Deerslayer, The (1943) – 486
Del Ruth, Roy – 272
Demarest, William – 174p, 396p
Desert Fury (1947) – 136, 137, 443
Desert Hawk, The (1950) – 115, 437
Detective Kitty O'Day (1944) – 300, 319, 487
Devil's Doorway (1950) – 326, 327p, 328, 338, 340-342, 491
Devil's Squadron (1936) – 222, 223p, 461
Devils, Holiday, The (1930) – 23-24, 25p, 48, 415
Dexter, Anthony – 305
Di Caprio, Leonardo – 403, 404
Dickerson, Doris – 56, 76
Dickerson, Emma – 55-56, 74
Dickerson, Fred – 55-56

Dickson, Gloria – 54-76, 54p, 60p, 60p, 64p, 64p, 67p, 68p, 70p, 72p, 73p, 246, 247p, 266-267, 285, 419-423
Dies, Martin – 228
Dieterle, William – 273
Dietrich, Marlene 28, 32, 40
Dillaway, Donald – 165
Dinner at Eight (1933) – 216-217, 218p, 459
Divorce in the Family (1932) – 290, 477
Dix, Richard – 18, 107, 222, 226
Dix, Robert – 336
Doctors Don't Tell (1941) – 470
Doctors, The (TV) – 118
Dodd, Claire – 77-101, 77p, 80p, 82p, 83p, 85p, 86p, 88p, 88p, 89p, 90p, 90p, 92p, 94p, 96p, 96p, 99p, 100p, 423-433
Dodd, Ethel Cool – 79
Dodd, Walter – 79
Dodge City (1939) – 298-299, 315
Domergue, Faith – 368
Don Winslow of the Navy (1942) (serial) – 95, 433
Don't Bet on Blondes (1935) – 91, 430
Don't Take it to Heart (1944) – 110, 436
Donat, Robert – 296, 313-314, 315
Donnell, Jeff – 266p
Donnelly, Ruth – 84
Doomsday Circus (stage) – 242, 262
Douglas, Melvyn – 36, 37p, 69, 93, 380, 381p, 383
Downstairs (1932) – 458
Doyle, Arthur Conan – 106

Dr. Erlich's Magic Bullet (1940) – 250, 272-273, 285, 470
Dragonfly Squadron (1954) – 144, 446
Drake, Betsy – 329, 344
Drake, Oliver – 274
Dream Girl (stage) – 300
Dressler, Marie – 181, 216, 217
Driver, Minnie – 375
Du Maurier, George – 155
Dubin, Al – 387, 392
Duchess of Idaho (1950) – 326, 327p, 328, 338, 342-343, 491
Duck Soup (1933) – 387
Duncan, Isadora – 309
Dunn, James – 91
Dunne, Irene – 279, 290
Dupont Show of the Week (TV) – 368
Durbin, Deanna – 36, 37p
Dvorak, Ann – 83, 207-208, 366
Dwan, Allan – 272

E

East Side, West Side (1949) – 326, 491
Easy Come, Easy Go (1928) – 18, 413
Ebert, Roger – 404
Edson, Arthur – 385
Edwards, Cliff – 68
Egg and I, The (TV) – 38, 39p
Einstein, Albert – 180-181
Elam, Jack – 346
Eldredge, Florence – 37
Eleventh Commandment, The (1933) – 165, 451

Ellington, Duke – 347
Elmer the Great (1933) -84, 427
Emerson, Faye – 357p, 358, 365p
Emery, John – 365
End of the Road (1944) – 473
Enemy of Women (1944) – 398, 509
Englund, Ken – 69
Engsted, John – 27, 30, 50
Epstein, Edward Z. – 127
Erickson, Leif – 330
Escape in the Desert (1945) -358
Escape, The (1939) – 250-251, 468
Evans, Madge – 219
Everson, William K – 44, 380.
Ewell, Tom – 42
Ex Lady (1933) – 427
Experiment Perilous (1944) – 347

F

Fairbanks, Douglas 124, 149
Fairbanks, Jr, Douglas – 28, 30p, 48-49, 84-85, 85p
Fairways and Fouls (1929) (short) – 154
Family Classics (TV) – 368
Fan, The (1949) – 113, 437
Farewell to Arms, A (1932) – 32
Farmer in the Dell, The (1936) – 297, 298p, 481
Farrell, Glenda – 84
Fast Company (1938) – 93, 431
Fata Morgana (stage) – 203
Faulkner, William – 359, 368
Faye, Alice 109, 109p, 267, 271-272, 394
Fenwick, Jean – 152-153, 178
Ferber, Edna – 216

Ferrer, Jose – 328
Ferrer, Mel – 398
Fidler, Jimmie – 47
Field, Betty – 359, 360p, 361p
Fields, Gracie – 104
Fighting O'Flynn, The (1949) – 113-437
Finch, Fred – 377
Finch, Patricia Marie – 377
Fireside Theater (TV) – 257
Fisher, Frances – 408
Fisher, Terence – 117
Fitzgerald, William – 72, 74, 75-76
Five Bloody Graves (1969) – 336, 347, 494
Five Star Final (1931) – 158-160, 159p, 160p, 176, 181-182, 447, 448p
Flame of the Islands (1955) – 368, 499
Flamingo Road (1949) – 362-363, 496
Flaxy Martin (1949) – 343, 496
Fleming, Rhonda – 305
Fleming, Victor – 18
Flesh (1932) – 211, 214p, 459
Fletcher, Adele Whitely – 27, 31, 51
Fletcher, Bramwell – 156
Flight at Midnight (1939) – 482
Flight Into Danger (1960) – 503
Flight That Disappeared (1961) – 335, 337p, 494
Flood (1976) (TV) – 401, 510
Flying Blind (1941) – 300, 484
Flying Deuces, The (1939) – 298, 314-315, 483
Flying Fortress (1942) – 110, 436
Flynn, Errol – 114, 252, 298, 315, 321

Follow Thru (1930) – 23, 48, 416
Fonda, Henry – 40, 44, 46, 51, 144
Fontaine, Joan – 276, 364
Fontanne, Lynn – 189
Footlight Parade (1933) – 85-86, 88p, 88p, 428
For Heaven's Sake Mother (stage) – 37
Ford Theater (TV) – 144
Ford, Glenn – 146
Ford, John – 105, 214, 379, 393, 394, 395
Ford, Paul – 41
Ford, Ruth – 367, 368, 369, 371-373
Ford, Wallace – 173, 306
Forever Amber (1947) – 113, 437
Forgotten Women (1949) – 475
Forsythe, John – 175
Four Men and a Prayer (1938) – 105, 434
Foy, Brian – 62, 255
Framed (1947) – 226, 464
Francis, Kay – 62, 81, 83, 84, 91, 290, 379
Frankenstein (1931) – 380
Franklin, Chester – 294
French Without Tears (stage) – 104
Friedman, Phil – 378
Frontier Marshal (1939) – 250, 468
Fugitive from a Prison Camp (1940) – 455
Fulton, John – 385
Further Adventures of Ellery Queen, The (TV) – 38
Fury (1936) – 57

G

Gable, Clark – 138, 142, 254, 259, 274

Gabriel Over the White House (1933) – 216, 217p, 290, 459, 478
Gaiety George a.k.a. *Showtime* (1946) – 110, 436
Gambling Lady (1934) – 89, 90p, 91, 428
Garbo, Greta – 204-205, 206, 212, 235, 243, 243p, 262-263, 311
Gardner, Ava – 138
Garfield, John – 63, 64p, 64p, 65, 356
Gargan, William – 164p
Garland, Judy – 46, 134, 135p
Garmes, Lee – 208
Garson, Greer – 141, 223
Geist, Kenneth L. – 133
General Electric Summer Originals (TV) – 368
General Hospital (TV) – 407
Gershwin, George – 390
Gershwin, Ira – 390
Ghost Goes West, The (1935) – 296, 307, 310, 313-314, 319, 481
Gibbons, Cedric – 223
Gifford, Frances – 136
Gift of Gab (1934) – 389, 505
Gilbert, John – 263
Gilbert, Wolfe – 23
Gillie, Jean – 254, 277-278
Gilpin Jay – 361p
Girl From Alaska, The (1942) – 485
Girl from Scotland Yard, The (1937) – 222, 462
Girl in 419, The (1933) – 384, 503
Girl of the Limberlost (1934) – 166, 186, 452
Girl on the Front Page, The (1936) – 507

Girl Overboard (1937) – 507
Girl Thief, The (1938) – 455
Girls About Town (1931) – 81, 424
Gish, Lillian – 403
Glamour (1934) – 390
Glass Key, The (1935) – 91, 430
Glazer, Benjamin – 22
Gleason, James – 154
Gleason, Lucille – 154
Glennon, Bert – 393
Goddard, Paulette – 275
Going My Way (TV) – 38
Golddiggers of 1935 (1935) – 391-392, 505
Golddiggers of Paris (1938) – 62, 420
Goldwyn, Sam – 32, 80, 154, 222, 387
Gone With the Wind (1939) – 224, 299
Gooding, Cuba Jr. – 375, 406
Goose and the Gander, The (1935) – 91, 430
Gordon, Richard – 368-369
Gorilla, The (1939) – 250, 272, 469
Gough, Lloyd – 230, 235
Goulding, Edmund – 24, 28
Grand Illusion (1937) – 358
Granger, Stewart – 114
Grant, Cary – 28, 32, 44, 328-329, 330p, 343-344
Grayson, Kathryn – 328
Great Gambini, The (1937) – 173, 174p, 454
Great Impersonation, The (1942) – 471
Green, Louis – 270
Green, Mitzi – 34

Greene, Kathleen Gerard – 103
Greene, Richard – 102-121, 102p, 106p, 108p, 108p, 109p, 111p, 112p, 115p, 116p, 116p, 118p, 119p, 433-440
Greene, Richard (Richard's father) – 103
Greene, Ward – 54, 265
Greene, William Friese – 103-104
Greenstreet, Sydney – 357
Gregory, Paul – 144
Grey, Virginia – 144
Grot, Anton – 61
Grotter, Curtis – 299
Grounds For Marriage (1951) – 328, 347, 492
Gruen, C. H. J. "Jappe" – 40-41, 42
Guild, Nancy – 133
Guilty as Hell (1932) – 426
Guilty Bystander (1950) – 364, 365, 498
Gun That Won the West, The (1955) – 493
Gunfighter, The (1950) – 302-303, 317, 488

H

Hackman, Gene – 371
Haggot, John – 355
Hall, Ola – 67
Hall, Thurston – 223p
Hand of Death (1962) – 335, 494
Hanks, Robert Lowery – 305, 306, 319
Hard to Handle (1933) – 85, 427
Hardwicke, Cedric – 107
Hardy, Oliver – 298, 314-315, 321

Harlow, Jean – 72, 216-217
Harris, Jed – 316
Harrison, Rex – 333
Harryhausen, Ray – 332, 345
Hart, Lorenz – 23
Harvey Girls, The (1946) – 123, 134, 135p, 441
Harvey, Laurence – 333
Have a Heart (1934) – 294, 480
Have Gun Will Travel (TV) – 335
Hawaiian Eye (TV) – 335
Hawks, Howard – 206-208, 210
Hayes, Helen – 44
Hays, Will – 378
Hayward, Louis – 114
Hayworth, Rita – 268, 272-273
Healer, The a.k.a. *Little Pal* (1935) – 221, 460
Hearst, William Randolph – 97, 216
Heart of the North (1938) – 62-63, 420
Heartaches (1947) – 255, 256, 279, 475
Hecht, Ben – 206-208
Hecht, Harold – 280
Heckart, Eileen – 301
Hedda Gabler (stage) – 224
Hell's Angels (1930) – 154, 447
Hello Annapolis (1942) – 300, 485
Hemingway, Ernest – 40
Henderson, Clifford – 175, 192-193, 197
Henderson, Roy – 23
Henie, Sonja – 105
Henry, William – 302p
Hepburn, Katharine – 292, 292p, 310, 321, 326, 340

Her Kind of Man (1946) – 361, 363p, 495
Here Comes Elmer (1943) – 398, 509
Here Comes Happiness (1941) – 470
Here Comes the Navy (1934) – 390, 391p, 505
Here I Am a Stranger (1939) – 107, 108p, 250, 435, 469,
Hersey, John – 130
Hersholt, Jean – 18
Hi, Neighbor (1942) – 485
High Explosive (1943) – 300
High Stakes (1931) – 206, 457
Higham, Charles – 329, 343
Highway 301 (1950) – 256, 476
Hill, Craig – 337p
Hiller, Virginia – 242, 260-261
Hitchcock, Alfred – 127, 128, 129
Hodiak, Anna – 123-124, 131, 147-148
Hodiak, John – 122-150, 122p, 129p, 130p, 132p, 135p, 137p, 138p, 140p, 145p, 148p, 149p, 331, 440-446
Hodiak, Katrina Baxter – 142, 143, 147-148, 150
Hodiak, Walter – 123-124, 131, 147-148
Hodiak, Walter Jr. – 123, 131, 147
Hodiak-Sliva, Ann – 123, 131, 147
Holiday Affair (1949) – 491
Holliday, Judy – 302
Hollywood Canteen (1944) – 358, 495
Hollywood Legends (TV) – 407
Hollywood Playhouse (TV) – 144
Holmes, Phillips – 24, 25p, 27, 30, 31p

Holt, Jack – 18
Homecoming (1948) – 138, 138p, 443
Honey (1930) – 22, 23, 44, 48, 49, 415
Hopkins, Miriam – 378
Hot Saturday (1932) – 28, 417
Hound of the Baskervilles, The (1939) – 105-107, 108p, 434, 435p
House of Errors (1942) – 175, 456
House of Wax (1953) – 345
Howard, Leslie – 207p
Howes, Bobby – 165
Hoyt, John – 116p
Hoyt, Vance Joseph – 294
Hudson, Rochelle – 244, 245p, 264
Hughes, Howard – 87, 139, 154, 206, 208, 279, 364
Hull, Henry – 37, 127, 129p
Hull, Warren – 398
Human Jungle, The (1954) – 333, 493
Hunt, Marsha – 224
Hunter, Jeffrey – 346
Hurst, Fannie – 379
Huston, John – 229
Huston, Walter – 216, 217p
Hutchins, Will – 41-42, 46, 52
Hutchinson, Josephine – 133-134, 147, 150
Hutton, Betty – 254, 278-279
Huxley, Aldous – 223

I

I Dood It (1943) – 126, 440
I Like it That Way (1934) – 166, 167p, 389, 452, 504

I Live on Danger (1942) – 252, 275, 300, 301p, 471, 485
I Love That Man (1933) – 32, 418
I Must Love Someone (stage) – 36
I Sell Anything (1934) – 89, 429
I Used to Be in Pictures (TV) – 407
I Want a Divorce (1940) – 66, 69, 422
I Was a Communist for the F.B.I. (1951) – 256, 257p, 477
I Was a Male War Bride (1949) – 268
I Was an Adventuress (1940) – 109, 436
I'll Love You Always (1935) – 35, 48, 49, 418
I'll Tell the World (1934) – 389, 505
If I Had My Way (1940) – 95, 96p, 432
If This Be Sin a.k.a. *This Dangerous Age* (1949) – 113, 437
Illusion (1929) – 23, 415
In Spite of Danger (1935) – 169, 452
In the Glitter Palace (1977) (TV) – 401, 510
In the Navy (1941) – 95, 96p, 433
Incredible Journey of Dr. Meg Laurel, The (TV) – 510
Inescourt, Frieda – 93-94
Inside Straight (1951) – 330, 331p, 492
Inside the Walls of Folsom Prison (1951) – 256, 476
Inspiration (1931) – 204-205, 457
Invisible Man, The (1933) – 384-385, 386p, 504
Invisible Man, The (TV series) – 407

Irwin Allen's Adventures of a Queen (1975) (TV) – 401, 510
Island in the Sky (1938) – 508
Island of the Lost (1967) – 439
It Could Happen to You (1939) – 509
It's Great to be Alive (1933) – 384, 504
It's Only Money (1962) – 370, 501
Ivy (1947) – 276

J

Jagger, Dean – 148p
Jane Austen in Manhattan (1980) – 150
Janis, Elsie – 20
Janney, William – 386p
Jason, Sybil – 93-94
Javits, Senator Jacob – 39
Jealousy (1934) – 34, 35, 48, 418
Jealousy (1945) – 226, 462
Jeffries, Anne – 410
Jenkins, Allen – 84
Jenkins, Butch – 361
Jessell, George – 390
Johnson, Nunnally – 302, 359, 393
Johnson, Van – 139, 326, 328, 343
Jordan, Dorothy – 293
Joslyn, Allyn – 58, 59, 70p, 95, 247p, 266
Journal of a Crime (1934) – 89, 428
Journey's End (stage) – 104
Joyce, James – 400
Judge, Arline – 51
Julius Caesar (stage) – 104
June, Ray – 329, 343
Jungle Queen (1945) (serial) – 254, 255p, 276-277, 474

K

Kantor, MacKinlay – 127
Kaper, Bronsilau – 347
Karloff, Boris – 115, 160, 159, 170p, 186-187, 197, 212, 380, 383p
Katz, Lee – 62
Kaufmann, George S. – 216, 390, 398
Kaye, Danny – 51
Keel, Howard – 331
Keene, Tom – 219
Keep Smiling (1938) – 489, 508
Keighley, William – 62
Keith, Ian – 256, 280
Kellaway, Cecil – 332
Kelly, Jack – 335p
Kelly, Nancy – 105, 107
Kelly, Paul – 39
Kendall, Kay – 367
Kennedy, Arthur – 146
Kennedy, George – 239
Kentuckian, The (1955) – 256-257, 280-281, 477
Kentucky (1938) – 105, 223, 434, 462
Kenyon, Doris – 161
Key Largo (1948) – 328
Keyes, Evelyn – 250
Kid Millions (1934) – 387
Killer Shark (1950) – 476
King and I, The (stage) – 368
King of the Lumberjacks (1940) – 65, 421
King Richard and the Crusaders (1954) – 333, 334p, 345, 493
King, Henry – 107, 130, 132

Kirkland, Jack – 15-17, 22, 24, 27, 37, 44, 47
Kiss and Tell (stage) – 37
Kiss Before the Mirror, A (1933) – 32, 384, 418, 503
Knights of the Range (1940) – 483
Knowles, Patric – 276
Kohlmar, Freddie – 392
Kojak (TV) – 235
Korda, Alexander – 104
Koverman, Ida – 290. 308
Krauth, Alfred – 198
Krauth, Edward – 152, 168p, 178
Krauth, George – 152, 178
Krauth, Harriette – 152-153, 167
Krauth, Leo – 152-153, 155, 157, 177-178
Kruger, Otto – 34, 35p, 69, 172, 173p, 251p
Kumin, Irving – 57
Kung Fu (TV) – 235
Kuster, Sam – 377

L

La Hiff, Teresa – 15-16, 28
Lackaye, Wilton – 155
Laddie (1935) – 392, 506
Ladies Must Dress (1926) – 17, 413
Lady Escapes, The (1937) – 507
Lady For a Day (1933) – 291-292, 310, 319, 478
Lady Has Plans, The (1942) – 275, 471
*Lady in Question, Th*e (1940) – 250, 268, 272-272, 469
Lady in the Death House (1944) – 487

Lady Objects, The (1938) – 508
Lady of Burlesque (1943) – 71, 73, 423
Lady of Secrets (1936) – 172, 173p, 190-191, 453
Lady Without Passport, A (1950) – 141, 444
Laemmle, Carl Jr. – 379, 390-391
Laemmle, Carla – 410
LaHiff, Thomas – 14
Lahr, Bert – 42, 301, 316-317
Lake, Veronica – 367
Lamarr, Hedy – 141, 254, 278-279, 347
Lamparski, Richard – 175, 259
Lancaster, Burt – 256-257, 280-281
Land of Plenty (2004) – 407-512
Landers, Lew – 274
Lane, Lupino – 17
Lanfield, Sidney – 275
Lang, Fritz – 37
Langdon, Harry – 298
Langer, Lawrence – 355
Lansbury, Angela – 134-305
Lardner, Ring – 230
Lardner, Ring Jr. – 117
Lasfogle, Abe – 269
Lasky, Jessie – 153
Last Train from Madrid (1937) – 222, 461
Laughter (1930) – 24-25, 26p, 27, 48, 49, 416
Laughter in Hell (1933) – 384, 502
Laughton, Charles – 144, 145, 146, 380, 381p
Laurel, Stan – 298, 314-315, 321
Lawless Street, A (1955) – 305, 306p, 489

Lawson, John Howard – 230
Lawyer Man (1932) – 83-84, 83p, 426
Lawyer's Secret, The (1931) – 81, 424
Laye, Arthur – 71
Laye, Evelyn – 155
Lazy River (1934) – 479
Le Roy, Mervyn – 57-58, 60, 60p, 75, 159, 160, 246, 265-267
Lederer, Francis – 397
Lee, Canada – 127-128
Lee, Gypsy Rose – 71
Legend of Lizzie Borden, The (1975) (TV) – 401, 510
Leifert, Don – 154, 196
Leigh, Janet – 40
Leigh-Wood, Robert -- 121
Leigh-Wood, Shirley Alice – 121
Lennon, John – 367
Lenore, Jeff – 150
Leonard, Robert Z. – 223, 326, 342-343
Leslie, Joan – 361, 364
Let's Make It Legal (1951) – 366, 498
Levy, Ben – 34
Levy, Stuart – 368
Lewis, Jerry – 370
Lewis, Sinclair – 390
Life Begins at College (1937) – 395, 507
Life Begins With Love (1937) – 299p, 481
Lifeboat (1944) – 123, 128-129, 129p, 130p, 441
Lightning Strikes Twice (1951) – 366, 498
Lili (1953) – 347

Limehouse Blues (1934) – 294, 480
Linden, Eric – 297, 398
Lindsay, Margaret – 389
Linton, Elizabeth – 202
Linton, Walter – 202
Lipton, Leon – 339
Litel, John – 69
Little Caesar (1931) – 206
Little Darling (stage) – 224
Little Man, What Now? (1934) – 390
Little Old New York (1940) – 109, 109p, 435
Little Princess, The (1939) – 94, 105, 434
Little Women (1933) – 292, 292p, 307, 310, 318, 319, 479
Littlest Rebel, The (1935) – 222, 461
Livesey, Roger – 113
Loco (stage) – 300, 316
Logan, Josh – 47
Lone Wolf (TV) – 305
Long, Richard – 141
Loomis, Craig – 337p
Lord, Pauline – 225
Lord, Robert – 160
Lorenz, Dieter – 198
Loretta Young Show, The (TV) – 146
Lorna Doone (1951) – 115, 115p, 438
Lorre, Peter – 169-171, 171p, 172p, 188, 357
Losey, Joseph – 230
Louise, Anita – 105, 205, 272
Lourie, Eugene – 332
Love at Second Sight (1934) – 165, 452
Love Captive, The (1934) – 389, 505

Love From a Stranger (1947) – 136, 443
Love Letter, The (1999) – 406, 512
Lowe, Edmund – 32, 217, 218p
Lowery, Robert – 300, 302p, 305
Loy, Myrna – 34, 44, 48, 113, 212
Lubitsch, Ernst – 29-30, 31, 49
Lukas, Paul – 347, 385p, 386p
Luke, Keye – 308
Lund, John – 326, 343
Lunt, Alfred – 189, 355
Lux Video Theater (TV) 117, 368
Lyons, Chester – 294

M

M (1951) – 230, 464
MacDonald, George – 296-297, 299
MacMahon, Aline – 160, 182
MacMurray, Fred – 297
Macready, George – 141
Mad Doctor of Market Street, The (1942) – 95, 433
Mad Genius, The (1931) – 160-161, 176, 183-184, 449
Mad Love (1935) – 466
Made on Broadway (1933) – 478
Madison, Guy – 148p
Magic Box, The (1951) – 104
Magnificent Brute, The (1936) – 264-265, 467f
Maisie Goes to Reno (1944) – 126
Malaya (1949) – 141, 444
Mallory, Bolton – 27, 35-36, 47
Maltin, Leonard – 408
Mama Steps Out (1937) – 246, 467
Mamoulian, Rouben – 242-243, 262-263

Man About Town (1932) – 459
Man For Loving, A (1970) (TV) – 118
Man From the Alamo, The (1953) – 256, 269, 477
Man From Uncle, The (TV) – 336
Man of Sentiment (1933) – 165, 451
Man Wanted (1932) – 83, 426
Man Who Knew Too Much, The (1934) – 169
Man Who Live Twice, The (1936) – 173, 454
Man With Two Lives, The (1942) – 252, 253p, 275, 471
Manhattan Cocktail (1928) – 18, 19, 414
Mank, Gregory – 155, 156, 196
Mankiewicz, Don – 146
Mankiewicz, Herman – 216
Mankiewicz, Joseph L. – 133
Mann, Anthony – 330, 341-342, 349
Mann, Thomas – 150
Manners, David – 83
Manz, Paul – 272
Marcantonio, Vito – 231
March, Fredric – 24, 26p, 28, 29p, 36, 37, 48, 262
Marcin, Max – 389
Margulies, Edward – 363
Marian, George Jr. – 23
Marin, Edwin L. – 294
Marion, Frances – 216
Marriage is a Private Affair (1944) – 126-127, 441
Marsh, Joan – 165
Marsh, Mae – 154
Marsh, Marian – 151-199, 151p, 157p, 158p, 159p, 160p, 163p, 164p, 167p, 168p, 170p, 171p, 172p, 173p, 174p, 176p, 194p, 205, 206, 446-456
Marshall, George – 244, 264
Martin, Dean – 336
Martin, Jeanne – 336
Marx, Groucho – 387, 390, 398
Mask of Dimitrios, The (1944) – 357, 357p, 369, 494
Mask of Fu Manchu, The (1932) – 211-212, 215, 459
Mason, James – 326
Mass Appeal (1984) – 401, 511
Massacre (1934) – 87, 428
Massey, Raymond – 380, 381p
Mata Hari (1931) – 206, 457
Match King, The (1932) – 426
Mathews, Carole – 368
Matinee Theater (TV) – 333-334
Maverick (TV) – 335, 335p
Maybe It's Love (1935) – 291, 505
Mayehoff, Eddie – 371
Mayer, Louis B. – 126, 139, 215-216, 219, 270, 289, 290, 308
Mayo, Archie – 156, 157, 180, 379
Mayo, Virginia – 333
McCambridge, Mercedes – 366
McCarthy, Kevin – 343
McClelland, Doug – 358
McCormick, Robert – 229
McCrea, Joel – 89, 90p, 191, 197, 359
McDowell, John – 229
McGill, Barney – 156, 157
McGregor, Edward – 154
McGuire, Dorothy – 146
McHugh, Frank – 84
McLaglen, Victor – 264-265, 393

McNally, Stephen – 115, 116p, 116p
Medina, Patricia – 110, 112p, 113-114, 121
Meehan, John – 249
Men on Her Mind (1944) – 473
Menjou, Adolphe – 330
Mercer, Johnny – 134
Mercy Island (1941) – 69, 422
Merlene of the Movies (1981) (TV) – 401, 511
Merrill, Gary – 175, 192
Michael, Gertrude – 215
Middleton, Ray – 69
Midsummer Night's Dream, A (stage) – 390
Mildred Pierce (1945) – 358, 360p, 495
Milland, Ray – 141, 265, 275
Miller, Don – 70, 252
Miller, Marilyn – 81, 154
Million Dollar Hotel, The (2000) – 406, 512
Mind Twister (1993) 338, 494
Minesweeper (1943) – 486
Miniver Story, The (1950) – 141, 444
Miracles (TV) – 407
Missing Daughters (1939) – 455
Mission Impossible (TV) – 400
Mission Over Korea (1953) – 144, 446
Mission to Moscow (1943) – 233
Mississippi Gambler a.k.a. *Danger on the River* (1942) – 95, 433
Mitchell, Cameron – 331
Mitchum, Robert – 46, 368
Monkey Business (1931) – 387
Monroe, Marilyn – 46

Montez, Maria – 276
Montgomery, Douglass – 299
Montgomery, Robert – 203-204, 229
Moore, Colleen – 174
Moore, Eva – 380, 382p
Moore, Julianne – 375
Morella, Joe – 127
Morgan, Byron – 160
Morgan, Dennis – 65
Morgan, Frank – 126
Morley, Christopher – 203
Morley, Karen – 198, 200-239, 200p, 207p, 209p, 212p, 213p, 214p, 217p, 218p, 223p, 225p, 226p, 232p, 236p, 238p, 456-464
Morris, Chester – 78, 85, 169, 275, 296, 300, 301p, 316
Moseley, Roy – 329, 343
Mr. and Mrs. North (stage) – 37, 38, 397
Mr. Big (stage) – 397
Mug Town (1943) – 472
Muir, Jean – 38
Muni, Paul – 207-208, 209p, 221
Munson, Ona – 160, 251p
Murder By an Aristocrat (1936) – 92, 431
Murder By Invitation (1941) – 173, 456
Murder in the Fleet (1935) – 243, 296, 465, 480
Murder in the Music Hall (1946) – 254, 474
Murder She Wrote (TV) – 401
Murder She Wrote: The Last Free Man (2001) (TV) – 407, 512

Murder Without Tears (1953) – 256, 477
Murphy, George – 35, 139
Murphy, Ralph – 66, 69, 72
My Best Girl (1927) – 261
My Favorite Year (1982) – 401, 511
My Lucky Star (1938) – 105, 434
My Mother the Spy (2000) (TV) – 407, 512
My Three Sons (TV) – 401
My Wife's Best Friend (1952) – 143
My Woman (1933) – 85, 428
Mysterious Desperado (1949) – 255, 475
Mystery of Marie Roget, The (1942) – 252, 276, 472

N

Naish, J. Carrol – 359
Naked City (TV) – 38
Nancy (stage) – 17
Natchez Trace (1960)
Naughty Marietta (1935) – 243, 465
Navasky, Victor – 233
Navy Born (1936) – 91, 430
Navy Way, The (1944) – 300, 302p, 486
Neagle, Anna – 110
Negulesco, Jean – 357
Neill, Roy William – 169
Nemcek, Paul – 35
Never the Twain Shall Meet (1931) – 206, 207p, 457
Never Too Late (stage) – 41-42, 43p, 52
Neville, Gerald – 354
Newell, Gordon – 377-378, 380, 383, 388, 402

Newsboy's Home (1939) – 469
Nichols, Anne – 18
Nichols, Mike – 51
Night Angel, The (1931) – 27, 28, 29p, 49, 416
Night Club Girl (1944) – 473
Night has a Thousand Eyes, The (1948) – 490
Night Into Morning (1951) – 141, 445
Night of January 13th (stage) – 397
Niven, David – 105
No Hands on the Clock (1941) – 300, 484
No Place For a Lady (1943) – 472
No Place to Go (1939) – 65, 421
Nolan, Lloyd – 133, 145, 223
Norris, Edward – 58, 59, 60p, 76, 240-287, 240p, 243p, 244p, 245p, 247p, 248p, 249p, 251p, 253p, 253p, 255p, 257p, 259p, 287p, 464-477
Norris, Edward Jr. – 242, 258, 260, 282
Norris, Grace Vogt – 241-242, 261
Norris, Richard C. -241-242
North Star, The (1943) – 233
Notorious But Nice (1933) – 165, 451
Now Barabbas Was a Robber (1949) – 113, 437
Nugent, Edward – 166, 186

O

O'Brien, Eugene – 15
O'Brien, Pat – 90p, 94p, 384
O'Brien, Virginia – 134
O'Day, Molly – 155

O'Keefe, Dennis – 141
O'Neil, Nance – 154, 197
O'Shea, Michael – 71
O'Sullivan, Maureen – 41, 144
Oakes, Nancy – 114, 120, 121
Oakes, Patricia Luisa – 114, 120, 121
Oakes, Sir Harry – 114
Oakie, Jack – 398
Oboler, Arch – 136
Odets, Clifford – 398
Oh, What a Night! (1944) – 487
Oklahoma (stage) – 356
Old Dark House, The (1932) – 379, 380, 381p, 382p, 382p, 383p, 393, 501, 502p
Olivier, Laurence – 262
On Such a Night (1937) – 222, 462
On the Threshold of Space (1956) – 146. 148p, 446
On Trial (1939) – 468
On Your Toes (1939) – 65, 421
One Body Too Many (1944) – 300, 487
One Fatal Hour a.k.a. *Two Against the World* (1936) – 91, 92p, 431
One Last Fling (1949) – 363, 497
One New York Night (1935) – 465
One Step Beyond (TV) – 335
Only Yesterday (1933) – 389
Operator 13 (1934) – 294, 310-311, 479
Ostenzo, Martha – 203
Our Blushing Brides (1930) – 80, 423
Our Daily Bread (1934) – 219-220, 237, 460
Our Town (stage) – 397
Outcast, The (1937) – 222, 462
Outsider, The (stage) – 354
Over the Garden Wall (1934) – 165, 451

P

Paige, Janis – 363p
Paige, Marvin – 402
Palsey, Fred – 207-208
Parachute Jumper (1933) – 84-85, 85p, 427
Paramount on Parade (1930) – 22-23, 415
Parents on Trial (1939) – 483
Parker, Dorothy – 390
Parker, Jean – 275, 288-322, 288p, 291p, 292p, 293p, 294p, 295p, 298p, 299p, 301p, 302p, 303p, 304p, 304p, 304p, 306p, 322p, 477-489
Parks, Larry – 231
Parson and the Outlaw, The (1957) – 305, 489
Parsons, Louella – 394
Passing Show of 1924 (stage) – 15
Pate, Michael – 116p
Patterson, Floyd Leroy – 325
Patterson, Raeme Dorene – 325, 338, 348
Payoff, The (1935) – 91, 430
Pearce, Al – 398
Peck, Gregory – 302-303, 317
Penitentiary (1938) – 481
Penthouse Rhythm (1945) – 254, 474
People Against O'Hara (1951) – 141, 445
Perfect Tribute, The (1935) – 466

Periberg, William – 113
Perkins, Osgood – 209p
Perreau, Gigi – 364
Perry Mason (TV) – 257, 335
Personal Maid (1931) – 28, 32, 416
Personality Kid, The (1934) – 89, 90p, 429
Peter Gunn (TV) – 335
Phantom of Crestwood, The (1932) – 211, 459
Pichel, Irving – 202
Pickford, Mary – 44, 261
Picon, Molly – 37
Pidgeon, Walter – 138, 142, 331
Pine, William H. – 252, 275, 300, 301, 302-305, 316
Pirosh, Robert – 139
Pistols and Petticoats (TV) – 269
Pittsburgh Kid, The (1941) – 300, 484
Police Woman (TV) – 235
Politics (1931) – 206, 457
Pony Express (TV) – 257
Poor Little Rich Girl (1936) – 394, 506
Porter, Gene Stratton – 392
Powder River Gunfire (short) (1948) – 489
Powell, Dick – 66, 95, 96p, 146, 330, 343, 392
Powell, William – 83-84, 161, 182-183, 197
Power Dive (1941) – 484
Power of the Press (1943) – 70, 422
Power, Tyrone – 103, 104, 107, 265
Preminger, Otto – 113
Preston, Robert – 44
Pretty Baby (1950) – 364, 498

Prevost, Marie – 165
Price, Vincent – 113
Pride and Prejudice (1940) – 223-224, 235
Priestley, J. B. – 379
Princess O'Hara (1935) – 296, 400
Prison Nurse (1938) – 173, 455
Prisoner of Shark Island, The (1936) – 393-394, 395p, 506
Private Detective (1939) – 65, 421
Private Jones (1933) – 384, 503
Prodigal Son, The (1935) – 165-166, 186-186, 452
Professional Soldier (1936) – 393, 506
Pryor, Roger – 166, 167p
Public Enemy (1931) – 206

Q

Queen Christina (1933) – 243, 243p, 262-263, 285, 464
Quirk, Lawrence – 366

R

Racing Luck (1948) – 325, 490
Racket Busters (1938) – 62, 420
Radar, Dotson – 373
Raft, George – 91, 207-208, 209p
Rain (play) – 300
Raine, Norman Reilly – 130
Rains, Claude – 57, 58, 59, 64p, 247p, 385, 386p
Rainy Night in Newark (stage) – 371
Rankin, Ruth – 389
Rasputin and the Empress (1933) – 290-291, 294, 308-310, 477

Rathbone, Basil – 107, 108p
Rationing (1944) – 73, 73p, 423
Rawhide (TV) – 368
Ray, Aldo – 259p
Raymond, Gene – 44, 86p
Raymond, Paula – 115, 142, 323-351, 323p, 327p, 327p, 330p, 331p, 334p, 334p, 335p, 337p, 337p, 351p, 489-494
Razor's Edge, The (1946) – 136
Rebecca of Sunnybrook Farm (1938) – 394-395, 396p, 508
Rebello, Stephen – 363
Red Skelton Hour, The (TV) – 305
Reinhardt, Max – 390
Renoir, Jean – 358-359, 360, 371
Requiem For a Nun (stage) – 368
Revere, Anne – 128
Reynolds, Quentin – 39
Reynolds, Robert – 229
Ritchie, Ward – 402
Ritz Brothers, The – 250, 272, 395, 397
Road Show (1941) – 252, 471
Road to Reno (1931) – 424
Road to Singapore, The (1931) – 161, 182-183, 197, 449
Roar of the Press (1941) – 484
Robert Montgomery Presents (TV) – 117, 368
Roberta (1935) – 89, 89p, 429
Robin, Leo – 21, 22
Robinson, Edward G. – 158, 159, 160, 181-182, 197, 272-273, 305, 317-318
Robson, May – 291-292, 310
Rogers, Charles "Buddy" – 18, 20-21, 23, 23p, 44, 81, 242, 261

Rogers, Ginger – 44
Rogue's March (1953) – 115-438
Rogues, The (TV) – 371
Roland, Gilbert – 328, 330p, 368
Rolling Home (1946) – 488
Roman Scandals (1933) – 387, 388p, 392, 504
Roman, Ruth – 254, 276, 366
Romance in the Dark (1938) – 93, 431
Romance of the Limberlost (1938) – 297, 315, 482
Romance of the Redwoods (1939) – 482
Romero, Cesar – 192, 244, 264
Rooney, Mickey – 221, 224, 249, 271
Roosevelt, Franklin D. Jr. – 121
Roosevelt, John Alexander – 121
Rope's End (stage) – 203
Rosen, Phil – 273, 274, 275
Ross, Bob – 347
Rossen, Robert – 62
Roulien, Raoul – 384
Runyon, Damon – 296
Russell, Rosalind – 69
Rusty Leads the Way (1948) – 490
Rutherford, Ann – 224, 410
Ruthless (1948) – 362, 496
Ryan, Robert – 364
Ryan, Sheila – 255, 256p, 279

S

Sabotage Squad (1942) – 252, 472
Sailor Beware (stage) – 398
Sanders, George – 333
Satterlee, Mickey June – 252-253

Satterlee, Peggie – 252
Saturday's Heroes (1937) – 455
Scandal Sheet (1940) – 250, 251p, 469
Scarface, The Shame of a Nation (1932) – 206-209, 209p, 210p, 237, 458
Scarlet Dawn, The (1932) – 28, 30p, 48, 417
Schary, Dore – 139, 249, 328, 329-330
Schenck, Marvin – 125-126
Scott, Albert – 174-175
Scott, Albert Parker Jr. – 175, 195
Scott, Ann – 371
Scott, Catherine Mary – 175, 195
Scott, Lizabeth – 136
Scott, Randolph – 28, 254, 305, 364
Scott, Sallie Masterson – 353, 371-372
Scott, Shelley – 367, 369, 371-373
Scott, Sir Walter – 333
Scott, Zachary – 352-373, 352p, 355p, 357p, 360p, 360p, 361p, 363p, 363p, 365p, 370p, 494-501
Scott, Zachary Sr. – 353
Scott-Kaffaga, Waverly – 355, 357, 363p, 365, 369, 371-373
Scott-Kleiberg, Mary – 353, 371
Seagull, The (stage) – 378
Sealed Verdict (1948) – 490
Seaton, George – 69
Secret Call, The (1931) – 424
Secret of Convict Lake, The (1951) – 366, 499
Secret of Madame Blanche, The (1933) – 290, 478

Secret of the Blue Room (1933) – 384, 385p, 386p, 504
Secret of the Chateau, The (1935) – 91, 429
Secret Tent, The (stage) – 117
Secrets of an Actress (1938) – 62, 420
Segovia, Andre – 390
Seigler, Al – 169
Seiler, Lewis – 62
Sellout, The (1952) – 142, 331, 445, 492
Selznick, David O. – 216
Sensation Hunters (1933) – 218
Sequoia (1934) – 294-295, 295p, 307, 310, 311-313, 319, 480
Shadow of the Eagle (1950) – 114, 438
Shadow on the Wall (1950) – 364, 498
Shadows in the Night (1944) – 252, 474
She Married a Cop (1939) – 482
She Wrote the Book (1946) – 398, 509
Shearer, Norma – 24
Sheekman, Arthur – 387-389, 392, 397- 401, 400p
Sheekman-Thompson, Sylvia – 377, 392, 397, 398, 400, 407, 410
Sheridan, Ann – 246-248, 249p, 267, 269, 361, 368
Sherman, Vincent – 62-63, 76
Shertzinger, Victor – 18, 389
Sherwood, Robert – 296
Shilling, Marian – 205-206
Shootdown (1986) (TV) – 401, 511
Shopworn Angel, The (1928) – 19-20, 48, 414

Shotgun (1955) – 499
Show Them No Mercy (1935) – 244-245, 245p, 263-264, 283, 466
Sidney, Sylvia – 50, 134, 136
Silvers, Sid – 34
Sin of Madelon Claudet, The (1931) – 206, 457
Sin Sister, The (1929) – 414
Sing As We Go (1934) – 104, 433
Singing Kid, The (1936) – 93, 430
Singing Sheriff, The (1944) – 474
Singleton, Penny – 325
Skelly, Hal – 21-22
Skelton, Red – 126, 331
Ski Patrol (1940) – 250, 470
Skipworth, Alison – 28
Sleeper, Martha – 36
Slezak, Walter – 127
Slightly Honorable (1939) – 93, 94p, 432
Small Town Girl (1936) – 283, 467
Small, Edward – 37
Smarty (1934) – 428
Smiles (stage) – 81
Smith, Alexis – 313, 321
Smith, Stanley – 22
Smith, Stephen – 404
Society Doctor (1935) – 466
Some Came Running (1958) – 400
Somerset Maugham Theater (TV) – 117
Somewhere in the Night (1946) – 133, 441, 442p
Son of the Navy (1940) – 483
Song of Russia (1943) – 126, 233, 440
Song of the City (1937) – 247, 468
Sothern, Ann – 126, 364, 365

South of St. Louis (1949) – 363, 497
Southerner, The (1945) – 358-359, 360p, 361p, 364, 371, 495
Spellman, Cardinal John – 40
Sport Parade, The (1932) – 162, 164p, 191, 451
Springer, John – 38-40, 44-45, 46-53, 53p
Springtime For Henry (1934) – 34, 35p, 49, 418
Spy With My Face, The (TV) – 336
Stage Door (stage) – 37
Stahl, John – 380
Stallion Road (1947) – 361, 496
Stanley and Livingstone (1939) – 107, 435
Stanwyck, Barbara – 22, 71, 89, 90p, 301, 326
Starr, Frances – 158
Starrett, Charles – 325
Steel Trap, The (1952) – 332
Steinbeck, John – 40, 127, 365, 372-373
Steinbeck, John IV – 373
Steinbeck, Thomas – 373
Steiner, Max – 333
Stevens, George – 392
Stevens, Onslow – 386p
Stewart Finch, Alice – 376-377, 397
Stewart, David Ogden – 25, 216
Stewart, Frank – 376
Stewart, James – 141, 265
Stewart, Sophie – 37
Stewart, Tom – 376
Stolen Heaven (1931) – 27-28, 41, 416
Stone, Fred – 298p
Stone, Lewis – 204, 212

Storm at Daybreak (1933) – 290, 478
Story of Three Loves, The (1953) – 493
Straight is the Way (1934) – 219, 460
Strange Justice (1932) – 162, 449
Stranger in Town (1943) – 126, 440
Strangers May Kiss (1931) – 456
Strauss, John Michael – 93, 101
Strauss, John Milton – 81, 95
Street of Women (1932) – 379, 501
Street Scene (1931) – 32
Stricklyn, Howard – 332
Stritch, Elaine – 316
Stromberg, Hunt – 71
Stronghold (1952) – 367, 499
Stuart, Gloria – 374-410, 374p, 381p, 381p, 382p, 382p, 383p, 385p, 386p, 386p, 388p, 391p, 395p, 396p, 399p, 400p, 405p, 409p, 501-51
Studio One (TV) – 117
Submarine Patrol (1938) – 105, 434
Sugarfoot (TV) – 41
Sullavan, Margaret – 48, 389, 390
Sullivan, Jean – 358
Sultan's Daughter, The (1943) – 276, 472
Summers, Beatriz – 120
Sunday Dinner For a Soldier (1944) – 128, 138, 441
Surrender (1950) – 476
Susan and God (stage) – 37
Sutherland, Edward – 20
Svengali (1931) – 152, 155-157, 157p, 158p, 176, 178-181, 184, 196, 198, 447
Sweepings (1933) – 384, 502

Sweetie (1929) – 22, 26, 48, 49, 415
Swerling, Joseph – 127
Swing Shift Maisie (1943) – 126, 440
Sword of Sherwood Forest (1960) – 119, 439

T

Tabori, George – 328
Tailspin (1939) – 250, 271-272, 469
Talent Scout (1937) – 419
Tales From the Crypt (1972) – 120, 440
Tall Target, The (1951) – 330, 331, 338, 344, 492
Talmadge, Norma – 15
Tamang, Indra – 373
Tamiroff, Akim – 173, 242, 262
Taurog, Norman – 249, 270
Taylor, Elizabeth – 46, 51
Taylor, Robert – 107, 138, 141,, 229, 243, 245, 250, 263, 265, 296, 311, 326, 341, 343
Teacher's Beau (1935) (short) – 245, 466
Tear Gas Squad (1940) – 65, 421
Temple Houston (TV) – 346
Temple, Shirley – 94, 105, 222, 393, 394, 396p
Texas Carnival (1951) – 331, 492
Texas Rangers, The (1937) – 297, 481
Thalberg, Irving – 219
That Certain Age (1938) – 36, 37p, 419
The Gentleman from Dixie (1941) – 456
Theisiger, Ernest – 381p

There Goes My Heart (1938) – 36, 419
They Made Me a Criminal (1939) – 62, 64p, 64p, 420
They Won't Forget (1937) – 55, 57-61, 60p, 60p, 65, 75, 246, 247p, 248p, 265-267, 283, 285, 419, 468
Thirteenth Hour, The (1947) – 226, 463, 463p
This is the Night (1932) – 426
This Is Your Life (TV) – 41
This Side of Heaven (1934) – 243, 465
This Thing Called Love (1940) – 69, 70p, 422
Thomas, J. Parnell – 229, 230
Thomas, John Charles – 277
Thomas, William C. – 252, 275, 300, 301, 302, 305, 316
Thompson, Eugene – 400
Thompson, Kenneth – 83p
Thompson, Marshall – 327p, 330
Those Endearing Young Charms (stage) – 356
Those Redheads from Seattle (1953) – 305, 488
Three Loves Has Nancy (1938) – 432
Three Musketeers, The (1939) – 395, 397, 509
Through Different Eyes (1929) – 203, 456
Thunder in the Night (1935) – 222, 461
Tierney, Gene – 130
Time Out for Murder (1938) – 396, 508
Titanic (1997) – 402-406, 405p, 408, 511

Titanic Chronicles, The (1999) (TV) – 407, 512
Tobacco Road (stage) – 37
Tobey, Kenneth – 332
Todd, Richard – 366
Toler, Sidney – 73
Tomorrow We Live (1942) – 485
Tone, Franchot – 217p, 245, 250
Too Many Husbands (stage) – 37
Topics of 1923 (stage) – 15
Torpedo Boat (1942) – 484
Totheroh, Dan – 293
Touched By an Angel (TV) – 407
Tough Guy (1936) – 245, 467
Toughest Man in Arizona (1952) – 488
Tracy, Lee – 70, 384, 389
Tracy, Spencer – 107, 141, 249, 270-271, 326, 340, 343, 361
Traitor Within, The (1942) – 486
Transatlantic Merry-Go-Round (1934) – 34, 418
Trapped by Boston Blackie (1948) – 475
Treasure of the Ruby Hills, The (1955) – 368, 500
Treasure of the Sierra Madre, The (1948) – 362
Trenker, Luis – 165-166, 167, 185
Trent, John – 174p
Trial (1955) – 146, 446
Trilby (stage) – 155
Trotti, Lamar – 130
Truth About Murder, The (1946) – 254, 475
Tufts, Sonny – 305
Turner, Lana – 58, 126, 127, 138, 247p 248p, 361

Tuttle, Frank – 34
Twelfth Night (stage) – 377
Twelvetrees, Helen – 85
Two Alone (1934) – 293, 293p, 479
Two Kinds of Women (1932) – 425
Two Mrs. Carrolls, The (stage) – 37
Two Smart People (1946) – 133, 443
Two Worlds of Jennie Logan, The (TV) – 510

U

U.S. 90 (play) – 398
U.S. Steel Hour (TV) – 38
Ulmer, Edgar G. – 300, 316
Under Eighteen (1931) – 81, 162, 425, 449, 450p
Under-Cover Man (1932) – 28, 417
Undesirable Lady (stage) – 34
Unexpected, The (TV) – 325
Unfaithful, The (1947) – 361, 496
Unknown Woman, The (1935) – 169, 452
Unknown, The (1946) – 226, 226p, 463
Unpublished Story (1942) – 110, 436
Untouchables, The (TV) – 335
Up Pops the Devil (1931) – 423

V

Vallee, Rudy – 62
Vanderwilt, Jean – 361p
Variety Girl (1947) – 489
Vaughn, Robert – 343
Velez, Lupe – 83
Viceroy Star Theater (TV) – 368

Vidor, Charles – 215, 221, 224-225
Vidor, John – 237, 239
Vidor, King – 219-220, 297, 366
Vidor, M.C. – 237, 239
Vidor, Michael Karoly – 218-219, 236, 239
Vidor, Molly – 237, 239
Violation of Sarah McDavid, The (TV) – 511
Violent Stranger, The (1957) – 368-369, 500
Vogel, Paul – 139
Von Ditter, Michael – 150
Von Ditter, Tobin – 150
Von Eltz, Theodore – 165
Von Sternberg, Josef – 169-171, 187-188

W

Wagon Trail (1935) – 466
Wallace, Richard – 20
Walrus and the Carpenter, The (stage) – 224, 225p
Waltons, The (TV) – 401
Wanger, Walter – 93
Wanted Jane Turner (1936) – 507
Warner, H.B. – 160
Warner, Jack – 55, 63, 162, 229, 265, 278, 356, 358, 371
Warren, Harry – 134, 387, 392
Washington Masquerade (1932) – 211, 213p, 237, 458
Water Hole, The (1928) – 18, 413
Waterfront (1939) – 65, 420
Wayne, David – 326, 339
Wayward (1932) – 28, 30, 32, 416
Weaver, Tom – 378

Webb, Robert – 146
Wednesday's Child (1934) – 219, 460
Weil, Robert – 301-302, 320
Wellman, William – 71, 139, 142, 242, 261
Wells, H.G. – 384
Wenders, Wim – 406, 407
Westcott, Helen – 302
Westley, Helen – 396p
Westmore, Frank – 66-67
Westmore, Perc – 61, 63, 66-68, 69, 72
Whale, James – 32, 379-380, 381p, 382p, 384-386
Whalen, Michael – 393
What Price Innocence? (1933) – 478
When's Your Birthday? (1937) – 178, 454
Whiplash (1948) – 362, 496
Whistler, The (1944) – 398, 399p, 509
Whiting, Richard – 21, 22, 23, 34
Whitmore, James – 139
Who's Afraid of Virginia Woolf? (1966) – 51
Whoopie (1930) – 80p, 154, 423, 446
Whorf, Richard – 355
Wicked Woman, A (1934) – 243, 296, 465, 480
Wiegman, John – 140-141
Wilcoxon, Henry – 93-94
Wildcats (1986) – 401, 511
Wilde, Cornel – 113, 114
Wilder, Thornton – 397
William, Warren – 91-92, 162, 163p, 184, 197, 291
Williams, Esther – 326, 327p, 331, 343

Wings (1927) – 242, 261
Wings of Danger (1952) – 367, 499
Wings Over the Pacific (1943) – 252, 473
Winner Take All (1939) – 508
Winninger, Charles – 128
Winslet, Kate – 403, 404
Winston, Harry – 406
Wise Tomorrow (stage) – 61
Withers, Jane – 324
Wolf Hunters, The (1949) – 255, 475
Wolf of Wall Street, The (1929) – 414
Wolfson, P.J. – 69
Woman Accused (1933) – 32, 33p, 417
Woman Doctor (1939) – 93-94, 432
Women Men Marry, The (1937) – 431
Wood, Beatrice – 403
Woodbury, Joan – 94
Working Girls (1931) – 81, 425
World of Gods and Monsters, The (TV) – 407
Wouk, Herman – 144
Wrecking Crew (1942) – 485
Wright, Frank Lloyd – 134
Wright, Helena – 198
Wright, Marianne – 324
Wright, Paul Raymond – 324
Wyler, William – 229
Wyman, Jane – 65

Y

Yellow Canary, The (1943) – 110, 436
You Can't Beat Love (1943) – 473
You Can't Buy Everything (1934) – 479

Young America Flies (short) (1940) – 483
Young One, The (1961) – 370, 501
Young Sinners (stage) – 155
Young, Clara Kimball – 155
Young, Elizabeth – 243p
Young, Gig – 371
Young, Loretta – 105
Your Show Time (TV) – 325
Youth on Parole (1937) – 173-174, 454

Z

Zanuck, Darryl – 81-82, 104, 105, 128, 130, 246, 250, 264, 269, 271-272, 283, 392-395
Zenobia (1939) – 298, 482
Ziegfeld, Florenz – 80, 81
Zorina, Vera – 65, 109
Zucco, George – 93

Made in the USA
Middletown, DE
13 November 2023

42582981R00331